Constance

Also by Franny Moyle

Desperate Romantics

Constance

The Tragic and Scandalous Life of Mrs Oscar Wilde

FRANNY MOYLE

JOHN MURRAY

First published in Great Britain in 2011 by John Murray (Publishers)
An Hachette UK Company

2

© Franny Moyle 2011

A CIP catalogue record for this title is available from the British Library

Hardback ISBN 978-1-84854-162-7
Trade paperback ISBN 978-1-84854-163-4
Ebook ISBN 978-1-84854-461-1

Typeset in 11.5/14 Monotype Bembo by Servis Filmsetting Ltd, Stockport, Cheshire

Printed and bound by Clays Ltd, St Ives plc

John Murray policy is to use papers that are natural, renewable and recyclable products and made from wood grown in sustainable forests. The logging and manufacturing processes are expected to conform to the environmental regulations of the country of origin.

John Murray (Publishers)
338 Euston Road
London NW1 3BH

www.johnmurray.co.uk

To my mother Olga
and my daughter Rosa

Contents

Acknowledgements

I owe the greatest debt to Merlin Holland, whose great generosity has made this book possible. Not only has he shared his extensive knowledge of Oscar, Constance and their circle, but he has made his own immensely important manuscript collection available to me. And as a result of his allowing me to quote both from the letters in his own collection and those held elsewhere around the world, Constance's voice can be heard once again. I owe a great deal to John Holland, who allowed me to study those letters and manuscripts in his care. Merlin and John have also provided many of the rarely seen photographs featured in the book.

I am grateful to the Trustees of the Broadlands Archives and the University of Southampton, who have allowed me access to the huge, untapped resource they have in the form of the hundreds of letters between Constance and Lady Mount-Temple. Professor Chris Woolgar and the rest of the staff in the Special Collections unit there have been particularly kind. Thanks must also go to the William Andrews Clark Memorial Library at the University of California, Los Angeles, who have again been hugely accommodating in giving me access to their collection of Wilde manuscripts and meeting my numerous requests.

And of course, there have been other institutions and individuals who have contributed to this book. The British Library and the Morgan Library & Museum in New York have proven wonderful resources that I have tapped on a regular basis. In addition, I remain grateful to people such as the manager of the Royal Oak Hotel in Betws-y-Coed and the archivist at Bedales School, who so readily went out of their way to send me what precious information they had. It is this kind of open helpfulness that makes writing and researching such a joy.

The continuing support of my agents Georgina Capel and Anita Land, my publisher Roland Philipps and, of course, my family makes the chaos and upheaval of trying to squeeze writing into the rest of my 'portfolio' life and career worthwhile.

Introduction

'DEAR CONSTANCE . . . I am coming to see you at nine o'clock. Please be in – it is important. Ever yours Oscar.'[1] So went the note that Oscar Wilde, at that moment apparently the most successful man in London, dashed off in hurried pencil to his wife. It was the afternoon of 28 February 1895, and the forty-year-old playwright, wit and *bon viveur* was writing from the rooms in which he was temporarily resident, in the opulent settings of the Avondale Hotel at 68 Piccadilly, just off Dover Street. He was in a state of high anxiety.

The note made its way out of the hotel and into the wintry bustle of one of London's busiest thoroughfares, where horse-buses and carriages bustled to and fro. It weaved through the gents in bowlers and top hats and passed advertising boys whose sandwich boards, draped over the shoulders, promoted everything from the pleasure of the current 'Orient in London' exhibition at Olympia to Regent Street's International Fur Store, where 'a really good and serviceable Fur-Lined Overcoat, trimmed with Fur Collar and Cuffs', was available for £10.

When the note had left behind the splendid stone surroundings of central London, it found itself in the more modest but undoubtedly more modern domestic environs of Chelsea. Here it grew close to its destination in Tite Street, where a line of red-brick terraced houses found themselves overlooking the gardens of the Victoria Hospital for Children on one side and backing on to the slum dwellings so inappropriately named Paradise Walk on the other. At no. 16 it would have been Arthur, the Wildes' young butler, who attended to

I

the post boy's double knock and made sure that this latest missive was placed into the hands of his mistress, Mrs Wilde.

Houses in Tite Street were often beautiful, but they were generally far from grand, occupying a site that only a very few decades earlier would have been the haunt of the prostitutes and swells spilling out from the then notorious (and now demolished) Cremorne Pleasure Gardens. No. 16 had been Oscar Wilde's home for just over a decade. But although his wardrobe, dining habits and general lifestyle suggested an abundance of funds, Oscar was not even the owner of this relatively modest abode; he merely held a lease on it. Oscar and his wife, Constance, had secured tenure of the five-storey terrace back in 1884, when it had presented itself as merely a conventional new build, typical of the wider development of Chelsea in the last quarter of the nineteenth century.

The formerly insalubrious but fast-developing borough had acquired bohemian credentials during the 1860s and 1870s. By the early 80s the newly wed Wildes were following in the footsteps of several aspirant artistic householders, such as the painter James McNeill Whistler and the portrait artist Frank Miles, who wanted to secure their own patch of bohemia.

The Wildes had followed artistic protocol, and, like their friends Whistler and Miles before them, they had hired the fashionable avant-garde architect Edward Godwin to turn their conventional red-brick home into something more charming, surprising and aesthetically up-to-the-minute. And so 16 Tite Street, with its black iron railings and tradesman's gate leading down to the basement domain of Arthur and the cook, was remodelled. Its carefully designed rooms stood in contrast to the dark, cluttered style that had come to define Victorian taste. The interiors at Tite Street were shockingly pared down. The walls were painted white and polished, the floor covering kept pale and plain; internal dividing doors were replaced by curtains, and slim, sparse furniture contributed to a sense of space and calm. All this gave greater prominence to the art on display and the unusual decorative touches that Godwin and his clients had commissioned. In the drawing room, for example, prints and drawings were displayed as a frieze, boldly set off against a broad background band of gold. And in that same room peacock feathers had been pressed into the ceiling plasterwork.

But despite such flourishes, 16 Tite Street was a house that spoke not of riches but of aspirations. It was a home that placed those who lived in it in the set of liberal-minded, forward-thinking folk who found a frisson of pleasure in new territories, dangerously close to the old London slums, and who, rather than displaying riches by accumulating quantities of art and objects, showed their artistic appreciation of the few beautiful things they owned. It marked the Wildes out as pioneers, with more taste and intellect than money. And it pinned their colours to the mast of a movement being termed 'Aestheticism' by the chroniclers of the day.

Perhaps because of their far from infinite means, few concessions to art had been made to the exterior of the house, which, like those on either side, sported standard bay windows and a tiled porch that sheltered the shallow steps leading to the front door. Only the bold decision to paint this main entrance white amounted to a statement.

Now Oscar's note, entering through that unconventional white door, found itself inside a house little changed over the course of a decade. The birth of children had, of course, brought with it the attendant upheaval, and the telltale signs of its shared occupancy with two young boys could be discerned. Alongside prints by contemporary artists such as Whistler, Edward Burne-Jones and Walter Crane were photographic portraits of the boys, Cyril and Vyvyan, and a pastel of Cyril by the Wildes' friend and neighbour the artist Laura Hope.

Here Constance must have read the latest, brusque communiqué from her husband with a degree of concern. Although the Wildes were used to dealing with one another by post, and had made a habit of living apart from time to time when Oscar's business made it more practical, the note brought with it an air of panic. In addition to requesting that she remain at home, Oscar informed his wife he had telegraphed Mr Badley, the headmaster of Bedales School, and stopped a planned exeat for their elder son, Cyril. This was out-of-the-ordinary behaviour for a man who not only adored and relished the company of his elder child but who would rarely get involved with the mundane travel, school and holiday arrangements that were very much the domain of his wife.

Oscar had been staying at the Avondale for the best part of three weeks. It was a hotel that had the reputation of being 'a little Savoy in Piccadilly', offering excellent cuisine and theatrical décor to match: a marble-clad dining room with frescoed walls, and pillars complete with gilded capitals. But unlike the Savoy, which was inconveniently buried away on the Strand, the Avondale had unique appeal for Oscar. For Wilde found himself in the exceptional position of having two West End hits running simultaneously, and the Avondale placed him almost equidistant from the productions of *An Ideal Husband* and *The Importance of Being Earnest*.

Just a few hundred yards to the east of the Avondale, the Haymarket Theatre had been running Wilde's *An Ideal Husband* since early January. The play was about sin and blackmail, and the reputation of a public figure whose past came back to haunt him. London society was flocking to see how the fictional MP Sir Robert Chiltern would extricate himself from Mrs Cheveley, who was blackmailing him with the knowledge that he had sold political secrets in his misspent youth. How was he possibly going to square the situation with his wife, who believed that her 'ideal husband' was above reproach?

The play had been an immediate success. Oscar Wilde was 'the fashion' in those early weeks of 1895. London flocked to see the exquisite dresses in which the female members of his cast were clad and to be dazzled by the rich, bejewelled language and amusing epigrams that Oscar had wrought for them. Oscar had enthralled his audience with his wit and ingenuity; 'the whole of society' was 'engaged in inventing Oscar Wildeisms', an intoxicated press announced.[2] It was Oscar's ability to pepper his story so cleverly with aphorisms that 'the audience is kept perpetually on the *qui vive*', one journal opined. 'When all else fails, he knows how to shock or astonish – and a new sensation is all that *fin de siècle* society seems to want.'[3] He was quite simply the talk of the town, of the land even.

The ability to create sensation was something in which Oscar had become expert. Controversial and unapologetic, a man who captivated people with his magnetic personality, fabulous wit and magical storytelling, he was the embodiment of charm, genius and arrogance bundled into one. His whole career had been built on his ability to get himself noticed by shocking, provoking and then winning over his audience. It was not merely his pen that could provoke; he was expert in using his appearance and behaviour to market himself. His current pose was no exception. An image of the 'Great Oscar' as he was at this time, fleshy and languid, is easy to conjure. Noted for his dandyish outfits and unrepentant of his decadent behaviour, he was the subject of an abundance of caricatures, portraying a tall and somewhat over-fed figure, immaculately and expensively dressed with a cane and cigarette in his hand, an extravagant green carnation on his lapel and a withering expression.

It is less easy for us today to invoke a mental image of Mrs Oscar Wilde. Yet her contemporaries would have had little problem. She was a high-profile figure, whose beauty was widely acknowledged, whose activities were often reported in the press and whose appearances and outfits were also monitored for the sake of an intrigued public. In fact, ever since their marriage Oscar's charming wife had done nothing but enhance and complement his reputation. Constance Wilde balanced her husband. She was wholesome and earnest and provided the ideal foil to his determined flamboyance.

Née Constance Lloyd, she came from a moneyed background. Her highly respected family, although not aristocratic, had branches that had become entwined with the highest echelons of society. Stunning-looking and naturally stylish, with impressive chestnut hair and delicate features, she had been thrust into the limelight in 1884, when she wed a man who, at the outset of that decade, had managed to make himself famous even before he had achieved anything – an accomplishment in itself.

From the moment they married and Mrs Oscar Wilde came into

being, Constance had used her new-found celebrity to support the husband she adored but also to forge her own path. She had consistently encouraged Oscar's ambitions and contributed to his circle, and those who celebrated Oscar knew her well. But she had also pursued her own passions.

Those who admired Constance Wilde were discrete from Oscar Wilde's fans. In contrast to the self-proclaimed 'Aesthetes', of whom Constance would have undoubtedly considered herself one, she was nevertheless a role model for a more politically motivated circle of liberal women. They formed a section of society seeking both to be improved and to improve what they saw as the failings of the nineteenth century.

Those who subscribed to *The Young Woman* in January 1895 could see the latest photograph of Constance accompanying an article she had written on 'How to Decorate a House'. In contrast to Oscar, who posed so readily, his wife sat rather awkwardly in front of the camera, actually looking rather glum and insecure. This was her default expression in front of a lens, an involuntary look that she was all too aware made her appear 'solemnly tragic'. She was consistently surprised by such photographs. 'Do I really look like that?' she would ask.[4]

Her natural warmth and charm unapparent, nevertheless the photograph in *The Young Woman* reveals Constance's round, soft face and brown hair, worn in what was then the latest Parisian manner: crimped and drawn down over the temples and ears, then looped back into a bun behind. Her eyes seem dark in the photograph, belying their real-life blue-green hue. Constance is captured wearing one of her favourite 'Aesthetic' outfits: a full-sleeved dress with a loose pleated bodice that is drawn in at the waist. The silk she is wearing might be deep red or green, printed with a bold modern pomegranate pattern. Around her neck she wears two strands of 'art beads' shining like bright cough sweets. You have no way of knowing that in her stockings she stood five feet eight inches tall.

Very much the darling of the women's magazines, Mrs Oscar Wilde was renowned for her beautiful outfits, a regular complement to her husband's own attire. Constance, like so many other forward-thinking women of her day, used fashion to convey something of her political, feminist leanings. A hundred years before women burned their bras, she wore loose-fitting clothing in sympathy with the movement to reform female dress and emancipate women from the confines of corsets and hoops. She sported divided skirts, modelled Turkish trousers and talked about the hygienic virtues of cellular cloth.

But as much as her outfits could be 'political', they were also 'Aesthetic', worn to be beautiful and to express the value the wearer attributed to the importance of beauty and pleasure. Although her day dress was practical and pioneering, her evening dress could be show-stopping.

That January was no exception. What Constance wore to the opening night of *An Ideal Husband* became a story in its own right for the women's press. Her dress was 'composed of green chine moiré arranged with green chiffon and black silk muslin, and trimmed with velvet roses and ribbon to match', *The Lady's Pictorial* informed its readers.

> The full skirt is of green chine moiré with a black silk muslin round the hem, while the bodice is of green chiffon with sprays of roses and with long ends of ribbon reaching almost to the hem of the skirt. The sleeves are formed of two big puffs of black silk muslin, headed with green chiffon and moiré, while a garland of velvet roses may be seen on the shoulders.[5]

The very next day Constance sat down to convey to friends her delight in her husband's success. Formidable letter-writer that she was, she had a bespoke writing table in her bedroom, part of a larger set of fitted cupboards and shelves that had been specially built and were considered a complete innovation. One visitor to Tite Street described how, when opening the door to Constance's bedroom, one found oneself 'about to walk through the opening in a wall apparently three foot thick. When you get into the room you find that on the one side of the door forming a side of the doorway is an ideal wardrobe with every kind of drawer and hanging cupboard for dresses' and that 'on the opposite side of the door is a book case and writing table'.[6] All this was painted white.

'Oscar's play was the most tremendous success,' Constance wrote to her great friend Georgina, Lady Mount-Temple, 'and is, I think, the most beautiful play that he has written.'[7] Like many of her female contemporaries, she clearly approved of the way in which the play aired the question of morality and marriage.

An Ideal Husband quickly provided an excuse for widespread national debate on the nature of marriage. What constituted an ideal husband, and what was an ideal wife? The title of the play was like a red rag to a bull for the hordes of so-called 'New' or 'Advanced Women' emerging by the mid-1890s, a group of proto-feminists in whose cultivation women such as Constance and magazines such as *The Young Woman* played their part. These women, many of whom were associated with the latest craze for bicycling around London, expected more from men than their mothers had done. Not only did they challenge the dominance of men in society; they also challenged the assumption that moral divergences and duplicities were acceptable when perpetrated by men, but not by women. Husbands should adhere to the same moral rules as their wives, and marriages become transparent transactions. Wilde's farce could not have been better timed for them, and many of them reached for their pens, using the play's topicality to get letters and opinions into print.[8]

After the success of *An Ideal Husband* at the Haymarket, the actor–manager of the St James's Theatre, George Alexander, had decided that if you can't beat the opposition, you should join it. He had produced Wilde's *Lady Windermere's Fan* three years previously, and now, with a play by Henry James foundering, he decided to rush Oscar's latest work, *The Importance of Being Earnest*, into production. Billed to open on 12 February, it finally enjoyed its première just two days later, on St Valentine's Day. A week after opening, *The Illustrated London News* proclaimed to its readers 'the eclipse of Mr George Alexander's fortunes at the St James' theatre has been very brief. To the delicate but unhappily obscure comedy of Mr Henry

James has succeeded a piece of delightful nonsense by Mr Oscar Wilde.'[9]

A nonsensical tale of assumed identities, hilarious duplicities and babies left in handbags on station platforms hit the spot again, and within just six weeks of the new year Wilde found himself with two huge successes on his hands. This was something quite unprecedented. But then 1895 had been extraordinary from day one.

It had been a strangely momentous year. As if the old world was being prematurely washed away to make way for a new century still five years off, pillars of the cultural and political establishment tumbled within the first few weeks. The poetess of the nation, Christina Rossetti, passed away, as did everyone's favourite storyteller, Robert Louis Stevenson. Then the great statesman Randolph Churchill died too.

Britain was being bombarded by some of the most extreme weather for nearly half a century. New-year gales had cost ninety men their lives in the port of Hull, the Channel mail steam-packet had run aground in storms just off Calais, and Gravesend was drowned in flood water. Conditions had failed to improve by February, when wet conditions were replaced by a freeze over Europe the likes of which had not been seen for four decades. For the first time since 1854 the mouth of the River Medway, from Sheerness dockyard to the Isle of Grain, froze over. The Mersey and Thames were solid, and in Oxford coaches were running along the Isis. London had been transformed into a different city, and its parks were unusually busy with skaters packed ten-a-penny on to the frozen lakes and ponds.

Oscar had missed much of January's arctic conditions. After the opening of *An Ideal Husband* he had escaped to the warm sunshine of North Africa for a rest, at his wife's bidding. Since before Christmas, Constance had been worrying that her husband was overworked, and had suggested a recuperative visit to her great friend and Cyril's godparent, the adventurer Walter Harris, in Tangiers.[10] Oscar had embarked on such a trip on 17 January, although, rather than tracking down Harris in Morocco, he had decided to head to Algeria, so persuaded by his travelling companion Lord Alfred Douglas, or

'Bosie', as he was called. Constance, meanwhile, stayed behind, battling with the elements to return her children to their respective schools before closing up the house in Tite Street and heading off on her own holiday.

The day before she left, she hurriedly wrote a note to her and Oscar's great friend Robert Ross. Could he make sure Oscar reserved tickets for *The Importance* for her friends the Lilleys? And could he arrange for Oscar to send her some money on his return, since she was £38 overdrawn at the bank? 'I am writing this to you as you know what Oscar is about correspondence,' Constance explained. 'He would forget the Lilleys' address and send me no money!' 'My servants will be on board wages,' she added, 'and if he wants to come home tell him he must let them have a day's notice!' Knowing she herself would miss the first night of *The Importance*, Constance also asked Ross to send her 'some of the many papers Oscar will have about the play'.[11]

On 29 January Constance boarded the Great Western steam train from Paddington and made the journey down to Torquay, on the Devon coast. There she made her way to Babbacombe Cliff, the beautiful seaside home of her great friend the elderly Georgina Cowper-Temple, Lady Mount-Temple. If Constance felt a degree of disappointment at having to read the accounts of her husband's second first night in as many months in the press rather than enjoy them first-hand, she must have also felt her trip to Babbacombe was worth the sacrifice. For Constance's visit was not a mere escape. It was also intended to be recuperative.

Despite her relative youth, for some time Constance had been plagued by pains in her back, arms, legs and face. She had also been suffering headaches. What she commonly referred to as her 'neuralgia' had more recently developed into intermittent paralysis in her right arm and leg. She had sought relief from her symptoms with increasingly desperate measures, but the 'electricity treatment'[12] in which she had most recently invested was proving ineffective. By the end of January Constance was complaining that she could barely walk.[13]

Constance's intense friendship with Georgina, Lady Mount-Temple, had begun some five years earlier, and she had come to rely on the therapeutic effects of the calming, retreat-like holidays she would take at Babbacombe with its septuagenarian occupant. Constance adored Georgina's country home, and she also loved its lush, wooded gardens, which culminated in cliffs reaching out over the sea. In the summer she and Georgina would walk in the grounds and feed the birds, which Georgina had such a passion for. Often then they would slip into Torquay and indulge in Turkish baths together, an activity that seemed to improve Constance's aches and pains no end, and Georgina would massage Constance's aching limbs.

Even when the weather was freezing, as it was that February, and the garden paths too slippery to risk, Constance was able to find much to please her. She and Georgina could talk for hours on the subjects in which they shared a deep interest. Constance had a formidably inquiring and studious mind. She was entranced by knowledge. And in Georgina she had found a partner in conversation without comparison. Their interests in literature, the supernatural, religion and art were perfectly aligned.

All in all, Georgina Mount-Temple had become more than a friend to Constance. She was almost a second mother, whom Constance would playfully address as 'mothery', 'santissima madre', 'madre dolorosa' or 'darling Ani'. Georgina had become a drug that Constance needed on a regular basis. If Oscar could be accused of an apparently insatiable appetite for fine champagne, cigarettes and the company of his young, adoring fans, in her own way his wife pursued her relationship with Lady Mount-Temple with a similar voracious hunger.

Constance's trip to Babbacombe had always been envisaged as a month's sojourn. And so, as February drew to a close, she came home, probably on that 28 February, to find 16 Tite Street empty and the servants still on board wages, as she had left them a month earlier. Her husband had not set foot in the place, a fact that is unlikely to have surprised her greatly.

But the problem Constance faced in February 1895 was that she had grown very much out of touch regarding her husband's recent activities. With their respective holidays and Oscar's recent need to stay in the West End rather than at home, the pair of them had barely seen one another since the first night of *An Ideal Husband*.

To have Arthur press a worrying note into her hands the minute she was through the door must have brought home to her how isolated from events she had allowed herself to become. Her decision to steal herself away that February may not have been the wisest one, all things considered, not least because the life of the golden and celebrated Mr and Mrs Oscar Wilde had, in fact, been going noticeably awry over the course of the previous year.

Oscar had always been ridiculed. He had often suffered worse than ridicule from those envious of his talent. But in the last year Constance knew all too well that there had been terrible accusations levelled against her husband, worse than anything any critic or detractor had attempted before. Cocooned away in Babbacombe, she must have hoped that such accusations had died down, that the swell of her husband's recent success and public popularity had washed away the voices of those who had been trying to harm him. But now she must have sensed, in that hurried pencil note, a warning of imminent scandal.

On stage at the Haymarket the popular actress Julia Neilson, playing Lady Chiltern, was reminding her audience that 'We women worship when we love; and when we lose our worship, we lose everything'. Talking to the man she has considered up to that point her ideal husband, Lady Chiltern begs him: 'Oh! don't kill my love for you, don't kill that . . . I know that there are men with horrible secrets in their lives – men who have done some shameful things, and who in some critical moment have to pay for it . . . Don't tell me you are such as they!' With Oscar's note in her hands, Constance must have wondered whether her husband's play was about to prove some form of sickening rehearsal for their own impending drama.[14]

I

The sins of the parents . . .

IF YOU HAPPENED to dine at the Café Royal or the Savoy in the early 1890s, you might well have glimpsed the great Oscar holding court. A cigarette and wine glass in hand, enthroned in a corner, with a group of acolytes in attendance, he was the embodiment of blatant decadence. And many who witnessed this bacchanalian version of the man wondered how he and his political, campaigning but none-theless far more temperate wife had ever determined to marry. But Oscar and Constance were far more similar than has been generally acknowledged. The key to their compatibility was rooted in their own personal histories. On both of them the influence of Ireland, the scars of scandal and the impression of a domineering mother had made their mark. Their connection was Oscar's home town of Dublin, from where Constance's mother, Ada, also hailed.

Adelaide Barbara Atkinson, to give her her full name, was the daughter of Dublin's Captain John Atkinson, once with the 6th Rifles and subsequently Receiver-General of the Post Office there,[1] who with his wife, Mary, had brought up their family in an elegant Georgian town house, 1 Ely Place. Mary's brother Charles Hare, the first Baron Hemphill, Sergeant and QC, lived close by at 65 Merrion Square, where his neighbours included Oscar's parents, Sir William and Lady Wilde.

Ada Atkinson was a selfish and difficult woman, who when she was just nineteen married her cousin Horace Lloyd, an English barrister eight years her senior. Lloyd was the son of the eminent QC and one-time Radical MP John Horatio Lloyd. In choosing a husband from this branch of the family, Ada was marrying into a considerable fortune and perpetuating an already impressive lineage.[2]

The entrepreneurial Lloyds had grown rich on the back of the industrial revolution. John Horatio Lloyd was the son of the attorney John Lloyd, who played a leading part in suppressing the Luddite riots in the first quarter of the nineteenth century. Educated at Stockport Grammar, John Horatio went to Oxford and took a double first in Classics before being called to the bar and being elected Liberal MP for Stockport. He became an exceptionally wealthy man indeed, not least because his legal practice had become the favoured counsel for the fast-developing railway companies, but also because he invented a type of investment bond on which the development of the railway system became particularly dependent: the Lloyd's Bond.

Ada and Horace initially lived in 3 Harewood Square in Marylebone, close to Regent's Park and north of the busy Marylebone Road. On Wednesday 12 November 1856 the *Morning Chronicle* announced that 'On the 10th inst at 3 Harewood Square the wife of Horace Lloyd Esq., barrister at law' was delivered of 'a son and heir'. This was Otho Lloyd. Two years later the same column announced his sister Constance's arrival into the world, and the family was complete.

The birth of two children in quick succession did not, alas, signify domestic bliss in Harewood Square. Horace Lloyd's sense of his marital obligations quickly waned. As his professional success grew, so did his appetite for the pleasures of various gentlemen's clubs and his ambitions to rise to a position of prominence within the strange business of Freemasonry. Part of the Prince of Wales's social set, he developed the reputation for being a stop-out who could 'have taken on any expert in one of the three games, chess and billiards and whist, and beaten him in two out of three'.[3]

If a guiding paternal hand was absent in Harewood Square, so was maternal warmth. Ada also failed to show much interest in her off-spring. Otho Lloyd would later suggest that he and Constance were brought up 'against the will and determination of two most selfish and egotistical natures'.[4]

The one thing Ada Lloyd did do, however, was introduce her children to Dublin. Resentful and lonely, Ada's marital unhappiness prompted regular visits to her mother, 'Mama Mary', in Dublin's Ely Place. After Captain John Atkinson died in 1862, these trips became yet more frequent.

And so the young Constance and Otho found themselves often leaving the modern villas of West End London to spend time in the calmer, quainter Georgian environs of Dublin's Ely Place and Merrion Square. Here they had their cousin Stanhope Hemphill to play with as well as their youthful aunt Ellena, born in 1853. The Atkinsons, Hemphills and Wildes all moved within the same tightly knit Dublin community, and it is highly likely that the young Lloyd children would have encountered or heard tell of Sir William and Lady Wilde in Merrion Square, and of their two sons, Willie and Oscar.

Constance was not an entirely healthy child. Her brother described her as 'somewhat bilious'. Nevertheless she survived bouts of the standard juvenile maladies of the era, chickenpox and measles, and by the age of ten, by which time her father had become a QC, she found herself living with her family in the grand surroundings of London's Sussex Gardens.

The upwardly mobile Lloyds lived first at 9 Sussex Gardens and then, in line with Horace's burgeoning practice, they moved to an even larger villa at no. 42, where they enjoyed five servants: two housemaids, a cook, a kitchen maid and a butler. As the level of domestic help suggests, Sussex Gardens, just off Hyde Park, was an area associated with the well-to-do. It was also close to grandpa John Horatio, who lived in another huge and imposing villa at 100 Lancaster Gate.

Here Constance enjoyed a thorough education. Otho Lloyd remembered his sister as being able to play the piano well, able to paint in oils, a fine needlewoman and well read.[5] She also spoke French and could read Dante in the original Italian. The censuses of both 1871 and 1881 describe her as being a scholar. Although she was almost certainly tutored by a governess with her brother when they were small, when her brother was sent away to Clifton School in Bristol she clearly attended one of the few schools for girls that had been founded in London since the mid-century.

By the 1870s there were a number of colleges open to young women who wanted to continue their education, cherry-picking the courses and classes that appealed. The academic standards the mature attendees of the colleges were expected to meet were in fact very high. Young women, although unable to hold a degree, could, via these schools, study under the tutelage of university staff for examinations that were marked by the University of London.

Constance took one such course and university examination in English literature, specializing in the work of Shelley.[6] The intensity of the study required to pass the examination is suggested by Constance's complaint that the course 'ought to have been stretched over a year at least', although, practical as ever, Constance added that she was not going to bother 'worrying over it'. 'I intend to take it very quietly,' she told Otho, relaying that 'I shall not do any singing next week' in order 'to get what time I can for reading'. This strategy clearly proved successful, since Constance also noted that her tutor, a Mr Collins, was barely able to make a single comment on her Shelley essay, it was so good.

But regardless of their education, their impressive address and financial comfort, the emotional home life of the Lloyd children never stabilized. Horace Lloyd's weaknesses were not limited to billiards and cards: he also had a soft spot for women. Years later Constance witnessed a scene at her grandfather's house when a woman presented her son at Lancaster Gate and a 'row' ensued. Later Otho saw a young man at Oxford who caused him concern. Although Constance's correspondence regarding this is not explicit, the implication is that Otho felt sure he had spotted his illegitimate half-brother, the product of one of Horace's unwise dalliances.

> [Y]our letter distressed me very much for it seems so very probable, and yet I thought the boy was only about 16 or 17, also I thought she could not have afforded to send him to the University. After all if she can, surely they [sic] is less fear of any 'rumpus' since they could

only make an exposure in order to get money. Try and see him and see if you can trace any likeness – I tried a short while ago to find out something more about him, but grandpapa evidently thought I would tell Mama or someone about it so he said it was not a subject for me to talk about and shut me up completely, but he has heard nothing of them since they made the row at Lancaster Gate.[7]

The Lloyd family was particularly prone to the odd sexual deviation. It was not just Horace who had succumbed. John Horatio had also been at the heart of a sex scandal, of sorts. In the 1830s, when, as a politician, he had been assisting Lord Brougham in piloting through the House of Commons the first Criminal Law Amendment Act, a piece of legislation that would abolish capital punishment for certain offences, John Horatio was working until the small hours of the morning on a regular basis. His hard graft was not unnoticed, and he had, according to Otho, secured the promise of being appointed Solicitor-General in due course. But late nights and early starts wreaked havoc with John Horatio's well-being. 'His health gave way under the strain,' Otho explained, and then he did a very odd thing indeed. He 'exposed himself in the Temple Gardens . . . he ran naked in the sight of some nurse maids'.[8] Not surprisingly, John Horatio's career took a tumble. He lost the opportunity of becoming Solicitor-General and was forced to retire from political and legal work for four years, during which time he went abroad to Athens and became a director of the Ionian Bank.

Oscar's own background held similar, greater, scandals. Oscar's father, Sir William Wilde, was a self-made man. The son of a doctor, he became a highly esteemed and pioneering eye and ear surgeon, as well as a recognized scholar and statistician who had written widely not only on medical issues but also on archaeology and folklore. His decision as a young man to set up a free clinic to treat Dublin's poor had provided him with the publicity and experience to become Ireland's leading specialist in his field and had subsequently delivered him his fortune and title. But when Oscar's father married his mother, the fiery poet and Irish nationalist Jane Elgee, known as Speranza, he already had at least three illegitimate children in tow.

One, who went under the name of Henry Wilson, became a doctor and practised with his father. Sir William's two illegitimate daughters Emily and Mary Wilde were brought up by relatives. But it was not his premarital aberrations that were considered Sir William's scandal. Rather, it was an incident that happened during his marriage.

In the very year that Oscar was born, 1854, Sir William began an affair with Mary Josephine Travers, the nineteen-year-old daughter of one of his medical colleagues, Dr Robert Travers. Although they may have known each other socially, Miss Travers was also a patient of Wilde's. Their relationship was a long and relatively open one and resulted in another illegitimate child.[9] But after almost a decade, when Wilde ended the relationship, to his horror Miss Travers suggested that their affair had begun with a rape, carried out while, as his patient, she was anaesthetized. Although Travers did not attempt a court action based on her accusation, she began a letter-writing campaign, sending letters to Merrion Square as well as to local newspapers.

Travers's campaign heightened when, shortly after Wilde's knighthood, she published a scurrilous pamphlet, a cautionary tale about a girl raped by her doctor, barely concealing her own and Wilde's identities as Florence Boyle Price and Dr Quilp respectively. The whole of Dublin was scandalized, not least because Travers's coup was to publish the pamphlet under Speranza's name. Speranza wrote to Dr Travers, accusing his daughter of orchestrating the campaign 'in which she makes it appear that she has had an intrigue with Sir William Wilde'. Wilde's wife also alleged that Travers was attempting to extort money and referred to 'wages of disgrace'.[10]

In an event that Oscar would have been wise to have remembered when he faced his own weirdly similar trials, Travers now saw her opportunity to ruin her former lover by dragging the business into court and thus into the public arena and press. She sued Speranza for libel and in giving evidence revealed every detail of her affair with Wilde. Everything was reported. It became a national sensation.

The jury found in favour of Miss Travers, but awarded her just a farthing damages. But of course, the costs of the case had to be paid by the Wildes, and these were considerable. After the trial Wilde retreated to his country home, Moytura House in Galway, and pursued archaeological investigations there while Speranza, an indomitable character, faced Dublin's society alone with the boys. Sir William Wilde never properly recovered from the incident. He died in 1876. Constance's great-uncle Charles Hare Hemphill walked behind the coffin as part of the cortège that took the body to Dublin's Mount Jerome Cemetery.

Constance's father had met his own demise two years earlier, in 1874, from pulmonary disease. On Sunday 5 April that year *The Era* announced the death in its column dedicated to Freemasonry:

> The death of Br Horace Lloyd occurred on Monday last at his residence in Kensington, at the age of forty six. He had long been a distinguished Freemason and taken a prominent part in the affairs of the Craft . . . Latterly, however, his health failed, . . . but it was not suspected at that time that his sickness was 'unto death'. He did not however recover and . . . breathed his last on the 30th.

Constance was just sixteen. Her father's death would have a dramatic and devastating effect on her own life, and heralded another scandal that Constance, barely out of childhood, would have to face. This was not the kind of public scandal that had threatened her grand-father's and father's reputations. It was a private scandal, concealed by the family, but for that none the less shameful. This time it centred on the disgraceful behaviour of her mother.

After the death of her husband Ada Lloyd began to abuse her daughter. Behind the respectable white stuccoed façade of the villa in Sussex Gardens the teenage Constance suddenly found herself taunted, threatened and beaten by a woman who had turned from being uninterested and cold to downright cruel. Otho remembered the barrage of suffering his sister faced. It ranged from 'perpetual snubbing in private and public sarcasm, rudeness and savage scoldings' to physical violence that included 'threatening with the fire-irons or having one's head thumped against the wall'. No teenager could go through this 'without some mark on the character being left', Otho later recalled.[11]

Being made the butt of jokes in public and then slapped and threatened in private scarred Constance's personality and confidence. As a young woman she developed a pathological shyness when in public and a tendency to irritability and short-temperedness at home. The 'cruelty and contempt' Constance suffered in 'place of the care she ought to have received . . . fostered a natural irritability which I am sure she tried to overcome but never could entirely, but she would be sorry presently and would not be too proud to say so', Otho remembered. 'There is no question she was markedly critical, and was irritated by little annoyances which many another would have hardly noticed.'[12]

The damage was not merely emotional. If she already had something of a weak constitution, physical abuse did little to improve it. 'I went to see Mr Morgan yesterday,' Constance revealed to Otho in the summer of 1878, 'and he said that I was very weak indeed, with scarcely any pulse . . . He has given me tonic pills, . . . and also ordered me to lie down and sleep every day after lunch all of which Mama pooh poohed and declared it was only indigestion; she asked me if it was her cruel treatment of me that made me weak?!'[13]

One can only speculate why Ada became so cruel and abusive, but it's likely that sexual jealousy lay at the heart of it. Ada was still only in her thirties when her husband died. Although Horace Lloyd left a legacy of £12,000, which was made over in his will entirely to his wife, the supplementary income from his legal practice died with him, and Ada must have realized that to maintain her current high standard of living she must remarry.

Putting her life with Horace behind her, Ada moved to 1 Devonshire Terrace, Hyde Park, and began her quest to attract a new husband. It would become a search plagued by her own insecurities. She was clearly terrified of growing old. In the 1871 census she declared her age as thirty-five, but when the census called again a decade later, according to the figure given to the census official, Ada had only aged five years. How irritating it must have been for this relatively young widow to have a beautiful and much younger daughter who might deflect the attention of potential suitors from her.

And Constance was beautiful, with her unruly chestnut hair, brunette skin and large eyes. One story goes that she was once attending an exhibition of Pre-Raphaelite paintings by Dante Gabriel Rossetti at the Royal Academy and overheard the man in front of her remark that pouting lips such as Rossetti painted are never encountered in real life. But when the man turned and caught sight of Constance he was 'taken aback' and 'silenced' by the real-life Rossetti he suddenly saw before him.[14]

Constance's brother, Otho, could do little to help with the situation at home. After being away at school in Bristol most of the time, in 1876 he went to Oxford University with a 'demy' scholarship to Oriel College to study Classics. Here Otho became the first of the Lloyd siblings to become friendly with Oscar Wilde, who, also a Classical scholar, had gone to Magdalen College two years previously.

On hearing the news that Otho would be joining the university, Speranza dropped Oscar a line, urging him to look Otho up. But in fact it was in Dublin's Merrion Square that they first met, in 1877, 'my grandmother having sent me to call on the Wildes'.[15] Oscar amused Otho by recounting how he had just been on a trip to Greece and, returning to Oxford a fortnight late, 'was nearly sent down by the authorities'. Thereafter Otho and Oscar saw one another from time to time in Oxford, although it would be a little while before Otho's sister had the pleasure of Oscar's acquaintance.

Meanwhile, in 1878, Constance's fortunes encountered another dramatic shift when Ada Lloyd finally attracted an appropriate suitor in the form of George Swinburne-King, a man with some private means who also held a position in the accounts department of the Admiralty. A widower, he was a charming man and clearly thought he could take on the fiery yet insecure Adelaide. Constance sensed that matrimony might be on the cards and on 3 September wrote to Otho, who was staying with their grandmother in Dublin, to reveal her suspicions:

Miss Constance Lloyd present her compliments to Mr Otho Lloyd & begs to inform him that he has a sister still living . . . She also begs to give him a little hint that there is a 'Steparex' on the Tapis who may turn into something definite this day (this last hint is strictly private).[16]

Her instincts were corroborated by a proposal. In a subsequent letter Constance found herself outlining the challenging dynamics and potential conflicts that the proposed Lloyd/Swinburne-King union presented, not least because Mr Swinburne-King had a daughter Eliza, known as Tizey.

everything nearly came to a smash . . . so there was no good in writing till I knew how it was all going to end. I think it is all right but I do think that Mama should have more trust in a man she is going to marry. It drives me simply wild to hear her always wondering whether he likes her . . . and whether he has been colder the last two days, & whether he was not out of spirits at such & such a moment . . . and my greatest fear is the (I fear almost inevitable) jealousy of Tizey . . . am not sure she is not even a little jealous of me. Mr SK is charming really & devoted to M if she would only see it. We spent yesterday afternoon and evening at Ealing where they have a dear little tiny cottage and I like him very much . . . she (Tizey) is apparently not clever but takes an interest in dress and wants us two to be always dressed alike so you need no longer groan over your sister's ugly dresses. We are of course going to be dressed alike for the wedding our idea being Peacock Blue Dresses with . . . puffy sleeves & outer jackets to match . . . The colour of course depends eventually upon mama's dress, which we must not interfere with but I think she is inclined to a navy blue silk.

I tell you Mr King's idea about me. We were talking about mesmerism & I said I cd mesmerise grandpapa, upon which he turned to Mama & said 'how strange. I should have thought it required someone with a strong will and not a gentle girl (!!!) like Constance'. 'Oh Constance has got a very strong will, wait till you know her better' from Mama . . . he does not know the smouldering volcano beneath.

. . . I confess to you that I wld rather there had been no daughter as I think it will hamper all my actions & I shall never be able to go to the College to see all my friends there, & there will be a fuss every time I go to Lancaster Gate & leave Tizey.[17]

22

Apart from indicating the oppressive conditions under which she was living, this letter gives a telling snapshot of Constance at the age of twenty. Her interest in spiritualist experiments such as mesmerism is already apparent. Apart from her known college friend Lucy Russell, who was the younger sister of the barrister, financier, property developer and railway entrepreneur James Cholmeley Russell, Otho lists her 'friends' during this period as including Bessie Shand, whose brother Alexander (or Alec) went on to become a writer on philosophy and metaphysics. Then there was Mary Moore, the daughter of the Revd Daniel Moore, and Clara Monro, daughter of the famous mental physician Dr Henry Monro, who consulted at St Luke's Hospital. One can imagine the opinion and zest formed amid this group of privileged, educated, upper-middle-class young women.[18]

The reference to Otho groaning over her 'ugly dresses' alludes to her emerging enthusiasm for Pre-Raphaelite or 'Aesthetic' dress. Indeed the description Constance gives of the outfits she and Tizey might wear for Ada's wedding, in peacock blue with puffed sleeves, sound particularly 'Pre-Raphaelite'.[19] This development in Constance's taste and appearance was never wholly approved of by Otho, who, like other members of his family, never much identified with or saw the appeal of Aestheticism.

As a self-confessed Pre-Raphaelite – a term that by the 1880s was interchangeable with 'Aesthete' – Constance was carrying a torch whose flame had been lit in the 1850s by a group of women associated with the founding Pre-Raphaelite Brotherhood painters. Women such as Elizabeth Siddal and Jane Morris, the wives respectively of the painter Dante Gabriel Rossetti and the poet, designer and socialist William Morris, had modelled for the Pre-Raphaelite artists, wearing loose, flowing gowns.

But it was not just their depiction on canvas that sparked a new fashion among an intellectual élite. Off canvas these women also established new liberties for women that some twenty years later were still only just being taken up by a wider female population. They pioneered new kinds of dresses, with sleeves either sewn on at the shoulder, rather than below it, or puffed and loose. While the rest of the female Victorian populace had to go about with their arms pinned to their bodies in tight, unmoving sheaths, the Pre-Raphaelite women could move their arms freely, to paint or pose or simply be comfortable. The Pre-Raphaelite girls also did away with the huge, bell-shaped crinoline skirts, held out by hoops and cages strapped on to the female undercarriage. They dispensed with tight corsets that pinched waists into hourglasses, as well as the bonnets and intricate hairstyles that added layer upon layer to a lady's daily toilette.

Their 'Aesthetic' dress, as it became known, was more than just a fashion; it was a statement. In seeking comfort for women it also spoke of a desire for liberation that went beyond physical ease. It was also a statement about female creative expression, which in itself was aligned to broader feminist issues. The original Pre-Raphaelite sisterhood lived unconventionally with artists, worked at their own artistic projects and became famous in the process. Those women who wore Aesthetic dress in their wake tended to believe that women should have the right to a career and ultimately be enfranchised with the vote.

The flagship store of Aestheticism was Liberty's of London. By 1875 the brainchild of Arthur Liberty had opened in Regent Street and offered London's avant-garde set the opportunity to buy the best craft furniture and the finest oriental goods. It also specialized in 'art fabrics' which were made up into those loose-fitting, puffed-sleeved Aesthetic dresses, many of which were then worn at the bohemian Grosvenor Gallery. Constance was a regular at Liberty's. Her letters note deliveries from the store and also the fact she bought Otho a brown tie there, a gesture that it is unclear whether he appreciated, given his apparent reservations about Aesthetic wear.

And so Constance, with 'her ugly dresses', her schooling and her college friends, was already in some small degree a young woman going her own way. Moving away from the middle-class conventions of the past, where women were schooled by governesses at home, would dress in a particular manner and be chaperoned, Constance was already modern.

The letter she wrote to Otho in the autumn of 1878 includes another important insight, and that is about money. 'I want to know if you got your £10 from grandpapa', Constance continued,

> & if they told you the money arrangements. Grandpapa is going to make you quite independent of Mama & to give me an allowance of how much I know not yet. He will not give Mama a farthing, at which she is rabid. Would God I were independent too; I wld far rather work for my daily bread than have my mother make a compliment of keeping me in food and lodging. She says it is grandpapa's duty to keep the children of his only son and she says that his keeping you is no compliment as if he did not she is no longer bound to keep you, & you would have to leave Oxford & take a Clerkship. A nice look-out for the son of Horace Lloyd & for me with abilities like yours too![20]

With marriage for Ada on the horizon, the Lloyd family had been thrown into an ugly financial war. On Horace's death, Grandpa Horatio had agreed to supplement Ada's income to the tune of £400 per year, on the understanding that she was also supporting the children. With a new husband on the scene, Horatio was proposing withdrawing this allowance to his daughter-in-law. In retaliation Ada was refusing to support her own children. John Horatio was evidently less keen to see his grandchildren having to earn their own keep than their mother, and so had been forced to work out a plan to cater for them, as Constance began to outline to Otho. They would ultimately inherit a portion of his estate: 'by Grandpapa's will, having reached 23 we become possessed of the 4th share divided between us. Supposing Mama does not marry . . . we each give her half until her death, when it of course comes back to us.'[21]

Towards the end of September details had been finalized of further respective annual allowances that their grandfather was prepared to make. Constance, ecstatic to be financially independent of her mother at last, provided Otho with more information on her grandfather's proposals. Her ability to maintain something of a dry sense of humour amid this domestic turmoil speaks volumes for Constance's inner resilience, which would serve her well in years to come.

Your mother expected that you would write & condole with her on the loss of her income. You have not followed her unexpressed but oh! how expressive! wishes – in this respect. Was this right? Oh No . . . it was wrong. Was I say for there is no need now to write. The arrow smote deep but it has been stayed by the hand of whom do you think? – the aged Octogenarian who in spite of the storm of opposition raised by the assembly of Aunts & sisters in law has ventured to express his approbation of your humble servant's merits by bestowing on her £150 a year, £100 to be given to her guardian for her maintenance, £50 to be devoted to the purchase of her Dress, the payment of any studies or Concerts she may choose to attend & in fact for her 'menus plaisirs' in general.[22]

Rather amusingly, and entirely understandably, Constance suggested buying the meanest possible wedding present for her mother, within the terms of the brief that Ada had clearly set them. 'A propos of the honourable lady about to be married,' Constance informed her brother, 'it is necessary that we give her a present, & that present must be . . . costly . . . she has fixed her affections on a plain gold bracelet . . . I find the smallest is £7.7.6.'[23]

Ada Lloyd eventually walked down the aisle with George Swinburne-King on 19 October 1878 at St James's Church in Sussex Gardens. The newly-weds headed off for their honeymoon, and Constance was dispatched to one of her aunts in Norwood, south London.

Constance's grandfather John Horatio Lloyd had three daughters in addition to his sons Horace and Frederick. The family was close-knit and would remain so throughout Constance's life. Frederick died early; Emily never married and lived with her father in Lancaster Gate; Carrie had married a physician, Dr Kirkes; and Louisa Mary, known as 'Aunt Mary', married William Napier, second son of the Trafalgar veteran and former Lord of the Bedchamber to King William IV, Baron Napier.

It was in Aunt Mary Napier's cottage in the leafy, smoke-free environs of Norwood that Constance now found herself at the end of October 1878. If she hoped that her mother's attitude towards her would be changed by marriage, she was to be disappointed. 'I have not had a line from my parents have you?' Constance inquired of Otho. 'Affectionate people!! Before I left Ella had had two letters from Mama, one from Mr King & Tizey ... grandpapa one from Mama, and Aunt Emily one from Mama on Monday. Why is it I am always snubbed? However Aunt Mary is more than kind to me & Mr Hope too who admires you immensely.'[24]

The reference to Mr Hope is to Adrian Hope, a young nephew of William Napier, who would almost certainly have been invited over by Aunt Mary to meet Constance, perhaps with matchmaking in mind. At twenty, Constance was eminently marriageable. Her mother's recent marriage and subsequent lack of interest in her only contributed to her status as family burden, the responsibility for whom would now be shared out between her grandfather and his daughters. In the 1870s Constance was living in an era when middle- and upper-class women still did not work and were not expected to look after themselves. Despite any ambitions they might harbour, there was still no career path or opportunity for a stratum of society that had traditionally been supported by family or husbands. The era of the career woman remained far off, and those women who had found a living by writing or painting were still few and far between.

Adrian Hope must have been an attractive prospect as a potential husband, but there was clearly no spark. The irony is that later in life Adrian and Constance would indeed become intimately entwined, but in circumstances that neither of them could have foreseen in these early days.

It was not as if Constance was averse to marriage at this time; she simply lacked confidence when it came to young men. She had a tendency to lapse into what appeared to many to be a sulky silence when in company. This tendency, almost certainly an attitude she adopted when struck dumb by the extreme shyness that remained a lasting legacy of her abuse, was something that haunted her for the rest of her life. 'Sulky' was an adjective often applied to her by detractors. The photograph in *The Young Woman* in 1895 serves as a reminder that, years after she had conquered her nerves, she could still unthinkingly appear gloomy and melancholic.

'Oh me! When shall I marry me?' Constance moaned to Otho around this time. 'You say I shall have a chance of marrying. I see none. I have no beauty, no conversation, no small talk even to make me admired or liked . . . I shall be an old maid, I am doomed to it & you will see your Sister walking about with 6 cats and half a dozen dogs.'[25]

While Constance was staying with Aunt Mary, the debate raged over where the newly wed Swinburne-Kings would live and whether Constance would live with them. Constance suggested a move that would take them into South Kensington, into the artistic hub that surrounded the South Kensington Museum – now the Victoria and Albert Museum. Constance's friend Lucy Russell lived in nearby Queen's Gate, and Constance mooted a similar address. Ada's response was typically nasty: 'I suggested to Mama to take a house in Queens Gate but she nearly fainted at the idea, for it suddenly occurred to her that Miss R lives there & she said she would not be near any of my friends for £1000!'[26]

Although Otho had been unable to protect his sister from Ada's abuse up to this point, the marriage presented a new opportunity. He visited John Horatio and insisted that Constance must be removed from her mother. Ada put up no resistance. And so Mr Swinburne-King and his daughter moved into Devonshire Terrace, and Constance moved out. Her new home was to be that of her grandfather, 100 Lancaster Gate, with John Horatio and Auntie Emily *in loco parentis*.

Now it would be these two charged with the future of their shy, studious ward. That within the next few years she would metamorphose into one of the most talked-about women in London was hardly an outcome they could have foreseen.

2

Terribly bad taste

IN THE SECOND half of the nineteenth century Hyde Park had become a pleasure ground surrounded by the palaces of the rich. It was in one such palace that, by the age of twenty, Constance Lloyd found herself resident.

Grandpa Horatio's house at Lancaster Gate was enormous and imposing. Built as part of an ambitious scheme in the mid-1850s around the newly built Christ Church, it was one of a row of huge houses, set back from the road and overlooking Hyde Park, that had been described as the most handsome terrace in the whole of London.[1] John Horatio was a man who had made his mark, and his address was testimony.

From her new home Constance would have seen the full anatomy of London life. Early in the morning, from half-past seven, the so-called 'Liver Brigade' would be out riding. Taking their constitutional gallop, shaking the liver ahead of the day's toil, London's top judges, barristers, surgeons and millionaires would be seen clad in silk hats and black hunting coats, breeches and shining patent boots. When they had headed off for the City and Inns of Court, nurse-maids in their smart grey flannel uniforms would emerge with perambulators, and governesses would march smart children up and down.

Sometimes Constance would get a sight of a protest, since the park remained the arena for political manifestation since the great Chartist and reformist protests of the 1840s, 50s and 60s. And then in July she would have witnessed the municipal gardeners lay out thousands of potted palms and semi-tropical plants that would transform the park for its ten-week 'summer season' into something altogether more exotic.

But prestigious and well located though it was, Constance did not much enjoy 100 Lancaster Gate. Over-sized for its occupancy of three, it was an austere and un-homely place for a modern young woman to live and, as she later told Oscar, she never felt more than a guest there. Although Constance adored her grandfather, her aunt Emily was old-fashioned and disapproved of many of her ambitions. Nevertheless, beneath Constance's quiet exterior lay a determined soul. Perhaps not quite the 'smouldering volcano' that her mother had alleged, but certainly someone with her own strong mind, who was not prepared to toe the line just for the sake of convention. And so Constance pursued her interests as best she could.

She began to display an increasing passion for art and culture, most specifically the visual and decorative arts. Constance makes much mention of the controversial Grosvenor Gallery in her letters in the early 1880s. This was a temple to contemporary art in New Bond Street, designed as an Italian palazzo. The art lovers who worshipped there would pass through its imposing Palladian entrance salvaged from the demolished church of Santa Lucia in Venice, before entering a huge room adorned with a blue coved ceiling on which James McNeill Whistler had painted the phases of the moon and a sprinkling of golden stars. Below a green velvet dado, red silk walls punctuated by Ionic pilasters rescued from the old Italian opera house in Paris displayed the best avant-garde art money could buy.

But the Grosvenor was more than just a gallery: it was also the social nexus for the alternative, Aesthetic, liberal-minded set and was particularly women-friendly. Since its inception it had garnered a reputation for supporting, among others, 'feminist' artists, many of whom would go on to become firm friends of Constance and Oscar. Painters such as Emily Ford, Louise Jopling, Evelyn de Morgan and Henrietta Rae had their work shown here. They, like Constance, would have enjoyed the gallery restaurant, which specifically catered for ladies lunching unchaperoned, as well as its library and club, which had a dedicated ladies' drawing room.

Oscar, who even at university in Oxford was aligning himself with the Aesthetic group of poets and painters, had of course made a point of getting invited to the opening of the Grosvenor in 1877, and years later he summed up its enduring cachet in his novel *The Picture of Dorian Gray:* 'You must certainly send it [the painting of Gray] next year to the Grosvenor,' Wilde's Lord Henry Wooton urges the painter Basil Hallward.

> The Academy is too large and too vulgar. Whenever I have gone there, there have either been so many people that I have not been able to see the pictures, which was dreadful, or so many pictures that I have not been able to see the people, which was worse. The Grosvenor is really the only place.[2]

Constance dashed to the Grosvenor on occasion to meet friends, although there is a sense that she did so with some secrecy. In one letter to Otho she confided that 'as Grand Papa was in the City and Auntie at Windsor, I rushed off there in a hansom and . . . lunched there'.[3]

At the Grosvenor, Constance met like-minded friends and solicited introductions to some of the contemporary artists she so admired. One man whose friendship she cultivated in 1881 was the sculptor Richard Belt. Constance's fascination with Belt, a contro-versial figure, suggests a susceptibility to men whose character and profession placed them with at least a foot in the demi-monde.

In 1879 Belt had won a prestigious competition to create a monu-ment to Lord Byron, and in 1880 Constance would have seen his huge bronze seated figure of the poet unveiled close to Hyde Park Corner. Just after it was unveiled, an article in *Vanity Fair* suggested that, far from being by Belt, the statue had in fact been farmed out by him to foreign assistants, as had all the output of his studio since 1876. The source of this libel was another sculptor, Charles Lawes, whom Belt had once assisted and whom he promptly sued. This national scandal was in full swing when Constance and Belt began seeing one another. She visited his studio, had dinner with him and began to make her own investigations into this man, whom she clearly found fascinating and with whom she obviously shared some social connections.

'Miss Emily A is going to take me to see the Pennants in Westminster next Wednesday in order to ask them about Mr Belt,' she wrote to Otho.

> [T]he H's had not heard of the libel and are most deeply interested in it and of course having heard of his talents when quite a boy, don't believe a word of it . . . I've told Auntie that I am going but she does not remember the connection. Mr Belt, I daresay you will remember, was in Mr T's school, and it was he who first discovered his talents.[4]

Belt won his libel case, and Lawes was faced with £5,000 worth of damages. Just five years later, however, in another scandal involving the sale of fake diamonds to aristocrats that could easily have formed part of the plot of one of Oscar's plays, Belt was convicted of fraud and sent to gaol.[5]

It was not just art and its colourful characters that Constance also found herself drawn to. The Aesthetic movement had generated a new level of appreciation for the decorative arts, and craft skills such as embroidery, enjoying heightened status and recognition, became recognized outlets for female talent in the 70s. In 1872 the Royal School of Art Needlework had been established to provide suitable work for gentlewomen. The leading Aesthetic artists of the day supplied designs for the attendees of the school to work. Above and beyond this institution, the arts-led interior design practice of Morris & Co. – where William Morris's own wife, Jane, and daughter May took an active role in supervising and commissioning the needlework – had given embroidery a new aspect. No longer a pastime where ladies produced their samplers in the drawing room, art needlework was now fashionable and for public consumption, considered a vital contribution to modern interiors.

Constance, embodying this moment, explored her own needlework skills. Her staunchly Christian aunt Carrie marshalled Constance's help in decorating the new high school for girls in Baker Street. This school was the philanthropic project of Mr and Mrs

Francis Holland. A notable clergyman, Holland raised money and bought the site at 6 Baker Street and erected a modest building that could be converted into warehouses should the school fail. The great and the good from the local Christian community dived in to decorate the plain whitewashed walls in the weeks before the school opened in October 1878.

Constance prepared a series of embroideries to run the length of the school's 'Ambulatory'. She spent days working the words 'Hearken unto me, O ye children, for blessed are all they that keep my ways. Hear instruction to be wise' on blue sham leather, carefully stitching each letter in a gothic script some five inches high in black, red and gold. Constance's love of art needlework never left her. Years later she presented Otho with a fire screen that she had 'embroidered on blue Morris linen in pink and green silks' and mounted in a Liberty ash frame that was stained green.[6]

For her efforts for the new girls' high school Aunt Carrie took Constance to meet the great Francis Holland himself, but Constance performed poorly, 'simply shaking with fright' throughout the interview, despite the fact that Holland was charming and full of fun. 'I do think I am the greatest donkey that ever lived I am so afraid of people,' she noted afterwards.[7]

Eventually, however, distance from her mother and the benign effect of her grandfather's kindness allowed Constance to blossom. Slowly her sense of humour, her intelligence and her love of life began to surface, and her shyness began to recede. The girl who had found herself unable to speak in front of Francis Holland began to transform into a sharp, opinionated woman with a quirky sense of fun.

'In a discussion she was surprisingly quick at detecting the flaw and weak point in any reasoning,' Otho recollected. 'She could carry her own in an argument well, and always had the courage of her opinions,' along with a 'quiet humour and a sense of the ridiculous'.[8]

Constance's natural interest in the arts reflected that of her grandfather, who had a keen interest in painting and something of a collection. Once Constance was out of her mother's reach, John Horatio's influence's in this sphere began to be felt. A year after her mother wed, she found herself on a tour of Wales with her grandfather, Aunt Emily and Otho, staying for a few days in the Royal Oak Hotel, Betws-y-Coed.[9]

The small village of Betws had become an artists' colony in the mid-nineteenth century, with several eminent painters resident in the area and others flocking to capture the surrounding Conwy Valley. And when it wasn't painters, it was art enthusiasts, the fashion-conscious and intellectuals who were also holidaying there, hoping to soak up the painterly spirit that prevailed and perhaps secure a work of art too. Constance would have thumbed through the visitors' book at the Royal Oak and seen the sketches left there by the many artists who had stayed there before her, some of whom were the country's leading landscape painters.

Constance was fired up by the artists she encountered. She delighted in meeting the well-known landscape painter Frederick William Hulme, who was a regular visitor to the village, and while in Betws her grandfather bought a picture of Pont-y-Pair from another painter, named Stevens.

Constance flourished in this artistic atmosphere, and although her stay at the Royal Oak was relatively short, her newly emerging conversational skills managed to make an impression on another cultural tourist, Henry Fedden, a Bristol sugar merchant. He and Constance got along swimmingly.

> I was so sorry to leave Betws, I had just begin to feel at home there, and I had made a friend whom I need not say I have been teased to any extent about, because he was, well, a he! Mr Fedden. He was married tho' and lives at Bishop Stoke about 4 miles from Clifton . . . He has asked them to let me come and stay with him & his wife, which of course I should like to do immensely.[10]

Constance's desire to visit the Feddens in Bristol was granted a few weeks later. In October she found herself installed in their comfortable home in Stoke Bishop, just outside the city, and thus began what would prove a very formative visit for her. The Feddens had a strong appetite for culture. They took Constance to concerts and soirées; they visited a loan exhibition; in the evenings Constance played the piano and Henry Fedden sang, and afterwards they would listen to his wife reading.

During her stay Constance was taken aboard the training ship *Formidable*, anchored in the Bristol Channel. This marvellous old fighting ship was Henry Fedden's philanthropic project. He, along with other Bristol businessmen, had leased it from the Admiralty and had turned it into a training vessel, not for privileged children but for street urchins. The *Formidable* could take up to 350 'lost boys' and train them up into seamen, who could then find useful employment on one of the many commercial vessels that passed through the city's port.

Mary Fedden was also an impressive character. She was involved in the Ladies' National Association, and from time to time the Feddens' home hosted this group's meetings, at which various speakers discussed how women might also provide constructive action in the war against poverty and injustice.[11]

This cultured, inspirational and mutually supportive couple presented for their young guest a model of an ideal, modern marriage that stood in stark contrast to the unhappy, selfish and separate lives her parents had lived together. What is more, the kind attention that Henry Fedden, in particular, had paid to her and the personal interest he had taken in her must have also persuaded Constance that, far from being unattractive and doomed to spinsterhood, romantic opportunities could one day be available to her.

In fact, by 1879 Constance had already had some luck in love. She was becoming close to Alec Shand, the brother of her friend Bessie. According to Otho, Constance was even briefly engaged to him,[12] although it seems that this was a fact kept between themselves, since her extant letters reflect nothing other than secrecy and some elaborate lying where Alec is concerned. 'I am rather disturbed in mind about something,' a 21-year-old Constance wrote to Otho.

I got Tennyson's 'Princess' in the Summer for Alec, who wanted a copy, and did not pay for it. They have unfortunately sent in the account to Aunt Emily in a bill of hers and fearing so the questioning I said I had got it for you. I suppose you will be angry but I do not think you will be asked about it. I will go with you and pay it the first day you're in town, and then you can say it is paid, if you are asked.[13]

It seems that Alec returned Constance's token of affection with much of the same, sending Constance 'a beautiful bound edition of Tennyson', which he left with Bessie to pass on. Spoilt for choice suddenly by men bearing gifts, Constance discovered that the devoted Henry Fedden had already given her that very edition, and so it was returned to Bessie with a request for Alec to find a different gift. The poetical works of Keats was presented instead.

But although by 1879 Constance was at last coming out of her shell and enjoying the attentions of men, she had not yet caught the eye of Oscar Wilde. For the moment his sights were trained elsewhere. While Constance had been getting on with her studies, Oscar had managed to secure a reputation at Oxford for being something of a poet and critic. In his final year he had won the Newdigate Prize for poetry with his poem 'Ravenna' and had had poems and articles published, mainly in the university and Irish press.

Swept up by the Pre-Raphaelite legacy, just like Constance, Oscar was writing under the influence of the poets of that movement, Algernon Charles Swinburne and Rossetti. He saw an intense devotion to beauty in their work. And this cult of beauty was endorsed in the critical writings of Walter Pater, whose *Studies in the History of the Renaissance* had a formative influence on him. In the conclusion to these studies Pater essentially argued that in a world in flux, beauty provides a fixed, refined aesthetic that could supersede the transient world and, in so doing, offer the onlooker a form of higher experience.

Pater was a Fellow and tutor at Brasenose College whom Oscar met in the Michaelmas term of 1877. Pater's theories about the importance of beauty were expressed not only in his written work but also in his own domestic environment. Mary Ward, the wife of *The Times*'s art critic, Humphry Ward, lived opposite Pater in Oxford and described his 'exquisite' house in her memoirs, where 'the drawing room was decorated with a Morris paper; spindle legged tables and chairs; a sparing allowance of blue plates and pots, bought, I think in Holland . . . engravings if I remember right from Botticelli; a few mirrors, and very few flowers, chosen and arranged with "simple yet conscious art".'[14]

Oscar's own college rooms declared his similar allegiance to Aestheticism. He too looked to contemporary designers such as William Morris and furnished his rooms simply, incorporating antique blue china and beautiful art prints.

Aesthetic taste could extend to any field in which beauty, its object, could be applied. It didn't stop with fine art, literature or interiors. Floristry could have an Aesthetic aspect. Lilies and sunflowers were the Aesthetic flower of choice. Japanese or Chinese artefacts were admired. And, of course, fashion was Aestheticism's route into the mainstream.

Alongside the 'ugly dresses' that Constance made up from her Liberty fabrics, some ladies took Aesthetic dress to new extremes. The actress Ellen Terry, associated with the movement through her relationship with the Aesthetic architect Edward Godwin, wore Japanese kimonos. Aesthetic men wore their hair long in the tradition of painters like Rossetti, and their dress seemed to incorporate anything from the long Middle Eastern robes that painters such as William Holman Hunt wore to the loose velvet jackets with which Swinburne became identified. But the dress adopted by the male aesthete was considered 'effeminate' by the uninitiated. For his airs and graces Oscar was taunted by his college peers. One prank, with the aim of removing and breaking Oscar's furniture, ended in the pranksters themselves being thumped and thrown out by Oscar, single-handed. Another attempt to 'duck' him in a college fountain also failed.

Oscar left Oxford at the end of 1878 with ambitions to become a poet and critic. With the Newdigate Prize under his belt and a double first to boot, he moved to London and installed himself in rooms in Salisbury Street, off the Strand, in the home of his friend the painter Frank Miles. Miles had 'a curious old-world house looking over the Thames ... with antique staircases, twisting passages, broken down furniture and dim corners'.[15] But the well-connected, moneyed and charming young artist had already created there a nexus for the bohemian set, with everyone from the poetess Violet Fane, Ellen Terry and James McNeill Whistler to Rossetti, Swinburne and Morris dropping by. Oscar was the perfect addition.

London was a new exciting arena for the young graduate. When Oscar arrived, the metropolis was quite literally newly aglow. Electric lights were being tested in galleries, and for the first time the Embankment and Holborn Viaduct were illuminated at night. And the cultural scene was sparkling too. In almost every cultural arena there were exciting new developments.

The great actor of the moment, Henry Irving, having just opened a refurbished Lyceum Theatre under his own management, was performing his *tour-de-force* Hamlet opposite Ellen Terry's Ophelia; Lord Leighton, an Aesthetic painter of 'effeminate subjects',[16] had just been elected as the president of the Royal Academy of Arts; and the whole nature of contemporary art was under scrutiny as Whistler went head to head with the great critic John Ruskin in a groundbreaking libel case. Ruskin had seen a series of paintings by Whistler entitled 'Nocturnes' and 'Symphonies', which today can been seen as the clear forerunner to abstraction. But for Ruskin, far from being a new, exciting development, Whistler's *Nocturne in Black and Gold: The Falling Rocket* represented the work of a 'coxcomb' who was asking 'two hundred guineas for flinging a pot of paint in the public's face' – a criticism that Whistler considered worthy of court.

With the arts in a moment of change and debate, there were rich pickings for a budding young critic. But compared with the territories Oscar had vanquished before, London was vast. It must have dawned on him quickly that fulfilling his dreams of a literary career amid this noisy bustling city, where the competition was fierce, would be much harder than winning over editors of the university and Irish presses. Oscar understood that to rise above the noise of the city he must shout loudest. He amplified the attitudes and activities that he had rehearsed in Oxford. Within months he managed to cast himself as not just a follower of the Aesthetic fashion but as its embodiment.

Once Oscar was in residence in Salisbury Street, he and Miles began inviting people to join them for 'Tea and Beauties'. In their bohemian rooms Miles would display his latest portraits of society belles and Oscar would entertain as only he could, with his rolling, golden voice pouring out wit and stories. Miles had persuaded the supermodel of her day, Lillie Langtry, to pose for him, and his delightful sketch of her had earned him a tidy income when, in reproduction, it became something of a best-seller. She had become a friend of Miles's and was soon also on Oscar's arm.

During his university days Oscar's romantic attentions had been trained for two years on Florence Balcombe, a Dublin girl and future actress whom he adored. But by 1878 he had found himself usurped in her affections by another Dubliner, the writer, theatre manager and future creator of *Dracula*, Bram Stoker. She married Bram that December, to Oscar's great distress. Now the high-profile Mrs Langtry, who seemed more than happy to adopt Oscar as her mascot, went some way to easing this disappointment.

But it was not just Lillie Langtry with whom Oscar regularly flirted. He was also showing public devotion to the great actress Sarah Bernhardt. In May 1879 he travelled to Folkestone to meet Miss Bernhardt as she arrived in England. In a gesture that guaranteed press attention, as she stepped foot on British soil, Oscar threw at her feet the armful of lilies he had brought to greet her. He was becoming a study in self-promotion. The following month he wrote a sonnet to her that was published in *The World*. A month after that his poem 'The New Helen' in praise of Miss Langtry appeared in *Time*.

Laura Troubridge, then a young, aspiring artist but who would one day marry Adrian Hope and become Constance's neighbour in Tite Street, witnessed the frisson that surrounded Oscar in those early days in London. Her cousin Charles Orde, known as 'Tardy', was friendly with the young Mr Wilde. 'To tea with Tardy', Laura wrote on 30 June 1879. 'Met Oscar Wilde, the poet. Both fell awfully in love with him, thought him delightful.' Then in July:

> To the National Gallery, saw Sarah Bernhardt there, had a good stare at her. Met Tardy and went together to tea at Oscar Wilde's – great fun, lots of vague 'intense' men, such duffers, who amused us awfully. The room was a mass of white lilies, photos of Mrs Langtry, peacock feather screens and coloured pots, pictures of various merits.[17]

Lillie Langtry remembered that, 'on his arrival from Oxford, Oscar had longish hair and wore an outfit that spoke of bohemian credentials: light-coloured trousers, a black frock coat, brightly coloured waistcoats with a white silk cravat held with an amethyst pin and always carrying lavender gloves.' But as Oscar's charm worked its magic on London society and, as Langtry observed, he 'began to rise in the life of London, and his unconscious peculiarities had become a target for the humorous columns of the newspapers, he was quick to realise that they could be turned to advantage, and he proceeded forthwith to develop them so audaciously that it became impossible to ignore them'.[18]

Before long Oscar had grown his hair longer than anyone else, and his buttonholes were more unusual. And his outfits became even more outrageous. Caricatures of him in the press quickly became animated on stage. By the end of 1880 a satire on Aestheticism called *Where's the Cat* opened at the Criterion Theatre, in which Oscar clearly provided the inspiration for the character of the Aesthetic writer Scott Ramsay. The actor playing Ramsay, Herbert Beerbohm Tree, modelled his performance on Oscar. Then came another play, *The Colonel*, in which another Aesthete, called Lambert Stryke, was again played in Wildean manner.

In early 1881 the *Punch* cartoonist George du Maurier was running weekly caricatures of two Aesthetic types, the poet Maudle and the painter Jellaby Postlethwaite. Maudle transfigured over the weeks into Oscuro Wildegoose, Drawit Milde and Ossian Wilderness, and was teased for his interest in lilies, the Grosvenor Gallery and blue china.

And so within two years after arriving in London, Oscar had

landed the city. Despite his limited output in print, by 1881 Oscar's fame was secured when the great painter and social observer William Powell Frith captured him at the Royal Academy summer show amid the great and the good. A lily in his lapel, the young Wilde, tall, long-haired and not yet showing the weight that would define his later years, stands notebook in hand, surrounded by a group of admiring women. To the right of the canvas the figure of George du Maurier is depicted looking on. To the left a woman wearing a loose, puff-sleeved Aesthetic outfit with a sunflower pinned to her breast gives us some sense of the figure that Constance too must have cut at this time.

In the same year that Frith immortalized Oscar in paint, the masters of popular music Gilbert and Sullivan confirmed Oscar's celebrity with the production of *Patience*, an operetta in which an Aesthete was presented in the character of Bunthorne. Bunthorne's costume took Aesthetic dress to new extremes. He wore a loose velvet jacket, knee breeches, silk tights and patent pumps. These extremes of dress were ones that soon became associated not with the fictional Bunthorne but with the man Wilde.

The Lloyds must have looked on with a mixture of bemusement and disapproval at the progress of their family friend. Conventional and upright, the inhabitants of 100 Lancaster Gate would not have considered wearing one's hair long and becoming the target of ridicule the best credentials. But then again, Oscar's Oxford contemporary Otho was hardly turning out as they had hoped.

For one thing, Otho had become embroiled in a court case that captured the public's imagination. A report in the *Daily News* for 22 March 1879, under the headline 'The Alleged Frauds upon the Charitable Public', gives an idea of the case's appeal. It describes the accused Vernon Montgomery and Ethel Vivian in the dock, amid an unusually packed and rowdy courtroom. Much of the crowd comprised young professional men, attracted by the impressive appearance of the bottle-blonde Miss Vivian, who was parading in the witness box in 'a light silk dress of fashionable make'.

The prosecution alleged that Montgomery and Vivian placed

advertisements in *The Times* purporting to be on behalf of an embarrassed girl in need of financial assistance. When charitable individuals responded to the advert, Montgomery entered into a correspondence that invited donations.

However, far from being a genuine lady in distress, prosecution witnesses identified Miss Vivian as in fact a Miss Wilmore, a Pimlico-based prostitute for whom Montgomery was almost certainly a pimp. In her defence, Miss Vivian protested from the witness box, much to the obvious mirth of the courtroom, that, far from being her pimp, Montgomery (who was using the moniker Viscount de Montgomery) was in fact a 'poet' whom she had met at the Promenade concerts, and that she had subsequently left Pimlico to live with him in his 'country house' near Maidstone.

To the horror of some constituents of his Lloyd and Napier relatives, Otho found himself appearing in court as a witness for the prosecution. He was one of the charitable individuals who had responded to *The Times* advertisement. In what was evidently an act of utter naivety, Otho sent Miss Vivian £5, a not insignificant sum. To the continued mirth of those watching proceedings, Otho noted that, although he acknowledged the fraud, he did not regret his donation to a woman who, regardless of her means of soliciting it, was indeed a subject for charity. Like many of those in the courtroom that day, Otho Lloyd presented as a man too easily turned by a pretty face.

Leaving aside his rather embarrassing susceptibility to the charms of young women and lack of financial acumen, Otho was beginning to concern the family more generally. Despite having won a scholarship to Oxford, he was lackadaisical in his approach to his studies and was soon failing key exams. Constance had made a huge emotional investment in her brother. Unable to pursue a career herself, her natural ambition was bound up in his achievements. As she saw the potential for such achievements slip away, Constance was genuinely distressed.

My Dearest boy, I am so terribly disappointed that you're being plucked, perhaps the more so that Francis has passed his examination, and I think in all probability Charlie his. It cannot but force itself upon my mind, seeing Grand Papa's disappointment, almost unspoken it is true, but scarcely for that the less, that you have not worked or that you have worked only indolently, as we are both only too inclined to do. Do dear boy try to make up this future year and work steadily and try to attain the honours that I know with study you have the capability of attaining . . . Do not think I am lecturing you. You know that all my ambition, all my future hopes are bound up in you and it is really a keen disappointment to me to find that you have none for yourself and it is not only that, but also that it is Grand Papa's money that is being spent and if you do not profit by your college career it is wasted, is it not so? Is there any possible way by which I can help you? Remember that ignorant as I am, I will do anything in my power, or learn anything by which I could afford you any possible assistance.[19]

With Otho's prospects foundering, Constance must have felt all the more keenly what potential suitors might offer her in terms of success and achievement. Despite now having several men 'in various stages of devotion', none of them was right. In fact, all of them were, for different reasons, utterly wrong.

In the summer of 1880 Constance, her aunt and grandfather travelled to the coast ahead of a family holiday in Holland. Constance's Irish uncle Charlie Hemphill and her cousin Stanhope joined the party briefly before it sailed. Constance thought this was nothing more than a social get-together, made possible by the fact that two branches of the family fortuitously found themselves close to one another during their respective travels. She suddenly discovered, however, that Stanhope, whom she had known since his boyhood, had long been holding a torch for her, and the whole meeting had been engineered for a very specific purpose.

'I've been so terribly horrified and frightened that I cannot get over it,' she wrote to Otho.

Did it ever in your wildest dreams enter your head that Stanhope cared for me? I went out for a long walk yesterday with him and Uncle Charlie and we two stayed behind to pick some berries, and he informed me that he had come to ask me to be his wife. I do hope no

43

one will ever again propose to me, for it is horrid. He said that he had wished to speak to me in Dublin and also in London when he was last there, and he would have waited now to test my feelings but that our going away tomorrow had hurried him on. It was so dreadful. I could but refuse him and he came again this morning to get a final answer, and looked as white as a sheet and frightened me so and yet I could not do anything else, could I? He would insist that I cared for someone else, and I assured him I did not. I have sent him away, and I don't want to marry, and I do hope nobody else will ever ask me. I am shaking all over still with fright. Tear up this letter.[20]

With poor Stanhope dispatched, it was not long before another admirer was buzzing around the Lloyd household. As London warmed up under the June sun of 1881, a Mr Fitzgerald began to hover. Despite his admirable persistence, he got short shrift. 'Mr Fitzgerald came . . . deep sigh, and requested to escort me somewhere this week,' Constance informed her brother. 'It ended finally in his arranging to come to Devonshire Terrace tomorrow and take Mama, Ella, Tizey and myself to the Fancy Fair at the Albert Hall. Poor man. I hope I shall meet someone I know and then I'll get rid of him. I left Zena and him to have a long conversation together but he made his way over after a time and I couldn't get rid of him.'[21]

Three days later the hapless Fitzgerald, failing to take a hint, tried his luck once more, as Constance once again relayed. 'Mr Fitzgerald was with me the whole afternoon and to my horror . . . went to the Arbuthnots[22] at home in the evening. I positively loathe him now. Isn't it horrid? He came last Monday and asked to be allowed to escort us on Wednesday, so I couldn't get off it.'[23]

Mr Fitzgerald's timing was poor. Unbeknown to him, his attentions were in competition with those of someone in whom, unlike himself, Stanhope and presumably the now defunct Alec Shand, Constance found herself passionately interested. Like Henry Fedden, whom she found so enthralling, this other suitor was cultured, and, like the fascinating Mr Belt, he was artistic and rather risqué. The man was none other than the newly famous Oscar Wilde.

It was Constance's Irish grandmother who engineered an

opportunity for Constance and Oscar to become properly acquainted in the early summer of 1881, somewhat by default. Grandma Atkinson's intention was to do a little matchmaking on behalf not of Constance but of her young aunt Ellena. 'Ella' Atkinson came to stay with her sister Ada Swinburne-King at Devonshire Terrace in the early summer of 1881. She was twenty-eight and still unmarried. Grandma Atkinson, well acquainted with Lady Wilde, suggested that Oscar, just a year Ella's junior, might come to tea during her stay. Lady Wilde was only too happy to oblige.

When Sir William Wilde died, Lady Wilde had been left in financial difficulty. Although the gross estate left by the surgeon was some £20,000, he had had debts, and since a substantial £2,000 was left to each of his three sons, William, Oscar and Dr Wilson, Lady Wilde was left with a sum that was quickly deemed not enough to live on in style in Merrion Square. Given both her sons' ambitions to seek careers in London, the decision was made that she would move to the capital, where she and Willie, Oscar's older brother, would combine their resources. And so in 1879 Speranza decamped to rented accommodation in Ovington Square, just off the Brompton Road, the plan being that Willie would take a house for himself and his mother once he had succeeded in securing a staff job on a national newspaper. Speranza was devoted to both her sons and, with them both now in London with her, securing a good match for them had become a priority.

At the tea party in Devonshire Terrace, held specifically for Ella's benefit, Otho recounts that Constance was 'one of the party too and was introduced for the first time to Oscar'.[24] The spark of attraction between the two must have been instantaneous. By 7 June, Oscar had paid a visit to one of Aunt Emily's 'at homes' in Lancaster Gate in order to see Constance again. Constance, suddenly all too aware of the celebrity attached to her new beau, found herself 'shaking with fright', something Oscar could scarcely have failed to spot. Nevertheless he persisted, begging her to visit his mother at the earliest opportunity.

Although the Irish side of the family were on very warm terms with the Wildes, the Lloyd clan in London held the notorious Oscar in general disapproval. 'Grand Papa I think likes Oscar,' Constance conceded to her brother, 'but of course the others laugh at him, because they don't choose to see anything but that he wears long hair and looks aesthetic. I like him awfully much but I suppose it is very bad taste.'[25]

Bad taste or no, Constance was determined. Despite or perhaps because of her past abuses, she had built up a steely resolve. Oscar's request to see Constance again as soon was possible was a 'little request I need hardly say I have kept to myself', she confided to Otho.

Constance's attraction to Oscar in these very early days reveals an aspect of their relationship that would remain fundamental to their later marriage. With Constance, Oscar dropped his public mask. As Constance revealed to an Otho who, less persuaded by the Aesthete, had obviously been relating something of Oscar's college history to her, 'I can't help liking him because when he's talking to me alone, he's never a bit affected and speaks naturally excepting that he uses better language than most people. I'm glad they didn't duck him, though you would have enjoyed it.'[26]

Shortly after this encounter, Constance and her mother paid a return visit to the Wildes in Ovington Square. Speranza had resumed her Saturday salons, which had become famous in Dublin society. Like her son, Speranza loved aristocratic society, and in London she did her best to attract the great and the good to her drawing room, along with Irish friends and literary folk. At that meeting the flirtations continued, with Oscar talking to Constance 'nearly all the time excepting when his Mother seized on him for somebody else. The room was crammed.'[27] On this occasion Oscar asked Constance to go to the theatre with him to see *Othello*.

Othello was playing at the Lyceum and was creating a sensation, thanks to its unusual proposition that the lead roles of Othello and Iago were being alternated between the famous American actor Edwin Booth and Britain's greatest stage star, Henry Irving. But more than this, Ellen Terry was starring as Desdemona. And this, Oscar must have known, would delight Constance.

Terry was, as the papers were reminding their readers that summer,

> something else besides a graceful, refined and tenderly emotional actress. She has the pre-Raphaelite facial angle, the pre-Raphaelite chest bones, the pre-Raphaelite eyes and lips. She is . . . justifiably dear to the dramatic but is doubly dear to the aesthetic heart.[28]

What better, then, than to take Constance to the most talked-about show in town, with the possibility of introducing her afterwards to a heroine? Oscar, already aspiring to become Miss Terry's recognized male counterpart, the High Priest of Aestheticism, had of course already made a point of getting to know both Irving and Terry personally.

Given her family's general suspicion regarding her latest beau, it was probably not just the social protocol of her time that encouraged Constance to present the theatre invitation as coming from the mother rather than the son: 'He [Oscar] or as I put it to the family, Lady Wilde has asked me to go to see Othello some night,' Constance wrote to her brother Otho in June 1881. 'Auntie looked *aghast* when I told her . . . I know she'll try and prevent me going and I shall be in a fury if she does.'[29]

It is not clear whether Constance managed to secure her exeat, but the fact that her suitor managed to see the production is evidenced by a note he sent to William Morris's daughter May, in which he included autographs of the full cast of that particularly celebrated production.[30]

As the love affair accelerated, barely a day went by when Constance wasn't either discussing or seeing Oscar. At a dinner with her sculptor friend Mr Belt, Constance sought his 'opinion of Oscar Wilde and yesterday got Oscar's opinion of him'. This, Constance noted, was 'the sort of thing I thoroughly enjoy'.[31]

By 10 June, Oscar had begun the process of inveigling himself with the elder Lloyds. He had taken Constance and her grandfather to see an exhibition by the Russian Romantic artist Ivan Aivazovsky at the Pall Mall Gallery. He specialized in seascapes, which Constance decided amounted to 'Poetry as well as painting on the canvas'. And it seems that even John Horatio was impressed:

> Grand Papa wants to buy the Moonlight scene on the Black Sea, price 700 guineas, which Auntie says is absolute folly but that Auntie has a soul above art, one that considers shillings and pence. She did not see the force of my argument that a thing of beauty is a joy forever. I told Grand Papa he might take it out of my money and leave me the picture instead for I never have seen anything I should like more, but he has no will of his own and Auntie will of course overrule him.[32]

Although John Horatio did not buy a major seascape, he did not return empty-handed from his excursion with Oscar and Constance that day. And, like his granddaughter, he proved himself more than capable of being a little sly when it came to dealing with Auntie Emily. Two major watercolour exhibitions were also on close to the Aivazovsky show at the Pall Mall Gallery. At 5 Pall Mall the Society of Painters in Water Colours had a selling exhibition, while at 53 Pall Mall the Institute of Painters in Water Colours was also exhibiting. It seems that after seeing the oil paintings by the great Russian, Constance, Oscar and John Horatio wandered through some of the other shows, and the temptation proved too much for the wealthy old man: 'However, he has actually bought 3 water colours of Aglaia Walton's for the drawing room for a 100 guineas,' Constance gleefully wrote to her brother, 'and he wrote and sent the money without even telling Auntie that he had made up his mind to it. She said he's mad.'[33]

Within just days of meeting Oscar, Constance had become so keen to continue seeing him that, rather than attend social invitations, she found herself staying in on the off chance of a visit from him. If ever there was someone Constance could see herself marrying it was Oscar, and she was going to make sure that she engineered every possible opportunity to realize this ambition.

'Aunt Mary has got a dance on Wednesday evening,' she told Otho, 'but I don't think I shall go to it, because the Wildes are coming to see Mama . . . some Wednesday and I want to be there when they come.'[34]

3

The sunflower and the lily

GIVEN HER OWN private ambitions towards Oscar Wilde, Constance must have been delighted to read in the newspapers, a year after they started seeing one another, that not only had her suitor's fame now spread internationally but that he had apparently also made a fortune. She must, in the same instant, have been devastated to hear that another woman seemed destined to become the beneficiary of Oscar's success.

The January after their summer of flirtation Oscar had travelled to America to undertake a lecture tour. Gilbert and Sullivan's *Patience* had opened in New York in September 1881, and within days of the fictional Aesthete Bunthorne delighting the American public, the opportunity to present the real thing was seized. An agent approached the producer of *Patience*, Richard D'Oyly Carte, who in turn cabled Oscar and proposed the tour. It was a massive enterprise that would see him travel the length and breadth of the United States and deliver readings on first 'The English Renaissance of Art', and then more fully on 'The Decorative Arts' and 'The House Beautiful'.

Constance had been delighted when the Wildes informed her about this important career break for Oscar the previous November. And regardless of quite how the tour had originated, Oscar's response to it proved that beneath the long hair and aesthetic pose was a man of substance and hard work. 'O.W. is going to be about 3 months in America firing 50 lectures and having all his expenses paid, not bad for him,' Constance proudly noted to Otho.[1]

Far from a three-month tour, what Oscar embarked on would in the end keep him away for a year. Adopting for real his own version of the velvet coat, knee breeches and silk stockings that had been designed for the fictional Bunthorne to wear on stage, Oscar was a hit with the American public. By September 1882 the gossip column of Dublin's *Freeman's Journal and Daily Commercial Advertiser* noted with glee how Wilde had been

> so completely filling all America with his renown that the country is absolutely bursting . . . and can hold no more. So he is about to depart for Japan. He will first of all however visit the still un-exhausted countries of Nova Scotia, New Brunswick and Prince Edward Island . . . Apart from all the ridicule there is much to admire and to wonder at in Oscar Wilde's career . . . He started from Europe, beneath the heavy burthen of ridicule . . . He was poor and dependent and laughed at. He has risen above every insult and con-demnation and will return home filled with respect for his own capacity and justly proud of his own perseverance . . . He is rich by his own labour, and will be respected now in spite of the strange attire he assumes.

But if this kind of report filled Constance's heart with pride and hope, the intelligence it offered next must have dealt a hefty blow. 'Moreover the great aim of his life is about to be accomplished (so folks declare) by a rich and laudable marriage with the daughter of the great American actress Julia Ward Howe. Miss Maud Howe was one of the beauties of the London season some three years ago, and obtained the honour of especial notice by one of the gallant sons of royalty.'[2]

Until this point things had been going well for Constance from a romantic point of view. Right to the moment of his departure, her and Oscar's mutual flirtation had been progressing, and although no correspondence between the pair while Oscar was overseas survives,[3] it seems likely Oscar would have been writing to Constance or, more appropriately, her family during his travels.

That Constance had revealed something of her unhappy private life to Oscar is evident. It is also clear that Oscar was moved by the fact that her circumstances had failed to erode Constance's capacity for kindness. By the time Constance heard that Oscar would be leaving for America, she was no longer bothering to conceal her feelings for him. She had become completely infatuated with him.

Just a few weeks after his flirtation with Constance began, Oscar had published his first book of poems. The edition had been roundly panned. The *Saturday Review* summed up the general tenor of the criticism that Oscar faced: 'Mr Wilde's verses belong to a class which is the special terror of reviewers, the poetry which is neither good nor bad, which calls for neither praise nor ridicule.' The *Review* informed its readers that 'The author possesses cleverness, astonishing fluency, a rich and full vocabulary, and nothing to say. Mr Wilde has read Messrs Tennyson, Swinburne, Arnold and Rossetti . . . and he has paid them the compliment of copying their mannerisms very naively.' But it warned its readers of Wilde's 'sensual and ignoble tone which deforms a large proportion of the poems for which a plea of youth is scarcely sufficient to excuse. So much talk about "grand cool flanks" and "crescent thighs" is decidedly offensive.'[4]

Far worse than the critical response, though, was the public humiliation that Oscar faced when an edition of his poems, specifically requested by the library of the Oxford Union Society, was then returned to him in what amounted to a rather public slap in the face. In a debate and vote held at the Union the majority of members found, like the *Saturday Review*, that Oscar's verses were immoral and derivative.

Quite what Constance thought has not been recorded. But it's more than likely that, like her contemporary Violet Hunt, who was an immediate rival for Oscar's affections, she saw only art and beauty in lines that others were interpreting decidedly differently.

Violet Hunt was the daughter of the landscape artist Alfred Hunt and something of a fixture within the bohemian art world. Beautiful, confident and attending the South Kensington School of Art, she had been courted quite aggressively by Oscar in the months before he met Constance. According to Violet, Oscar had even proposed to her, an offer that her father rejected.

Oscar sent Violet his book of poems, at a time when he sent copies to a number of people, including William Gladstone and the poets Robert Browning and Swinburne. It seems highly likely that Constance would have received a copy too. Despite the rumpus about their morality and originality, Violet thought that Oscar's poetry was beautiful. She wrote him a letter so full of praise that he felt moved to thank her, noting that 'In an age like this when Slander, and Ridicule, and Envy walk quite unashamed among us, and when any attempt to produce serious beautiful work is greeted with a very tornado of lies and evil speaking, it is a wonderful joy, a wonderful spur for ambition and work, to receive such encouragement and appreciation as your letter brought me.'[5]

Other immediate members of Wilde's circle had, however, taken a similar view to the Oxford Union – most dramatically, his house-mate Frank Miles's father. This clergyman, whom Oscar had known for years and visited on several occasions, found himself so concerned about the subtext of the poetry that he felt it necessary to write to Oscar and suggest that he and his son cease lodging together.

Since the days of 'tea and beauties' in Salisbury Street, Oscar and Frank had moved into 'Keats House', a property in that bohemian part of Chelsea, Tite Street, where Oscar would one day live with Constance. They were following the footsteps of their hero and friend the painter James McNeill Whistler. In 1877 Whistler had had the architect *du jour* Edward Godwin design 'The White House' in Tite Street for him. Here ebonized and gilt furniture stood amid Japanese cabinets and oriental carpets. But the house was sold just two years later, when Whistler went bankrupt.

In 1879 Miles commissioned the same architect to remodel 1 Tite Street into another temple of Aestheticism. Designing a studio at the very top of the house, Godwin created light airy interiors that, painted white, would display Miles's collection of exotic flowers and plants. A huge inglenook in the studio framed bespoke furniture, and throughout the house was indulged in exquisite detail such as door

and furniture handles in the form of swan's heads and glassware specifically blown by the famous Arts and Crafts glass manufacturers
Powell & Sons of Whitefriars.

In 1880 Miles and Wilde were installed in Keats House, where
their indulgence of things beautiful continued. Ironically Oscar's sets
of rooms included items he bought from the sale of the bankrupt
Whistler's effects, notably a painting of Sarah Bernhardt.

But more was going on in Chelsea than tea, painting and poetry.
Canon Miles's concern over Oscar's verse may well have been
heightened by wider worries over the moral well-being of his son.
With a reputation for being both a ladies' man, and also for keeping
the company of known homosexuals, Miles was living a sexually liberal life. Within a decade he would be dead from syphilis. Although
Miles's father did not accuse Oscar of similar misdemeanours, he
warned him that his poetry might suggest otherwise. It was an early
lesson in the power of appearances that Oscar would have done well
to remember.

'If we seem to advise a separation for a time it is not because we do
not believe you in character to be very different to what you suggest
in your poetry,' Canon Miles explained, 'but it is because you do not
see the risk we see in a published poem which makes all who read it
say to themselves, "this is outside the pale of poetry", it is licentious
and may do great harm to any soul who reads it.'[6] Oscar duly packed
his bags and left Keats House, moving temporarily into rooms close
to his mother and Willie, in Charles Street in Mayfair.

The moral laxity that those such as Canon Miles saw as part and
parcel of the Aesthetic proposition was either of no concern to
Constance or, far more likely, beyond her sightline. Leading a sheltered life in Lancaster Gate, Constance saw only the creative, artistic
aspect of the bohemian set. She had not yet had the opportunity to
comprehend that what went with this was a set of lifestyles that were
just as challenging to the social protocols of the day. Although
Constance understood adultery and violence, she had no direct
experience of the new sexual liberties that were being explored by
many of those whose art fascinated her.

On 18 November 1881 a letter from her stepfather, Mr Swinburne-King, arrived, and in it Constance discovered a poem teasing her about her infatuation with Oscar. Swinburne-King had penned what he termed a 'sonnet' entitled 'The Lily to the Sunflower' for his stepdaughter's amusement:

> One hour with thee, O Wilde,
> Would joy this longing Childe
> But she, tho' twenty-four
> To hear thy lips out-pour
> From depths of heart-born lore –
> What ecstasy she'd score: –
> To dream, Ah me,
> E'en I might be
> For age & evermore
> O Wilde with Thee!
>
> 2.
> Nor cease thy madding dream
> My Soul, until I scream –
> Not longer meek & milde: –
> By hopes deferement riled,
> By throbbing love beguiled
> And torturing passions piled
> I dream, ah me
> So this to be
> For age and ever Wilde
> O Wilde with Thee!

Constance, highly amused, penned her own poem by way of reply:

> Lyrics from the Childe to her Kinge
>
> Oh, do though gently singe
> To me, oh! Swinburne Kinge
> Of him I love
> With a passion Wilde;
> Until the very welin singe
> And all the bare-armed trees above

Do sigh as at an utter thinge
Moved by the sorrows of thy weary childe

Oh, could I be beguiled
With Terra-Cotta tiled
Or sunflowers gold
Or a lily white
The smell of verdant cabbage liked
Or sight of peacock feathers bold
And yet the thoughts of something wilde
Sootheth my aching spirit always quite.[7]

A week after receiving her sonnet from Mr Swinburne-King, Constance and her mother were yet again at home with Lady Wilde. Willie Wilde had finally secured a staff job on the *Daily Telegraph*, and so he and Speranza had moved from Ovington Square to a house in Park Street in Mayfair. A better address for a salon, perhaps, but a more expensive one. Lady Wilde's stretched finances could only accommodate the smallest house in the area, with the tiniest rooms, a fact not lost on Constance.

'We had such a joke yesterday,' Constance told Otho.

I went out with Mama to call on Lady Wilde having quite forgotten her address and in the pouring rain. I made Mama go down in a hansom to Number 70 . . . to find out then that it was shut up, so we went into all the shops on both sides of the way until at last at a bakers I reluctantly found the number and we went in and found Lady W all alone in her glory in such wee rooms that Mama and I puzzled internally how she'd got into them. No one had appeared though L.W. made us stay in to see Willie whom she was expecting. I heard all about Oscar. He is bringing out a drama which I see is advertised today in the Observer. *Vera or The Nihilists*, which is to be acted at the Adelphi on the afternoon of the 17th of December and Lady Wilde has said I must go because Oscar would expect me to go. I suppose she is trying to carouse audience. However I tried to make Mr King and Mama promise to go and Mama is quite willing.[8]

Vera, or The Nihilists was Oscar's first foray into drama. It tells the tale of a Russian female assassin who falls in love with one of her fellow nihilists, Alexis, only to discover he is in fact the heir to the Russian throne. When Alexis does in fact become Tsar, Vera is sent to kill him. But she cannot kill the man she loves, a man who is determined to use his birthright to bring democratic change to Russia. With her fellow assassins ready to follow in her steps and assassinate Alexis themselves unless Vera throws a bloodied dagger out of a window as a sign of the success of her mission, Vera chooses to sacrifice herself and throw a knife covered in her own blood to her colleagues.

The performance to which Constance was invited never took place. It was cancelled. A real-life Tsar had been assassinated in March and diplomatic pressures were afoot, possibly from the Russian Embassy. Meanwhile, preparations for Oscar's American lecture tour suddenly became all-consuming. Oscar had engaged George Lewis to act as his solicitor and negotiate his contract for the tour, and had been writing to important figures who might provide letters of introduction to opinion-formers on the other side of the Atlantic. On Christmas Eve, Oscar boarded the *Arizona* and set off on his adventure.

In Oscar's absence Constance continued to embrace the attributes of Aestheticism. It has often been suggested that she was a person whose adoption of Aestheticism was purely part of her enthralment to Oscar. But Constance was quite her own person. Oscar's appeal to her reflected her own predispositions.

Although an invitation to lunch at the club most associated with London's bohemian crowd, the particularly female-friendly Albemarle, felt like a step too far for Constance ('Mademoiselle Arbau and I went to the Temple Church on Sunday and did not get home to lunch until 2.30. Mr Short took us into the Hall and into his rooms. He was most anxious to take us to the Albemarle Club to lunch, but we were afraid to go'[9]), nevertheless Constance was making inroads elsewhere.

She began a collection of blue and white china, which was *de rigueur* for anyone pretending to Aesthetic credentials. She also continued to explore her own artistic talents, and now it was to ceramics that she turned.

If not before, certainly by, early 1882 Constance was taking pottery classes, probably either at the pottery studio at the South Kensington Museum or at the Minton art pottery studio in Kensington Gore. Both locations were close to the Royal Albert Hall, a place that Constance found herself passing regularly as she trudged from Lancaster Gate, across Hyde Park and into South Kensington. Her correspondence mentions her tendency to bump into friends there, including on one occasion Oscar, whom she saw there 'for about a second' one day.[10]

'Had two lessons in terracotta painting and I'm at present in a hopeless state of despair over it,' Constance reported in March 1882, 'but I'm going to have a private lesson on Friday. There's no use in joining a class unless you know something about it first, and I of course have been working all wrong.'[11]

In the late 1870s female amateur potters working in these South Kensington studios made their contribution to what became known as the Arts and Crafts movement, a revival of craft skills that went hand in hand with the so-called Aesthetic movement. By 1878 these potteries had established a commercial outlet via Howell & James, in Regent Street, and that year they staged an exhibition that 'contained upwards of one thousand original works, mostly by ladies, and was frequented during its two months duration by nearly 10,000 visitors'.[12]

A year after the first mention of ceramics in her letters, Constance was working towards a contribution for another similar show and had high ambitions. 'I want to paint two plates for the Amateur Exhibition on the 21st in Regent Street and to sell them, if possible for 30 shillings a piece,' she revealed in a letter. 'They cost me 10 shillings without paint, but I'm afraid I cannot do them well enough and then they will not accept them.'[13]

Constance's plates were essays in 'barboline' painting, a technique, as she herself explained, of 'painting under glaze on pottery with a thin kind of clay called slip mixed with the colours to make them opaque like oil. Consequently it can be painted boldly, unlike the ordinary enamel china painting, and is fired and glazed afterwards. You paint it on the bisque ware.'[14]

It is also evident that Constance was working away at her fine art skills. She had enrolled in the St John's Wood School of Art, based in Elm Tree Road, not far from Lord's cricket ground. Founded in 1878, this was an art school where women could study those drawing skills and take the life classes that would, among other things, prepare them for entry into the Royal Academy Schools – an institution that had admitted its first female student in 1860.

Art classes were becoming increasingly popular in the 1880s. For those young women like Constance who instinctively felt the need to do something with their lives, periodicals such as *The Girl's Own Paper* explained the potential appeal of what might lead to a career, if not as an artist, then most certainly as a tutor.

Between true artistic geniuses and those destined to be viewers of works of art rather than creators of art was 'a powerful and energetic middle class', explained the paper, 'who . . . are yet gifted with a vein of talent, more or less generous, which would well repay cultivation, and which would fill the lives of those who possess it with healthy interests and sufficiently lucrative employment'.[15]

The St John's Wood School, under the tutelage of a Mr Calderon, cost its pupils 15 guineas a year or 10 guineas for two terms. Girls had to buy their own equipment, but models were supplied. Apart from full-time tuition, the school offered part-time and evening classes, and it's likely that Constance, with all her other activities, opted for the latter. One convention of the school was the expectation that students should join the St John's Wood Sketch Club and enter their work for regular viewings where invited practitioners and celebrities came to judge the pupils' work.

In August 1882, while Oscar was introducing residents of the state of New York to the joys of the artistic movement in England, Constance was planning her contributions for the sketch club exhibition. She was on holiday at Delgaty Castle in Aberdeenshire. The imposing sixteenth-century castle, with its white-harled five-storey tower, had come into the ownership of the local Ainslie family, who were resident there that summer in their latest incarnation as Mr and Mrs Grant-Duff-Ainslie. Amid the magnificent setting of the imposing castle and its sumptuous grounds, the house party comprised a Mr Huxley, a Miss Michelle, Mrs Ainslie's cousin Mr Morgan and his family, a Colonel Forbes and the main Ainslie clan, which included sixteen-year-old Douglas.

On arrival Constance realized that Delgaty provided plenty of opportunity for sketching and immediately dispatched instructions to Otho in Lancaster Gate to send her 'my spectacles which are lying somewhere in my room in a case . . . Next is a small sketch book, thickish paper about 10 inches by 6 which I shall be awfully obliged if you can get to me . . . Also a medium sized, rather large camel's hair brush, a good one. I am very anxious to try and take some sketches here, though I expect not to succeed.'[16]

Constance quickly discovered that any ambition to make a series of sketches for the St John's Sketch Club would be hard to realize. She was having far too much fun. There were billiards, tennis and chess tournaments, punctuated by picnics and outings. She was even being taught how to shoot. And of course, there were those mystical activities in the evenings that she so adored. She was mesmerized one night by one member of the group and 'upset Mrs Ainslie dreadfully. She thought I was awfully ill!' In fact, Constance revealed that she had 'never enjoyed myself so much anywhere' as during that wonderful summer in Scotland.

But something else happened during that holiday. The happy radiance that Constance exuded proved irresistible to the male members of the party and quickly ignited the jealousies of women in the group. If the growing number of admirers to date gives a picture of Constance as clearly attractive, this account shows that she was something far more than commonly attractive. She was, frankly, sexy and unconventionally precocious. In short, whether she was conscious of it or not, she was a magnet and a flirt.

At first it was Mr Huxley who fell under Constance's spell, much to the annoyance of Miss Michelle, who became jealous of me because for 3 days before I came, Mr Huxley devoted himself to her. I think she is about 45, of Italian descent, the daughter of a diplomat, and consequently has been all over Europe and is very amusing, but she's terribly superstitious and too fond of chat. She never knows when to stop and riles everyone. I have offended her mortally and she will not forgive me, which is rather a nuisance.[17]

But it was not just Mr Huxley who found Constance Lloyd so compelling. Once Huxley had left the party, the teenage Douglas Ainslie confided that he too was utterly smitten with Constance, despite the fact she was a good eight years his senior. 'Douglas says that he was so jealous of Mr Huxley that he didn't know what to do,' Constance told Otho, 'and used to go and bemoan himself to Miss Michelle, and ask her what he should do to make himself agreeable.'[18]

Constance's and Douglas's flirtations were quickly noticed by the wider group, and a series of unfortunate incidents led to Constance being deemed a bad influence on the young man. In terms of his crush on her, 'I never saw anything to equal Douglas,' Constance admitted,

and the worst of this is that Mrs Ainslie has discovered this and I simply don't know what to do. Unfortunately tonight he began telling me of this scrape he had got into at school and I was advising him to the best of my ability, lecturing him he called it, and Miss Michelle who is perpetually interfering about everything, went and told Mrs Ainslie we were in his room together and so I have been told I am not to go there. I like Douglas a great deal, too much to snub him and I like Mrs Ainslie a great deal, too much to want to offend her but it strikes me that I shall be lucky if I am asked here again and I have never been so happy in all my life.[19]

Things went from embarrassing to farcical. Douglas, unable to conceal his massive crush, and with all the awkwardness one would expect from a boy of his age, began behaving strangely whenever Constance was near him, which left Constance 'awfully done up':

Mrs Ainslie's simply furious with me about Douglas and I am quite certain now that I shall never be asked here again. Everybody . . . is

... laughing at us ... What makes it so awfully difficult for me is ... this, which you must not tell a soul. Douglas has got into the most fearful habit of betting and has actually bet £60 on the ... race, ... that comes off on September the 13th ... Now for a lad of 16 it seems to me perfectly dreadful and my one great aim is to induce him to give up betting, and he says that I am the only person who could make him do it if I want to induce him to give me a promise not to bet anymore, the more so as he never loses ... You could not understand unless you were here how awfully disagreeable it is. Everyone in the house is making fun of it, and they say that Mr Grant Duff and Mr Huxley were just the same, and there is a Colonel Forbes here too, about 50 I should think or more, evidently an awful flirt, who has gone cracked too, and of course everything is noticed and talked about here, and I know they all think I flirt. Mrs Ainslie tells me that I have turned Douglas's head ... I must go to bed or I shall think my head off. Certainly I'm unlucky. For goodness sake write to me. I think I shall offer to go back to London next week and that will settle matters satisfactorily.[20]

But matters did not settle. In fact, they became even more comical. Douglas wrote Constance a note inviting her to his room after everyone was in bed. Clearly losing his nerve at the last minute, he never delivered his highly risqué proposal. Instead he left it in the blotter, to be found the next day by the disapproving Miss Michelle. The latter informed Mrs Ainslie, and Constance found herself returned to London.

Although Delgaty proved unfruitful from a sketching point of view, over the course of the next few months Constance did complete something that she felt was worthy of submission to the St John's Wood School. The following March she was in Torquay staying with relations, the Harveys, and was able to send a picture back to London by the night train. Otho was put on standby to collect it and get it to the school before eleven.[21]

Constance's craft and artistic endeavours, along with her university exams, show her as a young woman searching for a role for herself. Some two years earlier, at the time when her cousin Stanhope so inappropriately proposed to her, she had attempted to put into words this deep-seated desire to achieve something in life: 'I have no special objection to being married, excepting that I don't care for anyone and that I think I am rather afraid of marrying,' Constance had told Otho.

> At the same time I cannot say that I prefer the life I am leading at present. If I eventually do not marry, I will not live with Auntie all my life, I shall do something. I feel as though I am stagnating and it won't be so bad however if you are in London and I am thinking of going in for an examination. I shan't work my head off for I don't care much about the result, I just want something specific to do to prevent my continually dreaming 'til I get perfectly morbid.[22]

With her desire to achieve something in life, Constance was aligning herself with a group of women who since the middle part of the century had been fighting for social equality for women, as well as for their political enfranchisement. It would be a cause that in the fullness of time Constance would espouse more fully and formally.

Throughout the 1880s the voice of feminism was getting louder. The suffrage movement got under way with high-profile and aristocratic campaigners such as Viscountess Harberton leading national demonstrations for the right for women householders and rate-payers to vote. The question of the parliamentary vote aside, the dominance of men in other aspects of life was being chiselled away in tiny chunks. Women had already won the right to practise medicine, and in 1880 Eliza Orme became the first woman to obtain a degree in law. Then in 1882 the Married Women's Property Act marked a genuine shift in women's legal rights, since for the first time it allowed the notion that a married woman could in fact, legally speaking, be her own person.

Until 1882 all married women were defined as subordinate to their husbands, and any property and rights they might have held as single women were surrendered to his ownership. Horror stories in the press pointing out the injustice of this system cited men's ability to squander their wives' private fortunes should they wish, with the former having no recourse. But after the Act married women were suddenly redefined legally. They were given the right to their own wealth, as well as to buy and sell property in their own right. They could hold bank accounts and stocks. They could sue as individuals rather than rely on the offices of their spouse. The flip side was that they were now liable for their own debts and could be declared bankrupt, but few were complaining. Constance was living in an era when she could enjoy both liberty and responsibility above and beyond her mother's and her grandmother's generations.

Speranza Wilde may not have fully grasped the implications of this Act of Parliament. In her time Speranza had expressed views that diverged from that Victorian expectation that the sole purpose of a woman and a wife was to accommodate the wishes of her spouse. In her essay 'The Bondage of Women' she condemned an education system for women which solely prepared girls for 'husband worship'. Nevertheless, in spite of her published views, Speranza was also a pragmatist, and when it came to her own sons she was more than prepared to consider how wealthy girls might provide automatic financial security for them.

Money, or the lack of it, was a constant preoccupation for Speranza. Amid the letters that survive between her and Oscar there are few without mention of money or debt. While he was in America, Speranza bombarded Oscar with letters in which she reminded him constantly of her own precarious financial situation. She complained she was living 'in a fever of nerves' and remained perpetually on the brink of having to give up her house. She was, she told Oscar, scouring the papers to look for opportunities where the output of her own pen might bring in a few pennies.

Part of the problem was Oscar's brother Willie, who, far from providing comfort and security for his mother, was simply adding to her worries. Willie was a talented journalist and likeable raconteur who had secured work with *Punch*, *Vanity Fair* and the *Daily Telegraph* and had acquired quite a profile when he moved to London in the late 1870s. But despite what his peers recognized as a not inconsiderable talent and charm, he lived up to his surname. He was irresponsible and unreliable and drank like a fish. He had a reputation for partying hard and was a member of the notorious Fielding Club in London, which would open its doors at eight o'clock in the evening and then stay open throughout the night.

Far from contributing to the Wilde coffers, Willie was, if anything, a drain on them. He had run up debts of around £2,000 by the early 1880s. The relationship between Willie and Oscar was consequently strained. Oscar was angry with his brother for his professional failures and while he was away wrote to him in no uncertain terms. Speranza opened the letter.

> yr last from N York dated the 9th has arrived addressed to <u>Willie</u>. But he was away with a friend at Windlesham for a couple of days so I read it, but it was so severe & I did not give it to him, I burned it – he . . . feels at last how foolish he has been & he is really trying for work . . . I would rather you write a few kind words to him appealing to his good sense for something good.[23]

But it was not just Willie who was to blame for the Wildes' generally impecunious situation. While Oscar was away, Speranza found herself bombarded with bills from Oscar's creditors too. With his exploits in America racking up column inches, the impression at home was that Oscar was making a fortune. Some newspaper reports suggested he would make as much as £5,000. And so those he owed began to call in their debts.

On 10 July Speranza informed her son, 'Levers bill came here for you. I will send you the list next time I write – do pey [sic] them before you spend all the money.' A couple of weeks later it was 'North (of Dublin)' who was writing inquiring after Oscar's address, along with 'several people [who] have sent me your bills'. Then in August another 'bill came for you . . . you seem to have lived luxuriously at Tite Street – I never saw the rooms & can only judge from the items'.[24]

The actual profit Oscar made after close to a full year of lecturing was $5,605.31, a half-share of profits after costs of a tour that brought in $18,215.69. This would have amounted to just over £1,000. But with his debts to settle it's unclear how much of this money would actually end up in Oscar's own pockets, not least because, clearly despairing at his mother's situation, he also began to bail her out, sending cheques with almost every letter home.

'My dear child,' she wrote on 18 September 1882,

> Your letter and cheque £80 of Sept 6th has this moment arrived & my first impulse was a flood of tears over it . . . I feel deeply at taking your money; the product of hard work and . . . fierce strivings against a bitter world – Willie was expected home to night, but not come . . . I still trust he will . . . awake to the full meaning of his life and what has become of it . . . I will hold on to the house, at least over the winter . . . You are the talk of London – the cab men ask if I am anything to Oscar Wilde, the milk man has bought your picture! . . . I think you will be mobbed when you come back.[25]

For Speranza, a good marriage for Oscar was vital, and the sooner the better. 'What will you do on your return?' she wrote to Oscar while he was away, suggesting that 'you must bring home the American bride'.[26] Speranza was keen that Oscar set the bar high. Surely he could find an heiress with a '¼ of a million', then he could 'take a home in Park Lane – & go into Parliament'.[27]

His natural flirtatiousness heightened by Speranza's encouragement, Oscar became identified as quite the ladies' man while he was in America. And so it is perhaps hardly surprising that his name quickly became linked with that of Maud Howe when he stayed as the guest of her mother in Newport. But the newspaper reports were unfounded. Oscar and Maud may have been seen together, but there was no spark. It was Oscar's growing celebrity and the press's desire for a new story about him that generated news about an engagement. For once, Oscar was quick to quash the rumours, and he told his mother to do the same. 'I gave a decided contradiction to the report that you were to be married to the beautiful Miss Maud Howe,'[28] Speranza informed Oscar on 6 August, sounding perhaps just a bit disappointed.

Oscar arrived home in January 1883, and although he came

without the wife that the gossip columns had been predicting, he nevertheless stepped off the ocean liner *Bothnia* with the smell of success in his nostrils and a determination to build on his American experience. If not Parliament, then at the very least professional recognition was something he now craved. Sick of ridicule, he was intent on acquiring a new level of respect from those at home. He had cut the long locks that had been so mercilessly parodied before he left. Now, looking altogether a more robust proposition, he clearly considered that, after a haircut, marriage might also help.

While in America, Oscar had renewed his ambitions to become a playwright. He had befriended one of America's leading theatrical impresarios, Steele Mackaye, and together they had hatched plans to stage not only *Vera* in the USA but also a new play that Oscar would write: *The Duchess of Padua*. By the time Oscar returned home Mackaye had already brought one of America's leading ladies, Marie Prescott, to the table to produce and take the lead in *Vera*. And for *The Duchess* he had put Oscar in touch with another actress, Mary Anderson. By February financial terms for *Vera* had been agreed and Oscar had benefited from a lump-sum down payment. Meanwhile he was due to complete the *Duchess* by the end of March. To this end, just a few weeks after returning home he left for Paris, where he intended to write. With what was left of his American earnings and £200 in his pocket from the down payment for *Vera*, Oscar was for the first time in his life quite comfortably off.

By May 1883 both Oscar and Constance had returned to London for the season, Oscar from France and Constance from a brief stay in Torquay with the Harveys. Oscar, whose new, short hairstyle was now curled, stayed with his family in Park Street. The capital was once again in the grip of its annual social whirlwind, and he became intoxicated. Unable to focus on work amid the festivities, where 'the splendid whirl and swirl of life in London sweeps me from my Sphinx. I am hard at work being idle,' he explained to his friend Robert Sherard, 'late midnights and famishing morrows follow one another . . . However society must be amazed and my Neronian coiffure has amazed it.'[29]

To Oscar's distress, amid all this gaiety he found himself once again impoverished. He had managed to spend his recent earnings and discovered that he was still pursued by bills that had remained unpaid from his college days.[30] The disappointment of this financial position, in spite of a year's hard graft, prompted Speranza into action once again. She quickly reprised those visits in which marriageable young women were invited over for the benefit of her sons. On 16 May Constance and Otho found themselves in her tiny Mayfair rooms. And it seems that the relationship between Constance and Oscar took up where it had left off.

The very next day Constance and Otho returned to Tite Street to another of Lady Wilde's receptions. On 19 May Oscar was at Lancaster Gate. Constance was invited to visit Lady Wilde on 24 May. Unable to attend, she asked the Wildes to come to them on the 28th, when the Hope family were also expected.

Lady Wilde lost no time in responding. Sensing her son's renewed interest in Constance, she did not want to let the opportunity slip as it had done two years previously. 'Dear Constance (I trust I might call you Constance), We were desolated not seeing you yesterday,' Speranza wrote on 25 May. 'Oscar talked like Plato on Divinity . . . I shall go and see Miss Hope & Jenny, with great pleasure, on the 28th but hope meanwhile you will call on Saturday 26th. I like my rooms to be decorated.'[31]

Even if Speranza imagined that Constance would provide some adornment in her living room in Park Street, it's likely that few people would have noticed. Lady Wilde's salons were notorious for being held in such low-lit conditions that attendees quite often disappeared into the shadows. Speranza kept the curtains drawn in Park Street and, with candles muted by shades, luminaries from the artistic and literary world would be spared a clear sight not only of their fellow guests but also of their hostess's increasingly meagre means. Speranza herself and her household were becoming unkempt and second-hand, often wearing clothes that clearly belonged in a long-gone past. With only a single Irish domestic to polish and scrub her furniture, the artistic lighting was pragmatic.

If attending Lady Wilde's salon provided some candle-lit old-world flavour to Constance's season, elsewhere the wonders of modern technology were to be marvelled at. One of the spectacles of the season of '83 was the 'Great International Fisheries' exhibition held in South Kensington. With contributions from fishing nations from China to North America, it was a show designed to illustrate aspects of that industry all over the world. It quickly became the most popular haunt that summer. And thanks to the power of the new electric lighting, it was an event that could be visited at night as well as during the day.

One of the most popular attractions was the aquarium. Here live species of sea fish and crustaceans were on view in ten huge water tanks measuring fifteen feet long and over four feet deep. Some 70,000 gallons of seawater were kept in reserve to feed these tanks, with the water pumped through vulcanized India-rubber pipes. In addition there were a further nine tanks of freshwater fish! There was even a beautiful fishing pagoda and a waterfall in the Chinese court and an 'unrivalled collection of Indian fish preserved in labelled bottles' in the Asian pavilion.

Despite all these diversions, when Otho and Constance joined Oscar in a visit to this extraordinary spectacle on 7 June, Oscar talked away throughout the whole adventure, barely noticing the fish. Perhaps this was why he found it necessary to return to the show at a later date, on which occasion he bumped into the Swinburne-Kings and raised a few eyebrows among their party by referring to Constance by her first name. Writing from another house party out of town, Constance related the event to Otho, revealing that she had had a 'cheeky epistle two days ago from Mr King. I suppose you heard about their meeting OW at the Fisheries and his calling me Constance.'[32]

This style of address, which did away with traditional formalities, may have been as much an Aesthetic mannerism on Oscar's part as an indication of growing intimacy. But both implications were clearly welcomed by Constance, who in the same note revealed more of herself. She was continuing her habit of bringing up Oscar as a topic of conversation wherever she could. Every glowing account of the man with whom she was now head over heels in love simply served to enhance her devotion to him.

'There was a man dining here last night who was rather interesting,' she told Otho. 'He is a vicar and I should imagine very unsuited for clerical work . . . he . . . got out a couch and flopped on to it with his legs up in the air . . . flopped out of it onto the floor and asked me if I called that acting. He abused Oscar Wilde but acknowledged that he was awfully clever, said that his poems were very clever and very wicked.'[33]

As June progressed, Constance and Oscar continued to see one another as much as possible. According to Otho, they attended a reception held as a piece of advocacy for the women's rights movement. And then, on 10 July, Constance and Otho went to hear Oscar lecture on his 'Impressions of America' at Prince's Hall in Piccadilly. Shortly afterwards Oscar and his mother attended a large 'at home' in Lancaster Gate, where, according to Otho, despite sixty-odd guests Oscar spoke to no one but Constance.

It was hard to interpret Oscar's behaviour as anything other than romantic infatuation, but Otho did his best. At some profound level Otho was against the blossoming romance. In spite of Oscar's attentions to Constance, Otho wrote to his own sweetheart, Nellie Hutchinson: 'I don't believe that he means anything; that is his way with all girls whom he finds interesting.' Otho considered all this attention to Constance nothing more than another of Oscar's poses: 'If the man were anyone else but Oscar Wilde one might conclude that he was in love.'[34]

But if Constance hoped that their socializing might lead to a proposal, America once more proved the obstacle to their romance. Rehearsals for *Vera* were due to start in New York in August, and so after a brief lecture tour that took Oscar to Margate, Ramsgate, Southampton, Brighton and Southport, on 2 August he boarded the *Britannia* in Liverpool, bound for America.

Constance headed to the Continent with her grandfather while Oscar was away. John Horatio was in the habit of making a European excursion around August time. She returned to British shores towards the end of September and was at once keen to find out what Oscar had been up to in her absence. Writing to Otho from Folkestone, Constance noted:

> I've just got a *Western Morning News* . . . with an account of Oscar Wilde's lecture on America, at Exeter. It is the same that we heard apparently . . . they give a description of him, he is a handsome well-built man above medium height and wore his hair cut rather short, . . . he has a musical voice and good elocution and . . . easy self-possessed manner . . . when the lecture had been . . . delivered and Oscar had quitted the stage and the curtain had been dropped, no one showed any disposition to leave the auditorium. Loud applause called out the Lecturer who gracefully bowing, thanked the audience for their attention and courtesy and again retired.[35]

Constance's feet barely touched London soil. When she and her grandfather returned to Lancaster Gate, John Horatio fell gravely ill. Constance saw Oscar briefly in mid-October at Lady Wilde's Saturday salon but was then dispatched to Dublin to stay with 'Mama Mary', her maternal grandmother, where she arrived around 8 November. This time, however, distance did not get between Oscar and Constance. They wrote to each other avidly.

Before she left for Ireland, Oscar had given Constance a copy of *Vera* to read. The play had not gone well in America and had closed after just a week. Writing from her grandmother's house in Dublin's Ely Place on 11 November, Constance comforted Oscar as best she could over the play's lack of success. 'I cannot understand why you should have been so unfortunate in its reception unless either the acting was very inferior or the audience was unsympathetic to the political opinion expressed in it,' she offered. 'The world surely is unjust and bitter to most of us; I think we must either renounce our opinions & run with the general stream or else totally ignore the world and go on our own way regardless of all, there is not the slightest use in fighting against existing prejudices for we are only worsted in the struggle.'[36]

In the letter Constance continued an argument that she and Oscar had been having about the nature of art, one that set them distinctly apart: 'I am afraid you & I disagree in our opinion on art, for I hold that there is no perfect art without perfect morality, whilst you say that they are distinct & separable things.' But Constance was quick to offer a means of resolving their differences into a workable arrangement: 'I know that I should judge you rather by your aims than by your work.' And with this Constance wrapped up her letter with an invitation to Oscar to visit her in Dublin: 'I told the Atkinsons that you would be here some time soon and they will be very pleased to see you. I shall be here.'

Oscar headed for Ireland on 21 November. Constance was ready and waiting. The Irish family were primed to meet her beau: her Hemphill cousins had a note awaiting him at his hotel, the Shelbourne, inviting him to join the family the moment he arrived. And so Oscar saw Constance the very first evening he was in town. According to Constance, Oscar was 'extra affected'. She put this down to nerves.

The following day he was lecturing on 'The House Beautiful' at the Gaiety Theatre, and Constance and her clan attended. They were so thrilled with the lecture that, even though Constance had already heard it, they all decided to go to his 'Impressions of America' the next day.

Cenie and Stanhope & I went to the lecture yesterday afternoon and brought O. W. back to four o'clock tea . . . We three went again to the [American] lecture, which none of us thought as interesting as the former one. We also went to Oscar's box in the evening to see *The Merry Duchess* (stupid and somewhat vulgar thing!). He could not come himself as he was dining out. They all think him so improved in appearance, and he is certainly very pleasant. Mama Mary is so fond of him & he is quite at home here. We are having 40 or 50 people to tea this afternoon for <u>my</u> sake I believe, between ourselves rather a nuisance for I hate having to talk to dozens of people. Stanhope has started on a new tack and chaffs my life out of me about O. W., such stupid nonsense, & Cenie eggs him on . . . I have just read *Vera* through again, and I really think it very fine. Oscar says he wrote it in order to show that an abstract idea such as liberty could have quite as much power and be made quite as fine as the passion of love ... Please destroy this letter for as you know our family is not over-honourable in such matters as reading other people's letters.

Ever your loving sister

Constance M. Lloyd

Oscar praised you so much both to Cenie and me.[37]

And now something quite strange happened in the story of Oscar and Constance's romance. Otho, who throughout the summer had chaperoned his sister during her outings with Oscar, suddenly wrote to his sister confessing his doubts about the suitability of his Oxford contemporary as her suitor. His letter, no longer extant, related a story about Oscar Wilde, sufficiently unsavoury for Otho to feel he must raise an immediate alarm.

Otho's letter arrived at Ely Place on 27 November. It crossed with one that Constance had sent her brother the day previously. The two siblings must have been horrified as they opened each other's correspondence. For while Constance read with dismay Otho's warnings, on reading his sister's letter Otho realized he had acted too late.

'My dearest Otho,' his sister announced, 'Prepare yourself for an astounding piece of news! I am engaged to Oscar Wilde and perfectly and insanely happy.'[38]

4

'Bunthorne is to get his bride'

THE ENGAGEMENT RING that Oscar Wilde presented to Constance Lloyd remains in the possession of the Wilde family's descendants today: a heart formed from diamonds enclosing two pearls, surmounted with another bow of diamonds. The design was apparently Oscar's own.

In slipping this ring on to her finger, Constance knew that she was going to have to steel herself for a barrage of objections. When she informed her brother of her engagement, Constance revealed that, although the Dublin Atkinsons were delighted with the match, she held some concern that she would face opposition from the Lloyds, and specifically from Aunt Emily. 'I am so dreadfully nervous over my family; they are so cold and practical,' she worried. But in the same breath her determination to go her own way whatever was also clear. 'I won't stand opposition,' she wrote, 'so I hope they won't try it.'[1]

Constance felt sure that Otho would be her ally in negotiating any objections from the Lloyd camp, not least because she had spent recent months smoothing the way for his own somewhat unconventional matrimonial ambitions. Otho had fallen in love with a beautiful girl called Clara, whose background was socially dubious, to the minds of the conservative Lloyds at least. In the summer of 1882 Nellie, as Clara was known, was sent to a finishing school in Lausanne in Switzerland – possibly at Otho's expense, and as part of his longer-term ambition to marry her.[2] Certainly by the following March it seems that these ambitions had been aired, and Constance, who had a genuine fondness for Nellie, was being drafted in as her advocate.

Now, as far as Constance was concerned, it was Otho's turn: 'I want you now to do what has hitherto been my part for you, and make it all right.'[3]

Constance and Oscar had meticulously planned their assault on the Lloyd side. Oscar had left Ireland straight after proposing and travelled to Shrewsbury to continue his lecture circuit. On his arrival there he wrote to John Horatio, to Constance's mother and to Otho regarding his intentions. Constance had written a note for Aunt Emily, no doubt pleading how much she loved Oscar, and had sent this to Otho, with instructions that he should hand it over when Oscar's letters arrived, and 'not before'. Then the plan was that Constance would take a Friday crossing which would return her to London early on Saturday 1 December. That same Saturday, Oscar, with a temporary break in his lecturing, could return to London and then visit Lancaster Gate the following Sunday to repeat his intentions in person before setting off on his next round of lectures. His commitments would then keep him and his fiancée apart until Christmas, a prospect that Constance was already dreading.

The minute Oscar left Constance in Dublin he began writing to her. And two days after his proposal she wrote back in the most passionate terms:

My own Darling Oscar

I have just got your letter, and your letters always make me mad for joy and yet more mad to see you and feel once again that you are mine and that it is not a dream but a living reality that you love me. How can I answer your letters, they are far too beautiful for any words of mine, I can only dream of you all day long and it seems as if everyone I meet must know my secret and see in my face how I love you, my own love. If you had your magic crystal you would see nothing, believe me, but your own dear image there for ever, and in my eyes you shall see reflected nought but my love for you. Oh Oscar how shall I ever love you . . . for your sweet love for me, and yet I worship you my hero and my god! You may give up your lecturing if you will, for as long as I live you shall be my lover. You must come to me on Saturday, I cannot live til Xmas without you, & yet I know if you do not come you cannot. All thro the early watches of the night your image is ever present with me, & I cannot sleep.[4]

But Constance's and Oscar's plans were quickly challenged. First there was that unfortunate letter from Otho that suggested a potential lack of support on his part for the engagement. In addition to this blow came news that Oscar had forgotten a commitment to lecture on the very Saturday that he planned to travel to London to talk to Constance's family. And then there was further disappointment. Rather than giving his instant consent to his granddaughter's marriage, John Horatio had responded to Oscar's letter with the news that he intended to withhold his consent until Oscar could answer some important questions about his financial situation. After her initial elation Constance sank into a period of anxiety, fearing that it might be some weeks before she and Oscar secured the family blessing that was so preferable.

'You will have discovered by this that your observation that with regard to Oscar was rather ill timed,' Constance now wrote to Otho.

> I don't wish to know the story but even if there were foundations for anything against him it is too late to affect me now. I will not allow anything to come between us and at any rate no one can abuse him to me. I am sorry to say that he will not be up in town for 3 or 4 weeks because he has discovered that he has to lecture somewhere on Saturday. Please for my sake and because my happiness is dependent upon this thing do not oppose it, I'm desperately seedy with a very bad cold and can neither sleep nor eat now until this suspense is over.[5]

Otho replied by return. He had softened. He duly wrote to Oscar welcoming him into the family. With one of her concerns allayed, when Constance then heard that Oscar would cancel his Saturday lecture in order to meet the family, she was ecstatic.

More good news was forthcoming when the Swinburne-Kings gave their seal of approval too. Ada wrote to Lady Wilde explaining that she had already written to Oscar 'to say how pleased I should be to welcome him as my son in law'. Ada said the couple were well suited to each other. 'Both are . . . charming, gifted and what is to my mind even more essential to the beginning of married life, immensely attracted to each other. I have heard twice from Constance about the event and in each letter she says she is so intensely happy – I do indeed think that there may be a long and happy life in store for them both.'[6] Now it was just John Horatio who needed reassurance.

On Friday 30 November Constance packed her bags and headed for the steamer that would carry her across the Irish Sea. At seven the following morning, by her own accounts so radiant that 'all the fog in London will disappear', she met Otho on a frosty platform in Euston station. Constance had specifically requested that her brother have a muffin with him for her breakfast. Whether he remembered this detail is not known. That evening Otho invited Oscar to dine at Lancaster Gate, and much of Sunday was spent at home with the Lloyds, in frank conversation.

Far from objecting to the marriage, the Lloyds were in fact happy to support it, provided Oscar could prove himself sufficiently respon-sible. John Horatio, too ill to write when he received Oscar's letter on 27 November, had instructed Aunt Emily to lay out things as he saw it. John Horatio had 'no objection to you personally as a husband for Constance', she informed Oscar by return. 'He believes that you and she are well suited to each other. He has confidence you will treat her kindly . . . But he thinks it right as her guardian to put one or two questions to you . . . He would like to know what your means are of keeping a wife.' In addition, Aunt Emily pointed out that her father also insisted on knowing 'if you had any debts'. Only when Oscar could answer these points would Constance's grandfather 'give a considered consent'.[7]

Constance was not fully aware of Oscar's financial situation. She knew enough though to ascertain that he didn't have the resources to support a wife and start a household.[8] And so in the early days of her engagement she was working on the assumption that their marriage was not going to be possible until her grandfather died, a point at which she would be a beneficiary of his will.

John Horatio had written his will in February 1880. In it his per-sonal effects were split between his three daughters and Otho, who was to receive his library. The remainder of his property was to be sold, and the money raised divided into four portions for investment. The income from these investments was for the benefit of aunts Emily, Carrie and Mary, with the last to cater for Constance and Otho. Constance had no capital bequest *per se*. Aunt Emily had pointed out in her letter to Oscar that on John Horatio's death she might expect an income of £700 at least, but until then she had a limited allowance of just £250 a year.[9]

But John Horatio clearly wanted to help the couple. As requested, Oscar was transparent about his debts to the old man, which at that time were in the region of £1,500, and he must have made a good case for his capacity to earn an income. Perhaps knowing his own death was imminent and also, as Aunt Emily had conveyed to Oscar, making Constance's happiness his first consideration, he prepared a financial package for the couple that would allow them to marry more quickly than Constance had anticipated. They would not have to wait for him to shuffle off his mortal coil. John Horatio revealed he would forward £5,000 to a trust fund. The trustees of this fund would in turn advance Constance the interest generated by this capital, and this would provide her with an income immediately. When John Horatio died, this capital advance would be deducted from her legacy. It meant that the couple could go ahead and marry; the only remaining issue was when.

And so by the evening of Sunday 2 December 1883, when Oscar boarded the Scotch mail train that would return him to his lecturing commitments, his engagement to Constance had been thoroughly digested and approved. It was just the matter of a wedding date that remained.

On this topic, correspondence between Oscar and the Lloyds continued in early December, with Aunt Emily acting as scribe for the bed-bound John Horatio. Constance's grandfather was concerned that Oscar's debts would place a burden on a young couple. He wanted Oscar to manage to pay off at least £300 in the next few months. The wedding could take place only when this was done.

If Oscar was criticized for his high living and spending, at the same time he had a drive and work ethic that were hard to match. He had undertaken to make a lecture tour of Britain every bit as gruelling and intense as that he had made in America. Over the next two years Constance would have to get used to being without Oscar at least as much as she was with him. If there had ever been any sense that Oscar was marrying Constance for her money, the limits of her actual marriage settlement meant that he was never going to be a kept man. Determined to succeed in his own right, he set out to work hard and milk every opportunity that was offered him. He told John Horatio that he could pay off the £300 of debts by April. And with this pledge he and Constance began to make plans for a wedding in that month.

Constance was so deeply in love with Oscar at this time that every day his lecturing kept him away from her pained her terribly. She pined for him desperately.

> My darling love, I am sorry I was so silly: you take all my strength away, I have no power to do anything but just love you when you are with me, & I cannot fight against my dread of your going away. Every day that I see you, every moment that you are with me I worship you more, my whole life is yours to do as you will with it, such a poor gift to offer up to you, but yet all I have and so you will not despise it. I know it is only for 3 days, but – it is the wrench of the parting that is so awful, and you are so good to me I cannot bear to be an hour away from you: Do believe that I love you most passionately with all the strength of my heart and mind: anything that you asked me to do, I would in order to convince you and make you happy. I don't think I shall ever be jealous, certainly not jealous now of anyone: I trust in you for the present: I am content to let the past be buried, it does not belong to me: for the future trust & faith will come, & when I have you for my husband, I will hold you fast with chains of love & devotion so that you shall never leave me, or love anyone as long as I can love & comfort . . .[10]

Constance's reference to jealousy is intriguing. Had she and Oscar begun to discuss his past romantic and sexual histories? Was such a discussion prompted by the story that Otho had wanted to disclose

about Oscar and that Constance didn't care to hear? Had Otho suggested that Oscar had his eyes on other marriageable women at the
same time he was courting Constance? Or did Otho have an even
more controversial story – that perhaps Oscar was sexually interested
in men? One can easily imagine Oscar making an honest confession
about his past feelings for Florrie Balcombe and perhaps even Violet
Hunt. But would Constance have even dared raise any suggestion
that Oscar also had a penchant for men?

What Constance understood of homosexuality at this stage is
impossible to know. The stifling old-world atmosphere in Lancaster
Gate would not have been one in which such things were discussed.
But as a bright woman with an inquiring mind who was in touch
with the artistic community it also seems highly improbable that she
would have failed to grasp the sexual ambiguity that Oscar's Aesthetic
pose presented, or the implication that lay beneath the public ridicule
in which his effeminacy was so often held by publications such as
Punch. And that she understood the 'wicked' sexual allusions in his
poetry is clear.

The fact is that, in spite of his effete manner, Oscar's sexual orien-
tation in his twenties was predominantly towards women. He had
had a genuine and rather conventional love affair with Florrie
Balcombe at the very least. And his attentions to women elsewhere
had been well noted.

That's not to say that there was already an aspect of his personality
that was drawn to sexual experimentation, and more unconventional
or insalubrious sexual experiences. He had slept with prostitutes since
his Oxford days. And while on his writing trip to Paris in the spring
of 1883 he had continued this habit, as his friend the journalist and
author Robert Sherard would later attest. Oscar first met Sherard in
Paris in 1883, and they would remain lifelong friends. Sherard was a
firm heterosexual who himself regularly used prostitutes in Paris, and
he may well have introduced Oscar to the notorious Eden music hall,
where he paid for the services of the infamous Marie Aguétant.

Sherard is a key character. His attitude to Oscar seems very close
to that of Constance. Never for a moment did he consider Oscar's

'effeminacy' indicative of homosexual tendencies. Oscar had a habit of kissing Sherard on the lips when they met, and calling him and everyone else for that matter by their first names. Oscar would send him letters that others might well interpret as being sexually suggestive and homoerotic in tone. But Sherard persisted in reading Oscar's fruity letters and over-intimate behaviour as part of his Aesthetic affectation. It was his style. Sherard loved Oscar for all this. But not for a moment did he sense any predatory sexual attitudes on Oscar's part towards him.

And if Constance had any doubt in her mind about Oscar's behaviour, this is almost certainly the reassurance that she offered herself. Oscar was eccentric and shocking. He was playful and risqué. But at heart he was a conventional, 'manly' man. His devotion to her spoke for itself in this regard. Oscar was just as infatuated with her as she was with him, a fact revealed in Oscar's letter to his friend Lillie Langtry.

'I am going to be married to a beautiful girl called Constance Lloyd,' he wrote,

> a grave, slight, violet-eyed Artemis, with great coils of heavy brown hair which make her flower-like head droop like a flower, and wonderful ivory hands which draw music from the piano so sweet that the birds stop singing to listen to her. We are to be married in April. I hope so much that you will be over then. I am so anxious for you to know and like her. I am hard at work lecturing and getting quite rich, tho' it is horrid being so much away from her.[11]

Although Constance's life was taking a decided turn for the better, she was nevertheless haunted in these early days of her relationship with Oscar. Full of unspecified fear, she found herself sleepless and anxious at night. Her cousin Lizzie Napier, staying at Lancaster Gate, slept with her in an attempt to stop these night terrors.

'I get so frightened at night,' Constance confided to her fiancé. 'The wind was howling furiously and suddenly there came a crash as if the house were coming down, & after a few minutes another. We have not yet discovered what had happened. The wind always makes me think of death & separation and terrifies me into a state of horrors.'[12]

Oscar did what he could to comfort his bride-to-be. Wherever he was in the country, he telegraphed her twice daily and sent her flowers as often as he could, often lilies. If he had a day off from his talks and London was within reach, he dashed back to see her, sometimes forfeiting sleep or supper for the privilege of an hour with his fiancée. Although Constance was delighted with this devotion, it also concerned her. 'I wish you were not so tired,' she wrote to Oscar.

> Perhaps you had better not come to London next Sunday! You must not give up any more Saturday lectures, and if you won't promise to have a proper supper you are not to come & see me on Saturday evening. I am still very angry with you for not telling me you were starving last Saturday, I think it was so unkind: so it was, I should have insisted on your having something only I never feel at home here, I am only just like a visitor myself.[13]

In the first three weeks of December, Oscar travelled from the north to the south of England, gradually working his way through the north-east and Birkenhead, then to the midlands and Worcester, before returning to London to lecture at the Crystal Palace on the 21st. The minute he was back in London, Constance was at his side. She took Oscar to have lunch with her aunt Mary Napier in Norwood before the lecture. For the following Christmas week, which Oscar had as a holiday, the couple were barely out of one another's sight.

The engagement was announced in mid-December in *Society* and *Truth* magazines. The news spread quickly through a press for whom Oscar was now a regular topic, and Constance tasted the celebrity and public scrutiny that from now she would have to live with. By 20 December regional papers as far afield as Dublin, Liverpool, Manchester and Derby were carrying the news. 'Bunthorne is to get his bride,' announced the *Liverpool Daily Post*.

> Oscar Wilde is going to be married . . . she is a Dublin girl, a Miss Lloyd, a niece of the late Sergeant Armstrong, very well known and

much liked in Ireland. There was at first some fear lest London should lose its lion, and society its favourite source of admiration and ridicule. A terrible rumour had got about that Mr and Mrs Oscar Wilde were to settle down in Dublin. Happily this danger is averted. We keep Oscar.

Constance discovered that she was now something of a novelty. She and Oscar went to the theatre most nights that week. At the St James' the cast peeped through the curtains during the intervals to glimpse the future Mrs Wilde. On 23 December she found herself again the focus of fascination when Oscar's friend the painter Whistler held a special breakfast function at which Oscar 'and the lady whom he has chosen to be the chatelaine of the House Beautiful' were guests of honour.

Aunt Emily was having problems adjusting to her niece's new status. Constance was entering a bohemian, modern world that this spinster could barely grasp. Although a grown woman and now officially engaged, Constance had to fight for permission to attend every single event with Oscar. She barely made it to the Whistler breakfast. 'I am afraid you will have to go to Mr Whistler's without me,' she had written to Oscar earlier in the month. 'I am very sorry. Please don't let him be offended or think I did not want to come.'[14] It was Aunt Emily who was forbidding Constance to go. Oscar went into battle. Although Aunt Emily eventually gave in, she made her disapproval clearly felt in her letter to him.

'As Constance tells me Mr Whistler has arranged his luncheon party expressly for her & she is heartily disappointed at not being permitted to go, I have determined to withdraw my objection on this occasion on the distinct understanding that it is not to be made a precedent for any more visiting of a like kind. So long as she remains under her grandfather's roof it is also understood that her brother is to take charge of her.' Emily did not want Constance to do anything 'unbecoming to a young unmarried lady'.[15]

Despite the rather frosty and old-fashioned Aunt Emily, with whom he now had to negotiate access to his bride-to-be, Oscar was visibly delighted about his engagement. On Boxing Day he celebrated with the Sickert family and was so overcome with joy that he carelessly left two sovereigns behind him. Eleanor Sickert, the painter Walter's mother, was amused by this turn of events. 'We found two sovereigns on your chair,' she explained. 'I feel inclined to scold you for being so careless but you are too happy to mind even a severe lecture so I will not waste one.'[16]

Constance meanwhile found herself inundated with letters and cards congratulating her. Many of her friends and family prefaced their messages, asking whether the news was really true. Oscar was, after all, so famous, and Constance absolutely unlike the publicly visible Lillie Langtrys or Maud Howes with whom he was typically associated.

Constance responded to all who wrote with a brief note to which she attached a peacock feather – one of the motifs of Aestheticism. Whatever supply she had acquired was insufficient to meet a flood of interest in the news. In the end she cut up three of her own peacock feather fans as well as 'numbers of feathers that I collected at Mrs Ainslie's last year'. She tried offering one of these tokens to Otho, but he refused it, believing the peacock feather to be unlucky. Aunt Carrie, on the other hand, 'not being superstitious took them, so now we shall have no ill-luck'.[17]

One person who was far from surprised on hearing from Oscar of his 'Artemis' was Lillie Langtry. 'Oscar's contemplated marriage did not surprise me,' she said, 'as I knew that he had for some time admired the girl.'[18]

And then in January, Oscar was off again and Constance's life quietened. But Oscar did not leave before giving his betrothed a special gift, a pet marmoset to keep her company while he was away. It was christened Jimmy, possibly after Oscar's friend the painter James Whistler.

Constance took her new pet and headed for Bagshot in Surrey to stay with the Cochranes. Basil Cochrane, later Vice-Admiral Sir Basil, and his wife, Cornelia, were old family friends.[19] John Horatio was still very ill – if anything, his condition had deteriorated over Christmas – and Aunt Emily wanted Lancaster Gate vacated so she could be left alone to deal with her deteriorating father. Constance could read all the signs. She confided in Otho that she felt it unlikely the old man would survive the winter.

The philanthropic Cochranes kept Constance busy. They held a children's dancing class, for which Constance had to play waltzes on the piano. She went with Mrs Cochrane to help out at the annual Sunday school tea. But at night, when Windlesham House in Bagshot fell silent, Constance's trials continued. This time Mrs Cochrane crawled into bed with her, sleeping with her every night of her stay so that so she didn't feel so frightened in the dark.

Constance had a tendency towards clumsiness and misadventure when it came to everyday life. Throughout her life she was known for losing umbrellas or purses, or dropping or tearing precious things. Little Jimmy somehow fell prey to this unlucky aspect of Constance's life. Oscar's pet met its untimely end on 4 January 1884; it could only have been in Constance's care a matter of days. Constance broke the news to her betrothed. 'My sweet little Jimmy is dead, died at 1/2 past 5 o clock this morning: I am forlorn & miserable. Is it my fault that everything you give me has an untimely end? I don't think he suffered much as he looks so pretty. I can't bear to think of him; we are going to bury him presently.'[20]

Much of Constance's time away from Oscar was spent in imagining what married life would be like. Oscar, who was much parodied in the press for his heavy smoking, loved the very highest-quality cigarettes supplied from the Parascho depot in Mayfair's Park Street, conveniently close to Speranza and Willie. Constance began to wonder what it would be like to live with a smoker. She was not massively fond of the habit but told Oscar that 'I would never ask you to give it up: I see no reason why you should not smoke as much as you like, only if you over-do it, I should think it would become a morbid craving like that for opium.'[21]

If Oscar's fault in Constance's eyes was his addiction to nicotine, Constance began to wonder what aspects of her character would grate with him. 'Do get the list of my faults from Cenie!' Constance urged. 'I know two people who think I have none: one is Mrs

Cochrane who wrote to me yesterday, the other a lady at Oxford who told Charlie Napier so: Charlie did not agree!'[22]

No matter that at the heart of their relationship lay the simple concerns of any ordinary couple; as far as the public were concerned, Constance and Oscar were extraordinary. Now, with news that they would marry in April, the speculation began regarding the wedding itself. Just what would an Aesthetic wedding be like? And what would the bride wear?

Any such questions were quickly answered. Constance's wedding dress was made by March and went on show. This event in itself was enough to attract national attention. News travelled far and wide that the wedding attire of Mrs Oscar Wilde was 'saffron hued, the colour the Greek maidens wore on their wedding day'.[23]

Anna Kingsford, a friend of Speranza's, wrote to Lady Wilde keen to hear more about just this:

> I am coming to town for the season in about ten days . . . please write me a line and say WHEN and WHERE the wedding is to take place! I hear the bridal robe is on view somewhere and I should greatly like to see it. So please give me the address of the artist who is responsible for it. I hope the illustrated papers will do their duty noble in regard to the marriage and this 'sweetness and light' of which it will be the radiant point.[24]

Oscar's friend Robert Sherard alleged that Oscar himself designed Constance's wedding dress. Constance's son Vyvyan, however, later denied this. Oscar was often credited with matters of design at Constance's expense, and the anecdote of the genesis of this outfit may well be the first instance of this. Given her art schooling and her natural interest in fashion and embroidery, it is far more likely that Constance designed her own outfit, in conjunction with her dressmaker Mrs Nettleship.

Adeline Nettleship was the wife of the painter John Trivett Nettleship, a one-time solicitor who had given up his conventional career in 1870 to paint and who had subsequently become a successful and regular exhibitor at the Grosvenor Gallery.[25] Her business was based at 2 Melbury Terrace, St Marylebone, and it was probably here that Anna Kingsford and others would have gone to glimpse the gown ahead of the big day. While John Nettleship pursued his art on canvas, his wife created unique, dramatic and sometimes consciously bizarre outfits that were considered to represent the most outrageous and expressive end of the art dress market. Ada Nettleship was not dogmatic in her designs, but known for working with her clients, incorporating their own ideas into a final product that was always not only unique but also genuinely reflective of the wearer's personality.

While Mrs Nettleship and her girls were busy working on Constance's wedding and going-away gowns, Constance and Oscar got on with the pressing matter of where they should live. Oscar had already lived briefly in the exquisite Keats House that Godwin had designed for Frank Miles in Tite Street in Chelsea. Now there was another property coming up in that street. 'We have been looking at a house in Tite Street, which I think we are likely to take,' Constance wrote to family friends, the Harrises, at the end of March.

The problem for Oscar and Constance, however, was that, although they had found a house they liked, they still didn't have a sufficiently large amount of cash to secure it. Although Constance now had an annual income arranged, to lease Tite Street the couple would have to come up with a lump sum. It may well have been this final hurdle in regulating their affairs that encouraged Constance and Oscar to delay their wedding until May.

John Horatio once again came to the aid of his granddaughter. On 29 April an arrangement was made by which a further advance of £500, to be offset against her future legacy, was paid into the Union Bank of London. This sum would allow Constance to acquire a six-year lease on Tite Street and the cost of the modifications to the house that they wanted to make.

And so eventually, after a brief six-month engagement, the public were delivered the wedding that they had been so eagerly anticipating. The event had been kept as low-key as possible, not least because of the state of John Horatio's health. Only close family and friends were admitted to the ceremony by special ticket. The newspapers noted with disappointment that there were few literary or artistic glitterati amid the invitees. Whether Anna Kingsford made the ceremony is not sure. Jimmy Whistler telegrammed on the day that he would be late. People such as Oscar's solicitor and family friend George Lewis and his wife attended, the latter in a costume of black and amber. Ada Swinburne-King and Speranza were in brilliant shades of grey, the former in rich grey satin with black mantle and bonnet and the latter in silver-grey brocaded silk and satin. The actress Mrs Bernard-Beere wore a jet-covered dress with a black hat trimmed with yellow flowers.

Underwhelmed by the celebrity quotient of the guests, the large crowd of Oscar Wilde fans who had gathered to see Constance emerge from her carriage outside St James's Church, Sussex Gardens, at 2.30 p.m. on 29 May 1884 were then met with further disappointment. Those members of the public who had hoped to see her in that saffron dress which had been so talked about were instantly surprised. Rather than the deep golden yellow of the tip of the saffron crocus thread, Constance's dress had just the merest tint of yellow. The *Ladies' Treasury* described it as a 'rich creamy satin dress . . . of delicate cowslip tint', while the *Lady's Pictorial* thought it more of an 'ivory satin'. Oscar, meanwhile, 'appeared in the ordinary and commonplace frock coat of the period'.

There were, of course, some more obvious concessions to Aestheticism. Rather than being bustled, the skirt of Constance's dress was plain, with a long train. The bodice was low-cut with a Medici collar, and the sleeves were, of course, puffed. Instead of the traditional wreath of orange blossom, she wore a wreath of myrtle leaves, which the 'Metropolitan Gossip' column of the *Belfast News* informed its readers was 'a more poetical and highly classical adornment'. According to the press, the most unusual aspect of the outfit, apart from its surprising simplicity, was the veil. Hanging from the back of her head, it was Indian silk gauze embroidered with pearls. And around her waist Constance wore a silver girdle, which was Oscar's wedding gift to her. She carried a bouquet of lilies.

If anything, it was the bridesmaids who provided the spectacle that the crowd had been expecting. Six of Constance's cousins, two them children, were dressed in terracotta, 'after Sir Joshua Reynolds'. The elder girls had 'bodices and short over skirts of figured nun's veiling; the ground was pale blue, the flowers old gold. They wore high crowned straw hats trimmed with long cream feathers and knots of surah silk. All the bridesmaids wore yellow roses at the throat; amber necklaces, and carried bouquets of the fairest and most fragrant water lilies.' John Horatio was too ill to attend the ceremony, and so it was left to Constance's uncle Hemphill to give her away. Willie was Oscar's best man.

Oscar selected an extremely unusual wedding ring that he gave Constance that day. At first glance it is a simple gold band. But on closer examination it is sliced in half, so that it opens to form two interlocking rings. On the inside of one is the tiny inscription '29th May 1884' while the other bears the names 'Constance and Oscar'.

After the ceremony the party retired for a brief reception at Lancaster Gate. There they ate a cake covered with sprays of jasmine and lily of the valley. By 4.30 that afternoon Constance and Oscar were on a train from Charing Cross *en route* to a honeymoon in Paris. Constance was wearing what one publication described as a dark mahogany, and another reported as a deep crimson, travelling dress. Both press accounts agree that she wore a large-brimmed hat to match. What no one needed to report, but everyone took for granted, was that above all Constance was wearing a huge smile.

5

Violets in the refrigerator

THE 'ECHOES OF Society' column of the *North Wales Chronicle* carried a satirical sketch in its July 1884 issue that went like this:

> Mrs Oscar Wilde – 'Yes dear, dinner is ready. Which do you prefer, sunflower dried, or some toasted lily of the valley?' Oscar – 'Ah! Ahem! Is that all you have?' 'Oh no! There is a big dish of violets in the refrigerator.' 'My love haven't you got anything to eat?' 'Eat! Eat! Why what do you mean?' 'I should like some beef and potatoes and bread and a bottle of ale, and some' – But the bride of the aesthete had fainted.

When Constance married Oscar in May 1884, she became a celebrity. She also became an integral partner for her husband in what Oscar considered the next phase of his career. If as a bachelor he had lived life as the embodiment of Aesthetic principles, in marriage he saw the opportunity 'of realising a poetical conception . . . to set an example of the pervading influence of art in matrimony'.[1]

Since his return from America, Oscar had abandoned his silk breeches and long hair in favour of elegant suits and a short, curled coiffure. In doing so he had cast off any sense of boyishness that might formerly have been associated with his public persona. Marriage allowed him to develop this more mature character further in the public imagination. Instinctively Oscar understood the key to maintaining the interest of one's public is to offer them change. Constance could at once provide this, as well as amplifying and extending his profile.

But this is not to suggest that Oscar's and Constance's marriage was some form of publicity stunt, or merely something intended to benefit Oscar solely. It was a happy coincidence that allowed him his new ambition to explore how Aestheticism, and the liberal thinking that attached itself to this artistic movement, might apply in marriage. Far more importantly, his feelings for Constance were rooted in what was, according to the couple's friends, a very genuine love affair. Ada Leverson, one such friend, noted that 'when he first married, he was quite madly in love, and showed himself an unusually devoted husband.'[2]

On honeymoon in Paris they took reasonably priced rooms, no doubt with John Horatio and Aunt Emily's words about the need for economy and careful housekeeping still ringing in their ears. Their apartment in the Hotel Wagram, rue de Rivoli, was '3 rooms, 20 francs a day, not dear for a Paris Hotel', Constance explained to Otho. 'We are *au quatrième* quite a lovely view over the gardens of the Tuileries.'[3]

From here the couple would launch themselves out into Paris society on a daily basis and indulge themselves in art. They visited the annual Paris salon to see the work by Oscar's friends that was on display: Whistler was showing *Harmony in Grey and Green: Miss Cicely Alexander*, as well as *Arrangement in Grey and Black, No. 2: Thomas Carlyle*, and the sculptor John Donoghue a bas-relief of a nude boy playing the harp. They went to the opera and to see Sarah Bernhardt in *Macbeth*, a production in which Constance witnessed 'the most splendid acting I ever saw. Only Donalbain was bad. The witches were charmingly grotesque. The Macbeth very good, Sarah of course superb, she simply stormed the part.'[4] They held dinner parties and attended dinner, luncheon and breakfast parties by return. Constance met an array of new artistic people, among them the American artist John Singer Sargent. Then there was the French novelist Paul Bourget, the sculptor Donoghue (whom Oscar had befriended in America) and the writer Robert Sherard.

The evening before he married, Oscar had had dinner with some of his closest married female friends, the painter Louise Jopling and the wife of his lawyer, George Lewis. They gave him advice on how a 'young husband should treat his wife'.[5] If they told him he should be romantic, full of grand gesture and spoil his new life-companion, then he followed their advice to the letter. Oscar was enormously extravagant towards Constance. If he ventured out with his Parisian friends while Constance remained behind to write letters, the minute he left her, Oscar would send bouquets of flowers back to their rooms and shower love gifts on her the moment he returned. He played the role of lover extremely well, and not just for Constance's benefit. Robert Sherard found himself strolling along the Parisian streets with an Oscar full of nuptial joys and attempting to reveal in detail the delights of sleeping with his wife, details that Sherard squeamishly asked Oscar to desist from divulging.

But in spite of these grand gestures, even on his honeymoon Oscar displayed a characteristic that over the years of marriage to come would prove a thorn in Constance's side. It is obvious that Oscar enjoyed being apart from his wife as much as he loved being with her. He would disappear, and she would be left alone to her own devices.

Oscar was attracted by danger. He loved experiencing low life and would seek out notorious street haunts, where he would immerse himself in another world. Even on his honeymoon Oscar and Robert Sherard ventured out to some of the low-life bars in Paris, such as the Château Rouge, a notorious criminal haunt, above which was Paris's 'Salle des Morts'. This was a room in which the city's beggars and orphans, dropouts and cut-throats spent the night – a room full of ragged men who looked, in slumber, more like corpses than human beings, and upon whom Oscar gazed in horror and wonder.

Within a few months of their marriage Constance and Oscar would begin to talk about matrimony in unusual terms, consciously 'modern' in their approach to their new status. Adrian Hope recalled one dinner party with them in which Constance 'said she thought it should be free to either party to go off at the expiration of the first year'.[6] Oscar subsequently offered the proposal that marriage should be a contract for seven years, renewable as either party sees fit at the end of that duration.

It's intriguing to speculate whether these expressions on both sides promoting some form of trial period in wedlock, or some notion that marriage need not be eternally binding, indicates that the marriage suffered some teething troubles. What is sure is that Oscar and Constance, like so many other Victorians, barely knew each other when they married. They had met many times, but nearly always in public situations. And Oscar had spent much of their six-month engagement away on his lecture tour.

It seems likely, given the many accounts of a genuine love affair between the two of them early on, that they simply suffered a kind of shock reaction to the adjustments each had to make to accommodate life with the other. Oscar must have been surprised to find, beneath the delicate exterior of his violet-eyed Artemis, a rather steely resolve and something of a short temper. Later in life, after Arthur Pinero had written his stage hit *The Second Mrs Tanqueray*, Oscar's nickname for Constance would be Mrs Cantankeray.[7] Constance, on the other hand, had to accommodate Oscar's ego, his tendency to leave her alone and his utter uselessness with money.

In spite of this, the public profile that they presented was immediately, and for the next few years, fixed as one of utter union and single-minded purpose. If Oscar had an idea that there could be such a thing as an artistic marriage, then Constance was ready and prepared to explore it with him.

The first, instant evidence of this was Constance's wardrobe. Although she had in recent years adopted the loose dress that Otho so loathed, on her honeymoon Constance revealed a new wardrobe that took Aesthetic fashion to new heights and spoke not only of her allegiance but also of her preparedness to partner the high priest of Aestheticism in awakening a wider public to just how far art might be extended in life.

A sense of Mrs Nettleship's fabrications is given by *The Lady's Pictorial*, which reported:

> If the French ladies are more slaves to fashion edicts than are their English sisters, and are less indulgent to eccentricity in dress or manner, they yet recognize the superior right of grace inspired by taste to adorn itself with picturesque becomingness. Mrs Oscar

Wilde, in her large white plumed hats, in her long dust cloaks of creamy alpaca richly trimmed with ruches of coffee coloured lace, in her fresh and somewhat quaintly-made gowns of white muslin, usually relieved by touches of golden ribbon, or with yellow floss silk embroideries, is declared 'charmante' and to be dressed with absolute good taste.[8]

'My dress creates a sensation in Paris,' Constance proudly announced to Otho on the fifth day of her honeymoon. 'Miss R,[9] who is as I said, frightful . . . wants me to get Mrs Nettleship to make a dress for her exactly like the one of mine. Of course I promised. Imagine Oscar's horrors.'[10]

Constance had a passion for old lace and embroidery, and so pieces that she had collected over the years were now worked into her outfits by Mrs Nettleship. One description of Constance in the year of her marriage makes note of her 'in a very artistic looking gown of crimson and gold brocade. There was a Watteau plait at the back and the sleeves were long, full and puffed at the top of the elbows. A wide and falling collar of old lace complemented the chief features of this very elegant toilet.'[11]

Within a year the golden couple, effervescing with mutual devotion, dressed in their Aesthetic uniform, were the subject of a craze. Mrs Oscar Wilde, or 'Mrs Oscar', as she was often referred to, had certainly become the brand extension that her husband had hoped. By May 1885, when galleries held their important summer show previews, Mr and Mrs Wilde were offering Lillie Langtry some serious competition as the main interest for celebrity spotters. 'Mr and Mrs Oscar Wilde were the only rivals in public interest' to the 'rush and crush whenever "the Lily" was recognised'.[12]

While Constance seemed to prefer 'tea gowns' in lightweight and pale-coloured muslins for her day wear, for her evening wear Mrs Nettleship and Constance would often turn to green. At a preview of the Grosvenor Gallery's 1885 summer show

aestheticism culminated in Mrs Oscar Wilde's costume of a woollen stuff in dull reseda[13] trimmed with pink, a kind of Kate Greenaway dress, tied at the waist by a drooping pink sash. Round the neck she wore a wide Toby frill of two rows of ficelle lace with vari-coloured beads, and a large pink bow fastening a bunch of yellow marguerites; on her head a small Tam o'Shanter cap of the same greenish grey material was the accompaniment to this eccentric costume.[14]

A year later, at the same event, Constance was once again the focus of attention. This time she was dressed 'in every shade of green from the palest lichen to the fullest summer foliage – a lizard trimmed with beetles'.[15] Mrs Nettleship had sewn the iridescent green wings of the 'jewel' beetle on to Constance's gown, so that they glistened like sequins.[16] She would repeat this practice a year later, fashioning a hat for her client in which 'beetles' wings shone from unsuspected corners whenever the head was turned'.[17]

Anna, Comtesse de Brémont, remembered how startlingly original Constance always looked. On one occasion she would be

> purely Greek, on another early Venetian, in rich tints of old rose, with gold lace, high collar, trimmings and girdles. Again I would see her arrayed in draperies after the medieval style, or cerise and black satin with necklaces of quaint gems, all of which she wore with a shy air of depreciation, a bearing that was not quite in keeping with the stately, sumptuous style of dress.[18]

While the bohemian set considered her outfits charming, Constance's dress was generally considered eccentric and far too avant-garde by the wider public. Her new-found celebrity brought just as much ridicule as praise. One critic wrote that 'The least said' about her dress 'the better'.[19] The press aside, even some friends and neighbours found themselves utterly bemused by Constance's transformed appearance. The poets Katherine Bradley and Edith Cooper noted in their memoirs how they were 'received by Mrs Wilde in turquoise blue, white frills and amber stockings'.[20] Adrian Hope's fiancée, Laura Troubridge, met Constance shortly after she and Oscar returned from honeymoon. Horrified, Laura described her 'as looking too hopeless', dressed in 'white muslin with absolutely no bustle; saffron coloured silk swathed about her shoulders, a huge cartwheel Gainsborough hat, white, & bright yellow stockings & shoes'.[21]

Adrian Hope kept Laura up to date with news of Constance's wardrobe. That November he wrote to her, noting that, while visiting his Napier connections at Constance's old home of 100 Lancaster Gate, she and Oscar turned up for tea. 'He dressed quite like anyone else, she in mouse-coloured velvet with a toque to match looking horrid.'[22] Adrian recounts another instance when his friend Jo was introduced to the Wildes. 'Jo sat amazed at Mrs Oscar,' Adrian reported to Laura, 'and at Oscar who seemed to confound Jo's wits altogether.'[23]

There were occasions when Oscar and Constance wore planned, matching or complementary outfits that made something of a spectacle. Louise Jopling recalled an instance when they walked along the King's Road in Chelsea, with Oscar in a suit of brown cloth with innumerable little buttons on it that looked 'rather like a glorified page's costume'. Mrs Oscar meanwhile 'had on a large picture hat, with beautiful white feathers adorning it'. The couple were immediately taunted by a gang of street urchins, who, surprisingly well versed in the Bard, commented that they were like ''Amlet and Ophelia out for a walk'. On another occasion, at a private view at the Grosvenor Gallery, they were 'a harmony in green. The coat of the apostle of culture was of Lincoln green cloth heavily trimmed with fur, while Mrs Oscar had a very pretty and graceful velvet gown of exactly the same shade of colour.'[24]

But what seems clear is that, apart from such moments of collaboration, it was generally Constance who now took on the mantle of eccentric dress, while Oscar gradually began to adopt what would become his signature style: conventional attire with unconventional details. Although his dress may have had dandyish touches (Bradley and Cooper remembered him in a lilac shirt with heliotrope tie at around this time), it was more often than not now described as 'sensible'.[25] It was as if his marriage to Constance had bestowed a degree of respectability and maturity on the one-time rebel, who now seemed 'lulled into confidence . . . by the security ensured through his happy marriage . . .There was no longer any need for eccentric and startling self-advertisement.'[26] Oscar conversely gave his new wife permission to express the most extreme tendencies of her character.

Although fashion may appear superficial, Constance's collaboration with Mrs Nettleship represented a practical demonstration of serious thinking about dress that was circulating within certain circles. That Oscar would begin to explore the subject of dress in a new set of lectures devised within a few months of his marriage may well reflect the influence that Constance had on him and his subject matter.

On 1 October 1884 Oscar delivered his new lecture on dress to an audience in Ealing. He would repeat it on tour over the next six months. Oscar suggested that there had been a golden age of English dress. Harking back to a pre-1066 England, when ladies wore the loose medieval robes that the Pre-Raphaelite painters had re-imagined, he suggested that this era of beauty and simplicity was lost when William the Conqueror and his French court brought in new, exaggerated styles. Despite another brief period of beautiful clothing in the last quarter of the seventeenth century, the restoration of Charles II revived the French influence once again, and since then it had persisted. In the 1880s the French-inspired Watteau toilette, with its hourglass profile created by tight corsetry, its tight-fitting sleeves and heavy bustle, and its high-heeled shoes dominated English fashion.

Fundamentally his views on dress recognized the need to liberate women from the distorting and deforming clothing that moulded their bodies into idealized shapes. Oscar suggested that dress should be 'rational'. He advocated the wearing of high waistbands that did away with corsetry. He praised the Greeks, Assyrians and Egyptians for clothing that was supported from the shoulder rather than the waist, and he condemned high-heeled shoes that tipped the body of the wearer forwards. He even suggested that wool was the ideal fabric, able to provide warmth in winter but also feel cool in summer.

It's hard not to hear something of Constance's voice in these lectures. That she favoured dresses with high waistbands is clear. That she shunned high heels is also known, not least because of a comical note she wrote to her brother in 1882 in which she announced: 'I have ordered a pair of shoes to be made for me with broad soles and low heels. We have discovered that my left foot is a three quarters of a size larger than my right.'[27]

To the twenty-first-century eye, the considerations of where to place a waistband and whether or not to wear heels seem flippant. But in the nineteenth century these were considerations that had genuinely important social issues at their heart. The issue of restriction to one side, there were the health issues at stake: tight corsetry crushed internal organs and deformed ribs. The stiff ivory stays often included in corsets deformed muscles and created chronic spinal damage. There were safety issues too. The large crinolines that women had worn in the earlier part of the century were terrible fire hazards. Oscar's own family had had their share of tragedy in this respect. His father's two illegitimate daughters had died in hideous circumstances. The girls had attended a dance one evening. The crinoline skirt of one caught in a fire. When the other tried to save her sister she too caught ablaze. They became two human torches. Despite the frantic attempts of other party-goers to roll the girls on the floor and beat out the flames, both of them succumbed to their burns.

Working-class women, even in their simpler outfits, also found themselves at risk from their clothes. The long, cumbersome skirts that women wore were trip and catch hazards – something that working women in factory environments were all too aware of. A skirt getting caught in heavy machinery was a genuine danger.

The idea that Aesthetic fashion was also something altogether safer and more wholesome for women was soon being widely acknowledged. By 1885 the press were conflating the terms 'artistic' and 'hygienic' when it came to dress. When Constance attended a lecture that Whistler gave in March that year, the lady correspondent for the *Bristol Mercury and Daily Post* observed plenty of pretty dresses of both styles of fashion which now prevail in society, according to the taste of the wearer. Tight-fitting, well draped gowns, after the Parisian models, and some which might be called hygienic, or perhaps artistic, loose and flowing and very simple. Mrs Oscar Wilde of course wore one of the latter style, with a very high waist and a plain skirt. It was made of soft, creamy silk, embroidered with golden yellow flowers and she had daffodils in her hair and on her bodice.[28]

Health and healthier options in life were an ongoing fascination for Victorians in the mid-1880s, and they were not confined to dress. As a follow-up to the immensely popular 'Fisheries' exhibition of 1883, the Prince of Wales came up with the idea of a health exhibition. The 'Healtheries', as it quickly became known, was designed apparently to encourage healthy and hygienic modes of living, 'one of the first conditions necessary for the happiness and prosperity of a nation', as explained by the Duke of Cambridge in his address at the opening of the event.

In reality it was like an enormous handicraft show, featuring craft practices and handmade items from around the world. One of the most spectacular exhibits was a period street which saw lost buildings from London's past rebuilt, inside which the city's various crafts guilds showed off their wares and methods. There were working dairies producing milk and making butter on site, as well as areas devoted to the craft specialities of other countries, with Indian weavers demonstrating carpet-making and an Italian court featuring beautiful inlaid furniture as well as Venetian glass and mosaic. In this strangely eclectic assemblage the pump room from Bath had been rebuilt, and Royal Doulton had constructed a ceramic temple. In the section dedicated to healthy dress there were stalls featuring practical dress for various activities as well as displays of chemicals that might make fabrics less flammable and non-toxic natural dyes.

There was also a display of waxworks dressed in historical costumes dating from the Norman Conquest to the Regency period. The Times explained that this was intended to provide a comparative study of civilian dress in its bearings on hygiene at different periods in the nation's growth. The architect Edward Godwin, who was simultaneously busy modelling Oscar and Constance's new home in Tite Street, gave an address on this section of the exhibition. In fact, Godwin's address presented remarkably similar points to Oscar's lectures on the same subject, made some months later. Like Oscar, Godwin talked about Greek dress, about the need for clothes that emancipate rather than constrict a body and about the recommendation that shoulders rather than waists should carry the weight of a garment. And he too made the connection between health and beauty.

The 'Healtheries' loomed quite large in the first few months of Constance and Oscar's marriage. For a start Oscar had participated in a fundraising venture for the Chelsea Hospital for Women that was associated with the exhibition. He contributed to *The Shakespearean Story Book,* a one-off novelty publication that went on sale at the 'Healtheries' the day before his marriage, and which was intended to accompany some Shakespearean performances and costume displays occurring in the Royal Albert Hall, part of the wider exhibition site. Then later in the autumn Constance and Oscar both participated in a Royal Fête at the exhibition. At another charity event, this time supporting London hospitals, the couple manned one of many celebrity flower stalls. Amid other luminaries selling flowers of all kinds, ferns, exotics, fruits and refreshments, the Wildes' stall was, of course, offering lilies and sunflowers.

Perhaps with the theme of the exhibition uppermost in her mind, Constance made a point of wearing a divided skirt to the occasion. This was a very early form of wide-legged trouser that provided women with unprecedented freedom when it came to walking. She consequently became the focus of popular interest and found herself portrayed in the press in this novel outfit, along with a loose bodice tied with a sash, and a waistcoat.

The 'Healtheries' also provided a good source for hand-crafted decorative objects for the house in Tite Street. Just as Constance was now the living embodiment of the wife in an artistic marriage, so Tite Street would be the working precinct in which the marriage would operate. As such it too needed to be aesthetic, practical and healthy. The Wildes had come across A. B. Ya's stall at the

'Healtheries', which was selling 'Objets d'Arts du Japon'. A letter between Constance and Godwin indicates that they purchased a number of items from him.[29]

Godwin's remodelling of Tite Street took a while, and Constance and Oscar were forced to live for the first six months of their marriage in Oscar's old bachelor digs in Charles Street, Grosvenor Square. Not only were the renovations time-consuming, they were also chaotic and expensive.

Constance's grandfather, whose health had been failing so long, died just seven weeks after Constance and Oscar married. Consequently Constance inherited fully that portion of his estate of which £5,000 had already been invested for her. The Lloyd estate was finally valued at £92,392, of which some £23,000 was settled jointly on Otho and Constance.[30] And so within weeks of her marriage Constance's annual income doubled. It did so not a moment too soon.

No matter how great an architect and interior designer, Godwin was a poor site manager and seemed unable to assess builders' estimates properly. First he employed a builder called Green to work on Tite Street, but Oscar ended up firing this first contractor for shoddy work and refused to pay him. While Green sued Oscar, Godwin hired a second builder called Sharp. The work dragged on longer than anticipated. Not only did Constance and Oscar have to settle out of court with the disgruntled Green, but the second builder, Sharp, was also now charging more than his original estimate. In the end the changes to Tite Street would cost around £250 more than Constance and Oscar had bargained for.

The house was still uninhabitable in October 1884, when Oscar began his new lecture tour. And so Constance found herself suddenly taking over the reins of the project. What Constance brought to the project was a practical eye that Oscar and Godwin did not seem to have. Going back over the purchases and orders that Oscar and Godwin had agreed, she was quick to point out simple failings. The curtains for the first-floor landing were not wide enough and were not going to cross sufficiently to remove draughts; she asked if Mr

Godwin intended to put fringes on the curtains, in which case she needed to source these; she chased Godwin to see if there were patterns yet for the other curtains, and whether she could view the fabrics with Godwin; the kitchen needed a deal table; and Constance wanted a bath of 'any artistic shape' for her bedroom. She wrote to Otho to find out the whereabouts of their old 'nurse', whom she wanted to install in the house for reasons of security and practicality until she could secure a housemaid; and of course, she was going to be paying the bills while Oscar was settling his debts.

Oscar and Godwin are generally credited with the artistic vision for 16 Tite Street, an attribution that overlooks Constance's contribution. There was some acknowledgement among the Wilde circle that Oscar was in the habit of taking the credit for his wife's artistic talents. Later the writer Mary Braddon would model the fictional poet Daniel Lester and his wife, Sarah, on Oscar and Constance in her book *The Rose of Life*, rather pointedly noting that 'Sarah's good taste in chintzes and carpets, Chippendale chairs and Sheraton sideboards, generally went to the credit of Daniel'.[31]

In fact, Constance had plenty to do with the design of Tite Street, and it is better to see the house as a genuine collaboration between the architect and both her and Oscar. Apart from her own room, for which she was entirely responsible for the design and which was full of the lace curtains and needlework chair covers that Constance so loved, the drawing room in Tite Street owed more to Constance's taste than to Oscar's. Just as her passion for textiles made itself felt in her dress and her bedroom, so for this room Constance sourced old faded brocades for the upholstery rather than use contemporary fabrics. And it was she who had designed the dull gold strip along one wall which united Oscar's collection of etchings in a single frieze. This gentle nod to a faded past that Constance provided in the interior theme was complemented by decorative touches reflecting the latest avant-garde tastes. Two huge Japanese vases either side of the fireplace were perhaps the purchases from A. B. Ya's. And to add the latest contemporary twist, Whistler painted dragons on the ceilings, partly composed of exotic feathers pressed into the plaster.

Godwin's style was probably most felt on the ground floor: in the dining room, which lay at the back of the house and which was a symphony in white – white walls, white furniture and white carpet – and in Oscar's study at the front of the house, with its yellow walls and red woodwork.

Above the dining room and to the rear of the drawing room was Oscar's smoking room, which was North African in theme. Oscar's son Vyvyan was convinced this room had been inspired by Constance's great friend the traveller Walter Harris. With a dark red and gold Morris paper, it was furnished with low divans and otto-mans, Moorish lanterns, beaded curtains and latticed shutters, which blocked out the view of the rather unsavoury Paradise Walk.

Regardless of the worries over building work, one gets a sense that Constance and Oscar saw the first months of their marriage as noth-ing short of a wondrous adventure. By the end of their endeavours they had what Oscar's brother acknowledged was 'the prettiest house in London', they were the centre of attention and having no end of fun, contributing to events such as the Royal Fête. Constance had taken steps that just two years previously she would never have dared. It was not just her dress or the events she attended; she had begun joining clubs and societies too – not least the fashionable Albemarle Club, of which Oscar was a member, and which was innovative in its acceptance of women. And love itself was still a tantalizingly fresh and exciting feeling. As Oscar dashed off around the country once again, he sent Constance notes just as passionate as those he had writ-ten to her on their honeymoon. From his hotel room in Edinburgh in December he told his wife:

> Here am I, and you at the Antipodes. O execrable facts, that keep our lips from kissing, though our souls are one . . . I feel your fingers in my hair, and your cheek brushing mine. The air is full of the music of your voice, my soul and body seem no longer mine, but mingled in some sweet ecstasy with yours. I feel incomplete without you.[32]

Constance, meanwhile, was proud not only to be a married woman but to be the woman married to Oscar Wilde, and busied herself with some of the social formalities associated with her new status. At the end of 1884 she arranged greetings cards to send out over the festive season. One of these is in the British Library today. Gilt-edged, featuring a somewhat chocolate-box image of the Thames at night, it carries a poem that, popular, jaunty and sentimental, seems something of a contrast to Oscar's own poetry, as it declares to its recipients:

> A Happy Christmas
> How swiftly comes old Christmas
> With the quickly rolling years
> With the joy, and with the sorrow
> The laughter and the tears.
>
> Love makes the sorrows hallowed
> And the joys are not a few
> If we have thankful happy hearts
> And friends are tried and true.[33]

This Constance signed on the reverse, 'with best wishes from Mr & Mrs Oscar Wilde'.

Meanwhile, for New Year she chose a plain white card with italic writing announcing that the couple had finally moved into their new address:

Mr & Mrs Oscar Wilde
Send best wishes
For a Happy New Year
16 Tite St
Chelsea[34]

For the first five months of 1885, while Oscar was lecturing, Constance dutifully carried on applying the finishing touches to Tite Street. To compensate for his absence Oscar had once again bought Constance a pet – this time a puppy. Unlike the moments of separation during their engagement when Constance had hated being left alone, now she seemed happy on her own. Indeed, so determined was she to press on with their domestic arrangements that she even forwent a trip to Dublin when Oscar was lecturing there in January, instead busying herself over 'embroideries and housemaids'.

London, meanwhile, like a great unstoppable machine, churned on around her. By May the season was starting yet again. In a pause between lecture commitments Oscar and Constance attended all the gallery openings. Constance wrote to Otho and joked about the reception her 'Tam o' Shanter' hat had received. It had not gone down well. She suggested that the unkind report of it as 'indescribable' by one critic who claimed to have seen her in it at the Royal Academy private view might have been due to the fact that 'no one saw it', including said critic.

In the same month South Kensington was alive once again with the bustle associated with yet another international exhibition. After the 'Fisheries' and 'Healtheries' came the 'Inventories', or rather the 'International Exhibition of Inventions'. Constance and Oscar attended, of course. Constance provided Otho with a full account, not least of an exhibition of American watchmaking, which displayed the latest machinery designed to manufacture the tiniest mechanical parts.

'They were so minute that I could not see the thread of the screws without a magnifying glass,' Constance recounted, adding: 'It made me feel quite creepy, these wonderful sort of steel hands moving each in its twin in regular monotony with a feeling of dull fatalism. They can make 500 little cogged wheels in a day, one of the girls told me.'[35]

The replica 'Old London' street that had been constructed for the 'Healtheries' was still standing, and once again housing handicrafts. The Wildes liked the Donegal linen that was being worked there and placed orders for a tablecloth for their new drawing room. The faded dyes that were being used went perfectly with Constance's old brocade, and were

really quite beautiful . . . artistic in colour and much finer than what they used to make, but what specially attracted us was their embroidery on linen and we have ordered a 5 o'clock tea cloth to be made for us. The embroidery is done with flax thread on linen, old Celtic designs being used and the thread dyed the beautiful tints, yellow, pink, blue and green being the chief colours, green and pink, the chief combinations. The colours are dyed specifically for them and patented which is a very good thing. The cloth we have ordered is of ecru linen, worked with white, cream and olive green flax, the only colours we could have in the drawing room.[36]

One wonders just how interested Otho was really going to be in such detail about linen. But Constance would have been writing to him in the full knowledge that Nellie would get to read the letter. Nellie, who married Otho just days after Constance's own wedding, was now pregnant. In a postscript to her letter Constance mentioned two further things. First, that she was going to go to Whiteley's department store shortly to buy a bassinet, or cradle, for her expectant sister-in-law. Second, that the puppy Oscar had given her was thriving, 'fat as a pig and enormously strong'.

That Constance had managed to raise this animal successfully boded well. For in the same letter Constance mentioned to Otho that, in terms of bassinets, her own had 'come and is perfectly exquisite. I have never seen one so pretty.' Constance was eight months' pregnant. No wonder she had not travelled in Ireland in the new year, when her pregnancy would have been in its early stages. And no wonder she had been so frantically making Tite Street ready. Only six months in their new home, the Wildes were already expecting a baby.

6

Ardour and indifference

'My dear' said Mrs Oscar Wilde to her husband, 'will you not be happy if I some day present you with a little flower of a daughter!'

'I would prefer a son flower' was the quiet reply, and then for a few moments the silence was so deep that you could hear a gumdrop.[1]

Oscar's wish was duly granted on 5 June 1885. He telegrammed Otho and announced, 'Constance had a boy this morning at ten forty-five. She is quite happy and doing well but can not see anyone for some days. She sends her love.'[2]

The birth was, by the standards of the day, easy. Constance was anaesthetized with chloroform during the very final part of her labour and, according to Oscar, suffered hardly any pain. The baby was delivered by forceps in a procedure that was fashionable among higher-class women at the time – Queen Victoria had tried this method for the delivery of her seventh child. And like many accounts of women who 'slept' through the actual moment of birth, 'on coming to she absolutely declined to believe' her child 'was born at all! And was only convinced of the fact by the nurse producing a stalward [sic] boy.'[3] Constance's doctor, the amusingly named Charles de Lacy Lacy, pinned a note up in the hall at Tite Street reminding the household, such as it was, that Constance was to have utter rest for a few days.

Oscar had proved a considerate husband in the run-up to the birth. Writing to Lillie Langtry a few months before the baby's arrival, he gives a hint of his sensitivity to Constance's health. He and Constance could not dine out, he wrote to Mrs Langtry in April, 'as we dined out yesterday. And I don't like leaving her: you know she is going to have a child.'[4]

Once the baby arrived, his tone changed from considerateness and caution to jubilation and enthusiasm. 'The baby is wonderful,' he wrote to his friend the actor and dramatist Norman Forbes-Robertson. 'Constance is doing capitally and is in excellent spirits . . . you must get married *at once!*'[5]

The Wildes christened their son Cyril. Constance's friends and relatives predominated in the choice of godparents. Aunt Emily was godmother, while Walter Harris was appointed godfather. Although only twenty, Harris was showing every sign of being a living embodiment of action and adventure. He would become *The Times*'s special correspondent in Morocco, and with his perfect Arabic and Moorish garb would later live in North Africa with fellow adventurer Robert Cunninghame Graham and pass as a native. When Cyril was a little older, Harris returned from his latest travels and recounted how he had attended a cannibal feast and actually eaten human flesh. Perhaps Constance felt that Harris might present an alternative role model for her son, and an appropriate contrast to the artistic Oscar. Harris duly presented Cyril with a silver christening mug, which was placed in the dining room in a glass cabinet that contained the rest of the family silver.

Amid the excitement of appointing godparents and generally showing off their new baby, Oscar wrote to the author, polymath and eccentric Edward Heron Allen and asked him to cast the baby's horoscope. Heron Allen was one of those men who, like Douglas Ainslie, found himself mesmerized by Constance and fell rather inappropriately in love with her.[6] Perhaps this was why it took him six months to get around to the task. Or perhaps some instinctive sense of foreboding had prevented him doing so sooner. Just before Christmas he delivered the news that Cyril's life was not to be a rosy one. It was a strange warning, presented to Constance and Oscar at the height of their happiness, and not the first that they would receive. According to Heron Allen, the devoted parents were deeply grieved by the results.

Cyril was an utterly loved baby. Both Constance and Oscar had a passion for their first-born that comes through in references to this child again and again. The neighbouring Hopes were suitably scathing about the new arrival, wondering whether the Wildes' experiments in dress would be extended to the new addition to the family. Laura Hope wondered, 'Will it be swathed in artistic baby clothes? Sage green bibs and tuckers, I suppose, and a peacock blue robe.'[7]

The new arrival had another effect. If marriage had somehow been responsible for Oscar settling into a more mature persona, the arrival of a child prompted something further. Oscar decided he must get a job. Freelance journalism and lecturing were no longer enough when there was a child to feed. Just weeks after Cyril was born, he wrote to his friend the Hon. George Curzon asking if he might help him become 'one of her Majesty's Inspectors of Schools!' Curzon and Wilde were friends from Oxford days. When Oscar had sent his poetry to the Oxford Union, Curzon was one of the few voices to sound out in his defence. Now Oscar wanted Curzon to be his referee, not least because the Rt Hon. Edward Stanhope, the politician in whose gift the inspectorates were held, was not within Wilde's circle and Oscar was concerned that 'he may take the popular idea of me as a real idler'.[8] Oscar's bids for secure employment in this instance were unsuccessful.

Motherhood, however, did not suggest a more traditional, domestic wifely role to Constance. Far from it. The trajectory on which she had been placed in marrying Oscar was one she was determined to continue even after the birth of her first child. Artistic marriage amounted to more than conventional domesticity for women, even when children were introduced.

On her return from honeymoon Constance had written to Otho and expressed her firm intention to have a career. 'I am thinking of becoming a correspondent to some paper, or else going on the stage: que pensez vous? I want to make some money: perhaps a novel would be better.'[9] Babies were not going to get in Constance's way.

Her very first foray into published writing occurred a month before the arrival of Cyril. In the 'Correspondence' section of the *Pall*

Mall Gazette on 6 May 1885 Constance took issue with another lady correspondent on a subject she was clearly genuinely passionate about.

On the topic of 'Ladies' Dress – Esthetic and Artistic' Constance explained that she was a 'one of the much abused aesthetes' who a former correspondent had complained were untidy in their appearance. The correspondent in question had suggested women should be in tailor-made dresses. Constance was quick to retaliate with the point that these outfits are 'ill fitted for home occupation or home comfort'. With her current situation clearly at the forefront of her mind, Constance also took issue with the suggestion that 'a young matron should wear what is close fitting and appropriate to her duties' by pointing out that 'the duties most ordinarily assumed by our young matrons are those of childbearing, for which close-fitting dress is eminently unsuitable'. In a series of further comments Constance went on to demolish her opponent on a point-by-point basis. If some people look untidy in Aesthetic dress, it is because they are essentially untidy people, but even this must be better than the hideous distortion to female bodies effected by 'the high Paris hat and the ungainly crinolette'. Aesthetes were simply attempting to preserve the 'proper proportions of the human body while allowing as much freedom and ease of motion as possible'. And finally Constance declared her allegiance to the 'promoters of the rational dress movement' and added, 'the inconvenience of their dress is owing not to their eccentricity, but to the necessity they are under of trying to make the divided skirt look as though it were not divided, on account of the intolerance of the British public'.

In 1881 the enterprising Viscountess Harberton had founded a campaigning organization, the Rational Dress Society, 'to promote the adoption, according to individual taste and convenience, of a style of dress based on considerations of health, comfort, and beauty and to deprecate constant changes of fashion which cannot be recommended on any of these grounds'.[10] The Viscountess embraced the principles of the society herself, for it is she who is largely credited with the invention of the 'divided' skirt, which she herself wore with utter disregard for the ridicule that this costume widely attracted.

Constance joined the Rational Dress Society. Her activities for the organization would lead her into public speaking in 1886 and into editing in 1888, when she would take on the editorship of the society's *Gazette*. She may well have been a member from the inception of the society, although it is more likely that she would have joined when, as a married woman, she had greater financial and social freedom to do so.

The overlap between the Aesthetic and rational dress movements became clear in 1883, when the Rational Dress Society held an exhibition in the Prince's Hall, Piccadilly, in which Mrs Nettleship featured among the exhibitors. Who knows whether Constance, with her keen interest in dress, paid her 2s 6d entry fee to see, in that same venue to which she and Otho would go to hear Oscar lecture, stalls displaying a vast array of costume options for the modern woman and her children?

The first stall in the hall was taken by Messrs Liberty & Co. of Regent Street, where a range of their art fabrics was accompanied by an explanation of their inclusion in the exhibition. Art fabrics 'play an essentially prominent part in connexion with Rational and Healthy dress', a placard read, going on to explain how Liberty's had revived the materials so much in favour with ancient Greece, a time of healthy and liberal costume. Liberty's did not combine their fabrics with new materials; their fabrics were pure, their silk pure silk. As for colour, Liberty's argued that 'colour is generally acknowledged to be an invaluable agent in refining and elevating the mind' and revealed that the basis of the company's dyes 'were of old Persian origin, which for beauty and softness of colour are unequalled'.

But above and beyond this, the hall in general was greater testimony to the close connection between the rational dress and women's lib movements. The show presented costumes that would enable women to take men on in almost any activity. There were outfits that would allow women greater freedom to skate, boat, play tennis, ride a tricycle or play cricket. There was even one dressmaker who had imagined a mountaineering dress for one particularly adventurous client.

Mrs Nettleship presented, among other items, a 'Ladies' Walking Costume', which had wide trousers beneath it. The inclusion of trousers enabled the dressmaker not only to lift the level of the skirt from the ground but also to reduce the weight of an over-skirt by half. As another exhibitor explained in her marketing material, 'the trouser covers the body fully and evenly and thereby fewer layers are necessary'.

In addition to various trouser options, the exhibition also featured divided skirts inspired by Viscountess Harberton's own designs, and a stall dedicated to Japanese costume. Lilley and Skinner showed visitors options for 'sensible boots and shoes', while another exhibitor presented eight different outfits for working women. There were even some futuristic costumes for women, imagined by Mrs E. King, the secretary of the society. These included short knee-length dresses and loose jackets, underneath which ladies wore trousers or bloomers to cover their legs. Costumes such as these indicate how utterly avant-garde the rational dress movement was. And the press saw it as such, constantly ridiculing its ambitions and suggestions, and often depicting its members as, frankly, potty.

By March 1885 Oscar had spent more than three years on the road lecturing. Now he turned his attention more fully to journalism. He became a regular contributor to both the *Dramatic Review* and the *Pall Mall Gazette*, and his association with the latter no doubt eased the path to publication for Constance's letter. She enjoyed the novelty of seeing herself in print and wrote to Otho to tell him so, adding, 'Oscar is very pleased with it and sorry that I did not sign it.'[11]

Constance had been mulling over a literary career for some months. In July 1884 she had told her brother she intended to write a piece of fiction which she described as a 'practical romance'. If it was written, it does not survive. But it was not long before Constance did become a published author. First, however, she had some other ambitions to explore.

Apropos of her desire to go on the stage, an opportunity for Constance to try her hand occurred in 1886. Not least through his work on Tite Street, Constance and Oscar were, of course, on very close terms with Edward Godwin. And so when the architect turned impresario and decided to stage a spectacular Classical production, a reinterpretation of Sophocles' *Helena in Troas* that would accommodate both professional actors and amateurs drawn from his circle of friends, it was quite natural that Constance should be considered.

There had been growing interest in Classical subjects in the 1870s and 1880s. Aestheticism in its quest for beauty found much to admire in Classical precedents. Oscar had already likened Lillie Langtry to Helen of Troy in his poem 'The New Helen', and painters such as Burne-Jones were exploring Classical motifs in their art.

Moreover, new archaeological approaches were making the Classical world accessible in new and vivid ways. In the 1860s the innovative archaeologist Giuseppe Fiorelli, instead of just recovering artefacts from the sites of Pompeii and Herculaneum, as his predecessors had done for a hundred years, concentrated on clearing debris from the site so that for the first time the architecture and streets could be viewed. This new kind of excavation and display of private houses and civic buildings suddenly generated interest in the everyday life of the Classical world. Cities, and the people who once populated them, arose phoenix-like from the ashes.

No wonder, then, that the everyday wear of ordinary Classical Greek folk was being cited as a model for the reform of everyday wear for nineteenth-century Londoners. And no surprise either that throughout the 1880s theatre began to look back to its Classical roots.

In 1880 *Agamemnon* had been performed at Oxford, and then the production had come to London. It had been the first attempt to perform Greek theatre in an authentic historical manner. Other attempts had followed. In 1885 a young Cambridge Classicist, Harry Marillier, had sought Oscar out to invite him in his capacity as drama critic to attend a version of *Eumenides* in Cambridge's Theatre Royal.[12]

Although Marillier and those preceding him had set the tone and made great strides in imagining Greek costume, and the manner of Greek acting and direction, they had been handicapped by the theatres in which their productions were staged. Greek theatre performed on a raised oblong stage could never feel properly authentic. For that one would need an amphitheatre. Godwin understood this. His *Helena of Troas* was to be staged in a circus space, which with its semicircular arrangement could recapture something of the original amphitheatre performance.

And so Constance found herself heading into the centre of London on 17 May 1886 and making her way to the stage door of Hengler's Circus in Argyll Street, just a stone's throw from Oxford Circus.[13] Hengler's had a low-level, circular performance space and raked seating, and here Frederick Charles Hengler, the son of a tightrope artist, had been staging a circus with everything from acrobats on horseback to Rubin Raffin and his Porcine Wonder – a clown with a performing pig which not only jumped through hoops but also, to the delight of assembled Londoners, braved blazing gates.

Godwin boarded over the sandy floor and laid tiles in geometric patterns that would provide guidelines for the movement and dance of his fifteen-strong Greek chorus. In the midst of what he had now transformed into a semicircular Greek 'orchestra' he placed an altar to Dionysus. Behind the orchestra and opposite the audience he built a raised stage reached by two low flights of steps. Godwin decorated the lower part of the stage with reliefs featuring the battle of the Amazons and Centaurs. Two doorways framed by Greek pilasters gave on to painted scenes of the Greek coastline and provided the means of entrance and exit for the chorus and the other characters. This was King Priam's palace.

Constance had the elevated role of one of Helen's two handmaidens. Her companion was played by a Miss Hare. Helen herself was played by the actress Alma Murray, dressed in yellow silk. The handmaidens were in green and white linen. The clothes were as authentic as possible, the linen unbleached and, where dyed, done so with soft vegetable dyes for authenticity. Oscar's friend the painter Louise Jopling had a role, as did a number of the Wilde 'set', including Mr and Mrs Beerbohm Tree as Paris and Oenone respectively.

For six nights Constance and the rest of the cast braved the audiences. With the exception of *Punch,* which of course had a field day laughing at the Aesthetes undertaking their latest project, the newspaper reports were generally favourable. Oscar himself provided a positive write-up in the *Dramatic Review.* With professional propriety he was careful to mention all the leading ladies *except* his own wife. However, Constance was noted on at least a couple of occasions by other less compromised critics. Her notice in *The Era* is typical:

> The graceful form and appropriate action of Mrs Louise Jopling, who was Hecuba's tire woman were noticeable; Miss Hare's refined style and beautiful features drew attention to one of the Handmaidens; and Mrs Oscar Wilde's aesthetic poses and picturesque appearance were admired in the representative of the other. The performance was witnessed by an audience which included his Royal Highness the Prince of Wales and many artistic and dramatic nobilities; and was well worth seeing for once, simply as a curiosity of archaeological research and conscientious reproduction of the Past.[14]

This was the first and last time Constance took to the stage. If she had hoped that, like so many of Oscar's female friends, she might make her name treading the boards, she ultimately lacked either the talent or perhaps the genuine opportunity. With one child to manage, perhaps a stage career might have been conceivable, but with two children the notion of late nights and hard graft might have felt too much even for a woman as determined as Constance. For as Constance stood in King Priam's imaginary palace she almost certainly knew that her second child was already on its way. In May 1886, less than a year since the birth of Cyril, she was three months' pregnant.

The contrast between Constance's first and second pregnancies could not have been more profound. While the first was fired with a sense of excitement and adventure, the second was dull and laborious. Oscar, who only a year earlier had been so accommodating of his wife's bouts of prenatal sickness and frailty, was now less sensitive to these unavoidable symptoms. The journalist and author Frank Harris, a friend of Wilde's, claimed that years later Oscar recounted to him how during this period his sexual attraction to Constance plummeted:

> When I married, my wife was a beautiful girl, white and slim as a lily, with dancing eyes and gay rippling laughter like music. In a year or so the flower-like grace had all vanished; she became heavy, shapeless, deformed: she dragged herself around the house in uncouth misery with drawn blotched face and hideous body, sick at heart because of our love. It was dreadful. I tried to be kind to her; forced myself to touch and kiss her; but she was sick always, and – oh! I cannot recall it, it is all loathsome.[15]

The accounts of the graceful Mrs Wilde as she appeared in *Helena of Troas* fail to match Oscar's alleged picture of his wife with child, but nevertheless, as her second pregnancy progressed, Constance and Oscar's marriage suffered. With the first flush of sexual infatuation greatly diminished by its consequences, they cheered themselves with the notion that they might have a girl, the perfect complement to the adorable Cyril. They even had a name ready for her: Isola. Oscar had had a sister called Isola whom he had adored but who died when she was just nine years old, the victim of childhood fever. Perhaps Oscar had hoped that with a baby daughter the loss of his sister might finally be eased, or even replaced.

Constance went into labour on a miserable November day. Charles de Lacy Lacy barely made it in time from his home in Grosvenor Street to Tite Street, the fog was so thick. But instead of delivering the little girl that everyone wanted so badly, another boy was born. Unlike Cyril, who had been robust and healthy, Vyvyan, as he was christened, was a less than ideal infant.[16] He was small and ailing from the start. Instead of the flourish of activity that attended the arrival of Cyril, there was less fascination with the second addition to their family. While the exact moment of Cyril's arrival had been celebrated in the commission of horoscopes and a bout of letter-writing, no such activity seemed to attend Vyvyan's introduction to the world. In fact, Constance and Oscar didn't even register his birth for several weeks, and when they did, they could not remember the exact date of his birth other than it had occurred in the first week of November. The 3rd of that month was therefore registered without any certainty of accuracy.

Even the appointment of godparents hadn't gone quite according to plan. The Wildes asked the great critic John Ruskin if he would oblige. To have a figure of such high cultural esteem and social standing would have been a coup indeed for the newly arrived Vyvyan. But Ruskin wrote back and said he felt too old. So the services of the painter Mortimer Menpes were sought instead. Menpes was a great friend of Godwin and Whistler, with whom he shared a passion for things Japanese. Like Walter Harris, he had the spirit of an adventurer and explorer. Not long after Vyvyan was born, Menpes set off on a year-long tour of Japan, bringing back on his return not only a huge amount of artefacts but also an enormous collection of work he himself had produced in response to the country, which he subsequently exhibited.

Although Menpes, living close by in Fulham, probably proved to be a far more exciting and accessible godfather than Ruskin could ever have been, nevertheless things generally felt far less satisfactory than they had done a year earlier. The ideal frame within which Constance and Oscar had both envisaged their marriage and family life was changing.

When he grew up, Vyvyan acknowledged the fact that he was something of a disappointment. He adored Constance, he said, but noted that

> I was always conscious of the fact that both my father and my mother really preferred my brother to myself; it seems to be an instinct in parents to prefer their first born . . . I was not as strong as my brother, and I had more than my fair share of childish complaints, which probably offended my father's aesthetic sense . . . And most of all, both my parents had hoped for a girl.[17]

But it was not just the fact that their second child was a boy rather than a girl that was beginning to undermine the Wilde marriage. Vyvyan's arrival came at a time when, quite apart from everything else, Oscar had begun to feel a level of frustration with artistic marriage. While he had been on the road lecturing, the appeal of home and hearth was great. But once he was based in London, returning nightly to Tite Street, the novelty of domestic bliss quickly waned. He sensed that the venture he and Constance had so wholeheartedly and enthusiastically embarked on might not in fact be one that could fulfil him as he had originally hoped. He loved the company and companionship of his wife. But he also loved the attentions of young men. At a time when anything Greek was *à la mode*, Oscar was all too aware that Greek love, the attraction between men endorsed in Ancient Greek culture, was profoundly intriguing.

Ada Leverson told a tale about Oscar. According to Leverson, Wilde was an attentive, courteous and dedicated husband who, not long after he was married, took Constance shopping.

> He waited for her outside Swan and Edgar's while she made some long and tedious purchases. As he stood there full of careless good spirits, on a cold sunny May morning, a curious, very young, but hard-eyed creature appeared, looked at him, gave a sort of laugh, and passed on. He felt he said 'as if an icy hand had clutched his heart'. He had a sudden presentiment. He saw a vision of folly, misery and ruin.[18]

Swan and Edgar's was a famous department store that faced Piccadilly Circus. Elegant and suave, it nevertheless looked out on to one of the most notorious pick-up spots in the whole of the capital. Oscar, who so loved observing all walks of life, and with his particular fascination for vice, must have enjoyed watching the 'renters', or male prostitutes, who notoriously hung around this thoroughfare. That one of them could spot his predilection for young men almost before he himself had identified this sexual trait came as a shock.

That Oscar openly enjoyed the friendship of younger men was no secret, and this was an aspect of her husband that Constance was in fact proud of. Years later, in 1892, she wrote to Georgina Mount-Temple full of pride at the fact that

> Oscar had yesterday such a beautiful letter from the brother of a young man who has died lately in Australia. Beautiful to me I mean because it is so full of this boy's love for Oscar. I will write a copy of it and send it to you, I should like you to see how good O's influence is on young men, and the brother speaks of this young man as the purest soul he had ever known.[19]

In the early days of their marriage Constance was even party to Oscar's cultivation of young men, just as she was very much a part of almost everything in Oscar's life. One of the first visitors to the newly decorated Tite Street was none other than Constance's friend Douglas Ainslie. The love-struck teenager who had got Constance into such trouble was now entering his twenties. Just days after they had moved into their new home he came to see it. To her delight Douglas Ainslie was showing decidedly Aesthetic tendencies.[20]

'Douglas thinks our house the most charming he has ever been in,' Constance informed Otho, 'and could hardly tear himself away last night.'[21] Not so long after Douglas Ainslie had been entertained in Tite Street, it was Oscar who was asking Harry Marillier, the Cambridge student who had contacted him about his performance of *Eumenides*, to join him and Constance in town. Marillier's visit invigorated Oscar. 'I have never learned anything except from people younger than myself,' he declared, 'and you are infinitely young.'[22]

In November 1885 Constance and Oscar both went to Cambridge to visit the young Harry as well as other established friends they had there, including the poet Oscar Browning. On their return both the Wildes wrote thank-you notes to their hosts. Constance's notes to both were plain, polite and to the point: she returned a letter from their mutual friend Walter Harris to Browning, and in her note to Marillier she reminded him to come and see them again in London. Oscar, by contrast, found himself deeply moved by the youthful

Constance Lloyd by Louis Desanges, 1882.
The artist had painted the Prince of Wales just a few years earlier.

John Horatio Lloyd, Constance's grandfather who lived in Lancaster Gate. Wealthy and well connected, he invented the Lloyd's Bond: a type of investment bond on which the development of the railway system became particularly dependent.

Horace Lloyd, Constance's father. Part of the Prince of Wales's social set, he could 'have taken on any expert in one of the three games, chess and billiards and whist, and beaten him in two out of three'.

Jane Francesca Agnes, Lady Wilde. Oscar's mother was an Irish poet whose pen name was 'Speranza'.

Sir William Wilde, Oscar's father, was an esteemed eye and ear surgeon. He had a colourful private life and a brood of illegitimate children in addition to Oscar and Willie, his legitimate sons with Speranza.

Otho Holland Lloyd, Constance's brother, taken in about 1884 when he would have been twenty-eight.

Constance aged twenty-four, on holiday at Delgaty Castle, Aberdeenshire, August 1882. According to a note on the back, the picture was taken by 'Mr Burton, Son of the Scottish Historian'.

Above left Oscar the bachelor, wearing his hair long. According to Constance, her relatives in London disapproved of his appearance 'because they don't choose to see anything but that he wears long hair and looks aesthetic. I like him awfully much but I suppose it is very bad taste.'
Above right Constance in an 'aesthetic' dress in the period before her marriage to Oscar. Otho considered her loose dresses with wide sleeves ugly.

A Private View at the Royal Academy, 1881 by William Powell Frith. Oscar is featured in the foreground to the right, with a lily in his buttonhole. To the left, a young woman, dressed very much as Constance did at this time, wears a green puffed-sleeved dress, on which she has pinned the badge of Aestheticism: a sunflower.

Oscar the married man, photographed in 1885, with his hair curled in what he described as his 'Neronian coiffure'.

Consistent with the *Lady's Pictorial* descriptions of her honeymoon wardrobe, Mrs Oscar Wilde is seen here in one of her 'large white plumed hats' and 'somewhat quaintly-made gowns of white muslin, usually relieved by touches of golden ribbon'.

Suddenly in the spotlight after her marriage to Oscar, Constance featured in the press when she manned a charity flower stall at the 'Healtheries' in 1884. She is seen wearing one of the latest 'rational' outfits: a divided skirt.

As Constance and Oscar's home in Tite Street soon became acknowledged as a hub of cultural and social activity, the Wildes' 'artistic' marriage became the source of caricature in the press.

PROSE.

Little Wifey.—THEN THERE WERE TWO GREAT PAINTERS, AND TWO GREAT AUTHORS, AND AN EMINENT TRAGEDIAN, AND—YOU! WHAT A GATHERING TOGETHER OF CONGENIAL SOULS!

He.—YES! RATHER TOO MANY OF US, I THOUGHT, WHEN THERE WAS ONLY DINNER ENOUGH FOR FOUR.

Oscar photographed in 1889. While his private life took on new sexual dimensions, Oscar's public profile was essentially conventional in the mid to late 1880s. His dress was no longer bohemian, but traditional with just a dandyish twist.

Robbie Ross, *c.*1887, when he was the Wildes' lodger in Tite Street. At around this time he and Oscar embarked on an affair.

No. 16 Tite Street (*right*), which Oscar and Constance leased in 1884. In conjunction with architect Edward Godwin they converted the conventional new build into a 'House Beautiful'. The walls were painted white and polished; the floor covering kept pale and plain; internal dividing doors were replaced by curtains; and slim, sparse furniture contributed to a sense of space and calm.

Vyvyan Wilde in a Cossack costume aged about three.

Constance and Cyril photographed in 1889 when Cyril would have been about four. Cyril was the Wildes' favourite son, the mutual adoration between mother and child quite clear in this picture.

idealism he saw among Marillier and his student friends. For him, being in the company of young people was like being in a dream full of 'bright young faces, and grey misty quadrangles'. He found himself intoxicated by the enthusiasm of these young men.

In December 1885, when he was lonely in a Glasgow hotel room, having delivered another lecture, Oscar wrote and made a terrible confession to Harry Marillier. In a letter written almost exactly a year after the one he wrote under comparable circumstances to Constance, one where he had imagined their lips kissing, now Oscar confessed to a Cambridge undergraduate that for him there was no longer 'such thing as a romantic experience'.

Oscar revealed that for him

there are romantic memories, and there is the desire of romance – that is all. Our most fiery moments of ecstasy are mere shadows of what somewhere else we have felt, or what we long someday to feel. So at least it feels to me. And strangely enough, what comes of this is a curious mixture of ardour and indifference. I myself would sacrifice everything for a new experience, and I know there is no such thing as new experience at all. I think I would more readily die for what I do not believe in than for what I hold to be true. I would go to the stake for a sensation and be a sceptic to the last! Only one thing remains fascinating to me, the mystery of moods. To be master of these moods is exquisite, to be mastered by them more exquisite still. Sometimes I think the artistic life is a long and lovely suicide, and am sorry that it is so.

And much of this I fancy you yourself have felt: much also remains for you to feel. There is an unknown land full of strange flowers and subtle perfumes, a land of which it is joy of all joys to dream, a land where all things are perfect and poisonous.[23]

It is a letter, perhaps in response to a question about romance and marriage, that admits that the infatuation he once held for his wife is passed, that in its place is a loyalty or affection that amounts to a 'curious mixture of ardour and indifference'. The freedom and idealism of young single men reminded him of the compromise that marriage entails, and what pleasure might lie outside it.

There is unquestionably the possibility of interpreting Oscar's allusion to the land of strange flowers as homosexual code. To an extent the effusiveness of Wilde's language in his romantic letters to Marillier has to be mediated by context. Oscar was one of a number of Aesthetes who adopted excessively intimate language and gestures as part of the affectation of the time.

Nevertheless, the flirtation is palpable in the correspondence between Oscar and Marillier. Oscar was falling in love with the young man. Six months later another note to Harry seems to confirm both this and the fact that this love remained both tempting and unconsummated. 'I had been thinking a great deal about you,' Oscar wrote to him. 'There is at least this beautiful mystery in life, that at the moment it feels most complete it finds some secret sacred niche in its shrine empty and waiting. Then comes a time of exquisite expectancy.'[24]

Constance, accustomed to Oscar's affectations, saw nothing more in his liking of Harry Marillier than just that. She continued to encourage Oscar's young male friends, and he did not seek to conceal them from her. In fact, he continued to involve her in his socializing with them. The evangelistic enthusiasm her husband displayed in the recruiting of these apostles was, from her point of view, a positive thing. Within a month she was introducing these apostles to one another. In January she dropped Marillier a line inviting him to dine with her and Oscar at 7.30, noting 'I have asked Douglas Ainslie also.'[25] The boys were, after all, exactly the same age. It was perhaps on this occasion that Constance, Oscar and their young friends all drank 'yellow wine from green glasses in Keats's honour'. It was certainly at this dinner that Constance showed off a set of moonstone jewels that the couple were particularly proud of.

The Wildes' generosity towards young men culminated in them taking in a seventeen-year-old boy, Robert Baldwin Ross, at around this time. Robbie Ross was a young Canadian who, since the death of his eminent father, had been brought up by his mother in Europe. On his mother's side there were distant Irish connections which may have been the source of his introduction to Oscar and Constance. But Robbie's elder brother Alec, a founder and secretary of the Society of Authors, was also moving in London's literary circles and may have been the point of introduction. Whatever the connection, they were sufficiently friendly for Mrs Ross to ask if Robbie could lodge at Tite Street while she took a two-month sojourn on the Continent.

The stay must have proved a revelation for the young man, who had strong artistic leanings. Robbie was charming, intelligent and erudite. Both Constance and Oscar adored him, and in the fullness of time he would become one of Constance's closest male friends. One can imagine the Wildes indulging him with trips to galleries, talks and the theatre.

Robbie also proved a revelation to Oscar. Despite his young age, he was a practising homosexual. If Marillier had revealed to Oscar that there was an empty niche in his life, Robbie was the young man who actually filled it for Oscar. The two began a physical relationship.

Robbie shared Oscar's fascination with the underground world of vice and deviancy. Despite his youthfulness, he seemed to have been bold in his exploration of the opportunities there were for homosexual experiences in London at this time. During the day Robbie attended a crammer in Covent Garden that was intended to prepare him for entry to Cambridge. But at least some of his leisure time was, it seems, spent in cruising the public conveniences and alleys around Piccadilly in search of sexual encounters. Robbie was well known to the police. And this does add just a touch of credibility to a story told by Frank Harris that Oscar and Robbie had actually encountered one another in a public lavatory, where Robbie had importuned the older man.[26]

Robbie's introduction of Oscar to full homosexual sex could not have been worse timed. Although it was perhaps inevitable that Oscar would eventually explore this facet of his character, by doing so after 1885 he was committing a crime. In 1885 acts of gross indecency between males, even in private, were deemed criminal thanks to a new clause in the Criminal Law Amendment Act passed in that year.

At some level Constance sensed Oscar's infidelity, although she misattributed the object of his affection. Before they married, Constance had sworn that she would never be jealous, but just two years into the marriage she had begun to have doubts and was becoming resentful. In his capacity now as a drama critic Oscar was often away from home. Constance suspected Oscar of having developed an infatuation for an actress whose performances she considered he was following with rather too much interest. There is an anecdote of a dinner party at which Constance made a cutting reference to Oscar's current infatuation. When asked what he had done over the last week, Oscar, who had in fact been reviewing the actress in question, offered a typically obfuscating response. He 'had seen an exquisite Elizabethan country house, with emerald lawns, stately yew hedges, scented rose gardens cool lily ponds . . . and strutting peacocks'. Constance rather bitingly added: 'And did she act well, Oscar?', her suspicion being that 'The nearest he had got to a Tudor mansion that week was the Blank Hotel in Birmingchester, whither he had pursued the fair but frail leading lady.'[27]

Another event almost certainly contributed to Constance's insecurity around the time of Vyvyan's birth. Her brother became involved in another personal scandal that both alarmed and frightened Constance. Until this point in their lives Otho had pursued a series of choices that had closely mirrored Constance's own. He had married within days of his sister, and she thought that he had, like her, married for love. Now, just like Constance and Oscar, Otho and Nellie had had two sons. Otho Junior and Fabian Lloyd were born within months of their cousins Cyril and Vyvyan. But in 1887 Constance received an extraordinary piece of news regarding Otho. He was leaving his wife for another woman.

Otho's second child, Fabian, was born in May 1887. Within just two months of what should have been this happy occasion, Otho deserted Nellie and moved in with someone else. To make matters worse, this woman, Mary Winter, was a close friend of Nellie's whom she had befriended while at finishing school in Lausanne.[28] And it was in this Swiss city that Otho and Mary were now temporarily living together.

'What fatality has overtaken you? Will you not write and tell me how this all is,' Constance wrote desperately to her brother in July.

> If you care to write privately I will show your letter to no one, not even Oscar. I cannot think that you realise in counting the cost, what a burden you have thrown on poor little Nellie. She writes so very sweetly and kindly but she is such a child quite unfit to take charge of two children, two boys, entirely by herself with no father's care. I imagined that you had such an intensely strong feeling of the duties of parents that you would not have so deserted the little ones. Is it forever, or is there no chance that you will some day return to her? Do tell me. You have always been so dear to me that I cannot bear to think that you will not write to me now.[29]

While Otho's marriage fell apart, Oscar and Constance patched up the frictions that had emerged between them around the time of Vyvyan's birth. It would be a mistake to see Oscar's early frustrations and his affair with Robbie Ross as marking the end of his marriage in all but name. It would also be a mistake to think that Oscar would see his enjoyment of homosexual sex as being in conflict with his marriage. He managed to reconcile his different appetites and aspirations. Whatever distractions Oscar was finding, unlike his brother-in-law, he did have a strong sense of parental and marital duty. He also continued to love his wife.

Nevertheless, the sexual aspect of their relationship never properly recovered after the birth of their second child. Oscar's new sexual preference for men no doubt informed this, but there may have been post-natal medical issues on Constance's side that were also a contributing factor. Constance seems to have accepted the diminished physical passion in her marriage, reassured that at least the emotional and social bond between her and Oscar remained. She had a husband who was committed and affectionate, which was more than Nellie now had. Constance acknowledged as much somewhat pointedly when she wrote to Otho and told him that 'Oscar and I are very happy together now.'[30]

Whistler would note that Oscar was 'a bourgeois malgré lui',[31] and that was the nub of it. Oscar was the married man, his wife, children and home the cathedral he had built around him. His relationship with men would be kept both discreet and discrete. From now on a clandestine version of Oscar would quietly seek to fill that 'secret sacred niche'. This private version of Oscar, visible to us from the perspective history can offer, was apparent neither to the majority of his contemporaries at this stage nor to Constance. And it seems that once Oscar had realized that is was possible both to live a bourgeois married life and to have a secret existence, to have his cake and eat it, then his relationship with his wife improved.

In a gesture that must have reassured Constance of his sense of familial responsibility, Oscar redoubled efforts to secure proper full-time employment. Such reassurance came not a moment too soon. Constance confessed to Otho that their finances were spiralling out of control. In fact, they had borrowed money from Otho, agreeing to pay him back with interest.[32] Now that Otho found himself with two households rather than one, he needed evidence that the Wildes could meet their debts.

'Of course I will see that your interest is paid in future,' she calmed her brother. 'You shall receive this half year's in January and the rest shall, if possible, be paid off gradually also, but we have given up any hope of being able to let our house and I am afraid we shall still be living here rather too expensively as we neither of us have a notion how to live non extravagantly.' Constance added that she was 'obliged to have two nurses on account of baby and expenses flow . . . however, I hope that after next year we shall be able to get on.'[33]

That the Wildes were actually attempting to lease the house they had so recently moved into and in which they had invested so heavily seems extraordinary. This alone must have applied a pressure that would have brought the most romantic love affair down to earth with a bump.

Oscar finally got a job. In 1887, after being overlooked in his attempts to become first an inspector of schools and then the secretary of a charitable foundation, he was invited to become a magazine editor. In the spring of that year Thomas Wemyss Reid, a former editor of the *Leeds Mercury*, joined the publishers Cassell & Co. in London. Cassell's had begun publication of a magazine called *The Lady's World: A Magazine of Fashion and Society*. Oscar's lectures on dress and interiors had not gone unnoticed by Reid. The fact he had such a high-profile fashionable wife, well versed in the hot issues of the day such as rational dress, could not have hurt. Reid invited Oscar to look at the magazine and see if there were improvements that he thought could be made were he to edit it. It's tempting to consider that the letter he wrote to Reid in response was written in consultation with Constance.

'It seems to me that at present it is too feminine, and not sufficiently womanly,' Oscar wrote.

> No one appreciates more fully than I do the value and importance of Dress, in its relation to good taste and good health: indeed the subject is one that I have constantly lectured on, but it seems to me that . . . the field of mere millinery and trimmings, is to some extent already occupied by such papers as the *Queen* and *Lady's Pictorial*, and that we should take a wider range, as well as a high standpoint, and deal not merely with what women wear, but with what they think, and what they feel.[34]

Oscar went on the magazine payroll in May 1887 and immediately began recruiting writers from among the female intelligentsia of the day. The venture instantly realigned him and Constance. To be the successful man at the helm of *The Lady's World* Oscar must have known that his wife was going to play a crucial role. In accepting the job, Constance's and Oscar's interdependence was re-established. Their artistic marriage was back on track – for the time being at least.

7

A literary couple

Mrs Oscar Wilde entertains 'in a cream-tinted dining room, of which walls, furniture, and all things are in unison' – even the guests, who are of course the crème de la crème of society.[1]

Constance's 'at homes' were famous. From the moment Constance and Oscar moved into Tite Street in 1885 the great and the good had come to see the avant-garde interiors, meet the beautiful wife and, of course, hear Oscar entertain the room. 'To my mother's receptions came people of such widely different interests,' Vyvyan remembered, noting attendees including 'Henry Irving, Sir William Richmond, R A, Sarah Bernhardt, John Sargent, John Ruskin, Lillie Langtry, Mark Twain, Herbert Beerbohm Tree, Robert Browning, Algernon Swinburne, John Bright, Lady de Grey, Ellen Terry and Arthur Balfour. All the Pre-Raphaelite Brotherhood was constantly in attendance.'[2]

Ever the collector, and impressed by fame and success, Constance made sure that she captured the signatures of some of her visitors in an autograph book. Those she solicited provide an interesting insight into her own character and passions.

The first entry in the book, even before Oscar's own dedication, is from Oliver Wendell Holmes, the American poet and physician, friend of Longfellow and liberal reformer, who had championed the rights of women and blacks to attend university. Oscar's own contribution to the pages, written in June 1886, apart from being intended as an expression of his love for his wife for all subsequent signatories to see, seems to contain a very private message about the deeply intimate nature of their mutual understanding.

I can write no stately poem
As a prelude to my lay
From a poet to a poem –
This is all I say.

Yet if of these fallen petals
One to you seems fair,
Love will waft it, till it settles
On your hair.

And when wind and winter harden
All the loveless land,
It will whisper of the garden,
You will understand.[3]

After Holmes and Oscar, Constance made sure that Walter Pater provided his signature for her along with Jimmy Whistler, the painter W. B. Richmond and the critic and poet Theodore Watts. The latter, contributing a poem called 'Baby Smiles' in the summer of 1886, had obviously met an infant Cyril during his visit. Watts offered a rather saccharine and flattering observation that

> . . . a sight I saw outshine all other –
> Saw a woman kiss a lovely child –
> Saw the lovelier smile of her, the mother,
> When 'baby' smiled.[4]

the liberal politician and campaigner for parliamentary reform John Bright presented a much more sombre thought a few months later. He reminded Constance that 'In Peace sons bury their Fathers – In War Fathers bury their sons'.

Constance treated her twice-monthly 'at homes' as a theatrical exercise where scenery and costume were meticulously planned. She spent much time and effort in finding new surprising ways of decorating Tite Street to impress and please her guests, and the combination of this attention to detail with celebrity attendees quickly made Mrs Oscar's parties a matter of national news. In July 1887 the *Lady's Pictorial* took delight in listing those who attended one particularly successful party. Apart from family, including Aunt Mary Napier, Constance's mother, Mrs Swinburne-King, and Speranza, the Wildes managed to gather under one roof aristocrats such as Lady Nevill, Lady Ardilaun and Lady Monckton, alongside theatrical celebrities such as Mr and Mrs George Alexander and Mr and Mrs Bram Stoker, and artists such as Walter Crane and Waldo Story.

'Roses were the only flowers used for decoration,' the *Lady's Pictorial* noted; 'the hostess looked most picturesque in a lovely gown made with a bodice and train of dark green silk and outlined with small gold beads; long hanging sleeves from the shoulder lined with dark green, worn over tightly-fitting sleeves of gold gauze, completed this very charming and picturesque attire.'

Anna, Comtesse de Brémont, remembered the cachet that an invitation to Constance's 'at homes' carried. 'I was not prepared for the crush of fashionable folk that overcrowded the charming rooms of the unpretentious house in Tite Street,' she wrote.

> There was an air of brightness and luxury about it . . . A smart maid opened the door and I found myself in the wide hallway towards the dining room. There tea was served in the most delightfully unconventional manner from a quaint shelf extending around the wall, before which white enamelled (Chippendale) seats – modelled in various Grecian styles – were placed . . . I presently found myself sitting in one of the white Greek seats, drinking tea out of a dainty yellow cup that might have been modelled on a lotus flower, and being talked to by a young poet.

On finding Oscar in the smoking room, she was duly introduced to Constance, who was wearing 'an exquisite Greek costume of cowslip yellow and apple leaf green. Her hair, a thick mass of ruddy brown, was wonderfully set off by the bands of yellow ribbon, supporting the knot of hair low on the nape of the neck, and crossing the wavy masses above the brow.'[5]

In such circumstances it seems that Constance produced an event at which ultimately her husband could perform. The Comtesse noted that, once Oscar took the floor, Constance would slip back into the general hubbub of the event, mixing among the crush, 'a rapt expression of love and pride on her face; while her eyes were magnetised, on her husband's inspired features'.

Oscar did not underestimate Constance's 'at homes' as a recruitment ground for *The Lady's World*. His tactics are revealed in his letter to Helena Sickert, the sister of the painter Walter Sickert and a writer, lecturer and campaigner for women's rights. First he wrote to her and invited her to write an article for his new magazine, and then he followed this with an invitation: 'My wife is at home the first and third Thursdays in each month. Do come next Thursday with your mother and talk over the matter.'[6]

It's hardly surprising that Constance's autograph book also reflects the notable women who graced her living room *en route* to their contribution to *The Lady's World*. Mary Braddon, the author of the best-selling novel *Lady Audley's Secret,* and the American poet and critic Louise Chandler Moulton penned little epigrams and notes of affection for their hostess. The South African novelist and women's rights campaigner Olive Schreiner made her mark. The writer John Strange Winter (real name Henrietta Eliza Vaughan Stannard) wrote a strange little note in blank verse that reminded Constance that

> There are lions & there are tiger-
> Cats, but the balance is pretty
> Evenly kept between them:
> Man is not all lion; woman is not all tiger-cat.[7]

Constance must have felt inspired by these successful literary women with whom she now associated, not least because she had been progressing her own literary ambitions. Even during the personally difficult years of 1886 and 1887 Constance had exploited the literary opportunities that life within the Wilde circle brought, probably motivated as much by their financial mess as anything else.

While she was on honeymoon, Speranza had promised Constance that Willie Wilde was going to use his influence to get Constance appointed as a special correspondent for a women's weekly magazine. It was no idle pledge. While Oscar was a drama critic for *The Dramatic Review* and other periodicals, Constance was writing drama reviews of the plays they saw together for the *Lady's Pictorial*. These were all written anonymously. But on at least one occasion a beneficiary of Constance's comments wrote to Oscar, suspecting *his* authorship and thanking him for his kind words. The amateur singer and social phenomenon Georgina Weldon was flattered that in an account of Henry Irving's *Merchant of Venice* she had been described as 'radiant and young looking as ever'.[8] Oscar was forced to confess: 'The little note in the *Lady's Pictorial* on the Irving Benefit was written not by me, but by my wife.' This 'little note' was an article that stretched to close to a thousand words.

By June 1888 Constance was noted as one half of a 'literary couple' attending a gathering of 'Literary and Artistic Society' at the Royal Institute Gallery. But this literary acclaim was not down to her journalism alone. Although she had not realized the 'practical Romance' she had discussed with Otho, she began to write children's stories.

In 1887 Oscar had his first short stories published. 'Lord Arthur Savile's Crime', inspired by the amateur fortune-teller Edward Heron Allen, is the story of a young man who becomes the subject of a self-fulfilling destiny after a chiromantist (or palm-reader) called Mr Podger foresees a murder in the lines on his hand. Oscar's 'The Canterville Ghost' also reflects the fascination for other-worldly phenomena that prevailed in society at the time, and which held a particular fascination for Constance.

While Oscar was busy negotiating the publication of these stories, Constance was approached to write a children's story for *The Bairn's Annual*, a publication produced by the Leadenhall Press and edited by the writer Alice Corkran. Corkran's Irish family were established friends of Speranza's and by default Oscar's. Alice's sister the society artist Henriette had painted Constance's portrait two years earlier.[9]

For the third edition of *The Bairn's Annual*, released in November 1887 ready for the Christmas market, Constance wrote a story called 'Was It a Dream?' Her contribution provided instant publicity for the annual. '*The Bairn's Annual* . . . contains tales and poetry for children in every way worthy of the Leadenhall Press,' noted *Lloyd's Weekly Newspaper* in its 'Books of the Day' column, adding: 'among the contributors being Mrs Oscar Wilde'.[10]

The Leadenhall Press had built a reputation for publishing high-quality illustrated books and children's books, many of which were facsimiles of eighteenth-century editions. The firm was run by Andrew Tuer, who had a particular sympathy with the Aesthetic and liberal-minded set in which Constance moved. In addition to his children's literature, he published work by the feminist writer and poet Emily J. Pfeiffer, whom Oscar invited to contribute to *The Lady's World*. Pfeiffer's book was illustrated by none other than Edward Burne-Jones and Jimmy Whistler. Speranza's friend Anna Kingsford had written a Theosophical text, *The Perfect Way*, which was also published by Tuer. A passionate collector, Tuer had his own impressive stash of antiquarian books, which often provided the source of his company's facsimile reproductions. His own collection of Japanese stencils also allowed him, in collaboration with Liberty & Co., to produce a facsimile stencil book, enabling those Aesthetes who could not afford the services of a Godwin or Whistler a DIY alternative.

'Was It a Dream?' stands out among the other stories that Corkran assembled in *The Bairn's Annual* of 1887. Tonally it is quite different. The book generally features jungle animals, witches, moral tales of nursery tiffs and adventures featuring brave children. Constance's story, by contrast, takes art and dreaming as its subject matter. These preoccupations place it firmly as an 'Aesthetic piece'. Dream-like, somnambulant paintings were the mainstay of the movement's painters, such as Edward Burne-Jones. The adoration of 'Art for Art's sake' was articulated by the philosophers of the movement such as Walter Pater and, of course, Oscar himself.

Another aspect of the story that secures its claim to being part of the Aesthetic tradition is its fascination with Japan. 'Was It a Dream?' is about a Japanese fan, an object that could well have come from A. B. Ya's store at the 'Healtheries', or which could have travelled back with Mortimer Menpes from his own travels in that country.

In Constance's story the fan, decorated with a painted stork 'flying daintily' across it, is hanging in an imaginary nursery. One night the stork is magically brought to life by an angel who has come to bestow 'sweet dreams' on the nursery's two infant occupants. In the sleepy atmosphere that Constance conjures, where the children slumber 'with flushed faces and tossed golden hair on their downy pillows', the little stork complains to the angel, 'I am fastened here for ever; and though the sky is always blue, and the almond blossoms are always pink . . . I still long once more to see the dear home where I was born, and the wife who was given to me, and the little ones who came after I left, and whom I have never seen!'[11]

The angel releases the painted stork with the aid of a magic pink feather plucked from her wings. With this empowering feather attached to its head, the stork is able to leave the fan in which it is imprisoned and fly to its homeland, on condition that it returns before the two sleeping children wake.

Constance provides a highly visual, painterly and idealized description of the Japan to which the stork flies. There was plenty of reference material in her own home in Tite Street and other neighbouring Aesthetic homes that she could have drawn on. Not only had the Japanese fanatic Mortimer Menpes given Vyvyan some of his etchings of that country as a christening present, but his own nearby Chelsea home was an *hommage* to the East. Interestingly, the little girl in Constance's story shares the same name as Menpes' own child: Dorothy. If this was not enough inspiration, in August 1886 Otho had given Oscar a book on Japanese art, which Oscar described in his thank-you note as 'by far the best book on Japanese Art that I know', and one can imagine Constance studying this ardently before putting her own pen to paper.

Constance describes vistas of 'grey-tiled houses' that 'nestle in and out of the hill-side, each with its almond trees and its tiny rockery garden', a 'little stream with gold fish in it' and 'merry little girls clad in the richest rainbow hues, with eyes bright as stars, and smooth black hair dressed in butterfly fashion'.

The painted stork flies from one artefact into another. In the Japanese workshop in which he himself was painted he finds another

fan depicting 'a mother-stork and all her little ones', and this, he con-
cludes, is his wife and family. For 'many hours' the stork talks to his
family, and when the evening comes he realizes that he does not want
now to return back to the 'fog and the cold' of England. However, a
little Japanese girl who can conveniently see him and understands the
magic of the moment begs him to return to England to the children
there, and then bring them back to Japan with him so she might play
with them.

And so, because 'the child looked at him so piteously and her smile
was so winsome', the stork cannot 'bear to refuse her'. But when he
re-enters the nursery in London, the magic spell is broken. The
angel's feather becomes dislodged from the stork's head, his power to
weave between real and imagined worlds is suddenly gone and the
stork simply adopts his former place, back in the fan, finding himself
once more flying across 'the blue sky with pink almond blossoms
round him'.

Constance was delighted with the story and sent it to Otho.
Typically for a woman who had a tendency to clumsiness, she managed to send her own copy of the book by mistake, one in which she
had written an inscription, perhaps to Oscar or the boys. 'I found that
I've sent you my copy,' she wrote to Otho. 'Will you either send it
back when you have read it, and I will send you the other, or if
you like better, cut the inscription out and send it. Tell me what
you think of the story.'[12]

Constance's first foray into fiction proved successful. The publicity
her involvement in *The Bairn's Annual* solicited was quickly recognized. 'I have today got an offer for another story and if it appears I
shall send it to you,' she informed her brother. Quite what this subsequent tale was is unclear. If it was another single story, this author
has not tracked one published in 1887 or '88. But what is certain is
that within a year of 'Was It a Dream?' Constance wrote an entire
children's book, *There Was Once*.

This was for a different publisher, Ernest Nister. Nister came from
Nuremberg, at that time the centre of the toy and colour printing
industries, and he had built a considerable reputation as a publisher

and printer of highly coloured children's pop-up books. He ventured into the British market in 1888, with an approach to the children's publishing that was different from that of the more 'artistic' and refined Leadenhall Press. In contrast to the grey, understated jacket of *The Bairn's Annual*, books from the Nister stable had brightly coloured sentimental images of plump girls and boys holding fat little puppy dogs or playing together. It was an altogether more commercial and mass-market proposition.

Constance must have been one of the first authors Nister signed in the UK. She was in good company, alongside writers such as Edith Nesbit and the then very popular and prolific Mrs Molesworth.

There Was Once saw Constance re-tell a series of traditional nursery favourites that included the tales of Little Red Riding Hood, Puss in Boots, Cinderella, Jack the Giant Killer and The Three Bears – in which, incidentally, Constance wrote about 'Silver Locks' not the 'Goldilocks' we are more familiar with today.

'There was once, my children, a little girl who loved to coax her grandmother to tell her stories. She was not a fairy grandmother, but she could tell beautiful fairy stories,' Constance explained to her readers. 'The little girl is grown up now, and the dear grandmother is gone, but there are still children who love the old fairy stories, so the little girl has written them out for you just as they were told to her.'

Although the thrilling short stories that Oscar published in 1887, with their intrigues reflecting the fashion for spiritualism, could have offered little inspiration for the whimsical tales of magic and dreaming that his wife wrote for children, there is undoubtedly a sensibility in Constance's choice of imagery and poignant tone that resonates with a set of fairy stories that Oscar would publish the following May, *The Happy Prince and Other Tales*.

While he did not publish them until 1888, Oscar had been telling fairy stories for years. He had been rehearsing 'The Happy Prince' as far back as 1885, when he had related the tale to a group of Cambridge undergraduates when he and Constance went to visit Harry Marillier.[13] Apparently this was one of the first instances in which he tried out his tale of a statue of a Happy Prince standing high in an old town who sees nothing but unhappiness around him. Recruiting the services of a little swallow, the Prince asks the bird to pluck the jewels embedded in him and deliver them to the needy around him. The little swallow does so, but in carrying out this service to the Happy Prince he is delayed in his return to Egypt to such an extent that he misses his chance for migration. The swallow, now in love with the Prince, pays the ultimate price for his sacrifice. At the end of the story, when the statue is stripped of its former glory, the pair kiss each other once on the lips before the little bird falls down dead at the statue's feet.

Oscar's verbal storytelling could be almost mesmerizing. According to a friend of Harry Marillier, Mrs Claude Beddington, on the night Constance showed her moonstones to Harry and Douglas Ainslie, Oscar went on to invent a tale about the fairies and sprites that lived in the heart of the stones. Oscar 'wove fantastic legends of the mystical life within the cloudy shimmer', related Mrs Beddington, 'and when the youth went to bed that night he had a dream of the moonstone people which was all verse and which seemed to him the loveliest music he had ever heard'.[14] Instances such as this could not have failed both to inspire and to inform Constance's own endeavours.

Constance may well have been inspired by Oscar, but he was certainly reliant on her assistance when it came to his literary endeavours, at the very least at a practical level. At the outset of their marriage Speranza had suggested that Constance could be the sort of wife who might work alongside her husband, correcting his proofs. Certainly Constance did provide some assistance in Oscar's career. She often visited his publishers on his behalf when he was away, and would provide useful translation services for him. Oscar put into practice Constance's skills as a linguist a few years later, when he asked her to translate some Dutch reviews for him.[15] But there is compelling evidence that she also worked with him in an even closer capacity.

Only in 2008 did a manuscript come to light that suggests just how closely the Wildes may have worked on certain projects. In that year

Lucia Moreira Salles, a collector, gave the Morgan Library in New York a beautiful red leather-bound volume of letters and manuscripts. The whereabouts of this bound collection had been a mystery to Wilde experts for over half a century, and on examining it they realized that it contained a draft of Oscar's story 'The Selfish Giant', published as part of Oscar's *The Happy Prince and Other Tales*, which, although signed by Oscar, is written entirely in Constance's hand. The manuscript, written in ink, has some pencil corrections by Oscar that also differ from the final published version in certain details of grammar and expression.[16]

The question, of course, is whether Constance, at a time when she was writing children's stories herself, was in fact the author of the story and subsequently gave it to Oscar. Is the manuscript evidence of a genuine collaboration? Or is it simply an instance of Constance providing some secretarial support, writing up a fair copy from Oscar's initial draft for his publishers?

Tantalizingly, there are several aspects of the text that suggest that the manuscript may reflect collaboration. Even if the general plot of the story is not Constance's own, some of the telling of it may be. Oscar's storytelling in *The Happy Prince and Other Tales* is intricate and embellished. It incorporates images that feel surprising and unique, and are combined with brilliantly detailed observation. His characters, even with the minimal amount of dialogue, have crisp, characterful voices. He provides moments of vividly imaged back-story that give his fantasy realm terrific depth, but above all his narrative is woven with witticisms and comments intended to raise a smile with adult readers just as much as children. Oscar would later say that his stories were intended as 'studies in prose, put for Romance's sake into a fanciful form: meant partly for children, and partly for those who have kept the childlike faculties of wonder and joy'.[17] All in all, his narrative techniques add up to something very vivid, rich and sharp but also very witty.

This deftness and knowingness in the storytelling are missing in 'The Selfish Giant'. This story, by contrast, relies on a much more traditional narrative voice apparently directed more fully at children.

The imagery employed, although very similar to that in 'The Happy Prince', tends to be blunter and less embroidered. In fact, the narrative voice and broad-brush imagery in 'The Selfish Giant' are arguably closer to Constance's style in 'Was it a Dream?'

So could it be that Oscar told the story to Constance and that she then rewrote it from memory for him? The final, published version of the story shows amendments to this manuscript that Oscar must have made, some of them rather significant in the way they alter the story's meaning.

If this seems like a possible explanation for the Morgan Library manuscript, then one other conundrum remains. The story of 'The Selfish Giant' divides into two portions, the final section of the tale being overtly Christian and featuring a Christ-like child, bearing the stigmata, which revisits the giant at the moment of his death.

This Christianization is uncharacteristic of Oscar. It seems to contrast with the tale of self-sacrifice in 'The Happy Prince', which is more secular in tone, suggesting a personal, sensual love between the statue and the bird. And the clear Christian message seems at odds with a man who would go on to write that, far from being moral, art is 'useless because its aim is simply to create a mood. It is not meant to instruct, or to influence action in any way . . . A work of Art is useless as a flower is useless. A flower blossoms for its own joy. We gain a moment of joy by looking at it.'[18]

And so, one wonders, was this last portion of the story of 'The Selfish Giant' of Constance's invention? One of the more significant changes between the manuscript version of the story, in Constance's hand, and the final published version seems to be an attempt to tone down an overtly Christian message. In Constance's handwritten manuscript the child with the stigmata explains to the giant that his wounds were 'done many years ago that all men might be saved'. By the time this line was published it had been rewritten, as 'these are the wounds of love'.[19]

When Oscar's *The Happy Prince and Other Tales* and Constance's *There Was Once* were published in the same year, their reputation was cemented not only as a celebrated literary couple but as a uniquely suited one. Oscar and Constance had apparently successfully embraced the inclusion of children into the concept of artistic marriage.

'Novels are, comparatively speaking, easy work,' explained *The Weekly Irish Times*.

> But to be in sympathy with children, to know what will please them, and be capable of putting yourself sufficiently in their place ... demands students of juvenile nature for the work. Mr and Mrs Oscar Wilde possess charming children of their own, and they have utilised their acquaintance with the infant world in giving to it some delightful fairy tales, which even the elders must appreciate. *The Happy Prince and Other Tales* ... is one of the happiest works which Mr Oscar Wilde has ever produced; while Mrs Wilde's fairy tales, also published recently ... are a charming reproduction of the old stories, familiar to our childish days.[20]

Constance went on working with Nister until 1895. After *There Was Once* she contributed versions of Jack and the Beanstalk to *Favourite Nursery Stories*, and *A Long Time Ago*. In Nister's *A Dandy Chair* she wrote a story called 'The Little Swallow'. *Cosy Corner Stories* was a serial publication to which Constance contributed at least two stories across two different editions, one of which was called 'Far Japan'.

This last is heavily reminiscent of 'Was It a Dream?' and it is tempting to consider that it may well have been written at around the same time, even if it was published considerably later, in 1895. The story, beautifully illustrated, tells of a little girl called Isola, who on her birthday is given two gifts 'that have come all the way from that beautiful land of flowers, Japan'. One gift is a doll with 'almond-shaped eyes and straight black hair, dressed just like the real Japanese children in soft stuffs and gay colours. She has been told its name is Ai.' The other gift is 'a Japanese fan – with a garden painted on it – such quaint trees with a river running through them, and over the river an arched rustic bridge'. As Isola falls asleep, she thinks how delightful it would be 'to be a little Japanese girl and see Japan', and sure enough she dreams that she is dressed in a kimono like Ai and in a garden just like that painted on the fan.

Isola wants to see more of Japan than the garden surrounding her, and so she sets off and crosses one of the bridges leading out of the garden. But when Isola reaches the end of the bridge, 'there was nothing there, for she had got to the end of the fan! So down she fell with a bump, and woke to find herself safe in bed with Ai in her arms.'[21]

If Constance's and Oscar's careers were taking somewhat similar paths, with them both writing reviews and children's stories, the overlap in their professional activity would continue. It was not long before Constance would become a contributor to her husband's magazine.

In November 1887 Oscar launched *The Woman's World*. He had altered the proposed name of the publication from 'The Lady's World', a title both he and his feminist contributors considered far too vulgar for a magazine that 'aims at being the organ of women of intellect, culture and position'.[22]

The magazine was a careful mixture of conventional and adventurous elements. Like other magazines, it offered its readers a mix of features, a serial story and travel articles. The inaugural issue opened with a piece about pastoral theatre from a theatre producer and friend of Whistler, Janey Sevilla Campbell. Annie Thackeray, daughter of William Makepeace, wrote a historical item about an influential lady of the past, 'Madame de Sévigné's Grandmother'. The serial, 'The Truth about Clement Ker', is a mirage of assumed identities, purported to be written by one Geoffrey Ker. When this was bound and sold as a novel a year later Ker was revealed to be none other than the popular author George Fleming (the pen name of Julia Constance Fletcher). An anonymous piece on 'The Oxford Ladies' Colleges' was offered by 'a member of one of them'. And Oscar himself offered 'Literary and Other Notes', in which he reviewed the month's notable publications by women.

But filleted in between these perhaps more traditional items there were indeed more pioneering pieces that positioned the magazine as liberal, if not mildly campaigning. Eveline Portsmouth offered a piece on 'The Position of Women'. In an article that carefully navigated a path between the most advanced feminist thinking and more conventional beliefs on the role of the sexes, Countess Portsmouth noted

> Marriage ... is ceasing to be the only goal for girlhood. New resources are at hand and eagerly sought. Fresh possibilities are born, and in a widening horizon a wholesome and hopeful spirit is awakened. The workwomen of our large towns are those on whom all burdens fall most heavily ... but they are also stirred by the movement that is passing over other women, and may soon give it great impetus. The higher class of women ... are eager to use their faculties. With an increasing number a life of pleasure is losing is importance ... but it is in the middle class that the greatest change has taken place: there, not only the excellent education attainable by them, but the consideration of health and enjoyment put into the scale weighs heavily ... the present type of girl [is described] as altogether different to that [of] ... forty years ago, owing to her finer physical and mental qualities.[23]

Constance's first article for the magazine appeared in the July issue. Here she did her bit for rational dress by looking at 'Children's Dress in this Century'. Condemning the over-fussy, cumbersome and uncomfortable outfits that she saw children being squeezed into in the 1880s, she pointed out that the simple, loose clothes worn at the beginning of the nineteenth century had been far more 'rational' in terms of comfort.

Compared with the ornate and convoluted writing styles of many of the other contributors, by July 1888 Constance's journalism had attained a clear, succinct and personal aspect. Her scholarly inclination is also evident in an article that she has clearly thoroughly researched.

'At the beginning of this century the dress of English women possessed at least one merit, that of simplicity – simplicity of material, simplicity of form, simplicity of colouring,' she wrote. 'All these three things combined to render it a most charming costume

... and the children's dress was equally simple, giving us the pretty costumes of which Kate Greenaway has made such a charming study ... There is no doubt that the costume is at once light and graceful, the only drawback being that it is quite unsuited for our winter.'

Constance went on to remind her readers of the dangers of 'our rains, our fogs, and our treacherous winds' to children, and to promote the benefits of wool as a material that should be used more in clothing in British climes.

Constance's focus on wool chimed in with the latest thinking in the health movement. At around the same time as the 'Healtheries' was promoting healthy living and dress in London, in Stuttgart the zoologist and physiologist Dr Gustav Jaeger was developing his Sanitary Woollen System, which sought to encourage people to use wool in all domestic textiles, from their clothing to bedding. In a series of lectures in which he expounded purportedly scientific theories that wool allowed the skin to breathe properly, he encouraged people to wear wool next to their skin as a healthier alternative to vegetable-based fabrics.

Jaeger's theories, much discussed by a nation in the midst of a health debate, held sufficient appeal to encourage one entrepreneur, a grocer called Lewis Tomalin, to acquire a licence to open a clothing store in London under Jaeger's name in 1884. Within year the company had a West End branch at Oxford Circus.

Oscar is noted as having shopped at Jaeger, and it follows that Constance was a customer too. Her sons were also undoubtedly subject to the craze for wool, as per her advice to her readers: in terms of styles of uniform for little boys, she points out that 'At present it is the Navy that is predominant, and it is a very sensible dress. The woollen under vest, the blue blouse for winter, the white one for summer, and the blue serge trousers are very good dress for a boy. He is warmly clad and his limbs are free for movement.'

Constance continues: 'Nothing can be more charming than the rough, thick, Irish claddagh cloths and coarse flannels, with their beautiful vegetable dyes, for outdoor garments, while for indoor wear we have the most lovely woollen materials in every range of exquisite colour.'

For girls Constance recommended 'The Kindergarten costume introduced by the Rational Dress Society', which 'consists of woollen combinations; woollen stays – to button, not to lace – woollen stockings kept up by suspenders fastened onto the stays; a divided skirt either buttoned on to the stays or made with a Princess bodice; and a smock-frock overall'.

Despite the appeal of Constance's journalism (her contributions were well publicized in the classified ads for *The Woman's World*), she wrote only two pieces for Oscar, both on dress.[24] This is almost certainly because, just months after Oscar took up his position as an editor, Constance also found herself at the helm of a publication.

Throughout 1887 Constance's involvement in the Rational Dress movement had deepened, and her confidence in public was mounting. In February 1887 she presided over a meeting of the Rational Dress Society in Westminster Town Hall. It was an event to which, the press noted, only women were admitted, and at which Constance gave an introductory speech. After Viscountess Harberton had spoken, a number of women who were sitting on the platform, including Constance, modelled the divided skirt for interested onlookers. Showing how the item could be combined with elegance, Constance wore her divided skirt as part of a costume of striped cheviot wool, trimmed with blue fox and ornamented with birds' wings.

In the month that Oscar launched *The Woman's World* Constance once again caught the attention of the press as she attended the annual meeting of the RDS at the Westminster Palace Hotel. Now one of the most prominent leaders of the movement and noted as such, her literary successes and associations suggested Constance as the natural editor for the society's gazette. At first Constance declined to be called the publication's editor *per se*, and promised only to see the publication launch. The gazette duly went on sale in April 1888, at a cost of 3d per issue. It was published by Hatchard's in Piccadilly, and thus began Constance's relationship with a publishing house that in the fullness of time would have more significant personal ramifications for her. Despite her agreement to be a launch editor only, she ended up running the publication for all of its relatively short, two-year life.

The gazette could not have been more different from *The Woman's World*. A fraction of the size, more like a pamphlet in its dimensions, nevertheless its voice was loud, clear and unrelentingly campaigning. It was a political instrument for change and it set out its stall, in every issue, in no uncertain terms.

'The Rational Dress Society protests against the introduction of any fashion in dress that either deforms the figure, impedes the movement of the body, or in any way tends to injure health,' the pamphlet declares. 'It protests against the wearing of tightly fitting corsets, of high-heeled or narrow toed boots . . . It protests against crinolines or crinolettes . . . The maximum weight of underclothing (without shoes) approved of by the Rational Dress Society, does not exceed seven pounds.'[25]

The Rational Dress Society was attempting many things. Not just a campaigning body, it sold rational outfits and produced paper patterns. All these were available from the society's depot at 23 Mortimer Street. The need for money to support such initiatives put added pressure on Constance, who was tasked with turning the gazette into a commercial proposition and securing a solid base of subscribers.

It was a tall order. Hatchard's only managed to raise sufficient advertising revenue in the first issue to support a print run of 500. Constance quickly found herself in a Catch-22 situation, with too low a circulation to attract more advertisers and not enough advertisers to support an increased print run. Her letters indicate her unrelenting and thankless schedule of letter-writing to prospective subscribers in addition to her editorial duties. There was also an endless to-ing and fro-ing to Hatchard's, passing on the suggestions from RDS members of enterprises that might be prepared to buy space. Her work was complicated by the necessity of running editorial issues past the RDS committee. The committee's initial decision to deny prospective contributors by-lines was a constant thorn in the side of someone attempting to attract high-profile contributors.

During her editorship of the RDS gazette Constance tackled many issues. She oversaw articles on the 'Dangers of Women's Dress', she debated the term 'Dress', she commissioned a piece on 'Why Women Age Rapidly', which suggested that the inhibition of the lungs by tight lacing had much to answer for, and was constantly reminding her readers of the various forms of rational dress available, including the two most popular types of divided skirt, the Harberton 'which is narrow . . . and has a narrow box pleat round it', and the Wilson, 'which is about a yard and a half wide round each leg'.[26] She also related news of pioneering women who chose to wear men's clothing 'in the exercise of their profession', and published reviews on the more feminine 'trouser dresses'. 'Those who have worn these dresses have testified . . . to the delightful sense of freedom that results from the removal of petticoats.'[27] She was also careful to remind her readers of the genuine tragedies that still occurred to women wearing what Constance termed 'portable firetraps'. She recounted the story of Rosina Williams, aged thirty-six, from Camberwell, who 'was in the front room in a basement when a spark set her clothing alight', and of Eliza Dixon, aged fifty-five, who, when linen on a clothes horse began to burn, attempted to extinguish the blaze but herself caught fire.[28]

Interestingly, the fascination that Japan held for Constance and many of her Aesthetic contemporaries was also reflected in the magazine. Members of the RDS were concerned to learn that many Japanese women were adopting Western dress, and 'were anxious that they should first know that those who have studied the subject hold that there is great need of improvement in certain particulars'. The Japanese question was one that the RDS actively pursued. By the April 1889 edition of the magazine Constance was able to inform her readers that the RDS committee had met Mr Shimada, the Japanese editor of the *Daily News*, 'who had undertaken to ventilate the questions raised by the Rational Dress Society in the columns of the Japanese paper'. Constance adds that 'Letters have also been received from a lady doctor in Russia, requesting admission to the Society . . . This Lady states that the subject of Rational Dress is exciting much interest in her country.'

By mid-1888 the appetite for politics that her involvement with the RDS had sparked in Constance was fully ignited. If the first four years of her marriage had been essentially 'artistic', the years to come would be 'campaigning'. What, alas, she could not have foreseen was that as she pursued further rights and a higher profile for her own sex, her and Oscar's paths would begin substantially to diverge. The interests of *The Woman's World* had aligned Constance and Oscar both socially and professionally. But this alignment would prove brief. Oscar would soon succumb to different temptations and ambitions, ones that would quickly alienate him from the world in which his wife would continue to invest.

8

'Not to kiss females'

'**M**Y CHILDREN ARE growing and thriving splendidly, though unfortunately my nurse has taken it into her head to be married this July which is to say the least of it, annoying,' Constance informed Otho in March 1888.[1] Her brother, having left Nellie, was still in Switzerland with Mary. Brother and sister found themselves further apart from one another than ever before.

> Baby is quite strong and fat and long, and he can walk and is beginning to talk. Cyril adores me and Vyvyan more or less dislikes me and adores his father but I suppose this will come right in the end. People say he is pretty, but he was prettier when he was waxy and white and delicate. He is not as tall as Cyril was but is very much fatter. What you have lost by parting from your dear two boys, it's only the babes that keep one young and fresh and happy.[2]

Oscar and Constance were in some respects forward-thinking parents. Unlike many of their class and generation, they spent time playing with their children, and Constance certainly would do many of the domestic chores that others left to a nanny. Her letters are full of accounts of her taking her children to doctors, to tea parties and shopping for toys and clothes. Even when they were babes in arms, Oscar found his sons compelling,[3] and as they grew older, he indulged his own sense of fun in the games he enjoyed with them.

Vyvyan remembered his father playing with his sons with child-like delight, down on his knees pretending to be a lion or wolf. 'And there was nothing half hearted in his methods of play,' Vyvyan admitted:

One day he arrived with a toy milk cart drawn by a horse with real hair on it. All the harness undid and took off, and the churns with which the cart was filled could be removed and opened. When my father discovered this he immediately went downstairs and came back with a jug of milk with which he proceeded to fill the churns. We then all tore round the nursery table, slopping milk all over the place, until the arrival of our nurse put an end to that game.[4]

But alongside what seems like their modern approach to parenting, the Wildes could also be very Victorian. In addition to their parents' attentions, the children were attended to by nurses and governesses. And they were often dispatched to stay with friends and relatives, normally on the basis of some need, be it to do with a particular ailment that would benefit from better air or in connection with some character-forming exercise.

Constance took to heart the public debate on health. She was obsessed with the health of her children, and the effect of London fog on them was of particular concern to her. Constance worried particularly over Vyvyan, who she was convinced was sickly. He was often sent to Reading to stay with Constance's friend Jean Palmer, the wife of Walter Palmer, of Huntley & Palmer biscuits. Despite his tender age, these rest cures could mean weeks away from home on a regular basis, a routine that Constance described to Georgina Mount-Temple in her letters:

I am sending Vyvyan to stay by himself with Mrs Palmer for a month in hopes that complete change of surroundings may do him good. His nurse thinks he is going to have a 'St Vitus's Dance' as she calls it, but I don't think he is really so bad as that. Nurse will take him tomorrow, and stay with him till Monday and then come back to Cyril.[5]

Constance notes how furious Cyril would be with her 'for taking his little play-fellow from him'. Despite such rebellions, Constance was in the habit of separating the boys. They would often holiday in different locations, and when it came to their education later on, different schools were chosen for them.

With her nursery staff engaged, Constance had sufficient time to continue to pursue her interests. In addition to her writing for children, and her commitment to the cause of Rational Dress, as the 1880s drew to a close she began to focus on new projects. Constance's strident views about dress reform had revealed her as a truly political animal. The genes of one-time MP John Horatio Lloyd were surfacing not in Otho but in his sister, and now, along with a group of other pioneering women, she began to take on other high-profile political causes.[6]

'I have been political lately,' she informed her brother in March 1888. 'It has become the fashion to have political parties in London and some of the swells manage to get Gladstone, so I have seen a good deal of him lately and have heard him speak too, which was a real treat.'[7]

Just a month after this boast Constance found herself with Gladstone yet again. On the evening of 16 April 1888 the Marylebone branch of the Women's Liberal Association held a political party at the home of a Mr and Mrs Blyth in Portland Place, which enjoyed the attendance of 'the best known liberals in the Borough'.[8] Oscar and Constance were there, and one imagines that on this occasion Mr Wilde, finding himself on his wife's home ground, was there very much at her bidding.

The Liberal Gladstone held tremendous appeal for Constance. Not only was he a supporter of women's rights, but his wife Catherine was in the process of organizing the regional Women's Liberal Associations, of which Constance was a member of the Chelsea branch, under a national banner: The Women's Liberal Federation.

In addition to his sympathy for female equality, Gladstone was an ardent supporter of Home Rule for Ireland. And this was also a cause to which Constance subscribed. But Constance's version of Liberalism was far more radical than that of her hero Gladstone. A few months before this particular date with the great man, Constance had signalled just how extreme her liberal leanings might be when she attended the trial of Robert Cunninghame Graham.

Cunninghame Graham was a Scot who had been brought up largely overseas. But in the early 1880s he returned to the UK to pursue a political career. A regular attendee at William Morris's socialist gatherings, he quickly developed radical socialist ideals that placed him at the most controversial limits of the politics of his day. In the 1886 general election he became a Liberal MP on a ticket that called for the abolition of the House of Lords, universal suffrage, widespread nationalization of mining and industry, the disestablishment of the Church of England and Home Rule for Scotland. Within a year of his election he had gained considerable notoriety as the first MP to swear in the Commons, uttering the word 'damn', and subsequently found himself suspended.

But it was Cunninghame Graham's ardent belief in the right to free speech that put him in the dock in December 1887 and increased his notoriety further. On 13 November 1887 protesters in favour of Irish Home Rule had marched on Trafalgar Square. The protest had been prompted by the recent imprisonment of the editor of the Irish nationalist newspaper *United Ireland*, William O'Brien, who had been campaigning on behalf of Irish tenants against their forced eviction by landowners. Several British radicals, including Cunninghame Graham, joined the protest, only to find themselves at the heart of what would become known as 'Bloody Sunday'. As the protest apparently began to turn into a riot, the British police and military in attendance applied such force that there were over a hundred casualties. Cunninghame Graham himself was badly beaten, arrested and taken to Bow Street.

On 30 November 1887 Cunninghame Graham was tried alongside a Mr John Burns for their involvement in the riot. Constance was one of three women supporters that the national press noted as attending the trial in a show of support. The other women were Mrs Graham and Mrs Ashton Dilke, a notable campaigner for women's suffrage. Oscar, busy in Tite Street making plans for *The Woman's World*, did not attend. His own date with the Bow Street dock was yet to come.

Cunninghame Graham was eventually sentenced to six weeks'

imprisonment in Pentonville for his part in the Bloody Sunday riots. The friendship between Constance and his family never weakened. Cunninghame Graham would go on to live with Constance's great friend Walter Harris in Morocco, and Constance continued to mention members of the Graham family in her letters well after the event.[9]

These radical tendencies of Mrs Oscar Wilde soon found wider expression. Indeed on the very day that Constance had taken Oscar to meet Gladstone in Portland Place she had also attended a 'conference of ladies' in Victoria. This time it was the Women's Committee of the International Arbitration and Peace Association. And Constance was giving a paper 'in which she offered a number of practical suggestions to wives, mothers and school mistresses'.[10]

Like her journalism, Constance's public speaking was common-sensical and no-nonsense. She was an inherently practical person, who considered how political belief might be translated into practical action. Her thesis was that war might be avoided and peace promoted if instilled at the earliest possible opportunity, as children were educated.

The *Pall Mall Gazette* reported her suggestion that 'children should be taught in the nursery to be against war'. Constance did not want nurses and mothers to ban toy soldiers and guns, as some of her peers were apparently advocating, but she did believe that mothers could instil a dislike of war in their offspring. More importantly, she felt that as part of their schooling children should be exposed more 'to great international questions of the day'.

The Women's Liberal Federation quickly provided Constance with a regular public platform on which to express her liberal political views. It was not merely international peace that Constance dared to take on, but also the question of Irish Home Rule. At the 1889 annual conference of the WLF Constance gave a paper on this subject in which she pointed out 'that self-governing nations were not in the habit of tolerating outrages in their midst, and she was convinced that, given Home Rule, so far from the sister country aiding or abetting any foreign conspiracy against us, she would prove our best friend and virtual sea wall against invasion from the West'.[11]

In some ways, her appearance on political platforms had become Constance's response to her early desire to go on the stage. Serious and studious by nature, she must have worked hard to improve her stage presence and public speaking, efforts that some critics made note of. 'I was astonished and delighted to notice yesterday . . . how very much Mrs Oscar Wilde has improved in public speaking,' one critic noted after a WLF event. 'She was always graceful and always charming, but now there is an earnestness and an ease about her which is the result of practice in platform speaking, and I shall not be surprised if in a few years Mrs Wilde has become one of the most popular among "platform ladies".'[12]

But Constance the public speaker, whose activities were often reported nationwide, did not attract unanimous praise. One correspondent for the *Birmingham Daily Post* found himself horrified by Constance and her WLF associates, who took 'subjects most vital to the existence of the Government' and 'discussed and dismissed them' in what the ladies' maids denominate 'the twinkling of a stay-lace'. Mrs Wilde was accused of 'solemn trilling' upon subjects with which she had 'no concern'.[13]

The writer Marie Corelli first encountered Constance at around this time, and she too found the combination of high fashionable society and radical politics somewhat hard to reconcile. But Corelli, who met Constance at a lunch party held by the socialite Mrs Skirrow, could not deny, in spite of her scepticism about Constance's political efficacy, that Constance was strangely compelling. Just like Henry Fedden, Douglas Ainslie and many other admirers before her, Corelli, a lesbian, found herself falling under the spell of Oscar's 'pretty wife'.

On one occasion Constance and Marie found themselves at a 'grand crush at Upper Phillimore Place', and afterwards Corelli recorded Constance's extraordinary outfit in her diary. Interestingly, Constance was using a stick at the time, which suggests that she was already being troubled with her back and legs.

Oscar Wilde was present and kept me no end of time talking on the stairs. Lady Wilde, his mother, was there in a train-dress of silver grey satin, with a hat as large as a small parasol and long streamers of silver grey tulle all floating about her! She did look eccentric. Mrs Oscar Wilde, a very pretty woman, interested me, in a Directoire costume with tall cavalier hat and plume, and a great crutch stick.[14]

In the course of the late 1880s the two women were seeing quite a lot of one another, not least because they shared a passion for the popular Spanish virtuoso violinist Pablo de Sarasate.[15] Both made a point of attending soirées and parties where he was likely to be playing, and Constance certainly went to Corelli's home to meet him in person.[16]

Corelli's fascination with Constance comes across in one of her literary ventures. In 1892 she published *The Silver Domino, or Side Whispers, Social and Literary*, a series of satirical portraits of her famous contemporaries. Chapter 10, entitled 'The Social Elephant', presents a caricature of Oscar as a huge elephant and Constance as his dainty foil. Her account of Constance, portrayed as a fairy who sits on the elephant's back and is responsible for managing this cumbersome responsibility, not only restores a sense of the public profile that Mrs Oscar held before her husband's downfall but also gives an indication of the relationship that contemporaries observed between Oscar and his wife. Despite the condescending satire, it remains a vivid portrayal of a woman who was clearly captivating, not least to the author of the piece.

'As for the Fairy, it is not too much to say that she is one of the prettiest things alive,' Corelli notes.

> She does not seem to stand at all in awe of her Elephant lord. She has her own little webs to weave – silvery webs of gossamer-discussion on politics, in which, bless her heart for a charming little Radical, she works neither good nor harm. Her eyes would burn a hole through many a stern old Tory's waistcoat and make him dizzily doubtful as to what party he really belonged to for the moment. She has the prettiest hair, all loosely curling about her face, and she has a low voice so modulated as to seem to some folks affected; it is a natural music . . .

she dresses 'aesthetically' – in all sorts of strange tints, and rich stuffs, made in a fashion which the masculine mind must describe as 'gathered up anyhow' – with large and wondrous sleeves and queer medieval adornments – it pleases her whim so to do, and it also pleases the Elephant, who is apt to get excited on the subject of Colour . . . she does not talk much, this quaint Fairy, but she looks whole histories. Her gaze is softly wistful, and often abstracted; at certain moments her spirit seems to have gone out of her on invisible wings, miles away from the Elephant and literary Castle, and it is in such moments that she looks her very prettiest. To me she is infinitely more interesting than the Elephant himself . . . one never gets tired of looking at the lovely Fairy who guards and guides him. We could not spare either of the twain from our midst – they form a picture 'full of Colour'.[17]

On 28 April 1888 the colourful duo Constance and Oscar found themselves at a 'political conversazione' at 125 Queen's Gate, South Kensington, the home of Mr and Mrs Charles Hancock. This time it was Mrs Gladstone who had been invited to meet 'enthusiastic workers and friends in the Liberal cause', and the evening was under the auspices of the South Kensington Women's Liberal Association. One such enthusiastic Liberal attending the event was Margaret, Dowager Lady Sandhurst, an active member of the Women's Liberal Associations and subsequently the Women's Liberal Federation, and head of the Marylebone branch of the WLA.

Constance was susceptible to the influence of older women. She was already playing the devoted daughter–in–law to Speranza, whose company she clearly enjoyed. Constance visited Oscar's mother regularly. The two would go on drives together, and Constance would assist Speranza in domestic matters. Their shared interest in literature and liberal politics did nothing but make their friendship stronger.

Perhaps her disappointment in her own mother had encouraged her search for alternative maternal figures and role models. In addition to Speranza, Viscountess Harberton had also played her part. But around this time, and almost certainly thanks to the WLF, with which they were both involved, it was to Lady Sandhurst, thirty years her senior, that Constance now became particularly attached.

Margaret Sandhurst was an active philanthropist. She had her own home for sick children in the Marylebone Road, and under her influence Constance was quickly recruited to various fundraising activities to support this and other causes. But more than anything, her friendship with Margaret Sandhurst led to Constance's involvement in a landmark moment in the history of British politics, when she became instrumental in getting the first woman elected to the London County Council.

Since 1870 women had been able to sit on the School Board for London,[18] but without a vote the idea of women in Parliament was almost inconceivable. In 1888, however, a new Local Government Act offered the opportunity for female representation at local government level at least. With this Act, the electoral body was established as all occupiers and freeholders in the relevant borough on the parliamentary list, with the crucial addition of peers, women 'and a few others who are occupiers and ratepayers but who are not entitled to vote for members of Parliament'. With certain women able to vote, the press quickly raised the point that this 'seems likely to raise the question as to whether women are not qualified to become a candidate'.[19] This, in addition to the fact that the Act nowhere expressly said a candidate needed to be a 'man' – merely a 'fit person' – was the call to arms for which feminists such as Constance had been waiting.

Countess Aberdeen established a Society for Promoting the Return of Women as County Councillors and began seeking potential candidates. London became the battlefield. Jane Cobden, the daughter of politician and businessman Richard Cobden, put herself forward, as did the proprietor of the Old Vic Theatre, Emma Cons. And Lady Sandhurst determined to stand in Brixton.

Constance threw herself into Lady Sandhurst's campaign. Her network of political connections was quickly buzzing with excitement at the forthcoming challenge. Constance was confident that they were on the point of making political history: 'Lady Sandhurst was told that if her nomination was accepted . . . she would be returned by a large majority,' Constance informed her colleague Mrs Stopes.[20] Charlotte Stopes, a writer much interested in the issue of female suffrage and the mother of the birth control pioneer Marie Stopes, was a fellow member of the RDS and, like Constance, an active Liberal whose husband was standing for Norwood in the same election.

Oscar supported his wife's political activities in his own way. *The Woman's World* began to take on a more radical aspect in line with Constance's political activities, and Oscar began commissioning articles from his wife's political friends. Mrs Ormiston Chant – who shared the platform with Constance at WLF events – contributed an article on 'The Gymnasium for Girls', while Viscountess Harberton wrote an article on 'Mourning Clothes and Customs'.

The influence Constance could apply to her husband had its limits, though. Mrs Stopes found her manuscript returned by *The Woman's World*, forcing Constance to explain rather defensively, 'I have nothing to do with the editing of the *Woman's World* and did not know that my husband had returned mss of yours. I know however that he has enough for about 2 years hence, and his magazine, being an illustrated magazine he [sic] requires illustrated articles . . . I am sorry you should have been disappointed.'[21]

In the case of Lady Sandhurst, Constance was more efficacious. By far the most obvious concession to his wife's agenda was Oscar's inclusion of a speech delivered by Lady Sandhurst to a political society in Cambridge in the January 1889 issue of his magazine. With the council elections due in the middle of this month, Oscar's decision to print Lady Sandhurst's thoughts on 'A Woman's Work in Politics' was little short of propaganda for this prospective candidate.

Sandhurst's address encouraged women to become involved in politics. It encouraged them to read about politics, argue about politics and, when in the solitude of their own homes, at their needlework, to think about political issues. It suggested that, if they did not want to step into the front line of politics, women at least could make sure that they were guiding their husbands along the right political path.

Like Constance, Lady Sandhurst's politics were inherently bound up with her own sense of Christian, moral duty. 'Probably all will acknowledge that it is as much the duty of every woman as of every man to make the best use of every gift she may possess,' she argued, adding that 'the best use we can make of any gift is to devote it to the elevation of the human race . . . we must keep our minds fixed on the single object of good we can do, no matter the consequences to ourselves'.

Having urged women to engage in politics, having encouraged them to take 'any topic of the day and show the righteous side of it', Lady Sandhurst went on to practise what she preached, offering what she considered the right perspective on the Irish question. 'For this kind of effort there can be no theme more valuable than the great question which hinders at the present moment all true progress – the Irish difficulty, how to give peace, prosperity, and happiness to Ireland, and true Unity to our Empire.' Needless to say, the Sandhurst solution to this, much like Constance's own, lay in Home Rule, a point of view shared by Constance. Margaret Sandhurst's views in general, as they emerge in this speech, almost certainly offer arguments that Constance herself must have regularly presented.

To get a sense of some of the tactics Constance may well have employed when canvassing for her friend in the forthcoming election, the same issue of *The Woman's World* conveniently provides a portrait of 'Lady Canvassers at a Modern Election'. This article observed that 'While men merely form small local committees and often flounder about in the utmost difficulty to find suitable helpers, the women are members of great national organizations, working upon almost Masonic lines, and ready to send down talented and efficient aid for reproof, for correction and for sound doctrine politically.' The author recognized the value of organizations such as the WLF, far-reaching 'political nerve systems that vitalise and direct feminine movements in the great active life of the state'. All this, the author conceded, 'is rather humiliating to men'.

Certainly Constance's letters to Mrs Stopes confirm this sense of network. Mrs Stopes proposed to Constance that members of her Chelsea branch of the WLA could be harnessed to campaign for her husband, a request that was denied because these women were already engaged in the support of their local Liberal candidate. Mrs

Stopes then wondered if members of the New Somerville Club – exclusively for women – might serve a similar purpose on her husband's behalf. Constance apologised that she was not a memeber of that club.

Despite his support for her work, the time Oscar could devote to his wife's causes was limited. He was generally tired and over-committed, the pressures of editorship taking their toll. 'Oscar is overworked and is very miserable at times,' Constance confided to Otho. He needed 'a change of air very badly. I wish I could get him away.'[22]

Editorial responsibilities and the usual round of theatre trips and social engagements aside, Oscar was also fighting his own personal campaign to do with the continuing demise of his mother's finances. Income Speranza had realized in the past from her remaining prop-erty in Ireland had, according to Oscar, failed to be paid for some time, thanks to 'the unhappy state of things' in his homeland.[23] Consequently he had begun a series of petitions in support of his mother. One was to secure a pension from the Civil List; another was for a one-off payment from the Royal Literary Fund. He wrote to Gladstone, appealing to his pro-Home-Rule sympathies, and asked for his support and signature. If Oscar had hoped that his recent meetings with the politician at Constance's various WLF soirées might bear fruit, though, he was disappointed. Gladstone declined to play ball. Nevertheless, Oscar managed £100 from the RLF and eventually an annual pension of £70 from the Civil List.

Constance's campaigning proved successful too. In January 1889 Lady Sandhurst was returned in Brixton with some 1,900 votes. The other female candidates also won their seats. The jubilation in Tite Street and other drawing rooms around town was considerable. This was a huge milestone in the women's movement.

Their joy was, however, short-lived. One of the candidates who had stood unsuccessfully against Lady Sandhurst challenged her elec-tion. Mr Charles Beresford Hope, a Moderate candidate, took the case to the high court. By March 1889 there was a ruling that Lady Sandhurst's election had been illegal. Extremely complex, the essence of the ruling was that, despite the ambiguous wording of the Local Government Act, if Parliament had intended that women could be elected, it would have made this intention clear. No such intention was clearly spelt out, and therefore no such right endowed. In June, after an unsuccessful appeal, Lady Sandhurst's fate was sealed and her seat lost. Mr Beresford Hope took it over. To make matters worse, the Misses Cobden and Cons found themselves now caught in a political loophole. Technically also elected illegally, under the legislation of the time they faced a £50 fine each time they acted in their role as county councillor. They were therefore advised to attend meetings but refrain from voting. By the time the next county council elections came around in 1892, not a single woman bothered to stand. For the moment the cause was lost.

There were those who revelled in the failure of Constance and her associates. *Punch,* the magazine that had always been unkind to Oscar, offered his wife no sympathy whatsoever. In June, as soon as Lady Sandhurst's appeal was lost, the magazine published a satirical poem at Constance's and her fellow feminists' expense:

The (County Council) Paradise and the (Liberal) Peri teased:

At three a Peri at the gate
Of Eden stood disconsolate;
And as she listened to the Springs
Of talk within in torrents flowing,
And caught the light upon her wings
Through the half-opened portal glowing,
She sighed to think her subject race
Should e'er have lost that glorious place.
'How Happy' exclaimed this outcast fair,
'Are the many male members who wrangle there,
'Midst flowers (of speech) that freely fall;
Though I of the School Board now am free,
And parochial portals open for me,
The County Council were worth them all!
Though sweet an "At Home" graced by
Gladstone oration,

Of the Women's Liberal Federation,
In the Grosvenor or the Memorial Hall;
Though dear are the platforms your sweet tones haunt,
Mrs Oscar Wilde, Mrs Ormiston Chant,
Let the Earl of Meath make it clear – I can't –
How the County Council outshines them all!'

The Sandhurst affair proved a huge drain on Constance. The bouts of ill health and sleepless nights that had plagued her as a young woman had never properly left her. Now they were worse. There is also some suggestion that the mobility issues she suffered in the 1890s were already presenting. By March 1889, Constance found herself in the grips of an illness.[24] Exhausted, she dispatched herself to Brighton for ten days' rest, probably into the care of her mother, who lived there. But the poor relationship Constance had with Ada Swinburne-King could scarcely have been improved by the fact that Mr Swinburne-King had recently left his wife of ten years in favour of a solitary life in Hastings. Hardly surprising, then, that the sojourn did not provide the intended rest cure. Weeks later Constance was ill again.

'I am going to write a few lines,' she explained to her friend Juliet Latour Temple in June 1889, adding: 'if they are very stupid you must put it down to my having had 30 people here to talk to this afternoon. I have been very ill again, but I am going to try and mind-cure myself well this time.'[25]

As part of a programme of self-help Constance decided to read J. H. Shorthouse's *Golden Thoughts*, she explained to her friend. Based on the writings of the seventeenth-century 'spiritual guide' and 'Quietist' Miguel Molinos, this was a book that invited inward contemplation, meditation and reflection as a means to achieving a higher understanding. All one had to do was find a place that would enable quiet meditation.

Constance, earnest as ever, chose to try out some 'golden thoughts' in a church she increasingly frequented, St Barnabas, Pimlico, just a few minutes from her own home. But as so often seemed to happen to Constance, her best-laid plans were confounded. 'How can one be a Quietist in London? I never get a moment's real quiet,' she complained to Juliet. 'This morning I went to St Barnabas and thought I should be quiet there but carpenters came in and sawed wood till I went away!'[26]

What did seem to relieve her sleeplessness and anxiety were trips to the theatre with Oscar and his friends. Fortunately these were still frequent and a source of great joy for her. She was a regular at the Lyceum to see Irving and Ellen Terry, often dining with them after shows, and always enchanted by Terry, who was becoming a good friend. And humour helped Constance relax. She admitted that she laughed so much at one production of *Nerves*, an adaptation of *Les Femmes nerveuses*, 'that I had a good night's sleep which I seldom get, so I think I shall try this medicine again'.[27]

Finally an August holiday in Yorkshire with the journalists Emily and James Thursfield pulled Constance through this period of ill health. Constance got home on 31 August. Oscar was at King's Cross to meet her. He had had to wait since her train was an hour late. He discovered his wife 'looking extremely well – much better than when she went away'.[28] Constance was delighted to be home and full of fun. On seeing the boys she told a silly story that the voracious Oscar had eaten her bread and butter – which made the extremely sensitive Cyril burst into tears.[29] 'However he was consoled and sent to fetch some more.'[30]

Constance did not wait to throw herself into events once again, keen to show her socialist sympathies for any who cared to see. While Constance had been enjoying the Yorkshire moors with the Thursfields, London had become the battleground for a group of dockers, who, organized for the first time, were marching and striking for reform. A staggering ten thousand men downed tools. On 1 September the strikers, who had already been out for a fortnight, demonstrated in Hyde Park.

'This afternoon I dragged Oscar to the Park to see the great meeting,' Constance told Emily Thursfield. 'We saw a great part of the procession . . . with innumerable banners flying, all the people perfectly orderly with police marching by their sides. There were

representatives of all kinds of curious societies; one cart contained a
Neptune with a long beard and a trident.' Constance spotted Robert
Cunninghame Graham among the crowd of workers. Her political
friend apart, the crowd comprised strata of society Constance rarely
experienced, and never in this quantity. They 'were very much
in earnest', she noted, but also 'very <u>unsavoury</u>'. In the midst of the
rough workers she found herself almost overcome by the smell of the
great unwashed and their 'vile tobacco'. Nevertheless she was
impressed by them. 'One was in the presence of an immense power,'
she said.[31]

In the end the dockers had their day. Two weeks later, after striking for a month, their employers caved in to their demands and they
returned to work. They had secured a new pay rate of 6d an hour and
a hiring period of not less than four hours at a time.

More and more Constance saw political action in terms of her
own personal quest to find meaning and purpose in life. And more
and more she began to see parallels between Christian morality and
socialism. 'I have just been reading Tolstoy's *Work While We Have
the Light* and feel more depressed than ever,' she would write to Lady
Mount-Temple a little later; 'I am more certain than ever that I am
leading an absolutely useless life, and yet I don't see how to alter it.'
Constance went on: 'Mr Gurney says that the early Christians did
not all have their goods in common and that the scheme of Socialism
is a wrong one, but I am quite sure that the way we live now is
wrong.'[32]

And so, determined to right the wrongs of her day, it was not long
before Constance found yet another cause to take up – this time the
launch of a new club for 'progressive' women, one that might harness
their shared ambitions to effect social change.

Women had been noticeable as members of London clubs since
the early 1880s. And there were already a few all-female clubs. The
Alexandra Club in Grosvenor Street was grand and catered for high-
class women. The University Club for Ladies in New Bond Street
catered for university-educated working women of more modest
means. And the New Somerville Club in Oxford Street was a club

and college combined, providing lectures and talks alongside the standard offer of drawing rooms and a restaurant.[33]

One of the earliest gentlemen's clubs to accommodate women was that to which Oscar and Constance belonged, the Albemarle, founded in 1881. Constance was to be found there regularly, writing letters and meeting people. She and Oscar often dined there together. And she became involved in other aspects of club life too. In 1890, when the Albermarle expanded with the purchase of the neighbouring Pulteney Hotel, Constance was roped in as interior designer to fit out the new club house in suitably 'artistic taste'.[34]

Constance's aesthetic contribution to the Albemarle must have only heightened its appeal. Despite the extension of its premises, its members remained concerned about its over-subscription. This sense of demand outstripping supply no doubt informed the decision by Constance and her friends to set up a rival women-only institution.

In March 1891 Constance, along with Lady Harberton, Lady Sandhurst and a few other of her radical friends, announced their intentions in a series of advertisements intended to recruit potential members. 'It is proposed to start a Ladies Club with a view to furthering all movements for the advancement and enlightenment of women,' the notice in the *Woman's Herald* proclaimed. 'It is thought that such a club consisting at first of small but comfortable premises, in some convenient situation, would supply a want generally felt by women of intelligence, and provide them with a recognised centre and social rendezvous. The many and varied movements for improving and advancing women's work suffer from lack of esprit de corps.'

In the end the club, which initially was going to be called the Century Club, was launched as the Pioneer Club and opened in Regent Street. It quickly became embroiled in sororial controversy. The members of the Pioneer Club fell out with their sisters at the New Somerville Club when the latter labelled them 'political propagandists'. The Somervillians were duly punished. In August clubs typically closed for cleaning for a week or two. The tradition was for a system of reciprocal hospitality between institutions with members who found themselves temporarily inconvenienced invited to use the facilities of other establishments. But in August 1892 the press enjoyed the spectacle of 'the poor Somervillians wandering up and down . . . quite melancholy and homeless' after the founders of the Pioneer refused them such hospitality and took the Writers' Club instead, quite clearly out of spite.

'The Pioneer is very advanced,' a bemused journalist observed, 'to discuss its character in the current phraseology in which radicals and socialites love to describe themselves. The members are all women with opinions that agree as to the urgent necessity of reforming society by turning the world upside down as soon as possible, and a good deal of that readjustment of property-owning which is colloquially known as "robbing Peter to pay Paul".'[35] But even though its radical credentials proved unpalatable for some women, within a year the club had gathered a sufficient membership to support a move to bigger premises in Cork Street.

Israel Zangwill, the celebrated Jewish novelist and humorist, known to be sympathetic to the feminist cause, took the Pioneer Club as the inspiration for his comedic novel *The Old Maids' Club*. Zangwill's version was in fact the complete antithesis to the real thing, a club for young, beautiful, single women, who absolutely abhorred 'ideals' and vowed never 'to take part in Women's Rights Movements, Charity Concerts or other Platform Demonstrations'.[36] Zangwill's Old Maids' Club also swore 'Not to kiss females', a commitment that suggests that the genuine articles in the Pioneer Club were very much in the habit of kissing one another, much to the consternation of their peers.

9

Qui patitur vincit

IF YOU HAD walked down Oxford Street at lunchtime on
Friday 21 June 1889, proceeding from Oxford Circus to Marble
Arch under the almost continual canopy of coloured awnings that
once graced that thoroughfare, about half-way down you would
have found a cluster of folk blocking the pavement, vying to press
their noses up against the windows of no. 448. This group, drawn
from hoi polloi working in central London, were enjoying the spectacle of a great crowd of celebrated women milling about inside,
many of whom were smoking. This activity, normally the preserve of
men, was causing particular consternation. Constance Wilde, in her
signature Gainsborough hat and wearing a full-skirted velvet high-
wayman's coat, was in their midst. She, like a whole host of other
notable ladies, was attending the opening of a new Dorothy's
Restaurant.

Dorothy's was the initiative of one Mrs Cooper-Oakley, another
of London's leading feminists, who also ran a milliner's business in
Wigmore Street called Madame Isabel's. It was an innovation, a restaurant for women only. Although dining for upper- and middle-
class women was already available at the various women's clubs, and
although some conventional restaurants provided ladies' dining
rooms discreetly located in upper storeys or side-rooms, Dorothy's
was a bold modern proposition. Its door was right on the street, and
it was open to all classes of women, from shop assistants to duchesses.
Offering cheap wholesome fare for all, Dorothy's liberated the
former from having to eat a bun in a shop and offered the latter a new
kind of experience. You just bought an eightpenny dining ticket on

entrance, took a seat at one of the tables and waited for your 'plate of meat, two vegetables and bread' to arrive.[1] For an extra couple of pence you could also get pudding, and for a further penny tea, coffee or chocolate.

Dorothy's was a perfect example of how, in late Victorian London, Aestheticism, liberalism and feminist sympathies could collide. The first branch of the restaurant to open, in Mortimer Street, had cream-coloured walls with 'aesthetic crimson dados' and had been made 'gay with Japanese fans and umbrellas'.[2] The Oxford Street branch, which opened just months later, was a far more dramatic proposition, its windows hung with rich Indian curtains, its ante-room painted a deep red that offset luxurious couches, small tables and carefully selected ornaments, and its larger luncheon room featuring rows of simple tables set with glazed white cotton tablecloths surmounted by vases of fresh flowers.

Although men were not usually admitted within the hallowed walls of Dorothy's restaurants, an exception was made for the inauguration of the Oxford Street enterprise. And so Constance brought Oscar along. They found themselves seated next to the exotic Russian émigré Madame Blavatsky and her disciple Annie Besant.

Blavatsky proved a true rival for Oscar. Smoking just as heavily as he, until their table was defined by a blue cloud of tobacco, she held court talking about the position of women in Russia. Politically women were on a footing with men in Russia, Blavatsky told a fascinated group who had gathered around the rather exotic Wilde/Blavatsky table. What was more, women could smoke openly in Russia, just like men, she explained.

Her smoking aside, Madame Blavatsky had acquired huge fame at the time as one of the founders of the Theosophical Society. This society, which was created in New York in the mid-1870s, with the objective of studying and investigating spiritual activity, had become a phenomenon across the Western world.

It is hard to imagine the importance of mysticism and spiritualism in the latter half of the nineteenth century, but rather than lying on the peripheries of social interest, it lay at its heart. Séances were regularly held as the focus of social gatherings, and self-proclaimed mediums, professional and amateur, were highly visible. Constance's own interest in mesmerism as expressed in her juvenile letters, far from singling her out as unusual, merely shows the extent to which even the most conventional members of Victorian society were at least tolerant of and in some cases actively fascinated by the supernatural.

The Theosophical Society represented an intellectual response to spiritualism. It sought to provide credibility to spiritualism by grounding it in a system of belief. At the very core of Theosophy was the concept that that the material world cannot be separated from its spiritual counterpart. In fact, the Theosophists believed that there was a different natural order from that which separated the material and spiritual worlds. This alternative scheme of cosmogony was based on the idea of a constant flow and relationship between the material and spiritual dimensions.

Blavatsky herself promoted the study of Eastern philosophy as a means of grasping a higher understanding of the world, and of how the material and 'supernatural' worlds interact.

Mrs Cooper-Oakley was a Theosophical enthusiast and an evangelist for the movement. So was Constance. Constance's intro-duction to Theosophy lay in Speranza's friendship with Anna Kingsford. Kingsford, a physician, mystic, author, vegetarian and campaigner for women's rights, had eloped and married Algernon Kingsford on the firm understanding that he would support her determination to have a career in spite of her sex. She began writing and campaigning for female enfranchisement and used her not incon-siderable private income to become briefly the proprietor of *The Lady's Own Paper*. In the early 1870s she trained as a doctor in the Paris medical school, since at that time women were unable to qualify in the UK. But then in the early 1880s she experienced a number of mystical revelations which formed the basis of first a series of lectures, and then what became a popular and seminal mystical work explain-ing the deeper mysteries of religion: *The Perfect Way, or The Finding of Christ*. This publication gained her a sudden and considerable prominence in Theosophical and spiritual circles, and by 1883 she had become the president of the British Theosophical Society.

When Anna Kingsford wrote to Speranza back in 1884 to congratulate her on Oscar's engagement and secure her invitation to the big day, she was also proselytizing for the Theosophical Society, over which she now presided. Sending Speranza some of her latest writings, she had informed her of the imminent arrival in London of Alfred Percy Sinnett, who headed the movement's Indian branch:

> We shall shortly have a field day in the Lodge of the Theosophical Society for the President founder of the Indian Branch is expected in London about the end of this month; and we shall have a muster of all our Fellows to greet him. He and Madame Blavatsky are due today at Marseilles where they will stay a day or two . . . And Madame will then go on to Nice to visit Lady Caithness . . . My discourses, which I remember naming to you when I saw you in town, will probably be given under the auspices of the Theosophical Society as President of the London Lodge: and therefore it is not likely they will be quite public in their characters. They will be very grave and serious.[3]

In July 1884, Kingsford had also written to Constance confirming that the newly married Mrs Wilde would attend the Theosophical Society meeting the following day. 'I hear from Mr Sinnett that there will not be much "talk", only a short discourse by Colonel Olcott,' she had advised Constance. Constance had been a willing recruit from the start, providing Kingsford with a list of names of other people she knew who might be interested in the society. All of them had been sent invitations, Kingsford assured her.[4]

In fact, the much anticipated visit from Sinnett that Kingsford seemed so excited about proved deeply problematic for her. Unlike Sinnett's – and for that matter Blavatsky's – version of Theosophy, which looked very much to the East for answers, Kingsford's version invited the study of the Western mystery tradition and esoteric Christianity. The spiritual traditions that had grown up in the West, also known as Hermeticism, included alchemy, herbalism, the disciplines of the Tarot and astrology. Rooted in Western antiquity, in the ancient Hellenic and Egyptian belief systems, the Western tradition also extended to Rosicrucianism. This was a theology developed in medieval Germany by a secret society of mystics, which, again embracing the ancient past for profound answers to life, promoted a reformation of mankind according to new laws and knowledge.

When Sinnett arrived in Britain that spring, he and Kingsford found themselves at loggerheads. Sinnett had ambitions to head the London lodge himself, and Anna disagreed with his focus on Eastern mysticism. Sinnett got the upper hand, and the society attempted to mollify Anna by offering her her own 'Hermetic Lodge'. But soon the warring factions in the Theosophical Society forced Kingsford out of it altogether, and she set up her own independent Hermetic Society. And through this society Constance came into contact with yet another hermetic order, this one deeply secret, which would become notorious for taking the study of ancient mystical texts and beliefs a stage further. It was called the Hermetic Order of the Golden Dawn.

The Golden Dawn intended to revive ancient magic rituals that would unlock spiritual truths and experiences for its members. The founders of this extraordinary endeavour were three men: Mathers, Westcott and Woodman. Born in Hackney in the same year as Constance, Samuel Liddell Mathers was the son of a merchant's clerk who, after a short military career, found himself in Bournemouth caring for his widowed mother. He nevertheless claimed an impressive ancestry that reached back into the depths of the Scottish MacGregor clan, and by the later 1880s he was referring to himself as MacGregor Mathers. Despite his flamboyant style, Mathers was essentially an impecunious scholar who scraped a living undertaking translations and specialized in occult matters.

Like Oscar, Mathers had become a Freemason in the late 1870s, and then in 1882 he had joined the Societas Rosicruciana in Anglia – an esoteric Christian sect linked to Freemasonry that sought answers to life's great questions in the teachings of the seventeenth-century German Rosicrucian Brotherhood. Through this order he had met Dr William Wynne Westcott and Dr William Robert

Woodman. Westcott was a coroner and also had an interest in a business called the Sanitary Wood Wool Company, based at 11 Hatton Garden, London, which made surgical dressings, 'ladies napkins' and sponges, among other things. Woodman was a former surgeon and ardent horticulturalist.

When Mathers' mother died in 1885, he moved to London and was taken under the wing of Westcott and Woodman. The two doctors, meanwhile, had both joined Anna Kingsford's Hermetic Society. By 1886 Westcott and Woodman had introduced Mathers to Anna Kingsford, and he had begun lecturing for her Hermetic Society. His lecture topics included the Kabbalah and alchemy.

Within a year of meeting Kingsford, Mathers was moving within her wider circle of literary friends, which included Oscar and Constance. George Bernard Shaw noted in his diary for 1887 that he attended a soirée at which Oscar was present, at the novelist and historian Joseph Fitzgerald Molloy's. Molloy was an enthusiastic occultist who in 1887 wrote the novel *A Modern Magician*.[5] A year earlier Shaw had bumped into Oscar and the chiromantist Edward Heron Allen at Molloy's, where Heron Allen read his palm. But in October 1887 Oscar was there, and 'Mathers was the name of the man who read my character from my hand'.[6]

By 1887 Westcott had gained possession of supposedly antique cipher manuscripts and had managed to translate them sufficiently to reveal the outline of five ancient mystical rituals. Westcott asked Mathers to do more work on these rituals, refining and expanding the outlines to a point that the rituals could actually be performed, not least because Westcott claimed that he considered them to be central to a new occult order that he had discovered. This discovery was in the form of the name and address of a certain Fräulein Sprengel, which he said he had found among the pages of the cipher.

Westcott wrote to Sprengel, who apparently wrote back and authorized him to found the English branch of a secret German Rosicrucian society called Die Goldene Dämmerung. Thus Westcott established the Isis-Urania Temple of the Hermetic Order of the Golden Dawn. The rituals revived by Mathers from the cipher were to be at the heart of the Order. He, Mathers and Woodman would be the founders and Chiefs of the Temple. Prospective members of the Hermetic Order of the Golden Dawn could apply via the offices of the Sanitary Wood Wool Company in Holborn.

The timing of the launch of the Golden Dawn was propitious. Anna Kingsford died in February 1888. The Golden Dawn came officially into being in March that year, and many members of Kingsford's group transferred to the new society.

It seems quite clear that Mathers, Westcott and Woodman were engaged in a venture based on a considerable element of fantasy and fraud. Nevertheless Mathers, a man who embraced fantasy, combined his brilliant imagination with his knowledge of alchemy and magic to create compelling rituals. At a time when an interest in other-worldly matters was gripping Britain's bourgeoisie, there seemed to be little appetite for scepticism when it came to such ventures as the Golden Dawn. On the contrary, there seemed a strong craving among the upper middle classes for adventure. Letters of inquiry began arriving at the Sanitary Wood Wool Company offices, alongside the company's standard orders for sanitary towels and surgical dressings.

Constance was one of the thirty-two members who joined the Order in its inaugural year, of whom nine were women. Mathers may have approached her directly. He was a compelling, romantic figure. Tall, dark, athletic and marked with scars from regular boxing and fencing bouts at his local gym, often sporting a scarlet tie and velvet coat, when he was not enthusing about ancient hieroglyphs he was dreaming of fighting brave fights in far-off lands.[7]

If not recruited through a direct approach, Constance would have been one of those interested parties who applied for membership by writing to:

G D Secretary
c/o Sanitary Wood Wool Co, 11 Hatton Garden, E.C.[8]

After making her initial application, Constance would have been sent a pledge form, explaining that the Order was established for 'the purpose of the study of Occult Science, and the further investigation of the Mysteries of Life and Death, and our Environment'.[9] The form demanded a belief in One God and warned that the society was not designed for those who only sought superficial knowledge. Candidates were then required to pledge that they were over twenty-one, that they would keep the Order secret and that they would study the Occult with zeal. They were required to provide their address and a Latin motto, which would become their name as far as their dealings with the Golden Dawn went. Constance chose 'Qui Patitur Vincit' ('Who Endures Wins').

All candidates were warned that they would have to 'persevere' a ceremony of admission, and Constance faced her own initiation on 13 November 1888. She was admitted alongside one other candidate: Anna, Comtesse de Brémont.

Many of the Order's ceremonies were held in Mark Masons' Hall, a huge Masonic institution in St James's. If Constance and her companion were initiated here, then, according to the practice of the group, they would have avoided using the main entrance to the building and instead entered through a more discreet entrance at the side.[10]

But initiations were not always in such grand and impressive surroundings. Sometimes the Order took its ceremonies into the drawing rooms, studios and offices of its various middle-class members. The poet W. B. Yeats, a friend of the Wildes who joined the Order in 1890, was initiated in Mina Bergson's studio in Fitzroy Street. Bergson was a young artist who had attended the Slade School of Art and would go on to marry Mathers. She was one of the very first initiates to the Order and had already been a member for some seven months before Constance joined the group.

The highly theatrical initiation ceremony was designed to fill the candidate with both wonder and fear, and any formerly domestic interior would have been significantly transformed for the event, as would any apparently ordinary man or woman who belonged to the secret Order.

A black tunic was the standard, though optional, uniform of the

Order. Other optional wear for members included the ancient Egyptian head-dress known as a nemyss, which appears on so many Egyptian sarcophagi, made of black-and-white striped linen, which was passed around the forehead and then allowed to fall down behind the ears. Members could also wear masks, and it was mandatory for every member to wear a sash or badge that denoted their rank within the Order.

For her initiation Constance put on a black tunic and red shoes, allowed herself to be blindfolded and had a cord wound round her waist three times. She was then led into a room, temporarily converted into a 'temple'. Here members wearing the yet more theatrical dress of the offices of the Order were standing in deeply symbolic arrangement, along with banners and props replete with magical symbolism.

Constance and the Comtesse held hands throughout the bizarre performance that ensued. The Comtesse was blasé and noted that the 'theatrical ceremony ... would have been amusing had it not been taken so seriously'. Constance, however, more impressionable than her colleague, was so nervous that she shook throughout. Her hands were like blocks of ice and 'her beautiful eyes were full of tears'.[11]

The two women, kneeling before the Hierophant, a senior officer who, sitting on a throne, was dressed in scarlet and carried a banner, placed their left hands in his, and recited a lengthy obligation to the Order. It included an undertaking to complete secrecy. Constance would have had to acknowledge that, should she betray the Order, she would be expelled 'as a wilfully perjured wretch, void of all moral worth, and unfit for the society of all upright and true persons' and submit herself 'to a deadly and hostile current of will set in motion by the chiefs of the Order, by which I should fall slain or paralysed without visible weapon, as if blasted by the Lightning Flash!' At the moment at which this last terrible oath was uttered the Hiereus, another officer dressed in black, would have pressed a sword into the nape of Constance's neck.

After this strange ordeal, blindfolds were removed and more

mundane paperwork sorted out. Constance paid a 10s admission fee, and then a further 2s for her annual membership. She bought a 'sash' to wear at Order gatherings, at a cost of 2s, and then paid a further 7s for necessary texts associated with the society: a copy of the rituals she would have to learn and the pamphlet written by Westcott entitled *The Historic Lecture for Neophytes,* which provided some history for the Order and contained an account of its structure and teachings.

The Golden Dawn was structured around three key stages through which members had to pass. The first of these was the society's Outer Order, which comprised an initiate or Neophyte grade, followed by four other grades of achievement. To move between grades members were required to study and pass examinations that tested their knowledge of ancient languages such as Hebrew, the key rituals of their grade and the fundamental theories on which the Order's beliefs were based. After study and passing crucial examinations the Neophyte could move to the Zelator grade and then through the Theoricus and Practicus grades to the highest rank of Philosophus.

Once one had achieved the status of a Philosophus, one could be initiated into the Second Order, where there were three further Grades of Adeptship. Adepts were sufficiently authoritative to be able to tutor Outer Order members and establish temples. The third and highest Order of the Golden Dawn had three further grades: Magister Templi, Magus and Ipsissimus. These grades were, however, reserved for beings that existed on the astral plane, not on mundane earth.

The Comtesse's account of her and Constance's introduction to the Order was written some twenty years after the event and to some extent may have been influenced by hindsight. Nevertheless Anna Brémont's recollections are intriguing. Studying with her, the Comtesse got to know Constance well:

> I learned to read in that clear mirror her noble beautiful character and discern her secret unrest and sadness, her weakness and patience under

the process of disillusionment through which she was passing. I divined that she was not serious in the pursuit of occult knowledge, that she had an ulterior object in becoming a member, and that her end was to use the curious lore for some purpose other than that intended by the Order, and that her frank, truthful spirit chafed under the deception she was practising.[12]

The implication is that Constance had become an initiate of the Golden Dawn as part of a research project for her husband. Brémont quite clearly accuses Constance of reporting 'the ceremony and all its details to her husband' and of 'giving away the lore so laboriously and enthusiastically acquired by the members'. She also notes that the disaster that would be visited on Constance and Oscar in the next decade was attributed by many members of the Order 'to the breaking of her pledged word'.

It seems hard to conceive that Constance would put in so many hours of study at a time when she was furiously busy with her politics, was writing stories, managing the *Rational Dress Gazette* and had a young family to care for, just for the sake of Oscar's inquisitiveness. Over the course of the next twelve months Constance, studious as ever, acquired a working knowledge of Hebrew, became familiar with alchemical and kabbalistic symbols, grasped astrology and divination, learned the mysteries of the Tarot, studied the significance of the rituals performed by the Golden Dawn (as well as memorizing the rituals themselves) and passed a series of exams to prove it. By November 1889 she had passed through all the grades of the Outer Order of the Golden Dawn and had attained the status of Philosophus.

It seems more likely that Constance, growing disenchanted with the conventional church, explored Theosophy, and its extension into the Golden Dawn, as a genuine alternative to conventional religious practice. It does seem credible, however, that, despite the terrible oaths she had sworn, Constance revealed the Order's secrets to her husband.

To get a sense of the kinds of events Constance may have

recounted to Oscar, it's worth turning to Yeats. He tells how Mathers once gave him a cardboard symbol which, when he pressed it to his forehead and closed his eyes, conjured extraordinary images in his mind, images that he could not control. He saw 'a desert and black Titan raising himself by his two hands from the middle of a heap of ancient ruins'. Mathers explained to Yeats that he 'had seen a being of the order of Salamanders because he had shown me their symbol, but it was not necessary even to show the symbol, it would have been sufficient that he imagined it'.[13]

Yeats went on to link this vivid dream-like world into which he had been plunged by Mathers' magic to the imaginary world created by artists. He enjoyed the idea that the potency of some artists' imaginations was so great that they themselves were like wizards.

'I had found when a boy in Dublin on a table in the Royal Irish Academy a pamphlet on Japanese art,' Yeats recalled, 'and read there of an animal painter so remarkable that horses he had painted upon a temple wall had slipped down after dark and trampled their neighbour's fields of rice. Somebody had come into the temple in the early morning, had been startled by a shower of water drops, had looked up and seen painted horses still wet from the dew-covered fields, but not "trembling into stillness".'

It's not hard to see how such a proposition – that inanimate things might be imbued with life by powerful, imaginative magicians – might appeal to both the author of 'Was It a Dream?' and her husband, who in the autumn of 1889 began to write his novel *The Picture of Dorian Gray*. The idea that this story, of a painting that develops a life of its own, growing older as its evil owner preserves his youth, may have derived specifically from conversations with Constance about the Order seems highly likely.

But Constance's romance with the Golden Dawn was short-lived. Having achieved the highest rank in the Outer Order just a year after joining, she decided not to seek entrance into the Second Order. The membership list of the Golden Dawn notes that by November 1889 her subscription was 'in abeyance with the sympathy of the chiefs'.

That she withdrew from the Order at the moment that Oscar began to write *Dorian Gray* remains an intriguing coincidence.

After leaving the Order, Constance did not drop her interest in Spiritualism. She commuted it. Within a couple of years she would join the Society for Psychical Research, having met one of the founders, Frederic Myers, at Babbacombe Cliff. She and Myers quickly became friendly, corresponding and seeing one another regularly. It seems likely it would have been he who encouraged Constance to join his society as an associate in 1892. By 1894 she was a full member and was promoting the society to her friends.[14]

That Constance believed in an afterlife is unquestionable. That her great friend Lady Mount-Temple was hoping to provide proof of an afterlife in an experiment with Myers is also indicated. Georgina, who since the death of her husband was expecting her own demise at any time, had given Myers some specific words or phrases that, if received after her death by a medium, would indicate her continuing spiritual existence. Later, in 1892, Constance would refer to his plan. 'Mrs Duncan wrote to me the other day to pray that you might not be taken away from us, and I answered that I could not pray this . . . How could I pray for longer life and more crosses, when I look forward to radiancy and joy on that lovely face . . . Have you sent your words to Mr Myers that you promised to him; I hope you will, so that we may have some sign of you given to us.'[15]

Later on, Constance also became a subscriber to *Borderland,* a publication that had been launched by the pioneering journalist and former editor of the *Pall Mall Gazette* William Thomas Stead, which featured tales of ghosts and other-worldly phenomena. Constance adored this publication and would pass it on with relish to her friends.

If Oscar had been inspired by his wife's occult studies in writing *Dorian Gray,* such moments of creative cohesion between husband and wife must have been relished by Constance, because in many respects her marriage was once again encountering problems. Although in the summer of 1887 she had assured Otho that she and

Oscar were 'very happy together now', within a year she must have sensed that she and Oscar were in fact growing apart again. The glue that the launch of *The Woman's World* had provided, binding them socially and aligning their careers, was beginning to thin. Oscar was quickly bored with his role as an editor, and by the summer of 1889 he had given up the helm of the periodical.

On the surface they were fine. Yeats, who joined the Wildes on Christmas Day in 1888, described Oscar's life in Tite Street as a 'perfect harmony . . . with his beautiful wife and two young children'. And yet Yeats, with terrific perception, added that his home life 'suggested some deliberate artistic composition'.[16]

Oscar and Constance most certainly presented themselves to their friends and their public as a loving, committed and essentially conventional family. Oscar, like many middle- and upper-class Victorians, clearly felt a moral obligation to his wife and family, although he may well have considered extramarital sex an indulgence that married men traditionally enjoyed and which wives and society more generally were expected to tolerate. Constance, meanwhile, despite her stance as a New Woman, saw loyalty to her husband, a trait embodied by Queen Victoria herself, as a primary virtue and duty of womanhood.

'To-day the Bowles were speaking of married life,' she wrote to her friend Juliet Latour Temple, the adopted daughter of Lady Mount-Temple,

> and of the relations between husband and wife and of the absolute importance of affirming the good in one's husband, of affirming in fact that which one has fallen in love with, and which must exist and does exist, if one has married for love, and I don't believe that anyone can be happy unless they do marry for love. I hope you will fall in love with some delightful man, and marry him and be very happy in loving him, and leading him upward. This is the woman's work 'par excellence!'[17]

Juliet had told Constance that she was about to read *The Kreutzer Sonata*, a highly controversial novella by Tolstoy about married life.

It is the story of a husband's carnal lust for his wife, a lust that ultimately leads not only to a great number of children but also to the man murdering his wife out of jealousy when she has an affair. The novella argues that the sentiment men and women mistake for 'love' is in fact nothing more than basic sexual attraction.

'You told me that you were going to read the "Kreutzer Sonata",' Constance wrote. 'Please don't imagine that all men and women are like that. I think and hope that very few are, and that very few lives are so absolutely sordid as these.'

For Constance, in contrast to Tolstoy, love within marriage could be based on something other than sex. At a moment when this element of her own relationship had waned, the perfect harmony Yeats perceived in the Wilde household stemmed from Constance's continuing admiration for the poet and freethinker who had so impressed her as a younger woman.

In return for such loyalty and love, Oscar fiercely guarded Constance and his family. His determination to protect her in public life is evidenced by an odd incident that happened in 1889. A journalist and writer called Herbert Vivian published a memoir titled *Reminiscences of a Short Life,* which was then serialized in the *Sun.* Vivian claimed that Oscar had encouraged him to write these memoirs and was to all intents and purposes the 'fairy-godfather of the work'. But to Oscar and Constance's horror, on reading the memoir they discovered that some very personal details of Oscar's family life had been included in it.

Vivian recounted that Oscar had revealed he plastered the nursery walls in Tite Street 'with texts about early rising and sluggishness, and so forth, and I tell them that when they grow up, they must take their father as a warning, and occasionally have breakfast earlier than two in the afternoon'.

'The story of Cyril's altruism is also well imagined,' Vivian went on. 'That youth, not a lustrum old, bewildered his family one morning by announcing that he did not mean to say his prayers any more. It was pointed out to him that he must pray to God to make him good, but he demurred . . . after a prolonged altercation, the young philosopher offered a compromise, and said that he wouldn't mind praying to God make baby good.'[18]

The story is amusing, but it distressed Constance immensely. Oscar wrote in the strongest terms to Vivian, explaining,

> Meeting you socially, I, in a moment which I greatly regret, happened to tell you a story about a little boy. Without asking my permission you publish this in a vulgar newspaper and in a vulgar, inaccurate and offensive form, to the great pain of my wife, who naturally does not wish to see her children paraded for the amusement of the uncouth.[19]

It is likely that Constance's objection was rooted in a concern that was wider than that indicated by Oscar. It was not just that Cyril was being paraded in the press, but it was the manner in which he was being paraded, as the heir to his father's perceived vices. Cyril wanted God to make baby good so that he could be 'bad' like Oscar.

Just before Vivian went to press with this story, Oscar had managed to stir up a level of controversy, and the notion of Oscar as a man of dubious morality was topical once again. In July 1889 he had published 'The Portrait of Mr W. H.' in *Blackwood's Magazine*. Taking its title from the dedication in Shakespeare's Sonnets, the story is an account of Cyril Graham and his identification of Mr W. H. as Willie Hughes, a beautiful, young actor 'whose physical beauty was such that it became the very corner stone of Shakespeare's art'.

Oscar had contrived the story in conjunction with Robbie Ross, and it is a barely concealed exploration of and apology for homosexuality. Not only is the object of Shakespeare's love a man, but Cyril Graham, who is described as 'effeminate' and 'wonderfully handsome', also becomes an object of fascination for another character in the story, his friend Erskine.

Oscar was all too aware of the story's explosive potential. Prior to publication he sought advice from two politicians in his circle, Arthur Balfour and Herbert Asquith. Both warned him against publication in the light of the damage that such a story could do to his reputation.

All the implications of his own 'effeminacy' that had been so widely bandied in the early 1880s and partially dispelled by his marriage were bound to be resurrected. But Oscar ignored the advice. Whether it was out of his own genuine infatuation with young men ignited by Ross, a more profound liberal belief that homosexuality could be noble and should not be outlawed or simply his sense that publicity, no matter how controversial, could be commercially beneficial, he decided to publish and be damned. His friend the magazine editor Frank Harris later observed that this move delivered Oscar incalculable injury, providing his detractors with the ammunition they had so long sought.

While some review magazines such as *The Graphic* saw nothing but a very clever and convincing story woven around a conundrum that had kept scholars guessing for years, others were quick to pounce. Oscar's indulgent descriptions of Willie Hughes were 'unpleasant', *The World* noted. His 'peculiarly offensive' work was not the kind of thing 'one would have expected' in *Blackwood's.*

Constance could not have been unaware of such comments about her husband's work. While she knew Oscar was more than capable of defending himself against such damaging implications, she most certainly did not want her husband's notoriety attaching to the rest of the family. In fact, Constance was adamant that Cyril would never suffer the abuse that perceived 'effeminacy' invited. Perhaps informed by the fact that her former house guest Robbie Ross had been so persecuted when he went to Cambridge that he had to leave, she had decided that Cyril was destined for a thoroughly masculine naval career.

Of course, those critics who interpreted 'The Portrait of Mr W. H.' as a reflection of the author's own sexual preferences were justified. Since his affair with Robbie Ross in 1887, Oscar had continued flirtatious relationships with several young men, some of whom may well have become sexual lovers. Robbie had made Oscar adventurous and bold. In fact, between 1887 and the end of 1889 it has been suggested that Oscar could count among his conquests: the artist Graham Robertson, the actor Harry Melvill, the clerk Fred Althaus, the young American playwright Clyde Fitch and the extremely handsome writer John Gray, who would inspire the title of Oscar's first novel.

With the exception of Fred Althaus, whom it seems Oscar picked up at The Crown public house in Charing Cross, most of the young men he became involved with were in the vein of the literary-minded Douglas Ainslie and Harry Marillier, whose friendship Oscar and Constance had so encouraged in their inaugural year in Tite Street. Constance no doubt considered the frequent visits of such men, whom Oscar's friend the writer André Raffalovich dubbed his 'sons', as part of her husband's commitment to encouraging and inspiring the younger generation. Oscar introduced her to them, and they often dined with her and Oscar *en famille*. There are indications that Constance was quite conscious that not only was the behaviour of Oscar and his friends, open to misinterpretation, but also that their conversation could stray into controversial territories.

One day in 1889 Raffalovich arrived at Tite Street to be greeted by Constance. 'Oscar likes you so much,' Constance told him. 'He says you have such nice improper talks together.' Raffalovich was apparently appalled by this comment and swore never to talk to Oscar again 'without witnesses'.[20] Perhaps he was all too aware of the danger Oscar was already courting, and terrified that Oscar's loose tongue might do his own reputation significant damage. Their friendship ceased.

Oscar's affairs took him away from his family more than ever before. Once again Constance suspected that Oscar had fallen for another woman. This time it was a young woman called Bibidie Leonard, Constance thought.[21] Speranza had brought Miss Leonard to Oscar's attention and had asked him to consider her as a contributor to *The Woman's World*. His frequent visits to see Bibidie at her home in York Terrace seemed to Constance excessive.

Despite that altruistic expression of marital loyalty in her letter to Juliet Latour Temple, Constance's more intimate letters to Juliet's mother reveal that this did little to offset her terrible, growing jealousy when it came to Oscar. This was becoming 'the almost greatest, if not the very greatest' of Constance's 'soul-temptations', an aspect of character that she was in 'constant warfare against'. And Constance was beginning to discuss this aspect of her marriage with her close female friends, not least Bertha Lathbury, wife of the *Guardian* editor, Daniel Lathbury, whom Constance visited regularly at her home in Witley in Surrey. She wrote to Georgina Mount-Temple:

> Darling, I have been for years thinking about this terrible passion of jealousy, and I am quite certain that Mrs Lathbury is right that the only way to conquer it is to love more intensely; love will swallow up even the pangs of jealousy. Surely if one is jealous of one's husband, it is because one thinks it possible to make him love one more, and the only way to do that is to love <u>him</u> more, and make him feel that no-one else loves him as much. It is comparatively easy to conquer jealousy when one has a claim and a right to the best love. One can demand it, and demand it by the power of love . . . Jealousy cannot be anything but a sin, for envy is at the root of it. When I am jealous of my friends, it is not so much that they may love me more, but that they may love someone else less for I have not very much faith at any time in my power of attracting love, and I know that unconsciously I really fall back upon that. And here it is surely that love comes in to help in the struggle.[22]

Constance never states who is the focus of her jealousy. Was it Bibidie or another female mistress she suspected Oscar of keeping? Or was she jealous of those 'sons' whose company her husband was increasingly seeking out in preference to her own? And when it came to his young male acolytes, was Constance just jealous of the time Oscar dedicated to these men and the inspiration he found in their society, or did she, at some subconscious, instinctive level, also acknowledge there was more to be green-eyed over? There is a slight suggestion in her letter that Oscar was forced to find sexual comfort elsewhere because she herself could no longer provide it. Tantalizingly, she admitted that the focus of her jealousy offered her husband something she was unable to provide. Again the notion that post-natal complications after Vyvyan's birth had left Constance unable to have full sex is just possible.

'For even I am not jealous when I know that the one I am jealous of fills a place that I <u>cannot</u> fill,' Constance said, 'and when one real-ises that everyone fills the place that they are needed for, and that if this place is not filled, the happiness of those we love is touched and marred, then truly unselfish love steps in and says I am satisfied.'

Constance, it seems, had an extraordinary capacity to adjust to circumstances.

10

My own darling mother

THE 1890S WERE not so much the ending of a century as the beginning of a new one. This was the observation of the poet Richard Le Gallienne, one of Oscar's 'sons'. Looking back in the 1920s, he saw that in the last ten years of the nineteenth century 'all our present conditions, socially and artistically, our vaunted new "freedoms" of every kind . . . not only began then, but found a more vital and authoritative expression than they have found since because of the larger, more significant personalities bringing them about.'[1] Victorian society was disintegrating as different factions re-evaluated its spiritual, moral and artistic aspects.

In fact, it was as if London had become a huge recruitment fair, with these 'personalities' in their respective booths inviting passers-by to join their cause. Amid all the competing schools and philosophies being bandied about, Le Gallienne remembered the 'mystic looking booth, flying a green flag with an Irish harp figured upon it', offering talk of 'Rosicrucianism and fairies', and then there were the 'Socialist Clergymen, preaching High Church Anglicanism, and pre-Raphaelite art for the slums of Whitechapel'.

For Le Gallienne, Oscar was assuming a unique place amid such chaos. He was becoming a living synthesis of all the new, emergent ideas, borrowing from everything and combining all in a personality that defied definition. As such, he was becoming perhaps the most potent personality of the era – the individualist.

In contrast to her husband, Constance was by nature a fanatic who would throw herself wholeheartedly into one fad or craze before moving on to another. After her profound commitment to occult mysticism in the late 1880s, in the '90s Constance moved on from 'Rosicrucianism and fairies' to the booth presided over by the socialist clergymen. In her pursuit of Christian socialism she became, according to Le Gallienne, 'almost evangelical'.

As Oscar pursued individualism and Constance became involved in Christian socialism, the couple that had once been welded together through joint ventures and common interests were now following decidedly different interests. With both jealously guarding their right to their own intellectual freedom, their marriage took on a new shape: they began to lead increasingly separate lives.

Constance's renewed interest in Christianity was prompted initially by the work of Professor Henry Drummond, whose writings attempted to reconcile a belief in God with Darwin's science.[2] But if it was Drummond who opened her eyes, the person who sustained this renewed interest in Christianity was Georgina Cowper-Temple, Lady Mount-Temple, the stepdaughter-in-law of Lord Palmerston. The wife of the deceased William Francis Cowper-Temple, Lord Mount-Temple, a Whig statesman and philanthropist, Georgina was not only a significant friend to and patron of many of the great Pre-Raphaelite artists of the day; she had also become well known in public for her campaigning for sanitary knowledge for women. She was an ardent anti-vivisectionist and a promoter of vegetarianism. Bereaved in 1888, by the outset of the 1890s she was looking to fill the hole that her husband's death left in her life. Constance was a perfect cause.

Constance's friendship with Georgina Mount-Temple crystallized in the autumn of 1889. Her main point of introduction was through Georgina's daughter Juliet Latour Temple, with whom Constance had already developed a warm friendship. Her association with Juliet led to an invitation to stay at Babbacombe Cliff in September 1889. She was 'dreadfully shy about going', she confided to Emily Thursfield. But she added, 'Perhaps I shall make my mind to go next week.'[3]

Constance's first visit to Babbacombe began a love affair with the place and its elderly owner. Everything about the house held a kind of magic for Constance. Babbacombe Cliff was a temple to Pre-Raphaelitism and full of the most exquisite treasure. Georgina Cowper-Temple and her husband had spent a lifetime building one of the best collections of Pre-Raphaelite paintings in Britain. To house them they had created a seaside retreat that was in itself an architectural delight. On approaching the house one could see Crow's Nest, a tower built specifically for people to look out and pretend they were at sea, gazing out from the masts of some ancient ship. Referencing the medieval scenes that Pre-Raphaelite art so often featured, 'Babb' also had its own gated archway with mock portcullis.

Once inside, further wonders met the eye. The entrance hall was decorated with tiles designed by William Morris, and its staircase led to a corridor illuminated by stained glass designed by Edward Burne-Jones. Each room was papered and carpeted by Morris's famous interior design company, Morris & Co., and then named after the featured design: Marigold or Lily.

Then there was Wonderland, a room at the very heart of the building, designed to be sun-filled all day long, decorated with scenes from Lewis Carroll's *Alice's Adventures in Wonderland*. It was surmounted by a huge vaulted ceiling of turquoise Morris tiles and sported an enormous marble inglenook fireplace.

By June 1890 Constance was meeting Juliet's mother regularly at Sunday lectures,[4] possibly at St Barnabas Church, which was close to both Georgina's London home at 9 Cheyne Walk and Tite Street.[5] By the end of 1890 Constance and Georgina had become so close that Constance was referring to the older woman as her 'mother'. And when Constance fell ill on Christmas Day, Georgina came to her aid, a gesture that delighted Constance and prompted expressions of friendship so passionate that it is clear Georgina had now surpassed Viscountess Harberton, Lady Sandhurst and even Speranza in Constance's collection of matriarchs.

'Beloved Mother, my throat is a little better, but having begun to be wise, I am going to continue, and stay in bed to-day!' Constance wrote on Boxing Day.

Darling, how beautiful you made my Xmas Day for me, as you do
everything that you touch. I had been trying all the morning to feel
happy and to be with you spiritually in your communion, and then
you came and set the seal to my uncertain efforts, and made even
belief seem possible to me. My little room is consecrated to me by
your beloved words of peace.[6]

The following day Constance sent her friend a further note to
reassure her that 'Oscar says I no longer look tired'.[7]

The timing of Georgina's arrival in Constance's life is key. Having
given up the secure position he had enjoyed at *The Woman's World,*
Oscar was pursuing his other literary ambitions, to write more stories
and novels and also to write for the theatre. In doing so, he had
thrown the Wilde household back into the financial uncertainty that
goes hand in hand with a freelance career.

In addition to this, Oscar was spending more time away from Tite
Street and his wife. Apart from the socializing that was necessarily
linked to his business, and his liking for the theatre crowd which
often led to his 'talking witty nonsense in the dressing-rooms of his
friends' of an evening,[8] Oscar was also increasingly combining
his passion for young men with that for fine wine and food by using
the finest hotels and restaurants in London as the arenas of his
flirtations.

Oscar's late nights out were causing noticeable rows and friction.
One associate of the Wildes at the time, the opera diva Nellie Melba,
recounted Oscar warning his boys one day that dreadful things happened to naughty boys who made mothers cry. One of them
responded by asking what happened to naughty fathers, staying out
until the early hours, who made their mother cry far more.
Constance's tears often turned to accusation and anger.

Her own domestic problems came at a time when the wider Wilde
and Lloyd families were also buckling under various stresses. Oscar's
brother Willie was still suffering financial difficulties. Still unmarried,
and with drink problems, he was considered a drain on Speranza's
limited resources and a general liability. But it wasn't just her brother-
in-law who was a concern: Otho also continued to worry Constance.

With his second family he had returned to London, where he had all but given up the notion of a career *per se* and was attempting to live off the income from John Horatio's legacy. He had invested in a property development company called the Leasehold Investment Company. But rather than delivering a return, the LIC was running into difficulty.

Constance was in desperate need of both good counsel and maternal affection amid all these troubles. 'My mother sends me to-day an icy cold letter from Dublin,' Constance wrote to Georgina. 'Darling if you saw how she writes, you would not wonder that I turn to you for love, and claim a Mother's love because I need it so desperately.'[9]

The two women fell into a close routine that could involve daily visits to one another as well as church visits. They made a point of taking communion together, a ritual that they referred to in their own special code as a 'tryst'. They embarked on literary projects together, reading Thomas à Kempis and the apocryphal Gospel of St Peter, which had been discovered just a few years earlier, in 1886. At a time when Oscar was arguing that art needed no moral basis, his wife and her friend began scouring Dante for moral lessons that they might apply in their day-to-day lives.

Constance had experimented with the notion of an artistic life in the first couple of years of her marriage, and had become half of an intertwined literary couple in the later 1880s. But at the cusp of the 1890s she became intrigued by the idea of Utopian living, in which one could lead a good, moral, purposeful existence. Georgina told her stories about her friends Laurence and Alice Oliphant, British Victorians who had given up their all and moved to join the Utopian community founded in the United States by the American Thomas Lake Harris. Constance admitted that she would have joined such a community. But Georgina urged her that, rather than seek refuge from unsavoury realities within the walls of an idealistic commune, she should apply some muscular Christianity by going out and doing good deeds. And so Constance began to visit the underprivileged residents of Paradise Walk that, when they arrived in Tite Street, she and Oscar had concealed from view with latticework shutters. Within two or three years of knowing Georgina, the residents of that pitiful place were regularly knocking on Tite Street's white front door, a fact that must have mortified Cyril and Vyvyan, who remained terrified of the urchins who lurked in the slums.[10]

In the evenings when she wasn't dining with Oscar or going to the theatre with him Constance would often dine with Georgina. Even when she did dine with Oscar, she could still find time to drop in on Georgina to read to her before bedtime. On days when they did not see one another, Georgina and Constance wrote to each other instead. Constance, now attending church every day without fail, often made a point of noting particular details of a sermon or service she had attended. Cyril was sometimes tasked with playing postman between the two Chelsea homes.

For Oscar, Constance's friendship with Georgina could not have been better timed, since it not only provided her with the spiritual and maternal sustenance she craved but also gave him more licence to pursue those social engagements at which his wife's presence would have been inappropriate. But the extraordinary attention that Constance paid Georgina gave others cause for concern. The stockbroker Frank Sumner, a close friend of Lady Mount-Temple's, had clearly said something to this effect.

'Lest Mr Sumner imagine that I am neglecting Oscar, he is dining out!' Constance told Georgina one day.

> And in self-defence I must deny that I ever neglect him, or put him anywhere but first in my life-duties. Oscar has, I am sure, told you what he feels that you have been to me in my life, and he would not be a true husband if he were not grateful to you, and anxious that I should give you what I can, that can be of ever small interest to you ... If I had a mother who cared for me, an earth mother, I should most certainly go and see her every day, and why therefore should I not come and see my spiritual mother?[11]

Mr Sumner's comments may also have been a disguised signal to Constance regarding not so much her own behaviour as her husband's. Might he also have been suggesting that she should be keeping more of an eye on Oscar? Society has the habit of blaming wives for their husband's deviations, and the nineteenth century was no exception.

In 1890 *The Picture of Dorian Gray* had appeared in *Lippincott's Magazine*. Just as 'The Portrait of Mr W. H.' had done, it drew both praise and harsh criticism. The novel tells the tale of Dorian Gray, a beautiful young man who is the subject of both a painting by, and an infatuation on the part of, the artist Basil Hallward. Dorian, meanwhile, is simultaneously enthralled by the hedonistic life of one of Basil's older friends, Lord Henry Wotton. Dorian, enjoying the indulgences of his youth, wishes that his portrait might age rather than the real thing, and in doing so inadvertently casts a spell that realizes just this. So while Dorian plunges headlong into a life of debauchery and murder, remaining young and beautiful, his portrait becomes more and more disfigured.

The novel's focus on male beauty and the indulgence of the senses once again raised eyebrows. Oscar found himself engaging in bouts of public letter-writing to various newspaper and magazine editors whose publications had branded the work immoral. The criticism in the *Aberdeen Weekly Journal* sums up the general arguments offered against the piece. 'Characters more fantastic and repulsive than those of Dorian Gray and Lord Henry Wotton were surely never drawn,' it wrote. *The Picture of Dorian Gray* 'leaves a bad taste in the mouth'.[12]

But it was not so much the criticism as the very public nature of it that must have been difficult for the Wildes. The *St James Gazette,* as described by Oscar himself, 'placarded the town with posters on which was printed in large letters: Mr Oscar Wilde's Latest Advertisement; A Bad Case'. W. H. Smith refused to sell the book.

Oscar may have been useless with money, but he had a nose for commercial success. The very controversial nature of the work provided it with free publicity. '*Lippincott's* has had a phenomenal sale,' Robbie Ross wrote to Oscar, congratulating him on the book. '80 copies were sold in one day at the Strand booksellers, the usual amount being about three a week in that part,' he added, noting that 'of course it is said to be very dangerous'.[13]

Constance remained wilfully immune to the insinuations that were being made about her husband and his work, and continued an admiration for it that many noted as being close to idolatry. She had a terrific capacity to filter out the worrying comments being made about Oscar and instead to focus on the praise of him, which was in fact equally available. She was also perfectly capable of sifting through his work to find those elements in its complexity that appealed to her, and somehow discard the elements that others considered risqué or controversial. When Georgina read *Dorian Gray* in *Lippincott's* in June 1890,[14] one imagines it was Constance who proudly urged her to do so. A little later she delighted in recommending to her friend an excellent review of the novel by Walter Pater in *The Bookman*.

In spite of her own not inconsiderable successes, and despite the fact that her interests were now diverging substantially from his, Constance never ceased to delight in her husband and remained his greatest fan. In February 1891 she and Oscar dined at the Houses of Parliament as the guests of Sir Hugh Low. Constance's sense of pride in her husband becomes clear:

> I enjoyed my dinner at the House so much – a dinner party in the private room, and Sir John Pope Hennessy & Sir Hugh Low spoke to me in the highest terms of praise of Oscar which is of course always delightful to me. I have never heard anything like the enthusiastic way in which they both of them spoke of his brilliance and charm, and a little reflected light fell also on me, which is not always the case. It is no wonder to me that Oscar likes going amongst people who treat him like this, and who are themselves delightful.[15]

It was perhaps because of Constance's continuing pride in him that Oscar took some heed of his wife's complaints and tears and redoubled his efforts to play the devoted, if somewhat absent, husband. Much of this show of devotion took the form of letters that he began writing regularly to his wife when he was away from her, particularly during the autumn of 1891. The degree of attention Oscar paid to his wife in spite of his sexual adventures with young men is rarely acknowledged. But it is crucial to understanding the commitment that the couple continued to have to one another in the first years of the 1890s.

Tite Street was now regularly empty. Constance was finding London life too busy and demanding, and the industrial smog was dreadful. With Oscar spending more time away from her, she herself got out of town whenever she could. Among what one imagines were many more visits, her letters reveal that in February she went to see the Cochranes in Windlesham while Oscar made a brief trip to Paris. In May she and Oscar were guests of the Grenfell family at Taplow Court. In July, Constance was in Salisbury with Lady Grosvenor. And then in early August she and Oscar were both guests at Wrest Park in Bedfordshire, the country home of Lord and Lady Spencer Cowper.

During August and September 1891 Constance's travels continued. She made trips to Reading to see her friend Mrs Jean Palmer, to Great Berkhamsted to visit her friend Emily Thursfield, and to Brighton, probably to see her mother. After the latter trip she began to crave a country retreat of her own: 'I would give anything in the world to have a tiny cottage where I could take refuge from London at times when I feel overburdened, and when being 600 feet above the sea would refresh me.'[16] And so it was not long before she went to Georgina's clifftop retreat at Babbacombe, where it seems that she spent a fortnight in September.

Constance would take the boys with her on her longer sojourns to the Palmers in Reading or to Georgina at Babbacombe, where perhaps she felt the children were particularly welcome. But many of the other house parties she attended without the children. Constance often used the Palmers' ample home as a drop-off and pick-up point, spending a few days with them and then leaving the boys while she continued her country visits before returning to collect them some days later. Otherwise they remained in Tite Street in the care of nurses and governesses.

Perhaps it is little surprise, given its frequent emptiness, that the house in Tite Street was burgled in August 1891, the first of two occasions on which the Wildes were broken into. Valuable items were removed from the glass cabinet in the dining room which held both Oscar's and Cyril's silver christening mugs, silver claret jugs that had belonged to Oscar's father and it seems other heirlooms from Constance's side of the family. Although extraordinarily Oscar's family heirlooms were untouched, Constance and the boys lost prized possessions. Cyril's christening mug had been given to him by his godfather, Walter Harris.[17] Harris fortunately provided a replacement for his godson, but Constance lost everything else. Speranza noted at the time that her daughter-in-law looked 'charming even without her jewels'.[18]

The burglars were apprehended in November, and their stash, the product of some sixty-five housebreakings, displayed at King's Cross. Constance dashed down to see if anything had been salvaged from the Wilde household but was dismayed when nothing of theirs had been recovered 'in spite of the newspapers informing the world that we have recovered all our things'.[19]

The break-in did not deter Constance from heading to Dorking in the second week of October, to another house party, which included esteemed literary guests such as the writer George Meredith, who lived at nearby Box Hill. Constance described him as talking agreeable nonsense and being 'very pleasant and genial, though a strange being like all geniuses'.[20]

She joined this social gathering only after having the distress of saying goodbye to Otho. He and his new, second, family were returning to the Continent, fleeing from mounting debts and various calls on him from the sinking Leasehold Investment Company. Perhaps all too aware of the distress that separation from her brother had caused her, Oscar made sure that he wrote to his wife almost as soon as she arrived on this particular jaunt. 'I hear this morning from London Oscar that Willie Wilde is married in America to the rich widow who has been longing for ages to marry him!' Constance reported to Georgina from Dorking. In a very un-Constance-like line, she may well have been quoting from Oscar when she continued: 'The news has much the same effect upon me socially that poor Mr Parnell's death has upon me politically – that is, that it is the best solution of a difficulty, and that things in both cases will now right themselves.'[21]

Constance had forgotten, in relaying this latest news to Georgina, that her husband was not in fact in London while she was away, but was staying in Brighton. There was an arrangement that Oscar would join Constance and her party in time to celebrate his birthday on the 16th. Constance was excited at the prospect of seeing her husband but was disappointed that, after a night of storms over the south coast, he overslept, failed to catch the right train and discovered himself back in London instead.

Whether or not Oscar missed the train to Dorking accidentally on purpose, he made up for his failure to show with more loving letters. 'He has been so dear in writing to me since I came here,' Constance assured Georgina, 'and I have written to him, as I found he did not at all like my not writing to him when I was away before!!'[22]

The pattern of separation was set to continue into October. Oscar had been writing the play that would become *Lady Windermere's Fan* since the beginning of the year. By October it had reduced him to a state of nervous exhaustion, and he was much in need of a break. He informed Constance that he was planning to go to Paris with a friend to recuperate. Quite who the friend was that Oscar was proposing to take with him to Paris is not noted. But it may well have been Oscar's intention to take Lord Alfred Douglas with him.

Oscar had met 'Bosie' Douglas in June that year, as had Constance. Slight, blond and clean-shaven, he was an Oxford student and a Wilde fanatic. A practising homosexual who was himself exploring homoerotic themes in his own writing, he had become passionate about *The Picture of Dorian Gray*. When he had the good fortune to meet the author of this work, his admiration for Oscar, combined with his stunning looks, presented Oscar with the ideal formula for a new acolyte and lover. Bosie, instinctively controversial, captivatingly attractive and a genuinely talented poet, was just the ticket.

The poet Lionel Johnson made the introduction. The two young men had driven round to Tite Street after lunching with Lionel's mother in Cadogan Place. 'We had tea in his little writing room facing the street on the ground floor, and before I left, Oscar took me upstairs to the drawing room and introduced me to his wife,' Bosie remembered.[23]

Oscar was instantly smitten. Bosie, however, was not immediately attracted to such an older man. Nevertheless he met Oscar at the Lyric Club, where Oscar presented Bosie with a signed copy of *Dorian Gray*. Throughout the summer Oscar had continued to pursue Bosie, and the latter had continued to meet Oscar. It may well have been that Oscar was hoping that the romantic and exciting Parisian scene would be the one that would finally convert this budding, intense, new friendship into something with a sexual dimension.

Dutiful as ever, Constance left Dorking and returned to London in order to see her husband safely off. When she arrived at Tite Street on 22 October, plenty of news awaited her. To her dismay the doctor was recommending that Oscar take a six-week rest cure for his case of bad nerves. On the positive side, however, Oscar had finished his play and sold it to George Alexander at the St James's Theatre. 'This is a great pleasure to temper the sorrow at the separation,' Constance noted.[24]

Constance's return to London was brief. Practical as ever, she quickly fitted out the boys with winter clothing. She also made some moves to replace some of the valuables that had been stolen. With £10 from her insurers she bought a George IV silver teapot and sugar tongs. Her friends rallied round too. A Mrs Macpherson contributed a silver cream jug from the same period, and Jean Palmer promised to give Constance teaspoons.

On 23 October Constance took Cyril to wave his father off from Victoria station and was delighted that Oscar left her a copy of his new play to read. There is no mention of 'the friend' accompanying him. Perhaps Oscar had dropped his plans to take a companion at the last moment. Perhaps he had overlooked the fact that Bosie would be going back to Oxford for his Michaelmas term.

If Constance and Oscar acknowledged each other's right to pursue different lifestyles, accepting separation from one another, Constance still missed her husband. In that late October, when Oscar was in Paris and Lady Mount-Temple had not yet returned to London from Babbacombe, Constance began to suffer from depression. Although Constance was not technically alone – after all, she had both her children at home and refers to visits from friends, including the neighbouring Hopes – it was intimacy that she particularly craved. For Constance, Oscar and Georgina were the sole sources of this. With both of them away simultaneously, she felt adrift. 'I wish you would come back to Cheyne. London is unnatural without you, and I want you dreadfully now Oscar is away too . . . I can't live in the quiet <u>by myself</u>, and I am much more dependent than I was on fellowship and sympathy,' she explained to Georgina.[25] Constance's susceptibility to the blues would plague her for the rest of her life.[26]

By 26 October, Constance was preparing to leave the capital again, this time heading off to look after Aunt Emily, who had fallen ill. Emily Lloyd had moved to the seaside town of St Leonards after John Horatio's death. Constance was not looking forward to the trip, complaining to Georgina that she faced a 'fortnight's purgatory away from my bairns and all that I love'. Resentful that she faced missing Vyvyan's fifth birthday, she felt 'like a flower (a very weedy flower) transplanted into other soil that does not belong to it'.[27] When she arrived, Constance discovered she disliked the nurse Aunt Emily had hired and found herself sulkily knitting gloves for both her aunt and Georgina to pass the time.

But now Constance got ill again. She began to suffer from bouts of what she termed rheumatism. It was so severe in her arms that, like her or not, she was forced to ask this nurse to continually rub them for her. This episode of ill health would continue throughout the late autumn and winter months of 1891. She was regularly bedridden.

The one thing she looked forward to during her stay in St Leonards was Oscar's letters from Paris. 'Oscar writes in very good spirits from Paris, and never leaves me now without news, which is dear of him after all my grumbles,' she told Georgina, adding a few days later 'he really is very good in writing'. Oscar had told her she could read the play – which at this time still had the working title of *A Good Woman* – to her aunt. 'I think it very interesting, and hope it is going to be a great success, but one cannot tell unless one has great stage experience, how a play will <u>act</u>.'[28]

By mid-November Constance had waved goodbye to St Leonards and was back in Tite Street. Instantly her frantic London life resumed. Positive news from Paris buoyed her. Oscar had written to tell her that the French actor Coquelin thought *A Good Woman* 'faultless in construction and has recommended him a translator, and when it is translated will help him to get it acted in Paris!' Further news that her husband was embarking on 'writing a one-act play in French, and enjoying Paris and French people who are very kind to him seemed to cheer her further'.[29]

She took Cyril for portrait sittings – almost certainly with Laura Hope, a pastel artist of some renown who is known to have drawn him. She went to political meetings and she dined with the Palmers, who were in town, meeting Jean Palmer's Catholic father, Mr Craig. As a High-Church Anglican, Constance found Catholicism tempting, as did her husband and many other people moving in Aesthetic circles at the time.[30]

Once again it was not long before Constance made another excursion out of town, this time in connection with Vyvyan. She was worried about the general health of her younger son and she decided he would do well to stay with the Palmers for a month. Constance's determination to send a five-year-old away for a month feels brutal. It also adds credibility to Vyvyan's persistent feeling throughout his life that he was treated differently from his brother. In her letters to Georgina, Constance makes constant mention of Cyril. Vyvyan, by contrast, is rarely mentioned, except to express concerns. In 1891 alone Cyril has his portrait painted and Vyvyan does not. Constance sends Lady Mount-Temple Cyril's photograph, but no such picture of Vyvyan is offered. Georgina, who kept birds, sends Cyril two canaries, but apparently nothing to Vyvyan. Cyril sees his father off at the station, but Vyvyan does not. Cyril is referred to as his mother's 'Lovebird' in Constance's letters; Vyvyan is not described in such overtly passionate terms.

Cyril was clearly a deeply affectionate child. When Constance's aches and pains left her no alternative but to retreat to her bed, Cyril brought her hot-water bottles and proved attentive in a manner that his younger sibling did not and perhaps could not. 'He is my Dove now just come out of the egg,' Constance cooed.[31] Vyvyan was less demonstrative towards his mother, and generally more difficult.

The nurse who looked after both boys did her best to make up for what she saw as an inequality in their treatment. This did not go down well with Constance at all. Revealing the tougher, intolerant streak in her character, she complained to Georgina on this subject.

> I am getting more & more convinced that my nurse is not wise, and my cook tells me that she is ruining that dear little Vyvyan by indulgence, and that I should not allow it. What I am to do? She is so angry now at me sending Vyvyan away from her . . . She is kind and devoted to the child, but she is uneducated . . . it is becoming almost a monomania with her to think that every-one but herself is unkind to Vyvyan. She can never love Vyvyan as much as I do. I love him to the full as much as Cyril, but he is not interesting yet, because his soul has not awaked.[32]

When Constance returned to London, she came up with a plan that addressed the issues she had with the children's nurse. She sent her to Reading to assist in Vyvyan's care there. This, of course, left Constance more fully in charge of Cyril during the day. So now her already packed schedule was burdened further. In between visits to St Barnabas, attendances at lectures on Dante at University Hall, sessions with her phrenologist, Rational Dress Committee meetings at Lady Harberton's and visits to check on Speranza, who had now moved to nearby Oakley Street, she found herself also in charge of children's tea parties.

At this point Georgina lost patience with Constance. She could see a not very well woman rushing around and pushing herself to the limit. She told Constance to calm down and spend more time at home rather than being either endlessly out and about in town, or dashing up and down the country. Constance did not take kindly to being told some home truths.

'I have given up heaps of things since you asked me to do less,' she wrote at the end of November,

> and I don't want to live like a root! I am very well, and everyone says I am looking so well. I can't imagine what you want me to be like. I do a great deal of needle work and a fair amount of reading, and these things I can only do at home, and I spend dreary evenings by myself after Cyril goes to bed unless I go and see Lady Wilde. You talk to me as if I were never quiet and gadded about and I don't and I am very cross at your thinking so, and I shall not tell you any more what I do!!![33]

Georgina's concern seems to have focused on the fact that, in being away from home so often, Constance was not only exhausting herself but also contributing to her husband's absences. Georgina sensed a growing alienation between Oscar and Constance that matched their lack of time together. Georgina, like many women of her generation, believed that women's domestic duties were paramount. If a wife neglected these, then only she would be to blame if her household began to collapse.

Hurt by Georgina's criticisms of her, Constance was presented with what she considered proof of the love that still prevailed at the heart of her marriage when another letter from Oscar, who was still in Paris, arrived in the last week of November. If people were saying she was not paying sufficient attention to her husband, Constance was suddenly armed with evidence that, regardless of what they might think, Oscar loved her more than anything else in his life.

On Saturday 21 November 1891 a package arrived at Tite Street addressed to Constance. When she opened it, she discovered that it was Oscar's second book of fairy tales, *The House of Pomegranates*, hot off the press. On Oscar's instructions the publishers had sent Constance the first copy. She discovered the book was dedicated to her in the most loving terms. A day later a letter from Oscar in Paris revealed the full significance of the dedication.

'The book is dedicated to Constance Mary Wilde, and each separate story to one of his friends,' Constance wrote triumphantly to Georgina. She then dutifully copied out the private explanation Oscar had given her for the dedication. Her transcription provides one of the few remnants of the letters between Oscar and Constance that have been lost.

'And now see how the beloved Oscar writes this to me,' she continued.

> I shall not tell others, they would not understand, but you will: 'To you the Cathedral is dedicated. The individual side chapels are to other saints. This is in accordance with the highest ecclesiastical custom! So accept the book as your own and made for you. The candles that burn at the side altars are not so bright or beautiful as the great lamp of the shrine which is of gold, and has a wonderful heart of restless flame.'[34]

For Constance this was written testimony of the understanding on which her marriage now operated. Oscar had many claims on his affection and time, but in spite of this Constance remained at the centre of everything, the object of his profound and solid love. It was there in black and white. Joyous, she told Georgina that her feelings towards Oscar were entirely reciprocal.

'I have a cathedral for Oscar with a Lady-Chapel for the beloved mother, and there I always keep burning my lamp with its heart of restless flame, and there are times when one flies to the Lady-Chapel for sympathy and love, and here I fly now.'

Oscar also sent a copy of *The House of Pomegranates* to Lady Mount-Temple. In the accompanying note that he wrote, he explained how grateful he was to the elderly lady for the kindness she was showing his wife. 'You have allowed my wife to be one of your friends, have indeed given her both love and sympathy, and brought into her life a gracious and notable influence, which will always abide with her, and indeed has a sacramental efficacy over her days.'[35]

In light of the terrible scandal that would engulf Oscar within a few years, and in light of his persistent pursuit of men at this time, it is easy to assume that Oscar's words were quite hollow. With the letters he clearly dutifully wrote to his wife at this time lost, it is even harder to endorse Constance's belief that in 1891 her husband still loved her deeply. However, some of his unfinished work also suggests his continuing devotion to Constance in spite of his appetite for adventure elsewhere.

Before writing *A Good Woman,* or *Lady Windermere's Fan* as it would be re-titled, Oscar had begun a play titled *The Wife's Tragedy.* It was the beginning of an exploration of adultery with the plot involving a married poet by the name of Gerald Lovel who has an affair with another woman. While adultery was not, of course, an act confined to Oscar, there is perhaps a sense that he drew on his own relationship with Constance to deal with how marriage is not necessarily negated by extramarital affairs. 'Life is a stormy sea,' Gerald proclaims in the play, adding, 'My wife is a harbour of refuge.' And this was exactly true of Oscar's life with Constance. They now had different interests and were much apart, but there were still moments when Oscar was grateful for his family life with Constance and the children.

That Oscar still sought such quiet refuge in his deeply private life with Constance and his family is best evidenced by the holiday they took together the following year. On 19 August 1892 Constance wrote triumphantly to tell Georgina that she and Oscar were off to Grove Farm, Felbrigg, near Cromer, 'where Oscar will write his play and I shall vegetate and do nothing'. This play would be Oscar's follow-up to Lady Windermere, *A Woman of No Importance.*

Constance's sense of triumph was not misplaced. She and Oscar had left the decision to take a holiday by the English seaside far too late, and Constance, having found all the usual hotels and guest houses fully booked, had spent days 'telegraphing about' for accommodation.

The prelude to their holiday was a period of increasingly busy professional activity, and an increasingly precarious personal life, for

Oscar. In the ten months since Constance had opened the package containing that first copy of *The House of Pomegranates* the pace of Oscar's life had accelerated further, as had the controversy surrounding him. Oscar's sojourn in Paris had extended until late December 1891. He had become intoxicated with the intellectual life of the French capital and had grown bolder in displaying his homosexual appetites in a sexually liberated city. He had forged new flirtatious relationships with young poets and writers such as Pierre Louÿs and André Gide, and had indulged his hunger for experience, whether it was to be found in the 'lowest dives' or the most 'elegant cafés'.[36]

Not only was his social life acquiring a different dimension, but his professional career had also accelerated. After his return from Paris, Oscar was thrown into rehearsals for *Lady Windermere's Fan,* as the play was now called. On the play's opening night on 20 February, Oscar's friends flocked to see what would be quickly recognized as a triumph. Constance sat in a box with her aunt Mary Napier and the solicitor Arthur Clifton.

But Oscar's own performance on the night was indicative of the way in which his persona was changing. No longer the 'respectable married man' whom journalists had noted at Constance's side a few years earlier, he now presented himself as a more challenging figure. After the curtain fell on that first night, Oscar went on stage to be admired by his audience. But the tone he struck, rather than delighting an audience he should have had in his hands, astounded many of them. With his cigarette still alight in one hand and his mauve gloves pressed in another, Oscar complimented the audience on their good taste. It was a joke, of course. But for many the underlying egotism was too rich a taste, particularly when combined with smoking in public – an act considered by those outside the bohemian circles in which Oscar and Constance moved to be impolite and particularly discourteous to women.

The American writer Henry James was among the audience on that first night, and he also noted another distasteful aspect of Oscar's persona. He was wearing in his buttonhole a strange metallic blue flower. In fact, it was a carnation, dipped in a solution of malachite green dye, which, when absorbed by the flower, turned the white petals a green/blue colour.

But it was not just Oscar who was wearing this deeply unusual coloured flower. In the audience many of the young men to whom Oscar had given tickets were also wearing at his bidding what became known as green carnations. Robbie Ross was there, along with his friend More Adey. John Gray was there too. All were wearing the dyed flower.

In this one gesture the sea-change in his life must have been apparent to many. Once it was Constance who had dressed in outfits to match or complement her husband's. Once it had been she who had been paraded by him through galleries and premieres. But at the opening of his own play, although Constance was in attendance, it was Oscar's young male friends who were engaged in his theatrical antics.

After the show Constance and her aunt headed off. Oscar, however, was not staying at home. There were issues with the drains in Tite Street. Constance and Cyril were staying with Georgina Mount-Temple in her home on Cheyne Walk, and Vyvyan had once again been dispatched to stay with the Palmers in Reading. Oscar meanwhile had taken rooms at the Albemarle Hotel. And it was back to this establishment that Oscar went with another young man, the publishing clerk Edward Shelley. For the past few days Shelley and Oscar had been much in one another's company. Unbeknown to Constance, Shelley not only went to the Albemarle with Oscar that night, but he did not leave.

By May, Oscar's affair with Shelley had waned, and instead Bosie had once again come into the frame. In the spring of '92 Bosie was blackmailed and turned to Oscar for help. Oscar immediately sought the counsel of his old family friend the solicitor George Lewis and managed to pay off the blackmailers and extricate Bosie for the sum of £100. It was this act of salvage and generosity that finally clinched Bosie for Oscar. By June they were in a sexual relationship with one another, and from this moment Oscar embarked on what would become the most intense and profound love affair he had ever had.

Meanwhile the play he had written during his last trip to Paris, *Salome*, had gone into rehearsal at the Palace Theatre with Sarah Bernhardt cast in the title role, only to be shut down by the Lord Chamberlain's Office because of its combination of biblical and sexual content. With controversy once again surrounding him, in early July, Oscar, exhausted and stressed, headed for the German spa town of Bad Homburg, where, conveniently, Bosie was also on holiday. While he was away, the press speculated on whether Oscar would now leave Britain to live permanently in France, a threat Oscar had indeed offered on the banning of *Salome*.

Constance's friends rallied around her while Oscar was away. 'People are very kind to me,' she told Otho; 'I dine out, and go to the theatre and enjoy myself.'[37] But Constance was troubled at night. The boys had had whooping cough. Constance slept with one or other of them at night, but Vyvyan's coughing meant a broken night, and if she slept with Cyril he was wide awake by half-past six.

No wonder, then, that by the time Oscar returned to British shores Constance was desperate for a holiday. So on 20 August, after her admirable efforts to find rooms at short notice, Constance and Oscar arrived at Felbrigg with a view to staying there until the end of the first week in September. It was time for quiet recuperation, and time to regain that sense of family which had become diluted by recent activities.

The boys were on holiday together at Hunstanton in Cambridgeshire, and as she settled in, Constance began to make plans for the forthcoming weeks. It is clear that at this stage, although Oscar's relationship with Bosie had begun in earnest, it had not negated that with his family. Far from it: Constance was still a significant source of solace and calm for him, his sons a genuine font of joy. What is more, she was still very much in charge of arrangements.

'We are in such a fascinating farm in sweet air and country, 2 miles from Cromer,' Constance informed Georgina the day after they arrived in Norfolk.

> It seems difficult to get from here to Hunstanton, but I shall try and fetch Cyril for a week he will be so happy here with dogs and turkeys, and geese, and ducks and chickens, sheep and cows and all things to delight a child. The only thing I fear is that Oscar will get bored to death, but we have heaps of room and can ask people down to cheer him up . . . Cromer Church is far off but there is a little old church in the Park about a mile from here where the farm owner has taken me this morning.[38]

Mr and Mrs Wilde quickly settled into a routine. In the mornings and evenings they would work: Oscar writing *A Woman of No Importance* and Constance corresponding with the various societies and causes to which she was attached. But then in the afternoon they were together and would often go walking 'into Cromer where we generally come across some friend to have tea with. It is doing us both so much good, and I am already quite well, I recover as quickly as I get ill.'[39]

On 25 August, Constance left her husband to his writing and headed over to Hunstanton to see her children. When she arrived, she was disappointed to find them looking paler than she had hoped. Vyvyan was left in Cambridgeshire, and Cyril brought back to Cromer for some good Norfolk air. When mother and child returned to the farmhouse, they discovered that Oscar was so enjoying the rural idyll that he had decided to extend their stay there until 17 September. His morning writing was going well, and he felt he could finish the play.

'We go lovely drives all thro' the bracken and heather – scarcely any gorse – and Oscar thinks of Herrick's line "a green thought in a green shade". He says he must have been thinking of a place just like this when it was written,' Constance informed Georgina in one of many happy letters written across these weeks. She also revealed that Oscar had come across a new pastime. 'I am afraid Oscar is going to become bitten with golf mania. He played his first game on the links here yesterday and has joined for a fortnight.'[40]

On the last day in August Oscar's friend Arthur Clifton joined the party. He had married that summer, and he and his brand-new bride joined the Wildes as part of their honeymoon. And then, a day later, Constance received another telegram informing her that another of Oscar's friends was on his way for a visit.

'Having got all our rooms quite full yesterday a telegram comes from Lord Alfred Douglas asking to be put up for a night! I don't believe that even you have to contrive to put 7 people into 6 rooms. However, fortunately he put it off till to-day, and I think we can manage.'[41]

The day after Bosie arrived, Constance had to return Cyril to Hunstanton. When she got back to Cromer, she discovered that, far from staying for just a day, Bosie had installed himself for the duration. She didn't mind too much. The daily golf sessions Oscar began enjoying with Bosie were a source of amusement for her rather than concern. 'I am becoming what I am told the wives of golfers are called a "golf-widow",' she quite happily related to Georgina.

Before everyone went their separate ways, Constance arranged to commemorate these happy days. 'We are all going to be photographed in a group here tomorrow and if they are successful you shall have a copy.' She then headed for Babbacombe Cliff to see Georgina, while the rest of the party broke up. Oscar wanted a week alone at the farmhouse to finish his writing.

Some of the photographs from this session still exist. In one, Oscar, looking slim and handsome, stands with his arm on Cyril, while Constance looks down at a book placed on a small garden table. It is an image of contentment and calm. But for Constance, at least, this was her last happy summer holiday with her husband. In Cromer, Constance knew that, in spite of his myriad distractions, her husband remained at some level loyally devoted to her. It was, however, a situation that was about to change. Bosie Douglas would make sure of that.

The moment Constance and the Cliftons left Felbrigg, Bosie conspired to stay. Determined to place himself at the centre of all aspects of Oscar's life, Bosie suddenly became too ill to travel. This would be an illness that would conveniently place him and Oscar alone together for a whole week.

Constance was quite oblivious to Bosie's manipulations. 'I am so sorry to hear about Lord Alfred,' she wrote to Oscar from Babbacombe, 'and wish I was at Cromer to look after him. If you think I could be any good, do telegraph to me, because I can still get over to you.'[42]

Such a telegraph, of course, never came.

II

A dark bitter forest

THE SUMMER OF 1893 was peculiarly hot. The signs of an imminent heatwave began to emerge in the spring. In April residents of Coventry sweltered in 26.7° sunshine, while Cambridge reached an astonishing 28.9°, record temperatures for the time of year that remain still unbroken today. Between 4 March and 15 May not a drop of rain fell on Mile End in the East End of London, still the longest recorded run of consecutive dry days in the UK. By June local papers and magazines were celebrating the potential bounty that such a shift in the climate might produce for the nation's gardeners, naturalists and foragers. Butterfly enthusiasts would have more luck than usual if they took their nets out, since some varieties, such as the Duke of Burgundy, with its golden spots and white-tipped wings, were exceptionally producing second broods in the warm weather. There was almost certain to be a bumper crop of early mushrooms, the *Penny Illustrated Paper and Illustrated Times* announced to its readers – just as long as some heavy rains came to break the heat. And such downpours were indeed delivered as the summer reached its peak. In August, Preston in Lancashire saw the heaviest shower ever noted, when 32 mm of rain fell in just five minutes.

London's fashionable men responded to the heat by discarding the customary waistcoats that were worn in the summer months in favour of a new craze for colourful bandanas or cummerbunds. Women, meanwhile, could take to the beach in the swimming suits that were now available for them, with their long knickerbocker legs and tabard tops. By October that year these were publicized further in the hit musical *A Gaiety Girl,* in which the female chorus was clad entirely in bathing attire.

But the heat had its tragic consequences too. Businesses began to suffer, not least the West End theatres. After calls by the public for the installation of electric fans to cool the insufferably hot auditoria, twenty-three venues eventually just closed. Far more serious than loss of business was loss of life. London's mortality rates increased significantly over the previous year. And there were sad accidents too – none more awful, perhaps, than the tale of young Emil Goth. This eleven-year-old boy took tickets at the Jubilee Public Baths in Betts Street in London's East End. That August the baths were swamped by hot working men who wanted to cool off, and the newspapers reported that consequently the officials supervising the bathing establishment were 'taxed to their utmost' – so taxed indeed that they failed to notice that on closure of the baths one day an exhausted Emil removed his own hot, sweaty clothes and jumped into the pool. He was unaware that the large, nine-inch drain had just been opened to empty the pool. The huge amount of water pouring into the drain took Emil with it, sucking him down into the great underwater pipe, where his tiny body lodged in its bend. He had drowned long before anyone was able to extricate him.

Since June, Oscar had been renting a cottage at Goring-on-Thames, a very picturesque riverside village between Reading and Oxford. Although better than broiling in London, even at Goring there was no escape from the heatwave. 'It is so fearfully hot that I can do nothing at all not even think,' Constance wrote to Georgina Mount-Temple.[1]

For Constance, the holiday in Goring could not have been more different from the modest stay in Cromer of the previous year, with its country drives and golfing expeditions. The stifling temperatures meant that she and Oscar were limited in the activities they could pursue. Tennis was out of the question, and croquet was just about all they could cope with. Constance described herself as being 'cross and horrid', not least because of the terrible Old Testament thunderstorms that were keeping her awake at night. 'The heat is so great here, and last night God's thunder-angels woke me and I had visions of his Splendour in the lightning flashes,' she told Georgina.[2]

Storms were catching the holidaymakers out during the day too. One day when Arthur Clifton's family visited, Constance and Clifton's wife, Marjorie, went boating, only to be caught in a downpour. The two women had got 'drenched to the skin, a lake was formed in the boat and pools of water in which ducks might have swum on our laps', Constance related.

The cottage was close to the home of the comic actor and author George Grossmith and his wife, who became regular visitors with their children. They would join in the croquet tournaments and on two occasions at least participated in evening 'theatricals'. But the local Grossmith family were far from being the only guests. Most of the other guests were there at the invitation of Bosie Douglas. He was playing host at Goring, and as a result there came a constant stream of his friends, whom he was indulging with the utmost extravagance.

Bosie's bacchanalian court was kept supplied with champagne and luxury foods ordered and delivered from London's finest food halls, again at Bosie's behest. The bills for these decadent indulgences were, however, being paid out of the Wilde coffers, newly replenished after a change in fortune. *Lady Windermere's Fan* had proved a financial triumph for Oscar. It is estimated that he had probably received £3,000 in royalties. In early 1892 Constance had also come into a legacy when Aunt Emily finally expired in St Leonards, leaving her £3,000. And then a year later her other aunt, Carrie Kirkes, died, leaving a further bequest of £5,500.

The sense of abandon extended beyond those who were guests at Goring. Unlike the relatively simple holiday in Cromer, where Constance had arranged just one cook to attend to their needs, eight servants had been engaged for Goring. Although in the past Oscar had always left the appointment of servants to Constance, this time it was Bosie who had chosen the staff for Goring. Harold Kimberley, the butler, had once served Bosie's father, the Marquess of Queensberry. Walter Grainger was a young man Bosie had got to know in Oxford, who had been invited down to become the under-butler. These, along with the parlour maids and cooks, proved a riotous crew. With the strange, stifling, oppressive and intermittently stormy weather, nature merely contributed to the equally stifling and stormy atmosphere within the cottage itself. Everyone was tense. Sometimes the staff would get drunk on the left-over champagne. 'More scenes in the house here,' Constance confided to Lady Mount-Temple, 'and I shall not be sorry to leave, for they worry me. All such excellent servants and yet they cannot get on together.'[3]

It was not just the servants who were being badly behaved at Goring. After his years of courteous devotion to his wife, Oscar had suddenly changed. Apparently, for the first time ever he was being rude to her in public. And after his years of telling her his plans and proposed movements, now he was declining to inform her of his whereabouts.

'I cannot make out whether it is my fault or Oscar's that he is so cold to me and so nice to others,' Constance wrote in despair to Georgina, adding, 'He is gone to Birmingham to see his play acted there tonight. His butler knows his other plans and I know nothing. Darling, what am I to do?'[4] Later she informed Georgina that 'Oscar is, I believe, up in London and returns to Goring tomorrow but now I am going to be mother to my children and leave my wife-hood to brood in darkness until sunshine comes again.'[5]

The simple fact was that Constance was no longer the heart of the Wilde household. She was no longer the cathedral of her husband's devotion, nor was she any longer considered a calm harbour of refuge for him. During the course of a year she had been usurped. Since their holiday in Cromer just a year earlier, Oscar had effectively entered into a new marriage, with Bosie Douglas. The fact he had not bothered to tell his wife of this extraordinary shift in his affairs was only just beginning to dawn on the woman who had always chosen to see the best in the man she married. In less than twelve months she had lost her husband. Although she scarcely comprehended it, the likelihood of the 'sunshine' returning any time soon was remote.

Things had really begun to change soon after Cromer. This holiday had persuaded Constance that being away from London was a

good thing, both for her and for Oscar. She began to look for a country retreat for them. In October 1892 Constance attempted, but
failed, to raise a £3,000 mortgage in order to buy a country house of
her own. Although this was after her legacy from Aunt Emily, one
can only assume that a substantial amount of those monies had gone
on paying existing debts. Constance had been helping Speranza
financially, and she was also repaying debts to Otho, whose own precarious financial situation left him little choice but to call them in.
Otho's business affairs were crashing.

'I wonder if you have heard there has been another call on the
Leasehold Investment,' Constance informed her brother that
October. 'Your secretary has told Mr Hargrove that they intend to
call up every penny and then the shares will be lost. I'm fiercely afraid
that this means swallowing up all your profits, Mr H says that you
should have evaded your last call so they might not find out your
address.'[6]

Otho did, in fact, finally heed the family solicitor's advice. Within
months he had dropped his family surname in favour of his middle
name, Holland. Constance meanwhile worked with Hargrove to get
what fortune he had left settled on Mary, his second wife. Thus,
living in Switzerland under an assumed name, Otho Lloyd Holland,
as he now was, began a long evasion of his creditors.

Throughout the autumn of 1892 the chasm between Oscar and
Constance widened. Their social circles became more and more different. Through Lady Mount-Temple, Constance reignited her passion for Pre-Raphaelitism. She began associating with the now aged
painters who still survived from this group. So while Oscar was
exploring the company of a group of younger men to whom he was
now extravagantly offering silver cigarette cases as tokens of his love
and affection, Constance was forming friendships with more elderly
people, for whom she had a real sympathy.

In her letters Constance talks about visiting Little Holland House
throughout 1892. This was the Kensington home of the painter
George Frederic Watts, a great friend of Georgina's. Constance found
herself acting as a messenger and courier between the seventy-five-

year-old Watts and her similarly aged friend. She took the painter some 'spirit drawings' from Georgina, and by return reported back to Georgina on the state of Watts's health. That August he was 'suffering from eczema in the foot that was mosquito-bitten the other day'.

Watts had painted Georgina Mount-Temple, and Constance now found herself in his home looking at the photograph of the original that Watts kept. 'Your face was there in the gallery,' Constance assured Georgina. It was no doubt in good company since Watts had also famously painted the poet laureate Alfred Tennyson, whose memorial service Constance would dutifully attend at St Paul's Cathedral in October 1892.

Another person with whom Constance socialized at Little Holland House was Henry Herschel Hay Cameron, the son of the Pre-Raphaelite photographer Julia Margaret Cameron. They spent an afternoon looking through an album of photographs together. Many Victorian photographs were staged, presenting moments from literary or biblical narratives. One such in Henry Cameron's collection, a depiction of the Prodigal Son, haunted Constance. She thought it 'the most touching and the most exquisite, abandonment of grief and misery, and . . . abandonment of love given and received'.[7]

Cameron and Constance had known each other for some time, certainly since 1889, when he had photographed Cyril wrapping his arms around his mother's neck with tender abandon, and had also taken a portrait of Oscar. It may well have been Constance's friendship with Cameron that inspired Constance herself to take up photography during the forthcoming year, but not before she returned to him with another commission. On her return to London from Cromer she took Cyril to have his solo portrait taken by Cameron. Vyvyan, it seems, was once again excluded from this experience.

Despite her disappointment in not securing a country retreat of her own, Constance's desire to get away from London remained, and so in November she rented Babbacombe Cliff from Georgina Mount-Temple, with a view to staying there for three months, until 17 February. After a very cold journey Constance and Cyril arrived at the clifftop house on 17 November 1892.

'My own darling,' she wrote to Georgina, 'I arrive at this sad sweet house . . . it seems more wonderful than ever to me that you should have let me have it . . . I had to part from husband and brother today and mother last night, so do not scold me if I seem sad.' The next day she continued, 'Bab is looking very well after much rain . . . I intend hiring a piano that the drawing room may look as it did with you, and I am going to try to teach Cyril to sing . . . and now I am going to meet Vyvyan. The air is so lovely and soft here, that I think he will be cured almost immediately . . . Cyril sends you feather from pigeons.'[8]

While she waited for Oscar to join her, Constance passed her time reading Dante's *Inferno* and making the house ready. She filled the rooms with branches of bayleaves that the gardener, Mr Hearne, had cut from the garden. The boys were boisterous. Cyril managed to run into Mrs Hearne, the housekeeper, and cut his face under the eye.

Every day Constance and the boys expected Oscar, and every day his arrival was delayed. Originally due to join his family at the end of November, he eventually turned up on 3 December after a brief trip to Paris. He came armed with tin soldiers for the children.

Within two days snow had descended on the house and its gardens, and Oscar was wrapped up in bed. He was ill and in retreat at the doctor's behest. His high living was reaping consequences. His nerves were in tatters, and one presumes he was suffering the effects of his massive appetite for alcohol and cigarettes. Lack of sleep was almost certainly also a contributing factor, since Oscar had fallen into the habit of staying up into the early hours.

'I fear darling, that exile from London comes nearer & nearer,' Constance informed Georgina, 'and Oscar has been so ill last week that again the doctor says he must not live in London.'[9] One wonders whether this advice was given as part of a wider concern for the company the patient was now all too noticeably keeping in the metropolis.

For a while the family settled into a routine of domestic bliss. Mr Hearne, who was also the local coast guard, agreed to take Cyril round the coast. Constance visited the Turkish baths to soothe her aching arms and legs. Oscar fed the pigeons, 'who are so cheeky now that they come flying if the window is opened to see whether it rains. They sit in rows along the branches of the fir trees now and look so pretty.'[10] And he began to tell his wife and children stories.

'Oscar has found a book that interests him of supernatural stories – he told me last night a story that I think would interest you. It happened to a cousin of his, Mrs Walker, one of Father Maturin's sisters, an entirely unimaginative person,' Constance related to Georgina. The Maturins and Wildes were related on Oscar's mother's side. Charles Maturin was a relative of Speranza. He had made his name earlier in the century as an author and playwright. Oscar was an admirer of his novel *Melmoth the Wanderer*. 'Father Maturin' was the novelist's grandson, a controversial High-Church figure with papist leanings.

Father Maturin's sister 'had a little boy who died when he was a child', Constance continued,

and when he was very ill was taken to Eastbourne where he lay in bed in the drawing room looking out of a window at the sea. One day they noticed a dove which kept fluttering up and down outside the closed window, and which attracted the child's attention and pleased him. At about 3 o'clock in the afternoon he died, and a few hours afterwards the dove was found dead on his breast, tho no one knew it had got in, and the window was still shut. So the boy and the dove were buried together. What do you think the white dove was? We are so surrounded with the supernatural; I wish I could have some experience of it.[11]

During their extended residence at Torquay, Constance and Oscar took a break at the end of December to attend to other matters. Cyril and Vyvyan were left at Babbacombe in the care of their French governess and the Hearnes. First stop for the Wildes was London. Constance spent New Year's Eve with friends in De Vere Gardens in Kensington, probably because the bulk of the servants had been let go at Tite Street. Constance was house-hunting in London now. Oscar did not share his wife's desire to leave the metropolis; regardless of what the doctors were suggesting, London life was key to him.

So Constance now sought a larger family home in Chelsea. The lease on Tite Street was coming up for renewal in June, and Constance probably felt there were many reasons to be moving on from it. 'I expect to be very busy while I am in London,' she had told Georgina earlier, 'for I want to look for a small abode for Lady Wilde, and also for something for ourselves, for I quite agree with Aunt Carrie. Oscar will never live out of London, & I shall live alone in exile if I take a house in the Country. And we must settle on something or we shall be turned out on the street next June!'[12]

In fact, Constance's stay back in London was short. As 1893 got under way, rather than reopen Tite Street, Constance headed to Witley to see her friends the Lathburys. She then returned to Babbacombe briefly in mid-January with Oscar and Robbie Ross, before heading on to Plymouth to stay with the Walkers, those cousins of Oscar's who had featured in his story about the boy and the dove. Another quick return to Babbacombe to see the boys was merely a prelude to a trip to Italy with her aunt Mary Napier and cousins Eliza and Lilias. They would be *en route* for the Continent in the last week of January.

If Constance and Oscar's relationship had survived their respective travels in the first two years of the decade, Constance made a fateful mistake in assuming it could survive similar separations going forward. She had not counted on the influence of his latest best friend. In leaving for Italy in early 1893, Constance left Oscar to his own devices at a time when his relationship with Bosie Douglas was just beginning to take on new depths. Her departure provided the moment in which Oscar's infatuation with Bosie, and the latter's extraordinary power over the older man, really cemented.

In fact, Oscar's delayed arrival at Babbacombe had something to do with Bosie. Oscar's friendship with the young lord had led to several other new acquaintances. Through Bosie, Oscar had become friendly with a young homosexual called Maurice Schwabe, and through Schwabe, Oscar and Bosie had got to know Alfred Taylor. Taylor, a good-time guy and committed homosexual, lived in Little College Street in Westminster, where he held soirées and procured 'renters' – young male prostitutes – for his friends. In the autumn of 1892 Taylor had introduced Oscar to one Sidney Mavor, a twenty-year-old who had ambitions to go on the stage. He was one of those youths who were given a silver cigarette case by Oscar. Meanwhile on 18 November, when Constance was filling the house in Babbacombe with bayleaves, Oscar and Bosie were having tea in Little College Street, meeting Schwabe's latest conquest, a young cockney renter called Fred Atkins. That evening all five men – Bosie, Oscar, Taylor, Schwabe and Atkins – dined in town.

Oscar was becoming consumed by this new circle of homosexual men. The notion of his 'sons' had taken on an entirely new dimension. The ease of sex with 'renters' was a temptation he seemed unable to resist.

On 21 November in Babbacombe, Constance was in the depths of reading Dante's *Inferno*. She felt in the midst of a crisis. 'I feel every word of it true to me. I am approaching the middle of the path of my life, and I am lost in that dark bitter forest. I certainly was asleep when I entered it and I know not how I entered it or when!' she wrote to Georgina. 'And then comes my bane the leopard of envy that pursues and torments me so much ... And you darling Mother must be my Virgil and seeing me weep have pity on me and guide me right ... You haunted me so last night that I thought you were in my room in spirit, winging me to get up and see the sunrise.'[13] Oscar, by contrast, had decided to whisk Fred Atkins off to Paris for a few days.

And now, in January, Oscar's socializing with Bosie and the Taylor set continued. Bosie had come across a replacement for Atkins, a young unemployed clerk called Alfred Wood, who was living in Taylor's rooms. Within days, while Constance was conveniently out of the way on her trip to Witley, Oscar began taking Wood back to Tite Street.

In late January, Oscar went back to Paris, almost certainly in connection with the publication of his play *Salome,* which was imminent. Constance had a 'delightful peep at Oscar in Paris' on her way to Italy. Oscar informed her there 'that he would like to stay on at Bab till March and write his play for Mr Hare . . . The children will come home on the 17th and this will be better for Cyril to go to school and for Oscar to be alone.'[14] The play Constance alludes to was *An Ideal Husband*. That Oscar would be writing this alone at Babbacombe was not, however, how things turned out.

Constance made Turin by 2 February. The journey was difficult, and her 'neuralgia' returned, felt this time in her head and back. In spite of her discomfort, she had enjoyed watching Europe unfurl, 'looking so wonderful in its garb of snow' from the windows of her warm wagon-lit. Two days later she and her party were in Florence, having taken in Pisa *en route*. Aunt Mary Napier and her daughter went on to Naples with the plan to rejoin Constance later in Rome, but Constance was far from alone in Florence. There was her other cousin, Lilias, who was also travelling with her. But then there was also a raft of friends who, like Constance, had chosen to escape wintry London in favour of Italian sunshine. Laura Hope was in Florence, as was Miss Cunninghame Graham. The George Wyndhams, relatives of Bosie, had a villa, and Constance's old schoolfriend Bessie Shand was staying with them. Robbie Ross's mother was not far from Florence, and the artist John Rodham Spenser Stanhope and his family were also there. Constance's days were packed. Alongside a rigorous schedule of sightseeing that she set for herself, she also enjoyed a whirlwind social diary.

Constance took a Kodak camera with her to Italy and began to photograph everything. Kodak had introduced a portable camera that took roll film in 1890, and in the following year they had developed daylight-loading film, ideal for tourists unable to access a dark-room. Constance's cousin Lilias, who was her companion in Florence, found the process of taking Kodaks tiresome. Constance preferred the company of her cousin Lizzie Napier, who had happily trudged the streets of Pisa with her.

My cousin Miss Napier (who is not with me here but has gone on to Naples with her mother) is much more 'sympathetique' to me than

Lilias and is ready to wander about and look for odd churches and wait while I take kodaks and I am looking forward to being at Rome with her. We saw the Duomo, the Campanile, the Battisteria (where I saw a funny little bambina Anna christened) the Campo Santo a wonderful little church on the banks of the Arno, Santa Maria Della Spina and an old church of St Paolo that Lizzie and I found in the afternoon. Don't you think that is good for half a day?[15]

Constance was not just taking photographs of buildings. She was also photographing some of the art around her, as well as exploring her own artistic talent. 'I hope you liked the two scrappy photographs I put in for you yesterday,' she wrote to Georgina. 'They were meant to be sunbeams.'[16]

Florence must have wooed Constance into a false sense of security. In a bizarre way the holiday did nothing but reinforce the social wealth her life and career with Oscar had brought. The people she was mixing with were a reflection of the friendships and interests they had built together. These cultural pioneers were not restricted to living in London; they could live in the greatest artistic cities of Europe if they wished. She began to persuade herself that she and Oscar might actually leave Tite Street and take up residence in the magical city of Florence too:

Don't be surprised if you hear of my flitting here . . . I love Florence with a passionate love and yearning as I have never loved any place before, only people. Still I don't know whether I shall get Oscar out here, though he does speak of it as a possibility, and to me it seems more than a possibility, a delightful future to look forward to.[17]

While Constance continued her education in Florentine art and culture, back at Babbacombe Bosie and a colleague, Campbell Dodgson, had joined Oscar. Bosie had been sent down from Oxford for failing his exams, and Dodgson was supposed to be tutoring him. Far from the solitary, studious atmosphere Oscar suggested in a letter to Georgina ('Babbacombe Cliff has become a kind of college or school, for Cyril studies French in the nursery, and I write my new play in Wonderland, and in the drawing room Lord Alfred Douglas

– one of Lady Queensberry's sons – studies Plato with his tutor'[18]), in fact the three men were having something of a riot.

After Dodgson left Babbacombe, Oscar wrote to assure him that 'I am still conducting the establishment on the old lines and really think I have succeeded in combining the advantages of a public school with those of a private lunatic asylum.' As a memento he added a brief prospectus for Babbacombe School, as follows:

Headmaster – Mr Oscar Wilde
Second Master – Mr Campbell Dodgson
Boys – Lord Alfred Douglas

Rules

Tea for masters and boys at 9.30am
Breakfast at 10.30
Work 11.30–12.30
At 12.30 Sherry and biscuits for headmasters and boys (the second master objects to this)
12.40–1.30 work
1.30 lunch
2.30–4.30 compulsory hide and seek for headmaster
5 Tea for headmaster and second master, brandy and sodas for boys
6–7 work
7.30 dinner
8.30–12 Ecarté, limited to five-guinea points
12–1.30 compulsory reading in bed . . .[19]

Now the house in Tite Street was burgled for a second time. This time nothing was taken. Which raises the question, just what were the burglars looking for? By associating with 'renters', Bosie and Oscar were laying themselves open to blackmail. Having also slept with Alfred Wood, Bosie gave him a suit of clothes, overlooking the fact that there was a compromising letter from Oscar in the pocket. Within a month Wood would attempt to blackmail Oscar with the letter. It's tempting to speculate that he may well have been behind the break-in at Tite Street a little earlier, looking for more compromising material against the fêted Mr Wilde.

Oblivious to the double life her husband was now leading, after Florence Constance headed for Rome. On 19 February she got up at the crack of dawn and attended Jubilee Mass at St Peter's. 'The enthusiasm of thousands of people waving hats and handkerchiefs in that enormous building while the beautiful "Papa" was carried through the nave and round the Tribune, she explained to Georgina. 'I was glad to have the dear old man's blessing.'

'Oscar writes to me every day & must be written to every day,' Constance also stated, adding later that 'Oscar has quite made up his mind to spend next winter in Florence.'[20] Although a regular exchange of letters with one another had gone on during their periods of separation across the two previous years, now that Oscar's life was becoming so geared around Bosie Douglas, Constance's revelation that she and Oscar were still writing regularly seems surprising. Many accounts of Oscar's life have failed to recognise how much his wife remained in his thoughts. The fact is, however, that in the spring of 1893, Oscar was still torn between Bosie and Constance.

Although enthralled by him, Oscar's relationship with Bosie was ambivalent. While he was hooked on Bosie, at another level Oscar understood how damaging the affair was. It was not just the money he was spending on Bosie and his circle, nor the danger that the 'renters' they shared presented, but Bosie's personality was twisted and difficult. Demanding and hedonistic, greedy and selfish, Bosie Douglas also had tantrums that wore Oscar down. In fact, when Bosie left Babbacombe Cliff, Oscar said he was 'determined never to speak to you again, or to allow you under any circumstances to be with me, so revolting had been the scene you had made the night before your departure'.[21]

His letters to Constance were Oscar's last attempts to throw a life-line back to his formerly stable family life. But it was one growing weaker and weaker. Oscar was increasingly under Bosie's power, and, although she clearly did not know it, every day Oscar was with Bosie diminished the bond between him and his wife. Despite the elder man's resolution to break with his young love and acolyte, he was weak. Later Oscar would recall to Bosie that after the scene at Babbacombe 'I consented to meet you, and of course I forgave you. On the way up to town you begged me to take you to the Savoy. That was indeed a visit fatal to me.'[22]

Returning from Devon at the beginning of March, Oscar took a suite at one of London's most expensive and prestigious hotels. He and Bosie had adjoining rooms. The renters continued to come and go. Constance was meanwhile beginning to make her way back from Rome. She stopped in Florence again, now with the express purpose of looking at apartments. She was quite certain that she and Oscar would be back there together the following September and October. Earnest and hungry for knowledge as ever, she made sure that, when not viewing rooms, she was continuing to see every splendour of Florentine art still available to her. She had with her Ruskin's guide-book *Mornings in Florence* and attempted as best she could to follow his recommendations.

'I went with St C[23] to Santa Croce yesterday,' she faithfully reported to their mutual friend, 'not at sunrise as he thinks right, but armed with an opera glass and studied . . . the Giotto *St Francis*. When I come back to London I shall read nothing but Italian Art; nothing can exceed the vastness of my ignorance about it all.'[24]

Full of the joys of Renaissance art she may have been, but when Constance's feet touched British soil again on 21 March, she was mortified. Oscar was not waiting for her in Tite Street. He was staying at the Savoy with Bosie. The house in Tite Street, full of unopened post, felt as if it had been deserted. Whatever sweet nothings he had written to her while she was abroad, Oscar no longer seemed interested in seeing his wife now she had returned home.

Some of Oscar's friends began to feel disenchanted with him in the spring of 1893. Oscar and Bosie presented new behaviours that the old established circle of Wilde admirers – even the homosexual ones – found not only unpalatable but dangerous. John Gray, the original model and dedicatee of Dorian Gray, terminated his friendship with Wilde. And the man to whom Wilde dedicated *Salome*, Pierre Louÿs, also ended their relationship, not least because he witnessed what he considered Oscar's shameful treatment of Constance.

After their stay at the Savoy, Oscar and Bosie moved on to the Albemarle Hotel, no doubt telling Constance that it was important to be close to the rehearsals for *A Woman of No Importance*, which were now under way at the Haymarket Theatre. Louÿs visited Oscar and Bosie in their hotel rooms. Constance came round to deliver some post to her husband. When she complained that he no longer came home, Oscar announced for all to hear that he no longer remembered his address. He did so without an ounce of guilt. Constance left in tears, and Louÿs was horrified.

A Woman of No Importance opened in April. As the press reported, the opening night was conspicuously well attended, with 'Mr Balfour . . . in a stage box, accompanied by Mr George Wyndham and the Countess Grosvenor, while in the corresponding box on the opposite side was Lord Battersea with Mr Alfred Rothschild'. The stalls were glittering with celebrities drawn from artistic and literary circles: 'Lord Randolph Churchill and Lady Sarah Wilson, the Marquess and Marchioness of Granby, the Earl of Arran, M. Henry Rochefort, Mr and Mrs Chamberlain, Mr and Mrs Shaw Lefevre, Mr Alma Tadema, Miss Florence Terry, Mr Justin H. McCarthy, and Miss Jenoure, Mr Swinburne, and of course Mr Wm Wilde represented his brother.'[25]

Constance is not mentioned in the press as one of the celebrity attendees, but given that she and Oscar had attended a reception at the New Gallery just six days earlier, it seems unlikely that Constance would have missed the opening of her husband's second play, in spite of the recent personal difficulties between the two.

The audience applauded the play, but this time there were hoots and hisses at the author when, clad in a white waistcoat with lilies in his buttonhole, he came to bathe in their praise. It was not just Oscar's close friends who were noticing a change in his attitude and behaviour. The general public, it seems, had picked up on the rumours about his personal life, and his scandalous relationship with Bosie Douglas. As if in acknowledgement of this, the actor–manager responsible for the production, Herbert Beerbohm Tree, announced, as he took his curtain call, that he was 'proud to have been connected with such a work of art', a statement that raised applause, one imagines, from the large number of Oscar's invitees in the audience.

In spite of the souring of his public profile, Oscar suddenly found himself the recipient of £100 a week. This income could not have come at a better time for a family still generally outliving their means. But to Constance's dismay the much-needed income did not seem to improve matters. Rather than plough it back into family finances, Oscar was spending it on a new lavish lifestyle, on Bosie Douglas, on hotels and, unbeknown to her, on rent boys.

And so as the hot summer of 1893 got under way, Constance had lost any sway she had formerly held over her husband. Oscar was out of her control and totally captivated by Bosie. While Oscar had resisted Constance's former suggestions that they should buy a property out of town, at Bosie's suggestion he now took a year's lease on the property in Goring and began a pattern of spending that, with the rental, cost the Wildes some £3,000. As a result, not only was Constance snubbed, but the likelihood of the proposed autumn in Florence was also greatly diminished.

Although she and Cyril joined Bosie and Oscar in Goring in June, Constance and her son were an odd adjunct to the heady goings-on. Antics at the house were causing something of a stir in the village. One day the local vicar called to discover Oscar and Bosie wearing nothing but towels, larking on the lawn and turning a hosepipe on one another in the stifling heat. The new governess, Gertrude Simmons, whom Constance had employed to replace the French governess the boys had had at Babbacombe, also felt uncomfortable. One evening, during a firework display at a local regatta, she spotted Oscar with his arm around the boy employed to look after the boats.

'I very much wish that Oscar had not taken the Cottage on the Thames for a year – things are dreadfully involved for me just now,' Constance moaned to Georgina.[26] It was the first of many complaints she would now begin to share with several of her female friends. If Constance had been in denial about her husband up to this point, it seems that the truth was now dawning on her. In August she visited Mrs Lathbury in Witley again and clearly confided some of her fears and troubles.

'Mrs Lathbury has given me what I believe to be very good advice, and the advice that she always gives me, I shall try & follow it for 6 months and let you know the result,' Constance rather gnomically relayed to Georgina after the visit.[27]

Despite the year's lease that he had taken, by September Oscar had done with Goring. He was exhausted by his three-month stint with Bosie and needed to escape. He fled to Dinard in Brittany, where he spent the end of August and the first week of September. 'I required rest and freedom from the terrible strain of your companionship,' Oscar would later write to Bosie.[28]

Some accounts place Constance and the boys with Oscar in France. But in fact her letters suggest that she stayed in England, moving between London and Goring. After returning from Witley, she entertained guests at Goring in Oscar's absence, including her friend the painter Henriette Corkran. On 1 September she dashed to pick up Vyvyan in London and returned to Goring with him. Whereas Cyril and Governess Simmons had been resident in Goring for most of the holiday, Vyvyan had been with the Palmers again for the summer.

Constance's continuing habit of moving Vyvyan from pillar to post in this period begins to feel like the actions of a woman who was not only neurotic about her younger son's health but had in fact lost the capacity to cope with the responsibility of a second child. Vyvyan was 'sweet and affectionate but so extraordinarily wilful and wayward that he gets more and more difficult to manage', Constance claimed.[29]

Vyvyan could not stay by the Thames in the current climate, Constance wrote to Georgina. After just a few days with his brother there began a new search for another household that could take on the youngest member of the Wilde family. Initially Constance wrote to the Burne-Joneses in Rottingdean to see if they would have him. When the reply came that there was no room immediately in their household, he was dispatched to Brighton to stay with Constance's mother.

When Oscar returned from France, he settled up his bills in Goring and returned to London life. On 9 September or shortly thereafter Constance and Cyril also returned to London to greet Oscar, and, after a fortnight in Brighton, Vyvyan moved to nearby Rottingdean where, finally, room had become available for him in the Burne-Jones household.

Constance left town to settle Vyvyan in with the Burne-Joneses and stayed a few days there herself. Her marital problems were now being widely discussed and it's clear that the Burne-Joneses had their own advice to offer too. 'I have taken Vyvyan to Rottingdean and Mrs Burne-Jones is going to look after him. As for Mr Burne-Jones I am quite in love with him! He sent his love to you and said that I was to tell you how I had last seen him – and this was wheeling his two grandchildren in their perambulators to save the nurse trouble,' Constance related to Georgina. '[H]e asked me if I had any religion to help me, and I said that no-one could get on without it. This family life is so beautiful, Mr & Mrs Burne-Jones, Margaret & the husband and babes!! There I am going off again into dreams of what might be, wrong and foolish of me.'[30]

By 28 September, Constance was on her way back to London but was dismayed that Oscar failed to meet her at the station, a courtesy that he had always extended to her in the past. In later years Bosie Douglas would ardently deny that his relationship with Oscar caused the deterioration of the Wilde marriage. He conceded that relations between the couple had become 'distinctly strained', noting that Oscar was now 'impatient' with Constance 'and sometimes snubbed her, and he resented, and showed that he resented, the attitude of slight disapproval which she often adopted towards him'. With the most appalling lack of self-scrutiny, however, Bosie would claim that 'to try and make out that this had anything whatever to do with me is simply dishonest and untruthful.'[31]

There is no doubt that Oscar and Constance's marriage hit its lowest point to date during that summer of 1893. And regardless of his inability to take responsibility for it, there is also no doubt that Bosie was largely the cause. And yet the sad truth is that Constance also helped exacerbate matters by allowing the chasm growing between her and her husband to widen. Her almost relentless absence from Tite Street at a time when everyone else around her could see Oscar courting very real danger is hard to explain, except perhaps in terms of her fleeing from a situation that she did not wish properly to confront. Constance was going out of her way now to avoid her husband. From Rottingdean she had attempted to negotiate a brief stay with Georgina in Babbacombe at the end of the month. If Georgina could not take her, she would have to return home to Tite Street, 'but for reasons that I will explain when I see you I would rather not go there!'[32]

Constance wrote a short children's story at around this time, and perhaps in it there is some clue to the approach she took to her husband. Entitled 'The Little Swallow', Constance's story was published in late 1892. It may have well been inspired by the pigeons that she often fed during her sojourns at Babbacombe, since it begins with an image of children 'looking at the birds eating the crumbs that nurse has thrown out in the snow to them'.

As the children watch the birds eating crumbs, their mother tells them another story about a 'little bird', this time 'a tiny swallow'. The swallow is discovered on the ground by a young girl called Beatrice. It is spring and the 'little swallow had tried to fly too soon, and so it had fallen down, and could not get back to its nest'. Beatrice nurses the swallow; she 'picked it up and kissed it'. The swallow grows big and strong and soon learns to fly around inside Beatrice's house. But one day, when Beatrice is out, someone opens a window and the swallow flies away, 'singing for joy at the fresh air and bright sunshine', and the child is heartbroken. Beatrice thinks she will never see the bird again, but then to her delight one evening the swallow comes back and visits her as she sits in an open window. Ever since then 'he has come twice every day to get his food quite regularly . . . and Beatrice is very happy again'.[33] Perhaps Constance felt that, in exchange for his freedom, Oscar, like the swallow in her story, would always return to the domestic security his wife essentially provided him.

At the end of September, Constance went into a religious retreat at the convent of St John the Baptist at Clewer, Windsor. She was *en route* to Eton, which she was considering as a school for Cyril. The convent was part of a wider High-Church religious community in the area. It was associated with the Society of St John the Evangelist, the first Anglican religious community for men to be established since the Reformation.

But Constance had specific associations with Clewer. Father Maturin, Oscar's relative, had also taken a retreat with the Society of St John the Evangelist in the 1870s. Two of his sisters, Fidelia and Johanna, were now members of the convent, and Constance almost certainly went to see them and to seek some answers to her troubles within the austere atmosphere in which they lived. 'Last night I was put ignominiously to bed and dosed with bromide and this morning I feel pretty bad!' she related to Georgina.[34]

Shortly after this she went to stay with the Thursfields at their home in Great Berkhamsted, before going on to spend some time in Leighton Buzzard with the medium Sarah Wagstaff, a homoeopath and clairvoyant who had treated and assisted both John Ruskin and Georgina in medical and spiritual matters, and who would have almost certainly been recommended by the latter to Constance. Cyril accompanied her on her travels while Vyvyan was still with the Burne-Joneses. At Leighton Buzzard Constance once again sought advice on how best to cope with and manage her domestic situation. And finally it seems that she was told some home truths.

'Just back from Leighton Buzzard and have been district visiting since and am so tired. Mrs Wagstaff has been so kind and helpful about the children and other things. When I see you, I will tell you, but it is too "intime" to write,' Constance informed Georgina on her return to London on 9 October.[35] She picked up the thread again the next day, revealing that 'What Mrs Wagstaff told me in trance has not comforted me, but it is best to know the truth and I know that I of my own power can do nothing. I must pray for my boys and when they are older teach them to pray & to struggle.'[36]

Otho would always deny that his sister knew about Oscar's homosexual adventures, right up until his trial. But in the aftermath of what was to come he was keen to protect Constance's moral reputation. Constance's determination to pray for her boys surely indicates that finally she admitted the likelihood that Oscar's friendship with Bosie was more than just that, and that her sons might one day be susceptible to similar sexual predilection.

Amid their rapidly deteriorating relationship Oscar and Constance still had moments of intimacy, but they were few and far between. Constance was becoming increasingly tempted by Catholicism, an inclination that had been nothing but intensified by her recent visit to Rome and her introduction to the Maturins. Oscar too from his earliest student days had always been attracted to Rome. In October 1893 the couple found themselves alone at Tite Street and began to discuss the matter.

> I have been having wonderful talks with Oscar lately and I am much happier about him. But he thinks that it would be ruin to the boys if I became a 'Cat'. No Catholic boy is allowed to go to Eton or to take a scholarship at the University . . . imagine my surprise to find that Oscar goes to Benediction at the Oratory sometimes & other things that he does surprise me more still! He will not go himself with me there, but he would like me to go & burn candles at the Virgin's altar and offer up prayers for him. Remember that I can never broach these subjects to him myself and it may be years before he speaks to me again like this, but I shall not forget that he has these moods, and last evening he said a great deal to me. I shall go to the Oratory tomorrow and I shall burn a candle for Oscar and one for Mother.[37]

Perhaps Constance failed to pick up that Oscar's request to offer prayers for him might have been, if not a direct plea for help, something close to an admission from him that he was now in deep trouble. Bosie had in fact left Oxford University in June, having refused to sit his exams. During the holiday in Goring, Oscar had tried to help his lover as best he could and had suggested Bosie translate *Salome*, which Oscar had written in French, into English, and share something of the credit when the work was published in its English edition. But a terrible crisis had occurred when, by the end of August, it was apparent to Oscar that Bosie's translation was less than good. Throughout September the two had argued over the book's proofs, with Bosie rejecting Oscar's corrections and Oscar refusing to accept a second-rate version of his work.

'After a series of scenes culminating in one more than usually revolting, when you came one Monday evening to my rooms accompanied by two male friends, I found myself actually flying abroad next morning to escape from you,' Wilde would later recall, 'giving my wife some absurd reason for my departure, and leaving a false address with my servant for fear you might follow me by the next train.'[38] The incident was particularly painful and embarrassing for Constance, since it coincided with a major family event. Her cousin Lilias was getting married to one Henry Bonar, who worked in the consular service in Japan. Oscar was naturally expected to attend the ceremony.

'Yesterday I made the acquaintance of my new cousin Henry Bonar . . . he had a godmother Constance and after her is called Constant, so . . . we made friends over the beautiful name. I do <u>love</u> my name so much, and think it one of the most beautiful names in the world; don't you? I think that one should have beautiful names given to one and that then one should try and live up to them.'[39] So began Constance in that day's letter to Georgina, before revealing rather desperately: 'I am unhappy because Oscar is not at all well, and had to fly off yesterday morning to Calais to meet a friend there; he declined to go to Paris to the friend so they agreed to meet half way. I have got a Liberty dress for the wedding and Oscar is not here to see it!'[40]

Constance's reference to Oscar's health in the same breath as mentioning his unexpected departure for France is intriguing. Her letters of this period are full of references to him being 'unwell'. It's tempting to see Constance's references to Oscar's health as some form of unconscious euphemism for his homosexuality. Just as some medics considered it a curable illness, it's just possible that Constance was discussing possible 'cures' for her husband's condition with her close female friends, such as Mrs Lathbury.

If Constance had resolved to accept her husband's homosexuality, whether its source was an illness or no, she was not prepared to absolve him of poor conduct. Constance was furious when Oscar announced he would not attend Lilias's wedding. When he returned to London the next day, he was still smarting from what had clearly been a fiery row between the two of them.

'Oscar is back in town but not with me,' Constance confided to Georgina. 'I hope he comes back tonight – all my old misery over again and another fiasco.'[41]

12

Modern-day Martha

LILIAS'S WEDDING PROVED a watershed moment. As Oscar was sitting on the train hurtling across France, he realized 'what an impossible, terrible and utterly wrong state my life had got into, when I, a man of world-wide reputation, was actually forced to run away from England, in order to try and get rid of a friendship that was entirely destructive of everything fine in me either from the intellectual or ethical point of view'.[1]

On returning home to face the music, he resolved to change. And change he did. In late October and November 1893 the signs Constance had desperately sought – that perhaps there was still hope for her marriage – began to emerge. For a start, Oscar refused to see Bosie. He even took steps to have Bosie sent abroad. He wrote to Bosie's mother, Lady Queensberry, who, as Wilde himself conceded, had 'on more than one occasion' consulted him about her wayward son, and expressed his concerns.

'Bosie seems to me to be in a very bad state of health,' Oscar wrote. 'He is sleepless, nervous, and rather hysterical . . . He does absolutely nothing, and is quite astray in life, and may . . . come to grief . . . Why not try and make some arrangements of some kind for him to go abroad for four or five months, to the Cromers[2] in Egypt if that could be managed?'[3] Bosie was duly sent to Cairo. And the minute he was gone it was as if a cloud had lifted in Tite Street.

Constance, sensing the change, acted on some advice that Georgina Mount-Temple had offered her in a previous year. If she had had plans to spend the autumn out of town she cancelled them, and instead sorted out Tite Street. It had been empty for so long, it was time to turn the house into a home once more. She began the search for staff, not least a cook. As always, her trials and tribulations were related in detail to Georgina: 'I am Martha today troubled with many things. My new cook comes in tonight & my temporary one left me yesterday in a rage. So I have had to cook breakfast & dinner for the household – very amusing for a change but tiring too. To-night Oscar and I feast at the club.'[4]

On another day it was not the cooking she was attending to, but the household laundry.

> I wish you could see me in my new capacity learning 'gracious house-hold ways' doing my housekeeping properly! This morning I have arranged all my house linen in a new linen cupboard which I have had made, and I am very proud and pleased at my household stores. I have got a charming cook & housemaid, and once more I am happy in my house. To-night Oscar and I . . . dine at the Club and go to hear William Morris lecture on Printing.[5]

Mr and Mrs Wilde began to resemble the society couple they had once been. They were dining together regularly and attending lectures together. They were noticeable as a couple at their club, and were once again visible in London's theatres. They saw *Love's Labour's Lost*, *Measure for Measure* and *School for Scandal,* all within one week in November, and discussed the performances with one another as they had used to. 'The Shakespeare play last night was very interesting but exceedingly badly acted,' Constance twittered happily to Georgina. 'Oscar says that he never for a moment missed the stage scenery, and believes that it is a quite unnecessary adjunct to a really good play. However we did not sit it thro', because the poor acting made it so dull.' *School for Scandal,* on the other hand, went down well with the Wildes, and Constance admitted 'it was nice being there with Oscar.'[6]

Constance also became involved in Oscar's work again. This time she used her not inconsiderable talents as a linguist to translate a review of *Salome* that had been noticed in a Dutch newspaper and sent to the Wildes. She and Oscar suspected that a Dutch translation of the play had been published without Oscar's permission. Constance turned detective, tasked with trying to acquire a copy of the book.

Oscar even paid Constance the compliment of attending some of her dinner parties. 'To-night I have some friends to dinner only 4, but this is quite an excitement to us, as Oscar never cares to have anyone,' a delighted Constance boasted to Georgina.[7]

As the Wildes worked to re-establish the family routine they had once enjoyed, Vyvyan was recalled from Rottingdean and reinstalled with his brother in the nursery they had scarcely seen over the last twelve months. Oscar took rooms in St James's Place, where at 11.30 each morning he could sit down to write, undisturbed by his sons. And Constance renewed her search for a large London family home. She persuaded Oscar to view one in Elm Park Road, which, she explained to Georgina, although 'not so near to you as Tite Street is, still I could get to you even from there'. Oscar decided he did not like the house, but the fact he had viewed it must have felt like an achievement to Constance.

The children had not been oblivious to the stresses in their parents' relationship. Cyril certainly just wanted his mother and father to be happy together again. Constance related a poignant story to Georgina without perhaps grasping the full significance of it. Just before Lilias's wedding Cyril and Constance began playing a game together which centred on the idea that Cyril's toy donkey should perhaps get married too. Over the next few days they bought another toy donkey to play the bride ('black but comely') and a toy tea set for the wedding tea. Finally, on 21 October, they staged the donkey wedding in Tite Street.

Cyril wanted the ceremony to be religious, Constance explained to Georgina, 'so I read him the psalm about the wild asses quenching their thirst in the wilderness with the streams of water that God had made . . . and this satisfied him, and he said "That's enough, now they are married". He refused to have donkey in bed with him last night "No he's married now, and must look after his wife!" '[8]

It's hard not to read this game as an expression of Cyril's own wishes: for his father to look after *his* wife. And for a few brief months this childhood wish was answered. 'We are both of us very happy at these times and he is writing a wonderful little play (not for acting but to be read).'[9]

By the end of November people were noticing the improvement in the Wilde marriage. Constance put Oscar's good behaviour down to more than just Bosie's absence. She felt supernatural forces were at play. In fact Oscar had been altered by a 'communication from ghost-land if you care to call it so (I do not) given thro' raps by a father to his son', Constance revealed to Georgina. 'The father had appeared at a séance to his son, but this communication was given when he was alone, and has so altered his life that his friends are noticing & commenting on the change, which I trust will last. What was said I will tell you when I see you alone; it seems to me so wonderfully true.'[10]

Whether or not it was the benign influence of Sir William Wilde from beyond the grave, nevertheless while Bosie was abroad between November 1893 and February 1894 Oscar finished *An Ideal Husband*, his third major play, which he had been struggling with throughout the holiday in Goring, and he also wrote both *A Florentine Tragedy* and most of *La Sainte Courtisane*. His behaviour most certainly changed, his excesses moderated, and he reinvested in his marriage.

And then Constance made a terrible mistake. Throughout his exile Bosie had been attempting reconciliation with Oscar, bombarding him with letters. Oscar had stood firm and resisted them. But in February 1894 Bosie changed tactics and telegrammed Constance, begging her to use her influence on her husband and persuade Oscar to see him. Quite why Constance acquiesced to the demands of the man who had nearly destroyed her marriage is a mystery. It may have been that the four happy months she had spent with Oscar back in Tite Street had lulled her into a false sense of security. But for whatever reason, Constance, in at once an act of extraordinary kindness and pity and incomparable stupidity and naivety, encouraged Oscar to travel to Paris and meet Lord Alfred Douglas there.

'Our friendship had always been a source of distress to her [Constance],' Oscar would later recall; 'she saw how your continual companionship altered me, and not for the better; still, just as she had always been most gracious and hospitable to you, so she could not bear the idea of my being in any way unkind – for so it seemed to her – to any of my friends . . . at her request I did communicate with you.'[11]

Within days Constance must have realized her folly. Taking advantage of Oscar's trip to Paris, she took Vyvyan to stay with her cousins, Mr and Mrs Harvey, who lived in Torquay. With her retreat there, all her former suffering resumed. The version of Oscar that she thought she had reclaimed over the Christmas season evaporated. The man who could write to her daily once more fell silent. Suddenly communications from her husband ceased. With no news in the post she had no idea whether he had yet returned from Paris.

Aware that Constance was hunting for a family home in London, and experiencing some financial worries of her own, Georgina Mount-Temple suggested the Wildes take a lease on her large London house in Cheyne Walk. In correspondence with Constance on the matter, Georgina must have read with some alarm the letters she was receiving from Torquay. Despite Oscar's recent successes, the Wildes were oddly still without means, and Oscar had vanished again.

'Alas! Your delightful suggestion is, I fear, impossible for us,' Constance explained.

> Both the boys must have to go to school this year, and this will cost me at least £200 a year, and O is making nothing. I wish we could take your lovely house not only for our own sakes, but to help you, and to have you to stay with us. I don't know where Oscar is; I have not had a line from him since he went to Paris, but when I can I will ask him about it.[12]

Finally, at the very end of February or in the first few days of March, Constance discovered that Oscar had returned home. 'Oscar is in London again,' she relayed to Georgina, 'but I know nothing about his doings and he does not write!' With the issue of renting the latter's house in Cheyne Walk still unresolved, Constance promised to 'write to him, but I know he will see the impossibility of it all even more than I do!'[13]

But dealing with family homes and the boys' schooling had lost its appeal for Oscar as he renewed his company with Bosie. In the week that Bosie and Oscar were in Paris they fell back into their former decadent ways. They had lived it up at the Hotel des Deux Mondes in the Avenue de l'Opéra. Their lavish wining and dining did not cease on their return to London.

'I am storm driven, but it is the storms of my heart that drive me more than the world's storms,' Constance wrote miserably from Torquay, 'and I am like the city without walls "because I rule not my spirit".'[14] By mid-March, Constance had returned to Tite Street. Oscar was once again icy. She was unaware that in the month Bosie and Oscar had been in town while she had been with her cousins, new, worrying events had occurred.

Bosie's father was beginning to make trouble for Oscar. John Sholto Douglas, the Eighth Marquess of Queensberry, was a noisy, notorious, brutish aristocrat. He disliked 'effeminacy' in men and particularly in his son. By 1894 Bosie's association with the notoriously effete Oscar had been well noticed, and he was becoming almost as much a star as Oscar himself. Bosie was now a rival for those column inches that, as the intimate of the successful playwright, had once been reserved for Constance. The Marquess was horrified by this and felt sure that Oscar was having an unhealthy influence on his son.

In the spring of 1894, just days after Oscar and Bosie returned from Paris, Queensberry saw them in a carriage together and thought he saw Oscar caress his son inappropriately. He also saw them at the Café Royal together. This prompted a letter to Bosie in which the Marquess threatened to stop Bosie's allowance unless he gave up his 'loathsome and disgusting relationship' with Oscar. The Marquess alleged terrible things in the letter: he had heard that Constance was to petition for divorce from Oscar. This last allegation seems to have had little firm foundation but probably reflects the level of society gossip that had been gradually growing since the previous year, when

Bosie and Oscar stayed at the Savoy together. Certainly over the Channel, Pierre Louÿs contributed to gossip in Paris that Oscar had left his wife and children and was living with Bosie instead. Combine this with perhaps comments from some of Constance's female friends who were aware of her distress, and it is not hard to imagine how 'divorce' would quickly spring to the lips of scandal-mongers.

Bosie did not care a fig for his father's concern and rebutted the Marquess's letter with a short telegram that read 'What a funny little man you are'. Queensberry's fury erupted into new threats to make public what was 'already a suppressed' scandal.

Constance and Oscar had been discussing the need to send the boys to school for some time, and now, with their parents' relations once again deteriorating, the spring of 1894 was a good time to pack them off to their respective establishments. Constance had taken the lead in the search for the right school for Cyril and Vyvyan. Her letters to Georgina Mount-Temple in September and October 1893 make mention of options under consideration, including Eton and an establishment at Ascot where her friend the socialite and journalist Lady Jeune sent her son. News that Constance was making the decisions about her sons' education spread far and wide. It was usually the prerogative of the male head of the household to determine where sons and heirs would get their grounding in life. But, of course, Constance and Oscar had always been pioneering and liberal in their approach to life, and this moment was no exception. Bizarrely, the press as far afield as America picked up on the story: 'Mrs Oscar Wilde . . . has won a place for herself in her husband's brilliant circle,' the *New York Times* noted, adding 'an hour's talk with her shows that she has read and thought on the problems of the day. Entirely to her Mr Oscar Wilde has left the training of their two sons.'[15]

Constance, as in so many other aspects of her life, proved faddish and pioneering in her choice of school, for Cyril at least. In mid-November she noted to Georgina that she had spotted a school described 'in the *Pall Mall* last week, of which I have now got full particulars . . . it seems to me to be on the proper lines of a school, tho' quite unlike the present system'.[16] The school was Bedales, the subject of an article entitled 'Schooling without Tears' in the 5 October edition of the *Pall Mall Gazette*. This 'new school' was billed as combining the virtues of 'Greek Particles and Potato Digging'. The brainchild of one J. H. Badley, Bedales in Haywards Heath was to be an alternative school where study was combined with manual work such as carpentry and gardening. Bedales set itself outside the traditional school system which, Badley felt, specialized far too early. Instead, boys at Bedales would learn good personal habits, character training and general culture alongside the more traditional scholastic disciplines, which would be limited to a mere four hours a day.

For Vyvyan, on the other hand, Constance selected a more traditional preparatory school, Hildersham House in Broadstairs. The estuary air was probably considered beneficial for the perpetually unwell Vyvyan, and the headmaster, Mr Snowden, was kind.

Oscar did eventually head out for the city of which Constance had become so enamoured the previous year – Florence. But in a move that must have felt particularly hurtful, he did not go with her. He travelled out to join Bosie there in May 1894. Lady Queensberry had dispatched her son to Italy in an attempt to weaken his revived relationship with Oscar. But the separation did nothing but strengthen resolves – a point not lost on Bosie's father, who decided to take matters into his own hands.

On the afternoon of 30 June 1894 Queensberry turned up at Tite Street, accompanied by a rough, burly bodyguard. Oscar was forced to confront the irate Queensberry, who had been shown into his study by the Wildes' hapless butler, Arthur. Oscar suggested that Queensberry had come to apologize for the statement he had made about Constance in the letter to Bosie. But far from it: Queensberry parried with new accusations. He suggested that Oscar and Bosie had been kicked out of the Savoy Hotel the previous year for disgusting conduct, and had consequently taken rooms together in Piccadilly. Oscar asked the Marquess outright if he was accusing him of sodomizing his son. The Marquess replied that he did not make that direct accusation, but that the couple posed as if that were the nature of their relationship, which he considered as bad as the real thing. He finished with a threat to thrash Oscar in public. Oscar retaliated with a threat to shoot Queensberry, and then ejected him from the house.[17]

Constance was in London that June. She may well have been at Tite Street to witness the confrontation at first hand. Oscar's study, on the ground floor of their home, was directly under that summer drawing room, with its Japanese vases and peacock feathered ceiling, where she spent much of her time. If Constance had been at home, it's inconceivable that the Marquess's ranting would not have been heard in that room at least. But even if she had managed to miss this spectacular confrontation, Constance could not have been blind to the wider emerging brouhaha that was being whipped up.

Throughout July, Queensberry made a point of hunting for Bosie and Oscar in their preferred restaurants, with a view to making a scene if he caught them together. Bosie bought a pistol, which he carried loaded. It went off in the Berkeley, an accident that only served to heighten gossip.

Despite his bravado, Oscar was genuinely concerned that the Marquess might carry out his threats. A public accusation of sodomy would ruin him. And so that July he sought to have the ranting aristocrat gagged. He approached his old friend and associate the solicitor Sir George Lewis to see if he could have a restraining order placed on the Marquess.

Lewis, who had after all attended Wilde's wedding, and who had over the years provided plenty of paternal advice and legal assistance, as well as representing Oscar in some of his earliest professional engagements, delivered a piece of shattering news. Oscar's adversary, the Marquess, had in fact already retained him in connection with the allegations.

Shocked, and no doubt feeling betrayed by an old colleague, Oscar was forced to engage the services of another lawyer, recommended by Robbie Ross, Mr Charles Octavius Humphreys. Humphreys duly wrote to Queensberry asking him to retract his libels or risk litigation.

The letters was utterly ineffectual. The choice of Humphreys as his legal counsel would prove one of Oscar's worst mistakes.

There seems little doubt that Constance had sunk into utter despair in the spring of 1894. The man she adored clearly infatuated with Bosie again, her boys away at boarding school, and now with the Marquess threatening terrible things, it is not hard to see how she might for once turn for solace not to one of her elderly ladies but to another man. And this is exactly what she did. The gentleman in question was someone she met professionally.

Constance had never been afraid of earning money. Far from it, she relished paid work. And in 1894, when, despite her husband's apparent success, the Wilde coffers were once more empty, she rolled up her sleeves again in an attempt to bring in more cash. She had been trying for a while to expand her repertoire as a writer beyond her theatre reviews and children's stories. As far back as 1892 she had suggested to Otho that they collaborate on a book structured around letters between 'a fiancé and fiancée . . . or a husband and wife, or brother and sister',[18] but this project was yet to take shape. In the meantime, however, another idea had presented itself: to compile a collection of Oscar's sayings and epigrams, under the title *Oscariana*. Determined to make this project her own, she approached the publishers she had been working with in connection with her *Rational Dress Gazette*, Hatchard's in Piccadilly.

Arthur Humphreys, who was the general manager of Hatchard's at the time, agreed to take on *Oscariana* and to oversee the publication. Meanwhile, Oscar, who had turned down similar proposals in the past, was clearly only too happy to give his blessing to anything that at once kept his wife occupied and brought in more cash.

Humphreys and Constance began work together. It's worth remembering just how beautiful Constance was at this time. She is rarely mentioned in the press or in memoirs without being noted as particularly pretty. Her tendency to coyness and her deep sonorous voice had already proved massively attractive to a number of men, both before and since her marriage. Humphreys, like several before him, quickly fell under her spell.

The timing of Humphreys' interest in Constance is crucial. She had rebutted advances in the past quite easily. But in the early summer of 1894 Constance was perhaps as unhappy as she had ever been. The interest that Humphreys expressed in Constance, otherwise neglected, must have reminded her of that interest that the young Oscar Wilde once had in the shy and much ignored Miss Lloyd. Moreover, she had not had a sexual relationship since the birth of Vyvyan in 1886. Constance fell madly in love.

In June, after one session working on the book, Constance and Humphreys began to talk about their respective marriages. Clearly the dissatisfaction with Oscar that she had shared with her female friends was now recounted to a man. And he in return revealed his own unhappy marriage. Constance wrote to him afterwards.

> Dear Mr Humphreys
>
> I feel as though I must write you one line to emphatically repeat my remark that you are an ideal husband, indeed I think you are not far short of being an ideal man! Forgive me if this seems in any way rude. You know that I am a hero-worshipper down to the tips of my fingers, and somewhere near the head of my list I now put you!
>
> It must have seemed horribly inquisitive of me to ask you so many questions, but I am not inquisitive, as you will see for yourself when you know me better, and I cannot explain what made me ask — certainly not any outside influence! But I liked you & was interested in you, & I saw that you were good. And it is rarely that I come across a man that has that written in his face. And so I stepped past the limits perhaps of good taste in the wish to be your friend and to have you for my friend. I spoke to you very openly about myself, & I confess that I should not like you to repeat what I said about my childhood; I am afraid it was wrong to speak as bitterly as I did. But if we are to be friends as I hope we may be, you must trust me. Indeed I can be trusted, as I believe that you can be. I am the most truthful person in the world, also I am intuitive.[19]

The last line suggests that Constance is feeling towards an affair. She instinctively senses a mutual attraction. She reassures Humphreys that she will be discreet. These signals were clearly responded to and acted on. After the last few years of misery Constance had found someone who loved and respected her once more. By August she was writing to 'My darling Arthur' and explaining:

> I am going to write you a line while you are smoking your cigarette to tell you how much I love you, and how dear and delightful you have been to me today. I have been happy, and I do love you dear Arthur. Nothing in my life has ever made me so happy as this love of yours to me has done, and I trust you, and will trust you through everything. You have been a great dear all the time quite perfect to me, and dear to the children, and nice to Oscar too, and so I love you, and I love you just because you <u>are</u>, and because you have come into my life to fill it all with love and make it rich.[20]

At the beginning of August Constance secured a house in the seaside resort of Worthing from her friend Miss Henrietta Lord, the educational reformer, translator of Ibsen and Christian Scientist. Miss Lord's means were comparatively modest, and she had made her home available while she was away in the spa town of Matlock seeking a remedy for rheumatic gout. It offered a holiday in stark contrast to the high life Oscar had been leading in London. But then it was exactly Oscar's entertaining at the Savoy and Café Royal that had forced Constance's hand in choosing the property. They were overdrawn again, and a budget holiday that cost 10 guineas a week was all they could afford if they wanted to spend the summer together by the sea.[21]

As the house was not even properly equipped, Constance had to take all her own linen and kitchen equipment from London in order to cater for her household, which at that time included a new Swiss governess, who had replaced Miss Simmons, a cook, a maid and Arthur the butler. The latter – so young that Constance described him as a 'page boy' – was tasked with taking the children to the beach and sailing, alongside his normal duties.

Her first guest at her holiday home arrived on 7 August. When Constance was barely installed, a young minister, Mr Lilley, called on her in Worthing. Lilley was a preacher whose name begins to feature quite heavily in Constance's correspondence in 1894 onwards, and it seems that there was a passionate friendship developing between them.

Lilley was an associate of the high-profile Revd Eyton, the rector of Holy Trinity Church in Upper Chelsea. Eyton and Lilley, like Constance, were signed-up members of the Christian Social Union, an organization that sought to find ways of applying 'the principles of Christianity to the social and economic difficulties of the present time'. Both men were radical and reforming. Constance's recent trips to do good in Paradise Walk had been encouraged not just by Georgina but also by the rousing sermons of the rector, who proposed engaging in the 'toss and tumble of this common life'. He warned his congregation that they must be prepared to be 'bothered by human unreasonableness, and saddened by human distress'. His protégé Lilley saw Christianity as a force for wider political change. In his lecture on 'Democracy and Government' he saw God at work in the new, emerging democratic landscape, the champion and saviour of the working man who was at last finding his voice.[22]

Constance was deeply impressed by the young, politically active Lilley, and were it not for the evidence of the love letters between Constance and Arthur Humphreys, it would be tempting to speculate that Constance and Lilley's friendship was verging on something more intimate. But it was Arthur Humphreys, who came and spent a Saturday night in Worthing a few days later, with whom Constance 'walked about and enjoyed the air and the sea', as she revealed to Georgina Mount-Temple on 11 August, adding:

I have been so busy with collecting passages from Oscar's books for 'Oscariana' that I have been obliged to neglect everything else including you my Darling . . . But it has to be, if possible, in Mr Humphreys' hands before he goes abroad next Saturday. I think I have collected all the passages, but now they must be put in order which, I am afraid, I shall find the most difficult part.[23]

Before Humphreys left, he gave Cyril some money, with which the boy bought a little tortoiseshell fish, for which he wrote a thank-you note.

Oscar, it seems, was well aware of Constance's new-found love for the manager of Hatchard's. In fact, while at Worthing he began to sketch out a play, provisionally entitled *Constance,* with a plot that told of a marriage which, having run into difficulties, sees the husband and wife both seek solace in extramarital affairs. He sketched the plot out in a letter to the actor–manager George Alexander.[24] In *Constance* the plot centres on a man of rank and fashion who has become bored with his wife. The husband holds a house party full of his more outré, *fin-de-siècle* friends, and warns his wife that she must not be prudish but allow Gerald Lancing to flirt with her.

At the party all the guests are horrid to the wife, with the exception of Lancing, who is 'nice and sweet and friendly'. The husband makes love in a dark drawing room to one of the female guests, unaware that his wife is also in the room. When the guest's husband begins to bang on the door, the husband is astonished that his own wife safeguards her deceitful husband by presenting herself and saying the three of them were 'trying an absurd experiment in thought reading'.

This gesture of selfless love reignites the passion the husband once had for his wife. But such passion comes too late. Gerald Lancing's flirtations have borne fruit. She has fallen in love with the man her husband encouraged her to entertain. In fact, she is carrying his unborn child. Gerald and the wife go away together. The husband kills himself.

It is enormously tempting to see Oscar as a combination of the husband and the friends who are horrid to the wife. Lancing, of course, is the kind Humphreys. It is also tempting to consider the outcome of his proposed play as a suggestion that at some level Oscar was jealous of Humphreys, regretful of his recent behaviour towards her, and sad that he had lost his wife to another man. Certainly his letters to Humphreys regarding *Oscariana* are perfunctory and cool.

His reaction to the first proofs of *Oscariana* was also extremely negative. 'The book is, as it stands, so bad, so disappointing, that I am writing a set of new aphorisms, and will have to alter much of the printed matter,' Oscar wrote later. 'The plays are particularly badly done. Long passages are quoted where a single aphorism should have been extracted.'[25]

But what is also fascinating about the play that Oscar sketched out to George Alexander is the tragic ending that he chose for it, because it suggests that he knew now that his and Constance's life had become so complex that any outcome other than a tragic one was highly unlikely.

Oscar joined Constance in Worthing after suffering yet another humiliation at the hands of Queensberry, as he described in a letter to Bosie. Queensberry was 'on the rampage again – been to the Café Royal to enquire for us, with threats etc.'[26]

Worthing, for all its inconveniences, offered some respite from persecution at the hands of the Marquess. Away from the influences of London, Oscar became momentarily a typical husband and father again. He and Constance pored over Miss Lord's books. Constance was delighted to find *Middlemarch*, which she determined to read once she finished the light seaside reading she had brought with her – Anthony Hope's *The Prisoner of Zenda*. Oscar meanwhile discovered a little book called *I Woke*. Constance, writing to Georgina, inquired whether her friend knew it. 'Oscar has been reading it and is much interested in it.'[27]

When he wasn't working on what would become *The Importance of Being Earnest*, Oscar was dedicated to his sons. They had an aquarium with them, into which the finds from the day's fishing and rock pooling would be proudly deposited. Oscar swam with the boys and, relieving Arthur from his maritime duties, delighted in taking them out in fishing boats with the local fishermen.

'Cyril went out with his father in a boat this afternoon, and this evening bought 150 prawns and two lobsters,' Constance relayed to her brother in a letter. She added details of a subsequent conversation with her husband that must have taken on a different hue in retro-

Lord and Lady Mount-Temple. Constance became very close to Georgina, Lady Mount-Temple in 1890. Georgina, by then widowed, had a house in Chelsea close to Tite Street, and Constance soon became a regular visitor.

Babbacombe Cliff, Georgina Mount-Temple's seaside home near Torquay, photographed by Vyvyan Wilde, c.1904. The house, full of Pre-Raphaelite art, held a kind of magic for Constance.

An interior shot of Babbacombe Cliff, also taken by Vyvyan.

Constance aged thirty-four, 1892.

Oscar aged thirty-eight, 1892.

Lord Alfred Douglas, or 'Bosie', taken in 1891 when he was twenty-one. Although Oscar remained loyal and devoted to Constance whilst pursuing other homosexual affairs, his affair with Bosie would have a catastrophic effect on his relationship with Constance.

Above left Constance and
Oscar in the garden of Mr
and Mrs Palmer in Reading.
Constance stands while her
friend Jean Palmer is seated
on the ground.
Above right A photograph of
Oscar, Constance and Cyril
taken at the end of their
holiday in Felbrigg, near
Cromer, summer 1892.

Oscar posed with Bosie
during the same session. He
had originally asked to
spend just one night with
the Wildes, however he
stayed on at Felbrigg with
Oscar after Constance and
the children had left.

As this cartoon from early 1895 indicates, Oscar's play *An Ideal Husband* prompted much debate – particularly in the women's press – as to just what might constitute the perfect spouse.

Right During Oscar's trials, the press had a field day. Vyvyan remembered his mother 'in tears, poring over masses of press cuttings, mostly from Continental newspapers'.

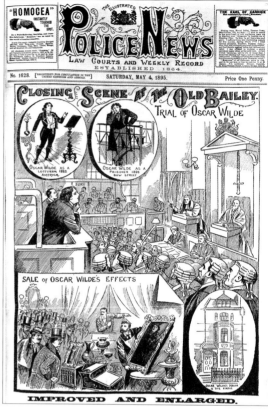

OSCAR WILDE   AND   HIS WIFE.

THESE pictures will be undoubtedly new to the great majority of our readers, especially as Oscar Wilde has not been seen in this country for less than ten years. When last seen by us he did not look the graceful man he is here shown to be, but of a fat and slightly unwieldy form. Oscar is all right, however. His enemies have a hard time trying to get ahead of him and they haven't as yet succeeded. He retorts at every point. Mrs. Wilde does not look happy here, but she is said to admire her husband very much.

The *New York Standard* ran this piece in early 1895. The photograph of Constance is the same as that published in January by *The Young Woman*, which Constance herself admitted made her look 'solemnly tragic'.

Otho, his second wife Mary and their
children Hester and Eugene,
photographed 'in exile' with Constance,
probably in Switzerland.

Constance in exile. This snap is
probably taken on her own Kodak;
the annotation is Vyvyan's.

Carlos Blacker and his wife Carrie, Cyril,
Vyvyan and an unidentified boy, almost
certainly the Blackers' son.

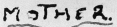

MOTHER.

Constance, aged thirty-nine, photographed in Heidelberg, 1897. She put the boys into school in this German town where her friend Lady Brooke was also educating one of her sons.

Cyril (*left*) and Vyvyan photographed in Heidelberg, 1896. Constance sent Oscar a copy of these photographs on his release from gaol in 1897. 'I have heard from my wife,' he wrote that May to Robbie Ross, 'she sends me photographs of the boys – such lovely little fellows in Eton collars.'

Oscar and Bosie in Naples, 1897.

Constance's sitting room in the Villa Elvira, near Nervi. Her treasured photographs are displayed on the mantelpiece.

Constance's letters refer to her making cushions for the villa. The picture on the right may be a print of Watts's portrait of Lady Mount-Temple, also mentioned in the letters.

Constance's grave in the cemetery in Genoa.
The line that she was the 'Wife of Oscar Wilde' was added later by Otho's family.

spect. 'I instantly said that I should like to go prawning with him one afternoon. After he had gone, Oscar explained to me the costume that the fishermen wear when they go prawning, which is indeed like the Emperor's New Clothes, so I think differently now about going!'[28]

His sons were not the only boys that Oscar was taking out in boats or swimming with. Despite attempts to keep Bosie away from Worthing, the young lord managed to inveigle his way into the holiday. To Constance's horror he joined Oscar. Together they courted local young men: Percy, Alfonso and Stephen flirted with the couple, and swam and drank with them.

While they were at Worthing, a scandal hit the headlines. A police raid at a club in Fitzroy Street had led to the arrest of Alfred Taylor – the man who had been procuring for Wilde. And now Taylor and one of his lovers, Charlie Mason, wrote to Wilde asking for his help. In the past Wilde had paid off blackmailers and bailed out many a young man. But now, for the first time perhaps, Oscar, already £40 overdrawn at the bank, found he was too strapped for cash to oblige.

If, by Oscar's own admission, Constance had always been gracious to Bosie, at Worthing she was fractious and annoyed by his presence. Bosie became a bone of contention, a fact that Bosie himself reported in a letter to their mutual friend Robbie Ross.[29] Her irritation must have been aggravated further by the fact that, rather than being able to escape temporarily from the burdens of celebrity, Bosie and Oscar, once together, began to attract attention in Worthing, creating much excitement among the locals. Perhaps unaware that the two men were not permanently joined at the hip, in early September, long after Bosie's return to London, Oscar and Bosie were invited to patronize a local concert, a patronage that was used to advertise the event with, according to Oscar, 'our names . . . placarded all over the town'. When Oscar took his son Cyril in Bosie's place, he faced a packed hall and was greeted with loud applause. 'Cyril was considered to be you,'[30] Oscar jested – a joke that Constance could scarcely have approved of under the circumstances.

Arthur Humphreys, meanwhile, was holidaying in Florence with his wife. But he wrote to Constance from the city she adored. With a new sense of confidence that Humphreys had brought, Constance now not only looked forward to new adventures of the heart but also to more creative and literary ones too. Once *Oscariana* was out of the way at the end of the summer, she wanted to start on another entrepreneurial literary project. She wanted to revive the literary project based around letters that she had proposed to Otho two years earlier. Oscar had helped her strengthen the plot. He suggested that the story should be based around two people discovering that they have committed to marry the wrong person, a theme somewhat pertinent to the Wilde household.

'I'm still thinking of that book that I suggested our writing of letters and Oscar has now given me a suggestion for a plot,' Constance wrote to Otho from Worthing.

It only needs to be a rather flimsy plot. A man and a woman, each engaged to a friend of the other's, write to congratulate one another, they have never met. These two first letters should cross each other, then each should write again, being rather interested in the other, perhaps describing where they are staying. You could describe Pisa, I Worthing and so we should gradually fall a little in love with each other and should at last suggest breaking off our engagements and marrying one another.

We are supposed never to have met and suggest a meeting place, then the last two letters should also cross each other, each saying to the other that he or she has made it up and is going to be married and hoping that the other will not mind so much. I think that a charming little book might be written in this way. Do tell me that you will try and let us write our first letters on 1 October, when the children will be gone and I shall have time. Write on one side of the paper and I should suggest that you, having much more wit than I, should write more humorous letters and that I should write very serious ones about books that I had read. These are to be imaginary books, not real ones and I think that we should each miss the point of the other's letters. Do let us try. We can both of us write letters about the only thing that we can do and we might make some money.[31]

Constance and the boys left Worthing on 4 September. Speranza was unwell and had been summoning her daughter-in-law. Constance was not just a regular companion for Oscar's mother but also did many chores for her, such as collecting her pension and sorting out disputes with servants. Oscar and Constance were growing concerned about the manner in which Willie Wilde seemed to be extracting money from the old woman. His marriage to the American Mrs Leslie had broken down, and by 1894 he was not only divorced but now married again to a former Miss Lily Lees.

Scribbled in the back pages of his own copy of a biography of Wilde, Constance's brother Otho made some comments about his sister years after the event: 'She was constantly short of money it is true, partly from Oscar's habit of expecting her (not I fancy himself) to pay off his mother's and brother's debts when the bailiffs were in their house in Oakley Street,' Otho notes rather bitterly.[32] And whether she sought it directly, Constance was certainly in receipt of handouts from friends such as Georgina, Lady Mount-Temple, to pass on to Speranza.

Oscar stayed on in Worthing while the family returned to London. He was well out of the way, for in September matters deteriorated when he became the subject of national ridicule with the release of a novel, *The Green Carnation*. The book, published anonymously, was a barely concealed satirical portrait of Oscar and Bosie, characterizing them as Esme Amarinth and Lord Reggie Hastings respectively. A caustic portrayal of the couple, the implication that they were not only practising homosexuals but also held unhealthy interests in young boys was clearly legible between the lines. To Oscar's and Constance's horror, the book was a huge success.

Oscar carried on his affair with Bosie regardless of the book, staying with him in the Grand Hotel in Brighton in October. Constance meanwhile continued to see as much of Arthur Humphreys as she could. When she visited the London Library, just off Piccadilly, she made sure she popped into Hatchard's to see him. They were both members of the Society for Psychical Research and also used its regular meetings as another opportunity to see one another. 'Are you coming to the PRS [sic] meeting on Friday?' Constance asked Arthur on 22 October. But their love affair was not without issues. The fact of their respective marriages aside, they held different political opinions and were finding themselves prone to fighting. They held radically different views on the cause of unemployment among the lower classes, for example – a point of difference that Constance found irksome.

'We must not talk of subjects we do not agree upon,' Constance warned Arthur.

> You have a very strong nature and perhaps it is natural that you should have no sympathy with the unfortunate of the world. I have had a long talk with the carpenter down here who has done all that work for us for the past ten years, and he spoke to me with grief of cases he had known of thoroughly competent citizens who were utterly unable to get work ... It is a subject I feel most deeply on, and that is not serious to you.[33]

By mid-November *The Green Carnation* had helped spawn a barrage of anti-Wilde feeling that was seemingly as strong in some portions of society as the enthusiasm for the author in others. Although publicly Wilde dealt with the situation with humour, privately he was rattled, as was his wife. Things were taking on a nightmarish complexion.

On the very day that a cartoon of Wilde and Bosie appeared in *Punch* Constance was moved to write to Georgina in despair. It was not just the personal humiliation that Constance was suffering at these depictions of her husband and his friend, but reading her letter one senses her mounting panic at their implications. 'I am very distraught and worried, and no one can help me. I can only pray for help from God, and that I seem now to spend my time in doing;

some time I trust that my prayers may be answered – but when or how I don't know. Destroy this letter please.'[34]

The cartoon, entitled *Two Decadent Guys: A Colour Study in Green Carnations*, depicts Bosie and Oscar, characterized as Guy Fawkes dummies called Sir Fustian Flitters and Lord Raggie Tattersall, bound and ready to be burned. Bosie's signature boater is worn by one, while the other wears a top hat. Both wear huge cauliflowers in their lapels in place of green carnations. The caption hints at a somewhat distasteful interest in young men: 'See Raggie, here come our youthful disciples! Do they not look deliciously innocent and enthusiastic? I wish though, we could contrive to imbue them with something of our own lovely limpness.'

The cartoon was just the tip of the iceberg. Only two nights before its publication Oscar, quite possibly accompanied by Constance, attended Haddon Chambers's play *John-o-Dreams* at the Haymarket Theatre. To his horror, he was snubbed by many members of the audience.

Whether it was naivety or a determined show of strength and faith in her husband, Constance dealt with the humiliating, distressing and embarrassing events that occurred that winter by ploughing on regardless with her round of social events and maintaining her 'at homes'.

An extensive interview with her in the 24 November edition of *To-Day*, a popular magazine edited by Jerome K. Jerome, must have served as some welcome positive publicity for the Wilde marriage, not least because the interviewer, on being shown Constance's autograph book, chose to relate the loving verse that Oscar had written to his wife in it.

Those around Constance could see the danger that she was now in. The satirization of Oscar and Bosie was doing nothing but play into the Marquess of Queensberry's hands, as was the mounting public distaste for the couple. Constance had been suggesting that she leave London in early December and spend two or three weeks with Georgina at Babbacombe Cliff. But, unusually, this suggestion was firmly rebutted by her friend. Although Constance claimed she found

Georgina's reasons for not having her 'puzzling',[35] Georgina was almost certainly indicating that Constance's place was by her husband's side at a time when insinuations about Oscar's sexual leanings were flying about.

Constance and Oscar began to pin their hopes on theatrical success as a means of regaining social approval. But although as confident as ever in public, at home with his wife Oscar revealed how extremely anxious he was that his next play, *An Ideal Husband*, would fail, at a time when he needed it to succeed.

'Oscar is very unwell,' Constance informed Georgina in early December, 'and altogether we are terribly worried ... but I hope that Oscar is going to make something by his new play, alas I doubt it, for he is so depressed about it.'[36] In the same breath she mentioned that her cheques were being bounced by the bank.

As the Christmas holidays approached, the boys came back from school. Constance busied herself with them, taking them to the usual seasonal children's parties, including one in Tite Street at the home of Adrian and Laura Hope. She also continued with other Christmas traditions, writing cards with greetings to all her and Oscar's friends.[37]

As an adult, Vyvyan would write down his memories of that Christmas. They are poignantly happy. 'In London my father always carried a gold-headed Malacca cane, about three foot six inches long, as was the fashion among the dandies of the day,' he recounted.

> This fascinated me and I would rush to take it from him when he came home. I asked him to let me have it when I grew up, and he said he would give it to me as soon as I reached its height. So the next time he came in I greeted him with books tied to the soles of my feet, so I was taller than the stick. This pleased my father immensely ... This ... was one of the last memories of my father. It must have been in January 1895 during the Christmas holidays.[38]

Constance must have worked hard to keep the boys shielded from her and Oscar's troubles. In fact, on top of every other worry they shared, there was also the issue of her health, which had deteriorated rapidly. According to anecdote, Constance fell down the stairs that

Christmas holiday, and as a result she could barely walk. If so, the fall only exacerbated a condition that her letters revealed had been plaguing her for years. On New Year's Eve she dropped Georgina a line to say that 'I am not well, in fact I have been very bad again, but my Doctor is coming to-day to give me some electricity and I hope I shall get better. I am alright when I don't walk, but then I can't go thro life sitting on a chair especially with two boys to amuse.'[39]

The events that followed that Christmas holiday have already been recounted in the first chapter of this book. Oscar took rooms in town as *An Ideal Husband* went into production. He took a holiday in Algeria with Bosie, returning to a different suite of hotel rooms for the opening of his fourth play, *The Importance of Being Earnest*. Constance, meanwhile, went to Babbacombe in an attempt to improve her health. Here she allowed herself to get lost in the old-world company of Georgina's elderly friends. On 8 February, while Oscar was making his way home from his African adventure, Constance and Georgina held a party for the critic John Ruskin's seventy-sixth birthday. Constance wrote to Vyvyan and told him all about it. 'I have had a lovely birthday cake,' she revealed, adding, as a good, inquiring mother should: 'you never told me whether *your* chocolate cake was a success.'[40]

On her return to Tite Street on 28 February, Constance found no Oscar at home, only the note that he intended to come around to see her, with something important to relate. When Oscar arrived at Tite Street at nine o'clock in the evening of 28 February 1895, just as his note had said he would, he delivered the news Constance must have been dreading. During the course of February 1895 Queensberry's behaviour had reached new lows. Things had come to a head, and Oscar felt he was going to have to sue.

Far away in Babbacombe, Constance had been shielded from a fiasco that had occurred on the first night of *The Importance of Being Earnest* and which the press had failed to report. Yes, Oscar had arrived triumphant at the theatre; yes, a full house that had braved a blizzard had worn lilies in his honour and applauded his success. But other things had also happened that night.

One of Oscar's friends, the Hon. Algernon Bourke, had heard that Queensberry had obtained tickets for the first night of *The Importance* and was planning to address the audience about Oscar's relationship with Bosie. Thanks to this tip-off George Alexander had written to Queensberry stating that his ticket had been issued in error and was not valid, and then he and Oscar had applied to Scotland Yard for protection. And so when Oscar stepped out of his carriage that night, mingling among his fans, twenty policemen were also there, stationed outside the theatre and briefed to prevent the Marquess from entering.

In spite of his ticket being invalidated, Queensberry had turned up carrying a bouquet of rotting vegetables and with a prizefighter to protect him. After his attempts to gain access to the theatre were thwarted by the police, he prowled around for the duration of the play, before eventually leaving the bouquet at the box office for Oscar.

The next day Oscar once again considered a restraining order against the Marquess, which his solicitor, Charles Humphreys, investigated. But the order would have needed witness statements from George Alexander and his staff at the St James's, and it seems that, though prepared to alert Scotland Yard to prevent affray, no one wanted to be implicated in a legal battle that was not essentially theirs. The statements were not forthcoming. Oscar's lawyer pointed out, however, in delivering this news to his client, that it was likely Queensberry would present them with another opportunity.

Such an opportunity now occurred on that very day, 28 February. While Constance was on the train, travelling back from the coast, Oscar's day had begun like any other, a mixture of professional meetings and social pleasantries. Early on he had been with the illustrator Charles Ricketts at his Chelsea home in The Vale, discussing proposed illustrations and typesetting for a new edition of *The Portrait of Mr W. H.* After leaving Ricketts, Oscar enjoyed a conversation with the latter's professional partner, lover and cohabiter, Charles Shannon, whom he bumped into as Shannon was making his way home along the King's Road. As a thick London fog descended, the couple exchanged a few words before Oscar jumped into a cab and headed for the Albemarle Club.

Despite its proximity to the Avondale, where he was staying, Oscar had not visited his club from some time. As he entered, he was handed an envelope by the hall porter, Sydney Wright. In it was the Marquess of Queensberry's calling card, on which had been scribbled in ink a brief message: 'For Oscar Wilde posing as somdomite'.

The Marquess had called at Oscar's club some days earlier, seeking to make the kind of public scene he had failed to achieve on Valentine's Day. When he was informed that Oscar was not at the club, he had scribbled the sentence on his card, mis-spelling the accusation that Oscar was a sodomite. He had handed the card to Wright, who was able to read the libellous accusation, before putting it in an envelope to await Oscar.

Oscar was utterly horrified by this event. After rushing back to the Avondale, he scribbled a note to Robbie Ross. 'Bosie's father has left a card at my club with hideous words on it,' Oscar wrote. 'I don't see anything now but a criminal prosecution. My whole life seems ruined by this man. The tower of ivory is assailed by this foul thing. On the sand is my life spilt. I don't know what to do. If you could come here at 11.30 please do so tonight . . . I have asked Bosie to come tomorrow.'[41]

The proposed rendezvous with Robbie late that evening gave Oscar the time to rush back to Chelsea to meet Constance, just back from her holiday. He allowed a couple of hours with his wife, accounting for the time a cab would then take to return him to his rooms in Piccadilly.

Now what Oscar had to explain to Constance was how he felt trapped by the note. Given that it had been read by Wright, and could have been read by other members of the club staff, this was no mere private accusation. As far as Wilde was concerned, although Queensberry had not made the public spectacle he had so long threatened, he had nevertheless made a statement that had been seen. It qualified as libel. If Oscar were to ignore it, he would appear to be accepting the libel and thus be damned; if he were to challenge it, the accusation would be made yet more public, another humiliation. Yet to defend his public face he had little choice but to take the latter course: to sue and have Queensberry arrested.

Oscar considered leaving the country. Continental Europe was littered with members of the British upper class and aristocracy who had defaulted on various social pacts. Some, like Otho, were fleeing debts, some were adulterers, some were cheats and many were homosexuals. When their respective scandals erupted, a lengthy stay overseas was seen as the appropriate action. After a year out of its glare, society tended to welcome its black sheep back again.

Somewhat bizarrely, Oscar faced some inconvenience if he chose this path. He would have to go without luggage. For the fact of the matter was that all his cases and effects had been confiscated by the Avondale Hotel in Piccadilly.

Ever since his most recent theatrical successes he had been served with writs from creditors to the tune of £400. Smelling his success and working on the basis that Wilde would now have money to pay his bills, everyone was cashing in. Among the cigarette merchants and jewellers, florists, hairdressers and wine merchants who suddenly wanted their accounts honoured, was the Avondale itself. The management had removed Wilde's luggage as security against the payment of his bill.

It was probably this confiscation that Oscar also used to justify his need to return to his hotel that night rather than stay at home with a wife he had barely seen for two months. As he headed out of the door and was subsumed by the London fog, Constance must have felt desperate, left alone in the house to contemplate the inevitable scandal she would now have to face.

After discussing his options with Constance, Oscar went to meet Robbie Ross at 11.30 as planned. When he got there, Bosie had also already arrived at his hotel. Bosie had lingered in Algeria after Oscar left at the end of January, but when his brother Percy, who shared Bosie's hatred of their father, telegrammed him alerting him to the fact that Queensberry was once more on the rampage, he returned to be at Oscar's side. His presence instantly undermined Oscar's ability to have a considered talk with Robbie.

Bosie was incredibly self-centred, and whereas Constance was always mindful of what was best for her husband, Bosie was always mindful of what was best for Bosie. Bosie's hatred for his father had become so intense that he was desperate to see the man humiliated and emasculated. Gaol seemed a most fitting and ignominious punishment. And so that night he delivered the most mind-bogglingly incautious piece of advice to Oscar. That night Bosie urged him to sue without hesitation.

Without properly taking into consideration the damaging effect that a legal case of this nature was likely to have on Constance and the boys, Oscar took Bosie's advice. He allowed himself to be persuaded that the loss of his luggage was a sufficient barrier to flight, and that action through the courts would prove fruitful.[42] And so while Constance was left to mull over the ramifications of what she had just been told, Lord Alfred Douglas and Oscar Wilde knocked on the doors of Mr Humphreys' offices in Giltspur Chambers, Holborn Viaduct. Humphreys asked if there was any truth in Queensberry's allegations, and on hearing Oscar's vehement denial he advised that Oscar did then indeed have a case.

In a moment of doubt over the wisdom of proceeding, Oscar pointed out that he could not afford the cost of a court case, given his current financial embarrassment. But Bosie instantly assured Humphreys that his family – that is, his brother and his mother, who was divorced and alienated from Queensberry – would meet the expenses. Oscar had no further excuse to prevent proceedings.

Humphreys, Bosie and Oscar hailed a cab that took them the relatively short distance from Holborn to Soho, and here at the Great Marlborough Street police station they applied for a warrant for the arrest of Queensberry. On the morning of 4 March 1895, Constance, along with anyone else who took *The Times*, was able to read how that arrest had been made two days earlier.

In the Police section of the paper, it was reported that:

At Marlborough Street on Saturday, the Marquess of Queensberry, aged 50, described as having no occupation and as residing in Carter's

Hotel Dover St., was charged before Mr Newton on a warrant of defamatory libel concerning Mr Oscar Wilde on February 18th. Mr C. O. Humphreys, solicitor, prosecuted; and Sir George Lewis, solicitor, appeared for the defence.

If Constance had not already been aware of the fact, the realization that George Lewis was not acting for them but for the other side must have come as a terrible shock. However, she may have felt momentarily reassured by the manner in which the paper seemed to be reporting events: 'Mr Humphreys stated that Mr Oscar Wilde, who was a married man and lived on most affectionate terms with his wife and children, had been the object of a system of most cruel persecution at the hands of Lord Queensberry.'

But if there was some solace to be found in the reference to her husband's married status, and the note of his victimization by Queensberry, reports of the warning shot that Lewis fired back across the courtroom at his adversary were ominous:

> Let me say one word sir . . . I venture to say, when the circumstances of this case are more fully known, you will find that Lord Queensberry acted as he did under feelings of great indignation . . . I do not wish this case to be adjourned without it being known that there is nothing against the honour of Lord Queensberry.

Queensberry's bail was set at £1,000, and the court was adjourned until the following Saturday. A week later the whole of London woke up to the scandal. The kind of crowds Oscar had formerly attracted outside theatres were now in Great Marlborough Street, waiting for his return to court and queuing for the limited number of places available in the public gallery. He did not disappoint. Arriving ten minutes early for the hearing, Oscar drew up with great style in a carriage and pair with a coachman and footman to boot, and with Bosie and Bosie's brother Percy in tow. Constance was noticeably absent.

On 9 March the same parties reassembled, but with one profound difference. Sir George Lewis was not present. In his stead a new solicitor, a Mr Russell, had taken over the defence of Queensberry and was now joined by Edward Carson QC. After the hearing, which went over similar ground to the first, the case was duly committed to trial in the Old Bailey.

Oscar's side may well have chosen to read Lewis's sudden withdrawal from the case as a positive indication of the likely outcome. Oscar and Bosie seemed to be ploughing ahead with utter confidence in their ability to win, and were blinkered to the realities of their likely success in the case. Almost somnambulant, they moved onwards without realizing that the whole of London was predicting that, on the contrary, Oscar was about to be exposed. For Lewis's resignation was less a sign of confidence in Queensberry than an indication that, with a sense of the evidence Queensberry was gathering, he was about to crucify his old friend and client. This was something he could not bring himself to do.

Constance had made statement appearances at court in the past. But she was absent now from a case concerning her own husband. That Constance did not want to expose herself to public ridicule or abuse would have been perfectly understandable. But another contributing reason was almost certainly her ill health. In spite of her restful stay at 'Babb', in March Constance's mobility problems had taken another turn for the worse. She had been temporarily forbidden to walk by her doctors and was consequently preparing to leave Tite Street for a short stay with her aunt Mary Napier in Lower Seymour Street, where she could be properly nursed. She was, she told Robbie Ross, preparing for an operation in the third week of March, though if Oscar wanted her in Tite Street before this date, she would postpone it until after the case.

Bed-bound at her aunt's house, Constance seems to have become reliant on Robbie's preparedness to play messenger between his two friends Constance and Oscar Wilde. Constance must have been mortified then to discover that Bosie, on seeing his father committed to trial, had suggested that he and Oscar head for Monte Carlo, and that her husband, seemingly prepared to accede to any whim presented by his young friend, had agreed. Resigned, Constance sent some correspondence for Oscar to Robbie, along with a note pointing out that she had arranged for someone to care for Oscar's mother, Lady Wilde while he was absent and she was incapacitated: 'I don't know Oscar's address . . . as I am forbidden to walk I shall not be able to come over to Oakley Street, but I will leave directions about his mother having everything she needs.'[43]

With a thirty-two-hour journey ahead of them, Oscar and Bosie must have left on or around 12 March to arrive in Monte Carlo, as noted in the *Pall Mall Gazette*, on the 14th. In spite of all the troubles at home, Bosie and Oscar launched themselves into one of the most fashionable, crowded, talked-about and written-about resorts in Europe, if not the world. They could not have appeared more publicity-seeking.

They stayed in the Hôtel Prince de Galles for a week. Back in London, society was scandalized by the audacity of this holiday *à deux*. While the *Pall Mall Gazette* was careful to separate Oscar and Bosie's simultaneous arrival at the Principality by a few lines in their foreign column, other papers were less afraid of innuendo. The *Aberdeen Weekly Journal* was quick to point out what readers of the *Pall Mall Gazette* might have missed: 'The following two paragraphs appeared in the *Pall Mall Gazette*,' it pointed out knowingly: ' "The Marquess of Queensberry [meaning here Bosie] has arrived in Monte Carlo via Paris from London." "Mr Oscar Wilde has arrived in Monte Carlo." '

Constance's aunt, meanwhile, seems to have dissuaded her from having the surgery that was scheduled for March to correct her mobility problems,[44] and apparently whatever home remedies and nursing she had provided her niece did some good, enough to get Constance up and about once more.

There is an account of her at this period that indicates that she did attempt some normalcy in her life and even continued her 'at homes'. One of her contemporaries encountered her at 'a little party for table-turning'.

On this particular occasion the charming but always a little clumsy Constance was carving a chicken, after communications with spirits had been completed. Suddenly the chicken slipped off its plate and ended up on the floor. Constance and her socialite friends laughed so much that they all ended up crying.

> 'I am weak with laughing!' she said, after this disaster, turning help-lessly to me as she sank into a chair. She was dressed in some soft shade of grey with a picturesque large brimmed hat, from beneath which her laughing face looked out framed, in its soft brown hair and lit by big luminous eyes. She looked a mere girl, and was merrier than us all . . . A few days later, my friend came to me and said: 'Constance Wilde told me she had taken such a fancy to you, and she did wish you would come to see her. Will you come on her next "At home" day?' I went, but my friend and I were almost the only visitors. Mrs Wilde received us with the gentle courtesy which characterized her, but we noticed that that she seemed depressed and distracted, and as we walked away my friend remarked to me: 'I cannot make out what has happened – usually the street is thronged with carriages and her rooms so full that one cannot even get near her – today there was no one there.'[45]

This particular memoir puts this 'at home' merely two days before the libel trial, on Monday 1 April, or April Fool's Day. It is entirely possible that memory has misted the exact timing of these events and that, although ringing very true in the description of Constance, they may have happened at an earlier date than suggested. But if accurate, it may suggest that there was a last-minute display of bravado by the Wildes as the full scale of Oscar's folly in pursuing Queensberry finally dawned on Saturday 30 March.

Oscar and Bosie returned from Monte Carlo on 25 March. Their initial action vis-à-vis the looming trial was to visit Mrs Robinson, a fashionable fortune-teller. It wasn't the first time the duo had sought her prophecies; indeed, it seems that visiting her was a little ritual they enjoyed. The previous summer the Sybil of Mortimer Street, as Oscar called her, had suggested that he and Bosie would travel abroad together in January, a prophecy that no doubt encouraged Oscar to include Bosie in his holiday plans when Constance had first suggested he sample North Africa. Now she predicted 'complete triumph' in the trial. Effervescing with optimism, the couple chose to believe her.

Despite her husband's ridiculous and insensitive behaviour towards her in the period immediately before the trial, Constance did what she could for Oscar. She went to friends and relatives to raise as many funds as she could to help him: £50 was forthcoming from cousin Eliza and £100 from Aunt Mary Napier, to which she added a further £50 from her own funds.

On 28 March the press reported that a trial date had finally been set and proceedings would begin at the Old Bailey on Wednesday 3 April. Queensberry was going to plead justification for the libel. Queensberry's legal team had intimated to Oscar's side the nature of the plea of justification, and promised that a full plea would be delivered by Saturday the 30th for the prosecution to study. In spite of these intimations, Oscar's team wished 'that this case should be speedily dealt with, and hence it was that the prosecution were not adopting the customary course of asking for a long adjournment in order to meet the plea of justification'.[46]

This act of legal folly, which committed Oscar to trial without time to consider properly the defence Queensberry intended to level against him came to haunt him when, on 25 March, Queensberry's team did indeed deliver their plea in full detail. In addition to accusations that Wilde's literature referenced 'the relations, intimacies and passions of certain persons of sodomitical and unnatural tastes habits and practices' there was the far more devastating accusation that Oscar had solicited and incited young men to commit 'sodomy and other acts of gross indecency and immorality'. There were fifteen different counts, in which Wilde was accused of soliciting more than twelve boys to commit sodomy, of whom ten were named. Edward Shelley's name was there, as was Sidney Mavor's. Freddie Atkins, Maurice Schwabe and Alfred Wood were all noted. Then there was a man called Charles Parker, another called Ernest Scarfe and yet another, Herbert Tankard. Walter Grainger, the under-butler from Goring, was cited, as was Alfonso Conway, whom Oscar had met during his holiday in Worthing.

While Oscar had been in Monte Carlo, Queensberry had been very busy. He had hired private detectives, who had turned over every stone in order to drag up the details of Oscar's clandestine homosexual activities, and their findings had leaked into the wider gossip-ridden society. The full nature of Oscar's friendship with young men, at which cartoonists and satirists had been hinting for so long, had been kept as an open secret for years within Oscar's circle of liberal friends. They had guarded it so well that it had never passed into the hands of those who could use such information against Oscar. They had even guarded against Constance discovering the full truth about her husband. But in the past weeks one of the circle had broken ranks. A disgruntled actor, Charles Brookfield, who astonishingly was playing in *An Ideal Husband,* had revealed all he knew about Wilde to Queensberry's investigative team. The news then spread like wildfire.

And this is perhaps why, if the account is correct, Constance bravely held her 'at home' on April Fool's Day. It is just possible that, knowing she was about to cancel it, Oscar had either written to her or visited her on that Saturday after he had seen the evidence against him and asked her to continue with her social engagements in a gesture of support and defiance. This is, of course, speculation. What is certain, however, is that he asked her to accompany him to dinner and then the theatre that evening. Oscar had finally realized that his wife was his greatest asset in this whole matter. Instead of visiting Monte Carlo, he should have spent more time with her, and certainly more time with her where the public could be reminded just how beautiful and loyal she was. Of course, Constance did exactly as she was asked. She put on one of her most beautiful outfits and made arrangements to go out. It was too little, far too late.

And so on 1 April 1895 Oscar Wilde and Lord Alfred Douglas arrived together at the St James's Theatre to see *The Importance of Being Earnest*. Constance, wearing white fur, was on their arms. The message was clear. If Oscar Wilde's wife had no issue with his relationship with Bosie Douglas, then neither should anyone else.

George Alexander, the theatre's manager, was starring as John Worthing, and the theatre was packed, as it had been ever since the show opened some six weeks previously. During the interval Oscar went back-stage to talk to Alexander but was horrified to find that, instead of supporting him, Alexander considered his appearance with Constance in the worst possible taste.

Earlier that very day Wilde had lunched at the Café Royal with his friend the journalist and editor Frank Harris, and the latter had pleaded with him to flee to France with Constance. Previously Wilde had asked Harris to provide evidence in support of his literature at his trial, a request that Harris was in principle prepared to grant. But when Harris began to make his own inquiries among his society friends, reporters and police contacts about the way the trial was likely to go, he was mortified to find that the die seemed to have been already cast against Oscar. 'Everyone assumed that Oscar Wilde was guilty of the worst that had ever been alleged against him; the very people who received him in their houses condemned him pitilessly . . . To my horror, in the public Prosecutor's office, his guilt was said to be known and classified.'[47]

Unpublished letters from Bosie's cousin and Oscar's old friend George Wyndham also indicate a widespread view that Oscar was going to lose the case.[48] Oscar's and Bosie's apparent confidence was leaving them utterly blind to how they were perceived and to the mood of the people. Just because Oscar's plays were a hit, this did not mean that he was. Many people were envious of him, and the public who knew him only by repute always loved to see a shining star fall.

With Harris's advice to drop the case and escape still ringing in his ears, Alexander's words must have felt like a double blow. But yet again Oscar failed to take heed. After the interval, rather than taking Constance home, packing their bags and summoning the children from school, he returned to his seat in the theatre.

According to Bosie's memoirs, Constance suffered terribly under the strain of that night. She must have felt as if the entire auditorium was looking at her. And perhaps now she looked at the auditorium in a new light.

Just a few weeks earlier the 'Call Boy' column of *Judy: The Conservative Comic*, a magazine that competed with *Punch* to amuse London's chattering classes, had carried an acerbic satire on Wildeans in general as they were observed in the auditorium on the opening night of *The Importance*. Presented as the foil to those 'New Women' among whom Constance would have counted herself were these 'New Men'. The article described them meeting after the show in the vestibule, where one

> was fastening a really charming silk wrapper round his delicate neck with a modest elegant diamond brooch, and to this same kindred spirit he suddenly gushed with pretty abandon 'I'm awfully glad Oscar made it a serious comedy for trivial people. I would never have gone if he hadn't, because my corset hurts me so when I laugh. Besides, Trixie, dear boy, violent laughter reddens the face so and makes one look such a shocking fright'.

This had been a seemingly harmless satire a few weeks ago, but now, with the public shame now being attached to Wilde and his circle, articles like these must have haunted Constance as she sat listening to her husband's wit played out on stage. All her adult life Constance had gone her own way. Determined and forthright, stubborn even – some had called her foolish – she was now about to pay a high price for the streak of rebellion in her character that had led her into the arms of the man that she now must have known was about to ruin her life.

It was the last time she ever went to the theatre with her husband. It may well have been the last time she saw him as a free man. And Bosie remembered that 'When I said goodnight to her at the door of the theatre she had tears in her eyes.'[49]

13

The strife of tongues

THE LIBEL TRIAL of the Marquess of Queensberry began on 3 April 1895 at the Old Bailey. Oscar put on a show, arriving at court in a brougham carriage with liveried servants in attendance. By the third day, after Queensberry's defence team had raked through the names of all the young men Oscar had associated with as part of their plea of justification, Wilde withdrew his libel charges against the Marquess. The judge ruled that the Marquess had been justified in calling Wilde a sodomite in the public interest. Queensberry was applauded. Oscar had not only lost the case but was faced with £700 of costs. He would almost certainly also now be prosecuted for indecency. His reputation was shredded, his professional life was in dire straits and his personal life was the talk not just of the town but of the whole of the Western world.

As the trial crumpled, Oscar returned to the hotel where he had been staying in Holborn to write a quick note to the press explaining his actions and then went on to Bosie's hotel, the Cadogan. He wrote to Constance begging her to 'allow no one to enter my bedroom or sitting room – except servants – today. See no one but your friends.'[1] But it was Oscar's friend Robbie Ross who went and broke the news to Constance in person. Oscar was beyond facing his wife. She was still staying in Lower Seymour Street with her aunt Mary Napier.

Oscar was arrested that night at around 6.30 p.m., charged with various counts of indecency. He was thrown into the cells at Bow Street. Robbie gathered some possessions from the hotel, a change of clothes and such like, but the police did not allow him to leave them for Oscar. Oscar was now on remand, and he would live like all the other prisoners awaiting their hearing with the magistrates.

That evening Constance's family were distraught. Mary Napier, who had been nursing Constance in Lower Seymour Street, went around to Laura and Adrian Hope in Tite Street. She was, according to Laura's diary, 'in a most frantic state about her poor niece Constance Wilde'.[2] Adrian Hope was well regarded within the Napier and Lloyd circles, and doubtless Aunt Mary was seeking both his advice and assistance. The very next day Bosie also called on the Hopes. He was not so interested in Constance. His mission was to raise bail money for Oscar. Interestingly, the Hopes were already showing their true colours with regard to Oscar. In Laura's diary he is noted as a ' monstrous husband' and a 'fiend'.

The Hopes' response to Oscar was typical of the wider public damnation of Oscar. Bile poured forth as newspapers produced ream after ream of hostile prose. 'We begin to breathe purer air,' declared the Pall Mall Gazette, a magazine to which Oscar had once been such a welcome contributor. Penny dreadful pamphlets were issued. The Great West End Scandal related in voracious detail the 'unnatural offences' and 'startling revelations' that the Queensberry libel case had brought forth. And of course, many of those who had once welcomed Oscar into their homes were quick to burn the telltale letters, photographs and calling cards that were evidence of their former association.

The day after Oscar's arrest the Pall Mall Gazette reported that his name had been removed from the playbills and programmes of his plays at the Haymarket and St James's theatres. It was noted elsewhere in the press that, although there had been no demonstrations outside the St James's Theatre, where The Importance of Being Earnest was playing, the audience was notably smaller, and remarks were shouted from the gallery at the mention of 'Worthing', a place now linked in the public mind in with Oscar's illicit sex sessions with Alfonso Conway.

In contrast to this surge of public hatred towards Oscar, there was a huge groundswell of public support for Constance. She was instantly identified as a victim of the terrible tragedy. She became from this point onwards 'poor Mrs Wilde' in the public's mind. Constance was inundated with letters, many from people she knew well, some of whom had met her merely in passing. Some people who didn't know Constance at all felt moved to put pen to paper. They were united in their pity for her.

'Dear Heart,' the actress Ellen Terry wrote in her large, loopy hand.

> Be of good cheer & when you can give me please a wee sign of you
> – I suppose I could be of no use to you or you wd have written? I
> could wish you were working hard – slaving – sweating – until a hard
> plank at night wd seem the softest bed – to hoe up turnips, or write
> verse, anything only to work – I hope yr little boys are ever so well. I
> send my dear love to you – if it can not serve you, it at least can do no
> harm. I don't quite know what rubbish I'm talking I only want to
> send you my love. Dearest Constancy.[3]

A Mrs Mundella, a woman not well known to Constance, also deter-mined to write: 'My impulse is too strong and so I act upon it and just send you a line to say how dearly sorry I am for you in your great trouble and how much sympathy I feel for you.' The Church Army sent a 'sympathetic word', asking Constance to join them, noting, 'No one shall know who you are.' Ruth Waugh in Oxford, who admitted she did not have the 'honour of your personal acquaint-ance', nevertheless wrote offering her help to Constance, despite 'my being at present a personal stranger to you'.[4]

While Oscar's close friends, Bosie and Robbie among them, moved fast to act on his behalf, Constance's intimate circle surged into action the minute news about Oscar broke. Oscar's and Constance's associates were already forming into two distinct camps, factions that would eventually be fiercely at war with one another.

One of the first of her closest friends to write to Constance was, of course, Lady Mount-Temple. On 5 April Georgina, who could only have received a telegram to alert her to the disastrous news, sent a note dictated by Mary Fawcett, who was at her bedside. 'You are always to remember how welcome you will be at the Cliff if ever you feel the "strife of tongues" too much,' she said.[5]

On 6 April, while Oscar was incarcerated in Bow Street and Bosie and Robbie Ross were working hard to secure his release, another of Constance's friends, Eva Roller, who lived at Clapham Common, wrote to Constance urging her that 'if you are still ailing as when I last saw you, will you come to this quiet place and stay here till your dear boys come home from their holidays?'[6]

The same day as Eva Roller's thoughts flew to Constance, so did those of the Burne-Jones family. Georgie Burne-Jones and both her son and daughter, Phil and Margaret, all wrote separately offering their services.

But for all those who instantly showed support and love there were almost certainly more who withdrew their association with Constance. Just as attendance at her 'at home' had fallen off in the prelude to the libel trial, now that Oscar was facing disgrace, many of those who had once called themselves her friends quickly distanced themselves. For many in society homosexuality was considered so vile that the wife of the man who was now confirmed in the minds of most as Britain's, if not Europe's, most notorious homosexual was also damned.

Even Juliet, Lady Mount-Temple's daughter, could not bear to have anything to do with Constance once the news broke. She announced as much in a letter to her mother. She may well have been encouraging her mother also to drop Constance. Juliet's letter does not survive, but Georgina's response does. She could not help but sympathize with Juliet's position, although she was determined to stand by her friend. 'I do not think there could be a greater trial with such disgusting shame . . . one cannot bear even to allude to it,' Georgina agreed with Juliet. 'Can one touch pitch and not be defiled? You are quite right in keeping aloof – so would I if I did not feel called upon to shelter her.'[7]

Constance, all too aware of the implications of the events unfurling around her, sprang into action too. Now that he had lost his libel trial, there is little indication that Constance was standing by her husband as he faced his own trial for indecency. In fact, her actions imply that, from the moment the libel trial was lost, Constance understood that her husband was doomed. She was not even waiting for further outcomes. From 5 April onwards her actions were entirely motivated by the need to protect her children's future.

As soon as the Queensberry libel trial got under way, Constance had taken the precaution of moving the boys out of their schools and sent Cyril to her family in Ireland. Letters from a relative, who signs herself simply as Susie, recount that, while elsewhere the world was having its full swing at his father's private life, Cyril, staying at Floods Hotel in the village of Borris in Co. Carlow, was having stories read to him and playing in the local streams and woods.[8] Vyvyan, meanwhile, stayed in London with his mother.

Constance was attempting to protect Cyril not only from public scrutiny but also from the truth. She would not explain to her sons the subsequent charges raised against Oscar. But Cyril was no fool. Later he would write to his brother and reveal that he had seen the newspaper placards and had persisted until someone, somewhere, explained to him what was going on. 'I never rested until I found out.'[9]

Constance swiftly explored options for her sons' futures. Even before Oscar's own trial had begun, she was formulating new futures for her children. She wrote to Bedales to secure references for Cyril, to which his schoolmaster responded with the pledge 'to do anything in my power for Cyril'. On 11 April a friend wrote to her from Admiralty House in response to her inquiries about the navy as a suitable career for her elder son.

'In reply to your letter of 9th,' the letter begins, 'I think that I shall be able to get a nomination for your boy Cyril when his age will allow of his going up for examination which will not be until he is thirteen years of age.'[10]

Constance was writing through tears. On 9 April, Laura Hope confided to her diary: 'to the Napiers where I sat with poor Constance, the most miserable woman in London, I should think'. Vyvyan remembered an image of his betrayed, humiliated mother during this period 'in tears, poring over masses of press cuttings, mostly from Continental newspapers'.[11]

Amid her grief, Constance was also being besieged by Oscar's creditors. With Oscar now incarcerated, the creditors who had been pursuing him were now writing to his wife with demands that their bills be paid. Constance had a private income, but it could not match the demands being made on it.

One man who proved of significant assistance to Constance during the terrible days of April 1895 was Philip Burne-Jones, the son of the elderly painter. Constance had clearly taken up his offer of service, and he now came to her aid. By 11 April – less than a week after Oscar's libel case had collapsed – Philip had run several errands on Constance's part.

For a start, he had been to see Sir George Lewis. If Lewis had failed to help the husband, he was at least prepared to help the wife. Philip reported to Constance that he had 'asked him all the questions you mentioned yesterday. As to any letters to you referencing Oscar's debts you can ignore them all – you have nothing to do with any debts incurred by him.'[12]

It was not just the tobacco sellers, florists and hoteliers who were baying for their dues: so too was the landlord who owned the freehold on the Wildes' family home in Tite Street. The ground rent had not been paid. 'If the landlord means to distrain for rent – let him – don't think about the house in Tite Street again – simply leave it – for the landlord to enter and distrain if he wishes,' Philip Burne-Jones told Constance.[13]

Burne-Jones knew that Constance must be thinking longer-term and continued with yet more dramatic news:

> Sir George was most anxious that as soon as ever the result of the trial is known, you should sue for a judicial separation . . . not only for the sake of yourself and your family but for the children's sake – the children must be made wards in Chancery and you could apply for the custody of them, & Oscar could never reach them or interfere with them. Something you should certainly do before Oscar is liberated – for he will be sure to come for money to you (who he knows has a

settled income) & you should protect yourself from this ... You <u>cannot</u> go on labelled as the wife of this man. I would urge you to change your name & that of the children as soon as ever you have got this separation ... remember you owe it to them to start them in life with a clean record – and if they bear their father's name this can never be. Also if anything were to happen to yourself, dear Constance – (which God forbid) Oscar could claim a life interest in your money, & might leave the children stranded – with nothing to support them at all. There would be nothing to prevent him spending all the money on himself.[14]

Philip's letter reached Constance in Torquay, where she had fled the day before, to her friend Lady Mount-Temple. He wrote to her again there three days later, assuring her that 'you are not intended to suffer always, as you have suffered. These dark days will pass away as some hideous nightmare.'

Despite practicalities and professional counsel, Constance, leaving no stone unturned, also sought advice from alternative sources. Ten days later, the day on which Oscar was committed for trial, Constance wrote to the same fortune-teller who had been so encouraging to Oscar and Bosie just weeks earlier. 'My Dear Mrs Robinson, What is to become of my husband who has so betrayed & deceived me & ruined the lives of my darling boys?' she wrote.

> Can you tell me anything? You told me that after this terrible shock my life was to become easier, but will there be any happiness, or is that dead for me? And I had had so little. My life has all been cut to pieces as my hand is by its lines. As soon as this trial is over, I have to get my judicial separation or if possible my divorce in order to get the guardianship of the boys. What a tragedy for him who is so gifted! Do write to me, & tell me what you can.[15]

The answer Mrs Robinson provided is intriguing. 'My dear Mrs Wilde,' she responded,

> I cannot tell you how much I am feeling for you in this terrible time. I said that there was a time of dreadful shock and sorrow coming to you, but I am certain that afterwards there is a bright time coming.

You have your dear little boys and their lives cannot be really injured by this. They will both live to comfort you I am sure. On your hand there is infinitely more peace and happiness coming after this terrible time than you have had for 8 years.[16]

Shortly after this communication Constance visited Speranza and broke the news to her that she intended to take Lewis's advice, separate from her husband and change the names of the boys, as advised. Lady Wilde, so proud of her son and their name, was shattered. She scrawled a sad note to Constance on 22 April.

'I am very poorly and utterly miserable,' she revealed. 'I do not like the idea of the boys changing their names – it would bring them much confusion. But at all events wait till the trial is quite over. Neither do I approve of the Navy for Vyvyan. I think it quite unfit as he is a born <u>writer</u>, made for literature alone.'[17] Lady Wilde's response, whether born from optimism or, by contrast, a reluctance to face facts, failed to grasp the reality that, whether Oscar was convicted or not, the Wilde name was already a byword for scandal rather than literary achievement.

On 24 April, Oscar's creditors moved in. There was an auction of the contents of Tite Street, attended – the press noted – by an unusually large number of cigarette merchants. Robbie Ross and Robert Sherard attempted to buy what they could of Oscar's. But in the un-policed scrum that ensued not only were things belonging to Oscar and Constance sold at knock-down prices, but many items were simply stolen. All Oscar's first editions, with his personal inscriptions to Constance and the children, which Constance kept in her room, vanished, as did all Oscar's letters to Constance, which she kept in a blue leather case. Constance had saved what she could, but she had not had time to collect the children's effects, and all their toys were sold. 'For months afterwards my brother and I kept asking for our soldiers, our trains and our toys, and we could not understand why it upset our mother,' Vyvyan later remembered. 'It was only when I saw the catalogue (of the sale), many years later, that I realised why my mother had been upset. The sale consisted of 246 lots;

number 237 was "A large quantity of toys"; they realised thirty shillings.'[18]

On 26 April, Oscar's trial began at the Old Bailey. He stood trial alongside Alfred Taylor, who had also been arrested shortly after the Queensberry libel trial. Between them they faced twenty-five counts of gross indecency and conspiracy to procure the commission of acts of indecency. Bosie by this time had fled to France. Robbie Ross was also now abroad, at the behest of his mother. Within a week the trial had collapsed with the jury unable to agree a verdict and a second trial had been ordered.

Cyril had stayed in Ireland with his relatives throughout April, but as May approached Constance was forced to find alternative arrangements for him as Susie was leaving for the mainland herself on 8 May. Constance determined that it was best to send the children abroad and get them completely away from the scandal.

Constance's friends and relatives had already made some provision for the boys. With Constance overdrawn at her bank, there was a whip-round to pay for a French governess who could care for the boys in an interim period and to cover their travel and living expenses abroad. Arthur Clifton, who had always been on good terms with Constance, was nominated as treasurer of the fund.[19]

And so either at the end of April or in early May a Mademoiselle Schuwer was employed, and along with her new charges she headed off for Glion, a remote resort in the Swiss Alps, above Montreux. According to Vyvyan's memoirs, Constance remained behind 'to be what assistance she could' to Oscar. But there is little evidence of a real effort on her part to secure her husband's release. It was to her own affairs and future that she was attending.

With Tite Street no longer in her possession, Constance was now living a nomadic life out of necessity rather than choice. After staying at Babbacombe Cliff, Constance also spent some time with her relatives the Harveys in Torquay before returning to London and residing at 22 Oxford Terrace, Hyde Park, as well as with the Napiers in Lower Seymour Street.

With a degree of irony it was the Christian socialism to which his wife had lately been devoting herself that came to Oscar's aid. On 7 May, Oscar got bail, posted for him by the Christian socialist the Revd Stewart Headlam. Hotels in London would not take him, and in the end he stayed with his friends Ada and Ernest Leverson, living in their children's nursery and keeping out of the glare of the press as much as possible. According to Ada Leverson, Constance paid him a visit. 'They were alone for two hours. I loved her very much and was grieved to see her leave in tears. I found afterwards that she had come with an urgent message from her lawyer imploring him to go away without fail before the next trial which would undoubtedly be his ruin.'[20]

Constance was not the only person still begging Oscar to go abroad. Bosie, now in Paris, wrote in the full expectation that Oscar would join him there. 'It seems too dreadful to be here without you,' he wrote from the Hotel des Deux Mondes, 'but I hope you will join me next week.'[21]

But Oscar refused to flee, and so Constance had little choice but to continue to pursue the course laid out for her by George Lewis. She began to prepare for a new life overseas, under an assumed name, legally separated from her husband. She began to make inquiries of friends living abroad with whom she and the boys might stay in the first instance.

Oscar's second trial began on 20 May. By 25 May he had been found guilty of committing acts of indecency. The judge was without mercy in his summing up. The crime that Oscar had committed was 'so bad that one has to put stern restraint upon one's self from describing, in language which I would rather not use, the sentiments which must rise to the breast of any man of honour who has heard the details . . . People who can do these things must be dead to all sense of shame . . . it is the worst case I have ever tried.'[22] Oscar was sentenced to two years' hard labour. It was devastating but by now anticipated news.

As the sentence was announced, Constance was ready to leave and had already written to most of her friends, including the Burne-Joneses and George Frederic Watts and his wife, to organize farewell visits. And then Constance discovered the new terms of friendship under which she was required to operate. The identity of her hosts is unknown, however Constance's letters suggest that at the last minute they seem to have imposed some kind of condition on her visit. Perhaps as the scale of the Wilde scandal dawned on them, they realized that having Constance and the boys to stay might prove just too controversial. Whatever this was, Constance was unable to accept it. She found herself writing to the Burne-Joneses again, apologizing for the fact that, despite her farewells, she still had not left the country.

Georgie Burne-Jones sympathized with Constance; she saw Constance could not 'go against' the wishes of her host, 'which probably represents the feelings of others also whom you would not like to vex. We both send love to you & quite understand you both in thinking of going & in deciding not to go!'[23]

Oscar had spent his first two weeks of incarceration in Holloway prison. He was wearing the standard prison garb, with arrows printed on the rough cloth, and began his new diet of barely edible prison fare. On 9 June he was moved to Pentonville, where he began working on the treadmill for six hours daily, twenty minutes on and five minutes off. His bed was a plank.

Constance, meanwhile, with her plans changing almost daily, took up Eva Roller's offer of a room to stay. On 10 June she wrote to Georgina from Roller's home in south London and updated her friend on her latest plans.

> I am staying with beautiful Mrs Roller whom you always admired so much . . . she has been to see the Watts drawing of you which is in the Academy this year. Mrs Roller and I went to call yesterday on the Lilleys and they are coming here to lunch on Friday . . . On Monday I am going up to town, and then I go abroad with the boys at Glion. I expect to be in England again at the end of the year when I have to give evidence in court. Do you know that I have to get a Divorce from Oscar? I meant to try & get a separation but I have no plea for that. I can either get a divorce or nothing and I have no choice . . . because if I died the boys would be penniless as matters stand now. I

have been kept in town to sign affidavits, but if they are ready in a week I shall go over to Geneva and swear to them before the Consul there . . . I shall be here till Monday, then at Mrs Napiers & I go on Wednesday or Thursday to Hotel du Parc, Glion, Switzerland.[24]

Before she left for Switzerland, Constance had one more important liaison. Although she was now pursuing divorce proceedings against Oscar for the sake of her children, she was still concerned about her husband's welfare. There were those in high places who were trying to help Oscar, and one such man was Richard Burdon Haldane QC, a friend of the Prime Minister, Lord Rosebery, who had recently been involved in a parliamentary inquiry into the penal system.[25] Haldane was also a friend of Margaret, Lady Brooke, the Ranee of Sarawak, who, as a good friend of both Oscar and Constance, had similarly used her influence on him. On 14 June, Haldane visited Oscar in Pentonville, and shortly after this he met 'his family'. In a subsequent letter Constance would inquire more widely about Haldane, and Arthur Clifton would reassure her that 'he is a very well known Q C . . . on the liberal side in politics'.[26] This may suggest that she was at this 'family' meeting with Haldane at which it seems some reassurances were made about arrangements that could be made to make Oscar more comfortable. On 4 July, at Haldane's request, Oscar was transferred to Wandsworth gaol, which was generally considered more lenient and comfortable than Pentonville.

Constance finally arrived in Glion later in the month of June, and thus began what her two sons considered a strange, long summer holiday. The village was close to Lake Geneva and was reached by a little funicular railway line from the nearby town of Territet. Constance and her sons were surrounded by water, mountains and woods. They explored the Gorges du Chaudron to their west, which was, according to Vyvyan's memories, filled with a carpet of narcissi.

Glion had become a fashionable resort in the nineteenth century, and it was not short of interesting Europeans. Constance and the boys particularly liked a couple of Russian countesses there who, according to Vyvyan, smoked perpetually.

Writing to Emily Thursfield from Glion, Constance allowed her feelings towards Oscar to begin to emerge. In spite of the horrors of the trial, which had left her 'broken hearted', the revelations about her husband's secret life and his recent treatment of her, she still felt desperately sorry for him 'confined within four walls'. At a profound level Constance could not stop loving Oscar, nor could she rid herself of the idea that, as his wife, she had sworn to never leave him. She did not want to break this oath now, despite the torments he had visited on her. Her decision to file for divorce was not about her and Oscar, she explained to her friend; it was about the children. 'I have to sue for divorce because the boys must be free and I cannot get a separation . . . and on account of the way he has behaved about money affairs no one would trust him to look after the boys if anything should happen to me and he got control of my money.'[27]

Otho travelled to Glion to meet his sister, and in August and early September stayed with her and the boys, assisting them as best he could. Extraordinarily, Otho had also managed to see Oscar in gaol, a visit that may well have been facilitated by Haldane. The effect of the visit was quite unexpected. Otho discovered Oscar to be utterly penitent when it came to Constance. His sentiments were persuasive and profound, for by the time Otho left the prison the two had agreed that Oscar should write to Constance and ask her to drop her divorce proceedings. In August, Oscar was allowed to write just one letter. Taking on board Otho's advice, he wrote it to Constance, begging forgiveness.

In the same month that he was allowed to write a letter, Oscar was also permitted to receive just one visit, and it was his old friend Robert Sherard who went to see him. Sherard, like Otho, believed that reconciliation was possible between Constance and Oscar, despite all that had happened. He discussed this with Oscar, and immediately after the visit he too wrote to Constance. The combination of Oscar's and Sherard's correspondence dissolved Constance's resolve to divorce her husband. The love that she clearly, astonishingly, still held for him was sufficient for her to forgive him, provided he was penitent. She would remain his wife, and somehow they would work out a future as a married couple. She wrote to Oscar to tell him as much.

And then, in early September, Constance received news that she had a visitor at the hotel in Glion. To her utter surprise it was her solicitor, Mr Hargrove. Although Constance had sought advice from Sir George Lewis in the first instance regarding her relationship with Oscar, Constance was now using the family solicitor, with whom she had liaised over the years regarding Otho's business dealings, to progress her divorce proceedings. Hargrove's decision to come all the way to Switzerland is extraordinary, but it may be that the amount of general business he had between the two siblings justified the journey. The Leasehold Investment Company had issued a final call in January, and no doubt Hargrove, in addition to Constance's affairs, had plenty of business with Otho.

Hargrove revealed that he too had received a letter from Oscar, so piteous and touching that he felt swayed. Suddenly he also suggested that divorce might be avoided. She and the boys would still have to change their names, but it was possible that Oscar might join them in doing so after his internment, and perhaps they could start afresh.

Given this turn of events, Constance now determined to return to London to see Oscar herself. This was not as straightforward as it might seem. Access to Oscar was very limited, as were visits to him, and many of his friends were making applications. Constance's distance from events only added to complications. Otho wrote to the Governor of Wandsworth prison in an attempt to make Oscar aware of Constance's intentions and to prioritize them.

'I have had a reply from the Governor of the prison,' Otho wrote to his wife, Mary, from Glion on 12 September 1895:

he says that my letter has been handed to Oscar; now by the ordinary rules, he may not receive another letter for the next three months, but, in special circumstances leave may be asked for from the prison commissioners. His letter and mine having crossed each other is very unfortunate, particularly if he should suppose as he could well

279

do, that mine was Constance's answer to his. Constance is waiting till tomorrow to see if it will bring a letter from the governor in answer to her enquiry whether she could have an interview with Oscar on the 18th of this month. This morning to make things still more difficult, a letter from Mr Clifton tells her that Mr Sherard is confident thro friends of himself and the Home Secretary of obtaining another interview with Oscar shortly, which of course if it were granted would lessen her chances of seeing him herself. She has therefore had to write to Mr Sherard asking him in her favour to forgo his claim, and that again is a nuisance because he is a journalist and sends everything to the papers. The next step probably for Constance is to write to Mr Haldane QC to interest himself in her letter being delivered. So it is all at sixes and sevens.[28]

In the end Constance's and Otho's letter-writing campaign bore fruit. Constance was allowed to visit Oscar in addition to Sherard, and she made preparations to return to London. Before she did this, however, Constance had to attend to Mlle Schuwer, the French governess, who had proved herself unfit to be in charge of two boys. According to Vyvyan, she had run up huge expenses and was in the habit of locking herself in her room rather than properly supervising the children. However, a comment from Otho to his wife suggests that she may have been devoting herself to a male companion rather than the children. 'It is said that Mlle Schuwer has rejoined her Corsican at the Hotel Victoria,' Otho informed Mary, 'and four servants have suddenly been dismissed.'[29]

Whatever new scandals Constance was faced with concerning her wayward governess, the solution was simple. She and the governess parted company. Now she packed Cyril and Vyvyan off to stay with Otho and Mary in their small chalet in Bevaix, not far from Neuchâtel, while she travelled back to London with a Miss Boxwell, whom she had met at Glion. Constance boxed up her sons' things and posted them on to her sister-in-law Mary Holland.

In a note she thanked her for 'taking charge of the 2 young monkeys for me while I go on this very sad pilgrimage to London. I am sure you will wish it to have a very happy ending both for his sake and for mine.' As part of this note Constance revealed that Oscar had written to her more than once, and that his 'letters are touching to a degree and I cannot think that the children will suffer more by seeing him than they must in any case by the very fact of being his children'.[30]

So, full of hope for her marriage and for a future where her children might see their father after all, Constance entered through the grim gates of Wandsworth gaol on 21 September. Afterwards she described the visit to Robert Sherard:

My Dear Mr Sherard

It was indeed awful more so than I had any conception it could be. I could not see him, I could not touch him, and I scarcely spoke. Come and see me before you go to him on Monday at any time after 2 I can see you. When I go again I am to get at the Home Secretary thro' Mr Haldane and try and get a room to see him in and touch him again. He has been mad the last three years, and he says that if he saw Lord A—he would kill him. So he had better stay away and be satisfied with having marred a fine life. Few people can boast of so much.

I thank you for your kindness to a fallen friend; you are kind & gentle to him and you are, I think, the only person he can bear to see.[31]

Constance returned to Switzerland after the visit, this time to stay in her brother's crowded home, where he lived very frugally since his financial demise. Otho, Mary and their children, Hester and Eugene, occupied the top floor of a two-storey chalet in Bevaix. The chalet was called La Maison Benguerel, after Mademoiselle Benguerel, the owner of the property, who lived on the ground floor, where she also made Gruyère cheese. It was a far cry from the life the boys had enjoyed in England, where they had had the run of huge houses such as Babbacombe and, even in Tite Street, had been used to the privileges of the upper middle class. Otho and his second family, by contrast, accessed their modest rooms via a wooden staircase that ran up the outside of the chalet and entered straight into the dining room, which also served as a study. Here the boys' education was resumed by Otho himself, who began tutoring them.

Constance's Kodak camera went with her to Bevaix. In the possession of Constance's grandson today there is an album with postage-stamp-sized photographs from his period depicting Otho, Mary and their children. There is just one image of Constance amid pages of images of the others. Gone are the beautiful dresses and hats. She wears a plain dark skirt and a white shirt. She looks like a governess.

The extraordinary loyalty and hope that defined Constance before Oscar went to prison re-emerged after her visit to her husband. From Bevaix she wrote to Emily Thursfield again, this time stating that Oscar 'cares for no one but myself and the children' and so 'by sticking to him now I may save him from even worse ... I think we women were meant to be comforters and I believe that no-one can really take my place now, or help him as I can.'[32]

Writing to Lady Mount-Temple, Constance revealed that her latest visit had made her determined to attempt another, more intimate visit to Oscar before the end of the year. 'I may even see him under more favourable circumstances than I did when I was in London a month ago,' she wrote.

> I saw him only as one is allowed by special permission to see any prisoner but I really could not go through it again. There were two gratings and a passage between us, and so we had to speak. It was awful, more awful than anything I have ever been through, and worse even for him I suppose. I came over to London for five days only to see him, but next time I shall word my request differently, and in a month's time I hope to see him face to face, tho even so, there must be a warden present all the time.[33]

If Constance did return to London in November for a second prison visit, it has gone unrecorded. In that month Oscar's name was once again splashed across the headlines when he had to appear at the bankruptcy court. With his hair cut short by the prison wardens, and wearing a short, unkempt beard, he stood to hear himself declared bankrupt and to see his affairs placed in the hands of the Official Receiver. This unwelcome publicity may have been enough to deter

Constance from returning to England as intended. But she may also have altered her plans because her health was yet again deteriorating. She was once more finding walking very hard indeed. Instead she decided that she and the boys should seek some sun for the winter. This news filtered back to her friends in England. Lady Mount-Temple's daughter Juliet, whose resolve to distance herself from Constance had melted, wrote to Constance from Babbacombe: 'Nervi sounds rather delicious for you for the winter.'[34]

Although life could hardly ever be delicious again for Constance, given her wider troubles, it is true that Nervi was a spectacular place. A village that clung to the cliffs surrounding an azure-blue bay, it lay close to Genoa on the Italian Riviera. Her motivation for wintering in Nervi was Margaret Brooke, the Ranee of Sarawak, who had a winter villa close by. Although Constance was enjoying her brother's company enormously, Bevaix was isolated. She missed her friends and the company she had always enjoyed at home. Margaret Brooke was one of many expatriates with villas in or around Nervi, and Constance must have hoped she could once again sample a little society.

Margaret Brooke was another older lady who would become a much needed shoulder for Constance. They had a great deal in common. The Ranee had gained her unusual title after marrying Sir Charles Brooke, the white Rajah of Sarawak.[35] But the marriage was an unhappy one, and she had lived apart from the Rajah for many years, in London and on the Continent. In London she had become friendly with many of the Pre-Raphaelite set that Constance knew – not least Ruskin and the Burne-Joneses. And when her son Bertram fell ill, she bought a villa outside Nervi where she could benefit from a better climate than London could offer.

'It was a nice little abode, painted white with yellow shutters and had a lovely view over the Mediterranean and its cliff-bound coasts to which clung olive woods, even rose gardens dipping themselves into the sea,' the Ranee wrote in her autobiography. 'Sometimes we were pleased, sometimes rather sorry that we were but one mile removed from Nervi, where an enormous hotel harboured portions of the beau-monde from Russia, Austria and elsewhere.'[36]

In the end Constance found an apartment just outside Nervi, in Casa Barbagelata at nearby Sori. This was still nice and close to the Ranee and allowed the two women to explore a friendship that had begun in London. The Ranee was also a keen photographer, but more advanced than Constance, since she could enlarge and print her work – skills she now began to teach her friend. With the studiousness and sense of purpose that Constance applied to everything, she now found an Italian maid and began Italian lessons.

Otho and his family joined Constance in the apartment in Sori that winter. But while Otho, Mary and the children were quick to explore the local countryside and its customs, Constance was housebound much of the time.

'I want to go and see all the lovely little villages around here. They look so sweet with their pink houses with the green shutters and their gardens full of orange trees and palms and all the lovely pergola,' she told Georgina in early December. But the fact was Constance could barely move. 'There is a large garden here, but I have not been into it yet,' she complained.[37]

Confined to her apartment, Constance had begun making new plans for the boys' education. She determined to return to Britain in the spring and bring the boys back with her. She had decided to send them to school in 'Gt Berkhamsted to be under Mr Gowring first and then I hope with Dr Fry the headmaster'.[38]

It seems likely that this plan was forged with her friend Emily Thursfield, who lived in Great Berkhamsted. Constance was also good friends with Lady Lothian, who lived at Ashridge, just outside Great Berkhamsted. At the heart of her thinking seems to have been a notion that she could reintroduce her sons to their homeland under the protection of new identities, because since October 1895 Constance, Cyril and Vyvyan Wilde had ceased to exist. Constance had determined to change her and her sons' names, and she had chosen the same family name that Otho now used. One day in October the documentation had arrived that changed Constance, Cyril and Vyvyan Wilde to Constance, Cyril and Vyvyan Holland.

14

Madame Holland

JUST BEFORE CHRISTMAS 1895 Madame Holland, as she was now
known, checked into a clinic in the Italian town of Genoa. The
clinic was the private concern of Signor Bossi, a gynaecologist who
was more than amenable to dealing with some of the less savoury
medical procedures that some Englishwomen could only have
undertaken on the Continent.

Mme Holland was not the only person in the clinic concealing a
former identity. One of her fellow patients, apparently delivering an
illegitimate child, was

> only 22 and is here evidently under an assumed name, she is the
> daughter of very rich people in London, she's more French than
> English and she doesn't want the nuns to know who she is. The
> Doctor posts all her letters for her and fetches those addressed to her
> ... She told me that she would tell me her mother's name, but I
> don't want to know it and I think she is suspicious and thinks always
> that the Sisters want to find out her secret. She is very pretty and very
> young. She's operated, as she calls it yesterday and today she is
> very unwell.[1]

Constance had come to the clinic because Bossi had claimed that he
was able to treat her mobility and the creeping paralysis in her right
arm and legs. His treatment included an operation, followed by a
month-long stay in his private clinic and complete bed rest. The
indications are that the operation had a gynaecological aspect.

Constance was miserable that her stay in the clinic was over the
Christmas period, but she was genuinely hopeful that the medical

procedures could improve her walking, which had been failing for so long. She took a photograph of Lady Mount-Temple into the clinic along with a little crucifix that Cyril had given her, and she quickly became friendly with the Dominican Sisters who provided the nursing care there. They wore white dresses and black veils, and one, Soeur Catherine ('refreshingly quiet & serene and beautiful with a fair face and grey eyes that look straight at one without any arrière pensée'[2]), became particularly close to Constance. Bossi was also charming to his latest patient. Although he told Constance that he normally charged up to 3,000 francs for the treatment he had given her, he had agreed to accept whatever fee she was able to muster in her reduced circumstances. Otho and Mary made a fuss of her as best they could. Otho sent her a book, which Constance considered far too expensive, and Mary sent her a blue blouse that Sister Catherine made Constance try on, even though Constance insisted it was far too beautiful for her.

By mid-January, Constance, confident that her dreadful aches and pains had been substantially improved, was full of plans to return home. She still intended to be staying around Great Berkhamsted in the spring and was considering spending the summer back at Babbacombe with Lady Mount-Temple.

But if there was a new optimism in Constance, there were also new worries. Although she had seriously begun to consider reconciliation with Oscar, this had depended entirely on his assurances that he would put his past life, and former associations, behind him. But now Constance could sense that many of Oscar's old friends were encouraging him down different paths. She was not alone in her fears. *Her* friends and allies were becoming nervous too, and retrenching back to their earlier position that divorce was, on balance, better than reconciliation.

'I am again being urged to divorce Mr Wilde and I am as usual blown about by contrary winds,' she explained to Georgina.

Everyone who knows anything about him believes that he wants my wretched money and indeed it seems from his present actions as tho it were so. Poor poor fellow, if it is so, it is he who suffers most throwing away affection and everything else. I cannot understand the greed for money that makes men cast everything else to the winds . . . And I don't know what I am to do if I divorce him now. It will be his own fault and that of his friends who are forcing on me a step in connection with money of which I do not approve. However time will show, and nothing else, what is going to happen![3]

The 'step in connection with money' to which Constance alludes was a matter arising from Oscar's bankruptcy. In September 1895 Bosie's father, keen to recoup his court costs, had forced bankruptcy on Oscar. Oscar, in his prison garb, had been dragged to the bankruptcy court, where his debts were noted as standing at £3,591, most of which had been incurred on behalf of Bosie. However, the hearing was adjourned because Oscar's lawyers suggested that his debts could well be covered by subscriptions by his friends.

One of the assets that had been placed in the hands of the Official Receiver was a life interest in Constance's private income. This annuity entitled Oscar to his wife's income if she were to predecease him. If Constance had divorced or been judicially separated from her husband, Oscar's claim on his wife's money would have been dealt with as part of those proceedings. But Constance's delay in this had created an interesting situation regarding the life interest. The Receiver now held this policy, and it was technically up for sale. Constance could both buy back the annuity herself and settle it on her children, or Oscar's friends could buy it for him, thus securing him an income if Constance were to die.

More Adey, an art historian, gallerist and close friend of Robbie Ross, had taken on the task of looking after Oscar's legal affairs and was determined that the policy should be Oscar's. The move chimed with those warnings George Lewis had offered Constance at the time of Oscar's trial: that eventually her husband would come after her for her money. After all that her husband's actions had put her through, this latest development was unwelcome, to say the least.

An opportunity to meet and discuss the matter face to face with Oscar presented itself in an unfortunate guise. In February a letter arrived from Lily Wilde, Willie's wife. Lily had shown particular kindness to her disgraced in-law during and after the trial. She had proved considerate and thoughtful, and this letter was no exception. It contained the news that Lady Wilde had died on 3 February. She had never managed to communicate with Oscar since his incarceration, despite several attempts on her part.

Lily knew enough of Oscar's relationship with his mother to understand that news of her death would come as a particularly terrible blow. She knew that it would have to be broken to him very carefully.

'I have written to Mr Haldane for leave to see O,' Constance responded to Lily. 'I quite agree with you that it must be broken to him and I believe it will half kill him. Poor Oscar has been bitterly punished for breaking the laws of his country. I am not strong but I could bear the journey better if I thought that such a terrible thing would not be told to him roughly.'[4]

Despite her frail condition, for the second time in six months Constance travelled back to London to see her husband, who had now been moved to Reading gaol. Now using her new name, she was sufficiently courageous to stay at the Grosvenor Hotel, from where she wrote to Otho on 21 February.

> I went to Reading on Wednesday and saw poor O, they say he's quite well, but he is an absolute wreck compared with what he was. On Wednesday I dined with the Macebrys and yesterday I saw the Lows, the Simons and the Burne-Jones who all asked after you. I cannot write now, I mean to write long letters but I seem to have lost all power. Mrs Christian's coming to see me this morning and I am lunching with the Millais. I'm dining with the Wilkes, your loving sister Constance.[5]

The letter is an interesting mix of tea and scandal, social parties arranged around a prison visit to a dishonoured husband. But it's also indicative of Constance's extraordinary ability to accommodate events, cope and move forward. Few people could have shown such mettle. For a woman once cripplingly shy, the brazenness of taking rooms at one of London's most visible hotels and then pursuing an energetic social diary is testimony to the sheer bravery that Constance was able to display under circumstances that might have reduced others to total breakdown. She could take anything in her stride, from cup cakes to prison, from art exhibitions to bankruptcy. These were facets of her life that she now dealt with equally.

The meeting with Oscar had been everything that Constance had hoped. In return for her kindness to him, Oscar confessed much to Constance that he had failed to admit in the past. Crucially, he confessed his fears for his children. Considering the failure of Bosie's own mother as a parent, he wanted to be sure that Constance was properly equipped to deal with her own children.

'I told her everything,' Oscar later revealed to Bosie in his confessional letter *De Profundis*.

> I told her ... the reason of the endless notes with 'Private' on the envelope that used to come to Tite Street from your mother, so constantly that my wife used to laugh and say that we must be collaborating on a society novel ... I told her that if she was frightened of facing the responsibility of the life of another, though her own child, she should get a guardian to help her.[6]

Oscar also made it clear to Constance that he absolutely approved of her acquiring the life interest so that it could be settled on the children and that he would not contest it. Constance consequently promised that, whatever happened, she would not leave Oscar penniless. On 10 March, Oscar wrote to his friend Robbie Ross confirming these wishes and asking his friends to act accordingly: 'I feel that I have brought such unhappiness on her and such ruin on my children that I have no right to go against her wishes in anything.'[7]

On 29 February, Constance visited her solicitors at the offices in Victoria Street and made a new will. In it she made her whole estate over to her family friend and relative Adrian Hope, with the express wish that on her death he should realize her assets and invest them, and then hold everything in trust for the boys until they were twenty-one. Hope was made her executor, and the will stated that it was Constance's 'earnest wish and desire' that he should also be the boys' guardian and have sole control over them.

Reassured, Constance returned to Italy. The tenure of the apartment in Sori had come to an end, so she moved into rooms at the Hotel Eden in Nervi. She had found London very expensive and had returned with a heightened sense of the limits of her finances and the need for economy. Consequently, after a few days at the Eden she changed to the Hotel Nervi, which was substantially cheaper ('I am very comfortable here and pay 26 francs, it would have been 36 at the Eden'[8]).

At the end of March, Constance's plans for the boys to be schooled in England were suddenly dropped. It seems likely that attempts to enter Cyril and Vyvyan at Berkhamsted School had been politely declined. Despite her best attempts to protect herself and her boys, scandal continued to follow Constance around. She and the boys were in Nervi for the annual festival of flowers and joined the Ranee, who had taken a suite of rooms at her hotel for the occasion. On the day of the celebrations the hotel proprietor kept calling Constance 'Mrs Wilde' rather than 'Mrs Holland', a fact that became more embarrassing when Cyril pointed out his mother's new name. It was a small mistake. But there were greater potential embarrassments close by. Constance had heard Bosie was staying in Genoa, 'so I don't feel much inclined to go over there', she told Otho.[9]

Since Oscar's conviction, Bosie had continued to proclaim his love and loyalty to the once celebrated Wilde. In fact, he was planning to dedicate a volume of poems to Oscar. Not only was this awkward for Constance, but Oscar also found it distasteful. A year in gaol had turned him against Bosie, whom he now referred to as 'Douglas'. Oscar wrote to his friends begging them to acquire letters and jewellery from Oscar still in Bosie's possession. 'The thought that they are in his hands is horrible to me, and though my unfortunate children will never of course bear my name, still they know whose sons they are and I must try and shield them from the possibility of any further revolting disclosure or scandal.'[10]

It was almost a year since Oscar's conviction, and although Constance had managed to keep her head above water, she was not without moments of despair. As her plans were forced to change yet again, she confessed to Georgina Mount-Temple that 'Some nights here I have had visions of how near the sea was and of how "life's fitful fever" might be soon ended, but then there are the boys and they save me from anything too desperate!'[11]

And so, after yet another disappointment, Constance once again thought on her feet and came up with a new plan. With Bosie far too close in Genoa, and English schools proving resistant to taking the children, she decided the boys would be schooled in Germany.

This decision was informed by the Ranee, who was planning to rent a villa in Heidelberg in Germany. She had a son who needed to improve his German in preparation for the diplomatic service. With the Ranee considering a sojourn in this German city, Constance suddenly decided that she should send her sons to Heidelberg too. She ordered Baedeker's guide to the town and began to make inquiries about schools and to explore the costs of a modest set of rooms for herself and the children. The Pension Anglais would offer her a single and double room for 75 francs a week, she told Otho. If the boys boarded, she could take a single room for substantially less, but this would have to be balanced against the £60 a year that Heidelberg College charged for boarders.[12] Constance was doing her sums.

The Holland family, as they were now, arrived in Heidelberg in April. As a renowned centre of learning and the home of the famous university, it was a city rich in schools. According to Vyvyan, his mother had managed to enrol the boys in a German school initially. The boys, who had so far had a very limited experience of school, were immediately troublesome. The schools practised corporal punishment. When Vyvyan was hit on the head with a ruler by one of his masters, Cyril apparently kicked the master on the shins. The boys were expelled from this first establishment almost instantly. Constance had scarcely more luck at a second school, where this time it was not the staff but the pupils who were attacked by the two young Holland boys.

Finally Constance settled Vyvyan and Cyril in the English school in the town, Neuenheim College. Most of the masters were British, and most of the boys were being educated in Germany because their own scandals and troubles had forced extractions from Britain. So in a sense Cyril and Vyvyan were in good company, and gradually they settled in.

Constance's life in Heidelberg became very simple indeed. Living in her small *pension*, reading became her greatest pleasure, along with small domestic chores. She began to teach herself German, of course, and she set herself the task of making cushions for Otho and Mary much of the time. She bought a photograph album and began to mount all her Kodak snaps.

She had very little in the way of society in Heidelberg. She was utterly astounded and delighted to hear that her friends Sir Hugh and Lady Low were passing through the city that summer and intended to see her. This was noted as a rare treat. Otherwise it was the Ranee who was Constance's most regular and loyal visitor. She would read to Constance from her diary about the life she used to lead in Sarawak.

Constance had joined the local English church and committed herself to being responsible for the flowers throughout July. But above and beyond small excursions to church and to town, she was essentially becoming housebound again. Signor Bossi's operation had failed.

'I'm afraid I've no news because nothing happens,' Constance wrote to Otho in mid-July. 'The Castle is always here and always looks beautiful and I have not yet been over it, because this entails a long walk and that I am not up to.'[13]

As an expatriate, Constance found that her life was becoming defined by the post. Her letters are full of instructions and information about things being boxed up and sent on, or having been safely received. Customs transactions, the cost of postage and the irritation of weight tariffs become part of her daily language. Many of her letters are concerned with cheques from her bank in England that need signing. It's small wonder that the boys became keen stamp collectors during this period. This in itself accounts for much of the correspondence between Constance and her friends and family, as she requests particular stamps for the boys.

Of course, much of her correspondence also concerned Oscar. After her arrival in Heidelberg, Constance's relations with Oscar's friends took a distinct change for the worse. As far as she was concerned, Oscar had agreed to allow her solicitor, Mr Hargrove, to buy the life interest in their marriage settlement. But the self-appointed group of friends who were taking care of Oscar's interests, specifically Robbie Ross and More Adey, were still attempting to block Constance's bid for the life interest and had lodged a competing offer for it with the Receiver. Constance was outraged. It felt like another betrayal. Robbie Ross wrote to her in June to explain the reasoning behind the move, claiming that rumours had circulated that Queensberry himself was planning to acquire the interest and that this had to be prevented.

Whatever the motivations of Oscar's friends, Constance was appalled by their actions, and now she threatened to withdraw her offer to support Oscar to the tune of £150 a year on his release. The business matters that were currently proposed were utterly incomprehensible to her, she told Robbie. She was, after all, a woman now 'obliged to live abroad'. She reminded him that 'the boys will be forced to make their own way in life heavily handicapped by their father's madness for I can consider it nothing else'.[14]

After Robbie, More Adey decided he must write to Constance. He was petitioning the Home Secretary for an early release for Oscar and was desperately keen that Constance's signature should be part of the petition. Hers was perhaps the most persuasive voice Oscar might have at his disposal. But after her departure from Nervi, and after the bid for the life interest by Oscar's camp, Constance's advisers had closed ranks around her. Her new address was not disclosed by Hargrove or Constance's family. More Adey was therefore forced to reach Constance through mutual friends. In doing so, further parties became drawn into Constance and Oscar's affairs.

At one time Margaret Brooke had lived in Wimbledon, where she had made the acquaintance of Adela Schuster – 'The Lady of Wimbledon', as she was referred to by Oscar. The socialite and literary enthusiast Adela was one of Oscar's supporters and was in regular contact with More Adey. Schuster now informed Adey that her great friend the Ranee was in close touch with Constance.

'I have heard from my friend at Heidelberg,' Adela Schuster wrote to Adey on 23 June 1896, 'a very kind letter evidently ready to do all she can – but she writes guardedly – she does not definitely say that she has or has not appealed to Mrs Wilde, but she advises me to write to her myself detailing exactly what Mrs Wilde should do.'[15]

The Ranee was clearly not being quite straight with Adela, for what is revealed next implies a very considered response which Constance must have almost dictated to the Ranee regarding Adey's request for Constance's signature on his petition.

> She then proceeds to tell me that she is quite sure Mrs W will do anything she can to affect her husband's release provided she is assured of one or two points: Mrs W wishes first to obtain some certainty of promise from Oscar . . . that O will not attempt to interfere with the boys; and secondly that she is to be allowed to have her own money to bring them up as she thinks best. Assured of these things (she says) she would 'tear herself to little bits' to get O's release.

Although Oscar had himself suggested that Constance must take charge of the boys, in light of the recent moves by his friends Constance clearly felt the need to restate this position. She was aware that what Oscar wanted and what those acting on his behalf were initiating were not necessarily the same thing. While at Nervi, Constance had even become nervous that some friends of Oscar might actually attempt to remove the boys from her. And she had become rather paranoid about their safety.[16]

It seems that the request for Constance to 'have her own money' represents a desire on Constance's behalf to have complete financial freedom from her husband, such as would be accorded her by the courts were she to divorce him. Constance was still seeking to avoid a formal divorce, the attendant proceedings, costs and publicity, but she wanted nevertheless the kind of monetary separation that a divorce would provide. And so, as part of this desire, the thorny issue of the life interest was raised again.

Adela continued: 'Can you get at the friends of O's who are bidding for the life interest, and will you get their consent and empower me to say that they will not attempt to bid against her if she will appeal for Oscar's release?'

More Adey did not comply with Adela's request. Instead he wrote a letter to Constance explaining the nature of the bid for the life interest. This letter was sent to Adela, who in turn sent it to the Ranee for Constance's attention. In the letter Adey revealed that, for those on Oscar's side of the fence, there were mounting suspicions that those advising Constance were hostile to Oscar. In effect, Adey was suggesting he did not entirely trust Constance's word and wanted more assurances.

'I am instructed by admirers of Mr Oscar Wilde to buy the Life interest under your marriage settlement for his benefit,' he explained to Constance.

> My clients are persons who have never had the pleasure of his acquaintance nor of yours. They are actuated by admiration for his talents and profound pity for his lamentable circumstances . . . They understand that you wish to purchase the life interest yourself and they are anxious to meet your wishes to the best of their power. It was their original intention to hand over to you upon what ever terms you pleased, one half for settlement upon your sons. The other half they proposed to settle upon Mr Wilde . . . As an alternative they would still be willing to withdraw altogether if you would secure to Mr Wilde in some other way the enjoyment of an annuity in the event of your predeceasing him . . . Mr Oscar Wilde has had no voice with my clients and indeed as far as I know imagines that their efforts have ceased.[17]

Constance replied, but her letter does not exist. Adela's comments on it do, however, and from them one can piece together that Constance was not interested in bargaining with people she did not know. Her conditions were that those attempting to buy the life interest must back off. She would not enter into promises about other annuities or be bargained with.

Constance had always been clear-headed when it came to business. As a young woman she had been through the details of financial settlements between her grandfather and mother; she had worked with lawyers to protect her brother's assets from his creditors; and now she was going to fight as hard as she could for her own. What is more, she had done her duty by Oscar. She had bailed out his debts more than once, and helped his mother financially. Otho had even loaned Oscar £500, of which some outstanding amount was still due. Her sense of indignation was strong in the matter of the life interest. And she had nothing really to lose. For what Oscar's side had not worked out was that, if she divorced Oscar, the life interest would be voided anyway. The stupidity of their position only served to inflame her further.

At first More Adey actually doubted that such a hard-nosed letter could be genuine. Bizarrely, he asked Adela Schuster if she thought the letter was some kind of forgery. Adey perhaps knew only a version of Constance informed by her somewhat shy and quiet manner. He was not, perhaps, familiar with the fiery, determined and highly intelligent version of Constance that Otho, Oscar and her close female friends, such as Georgina Mount-Temple, would have recognized. Adela, however, considered the letter genuine. What is more, she was in perfect sympathy with Constance and told More Adey as much.

'The opposition of O's friends sets her against her husband and will probably interfere with her being kind to him when he comes out,' Adela warned Adey in August 1896.

> In every way – financially and socially he is very dependent on her good will . . . Whatever O's friends may do or say she will certainly attribute their action in this matter to him, the more so as she knows that they have seen him several times, & she will soon naturally believe that they would not act in defiance of his wishes. All this is irritating her against him. This in itself seems to me cause enough to

drop all opposition to her, and then will you consider what is the advantage you gain for O – set against all this possible loss?[18]

Adey failed properly to heed what in fact was a very sound assessment of the situation. He wrote to Oscar and muddied the water further. This time, although he suggested that Oscar should perhaps accede to some of Constance's wishes, Adey warned Oscar against signing any legal documents that would in any way diminish his paternal rights over his children. He suggested that Constance's advisers were in fact now declared enemies of Oscar.

In the meantime, in July, Oscar petitioned the Home Secretary himself for an early release. He argued that his crimes were in fact 'forms of sexual madness' and that he had been suffering from 'the most horrible form of erotomania which made him forget his wife and children'.[19] He also complained that his health was deteriorating, he was becoming deaf and his eyesight was concerning him. His petition failed to deliver the early release he had sought, but the authorities did grant him permission for more writing and reading material in his cell.

In September, Oscar wrote to Adey. He had now obviously considered Adey's suggestions that Constance's family and advisers were hostile to him and suggested that, when it came to the guardianship of his children, someone from Constance's family should be resisted. He suggested Arthur Clifton, but Clifton himself declined this suggestion.

It is unclear whether Oscar's views regarding a suitable guardian were made known to Constance. If so, they would only have been another among several aggravations that had now placed her side and Oscar's in conflict. It is little surprise that, by October, Constance had had enough. She instructed Hargrove to write to Oscar directly and make the simple point: do as she required or she would divorce him. The divorce courts would annul any claim he had on her life interest and under current circumstances would award her the guardianship of the children.

Oscar's mental state had deteriorated greatly during his time in gaol. After suffering terrible health problems that ranged from bouts of dysentery to the problems with his hearing and sight that he mentioned in his petition, his mind was also becoming fragile. Arthur Clifton, who visited him in October 1896, noted how shockingly thin his appearance was. He was broken-hearted and felt the victim of the most savage punishment.

Malnourished, suffering from lack of sleep and hard labour, Oscar had become grateful for any tiny kindness and irked by any further distress visited on him. He had been greatly moved by Constance when she had visited him in gaol, and he was grateful for the time and effort friends such as Adey were spending on his behalf. But when cold, business-like letters from Constance's solicitors arrived, compared with the persuasive letters that Adey wrote against Constance and her advisers, Oscar far too quickly began to resent what he saw as the high-handed, dictatorial manner in which a wife who had once been utterly dedicated to him now behaved.

In December 1896, Hargrove received notice from the Official Receiver that indeed half the life settlement in the Wilde marriage was about to be sold to Oscar's friends. Hargrove wrote to Oscar and repeated the position that, if this sale went through, Constance would withdraw her offer to pay Oscar £150 a year on release from prison.

But now Oscar had become fully persuaded by Adey and others. Living under the misapprehension that his friends had raised a considerable sum of money for him that would take care of his expenses for a couple of years after his release from prison, he decided to thumb his nose at Constance's offer of an annual income and instead pursue the life interest against her wishes. He wrote to More Adey to this effect.

By the end of December, Oscar's position was emboldened yet further. He decided now that he wanted an income *as well as* the life interest, and he wrote to his newly appointed solicitors, Stoker and Hansell, to make this point clear.

'With regard to money affairs, the offer made to me by my wife of £150 a year is, of course, extremely small,' he wrote.

I certainly hoped that £200 would have been fixed on. I understand my wife alleges as one of the reasons for £150 being selected that she wishes to pay off a debt of £500 due from me to her brother Otho Lloyd at the rate of £50 a year. I think, with Mr Adey, that I should have the £200 if that debt should be paid off by me.[20]

Oscar was talking as if he were in a position to bargain. And he continued in the same vein: 'With regard to my life interest I sincerely hope that half at least will be purchased for me.'

Constance was left with little choice. She and her lawyers began once again to explore the divorce proceedings that they had delayed for eighteen months. She also moved forward with sorting out the custody of the boys.

On 12 February 1897 the courts awarded Constance custody of the children, and she became their legal guardian alongside a responsible person of her choosing: her relative and former Tite Street neighbour Adrian Hope. In terms of divorcing Oscar, matters proved more complex. Given the amount of time that had elapsed since Oscar's trial, from a legal perspective Constance could no longer divorce him for the 'crimes' revealed in the cases of 1895. Her reluctance to divorce her husband after such revelations amounted to her condoning them, in legal terms at least. If she were to obtain a divorce, Constance would have to bring about a new court case and prove new grounds. So now the prospect of a judicial separation was revisited.

By April 1897, Oscar was preparing himself for his release from gaol. He would have served two years by 20 May 1897. As he began to get his affairs together, the full folly of More Adey and Robbie Ross dawned on him. Finally it became clear to him what Constance had grasped from the outset: that judicial separation would mean he would have to relinquish any claim on the life interest anyway. He suddenly realized the stupidity of his friends in alienating Constance. This fact was brought home all the harder by news that, contrary to his belief that his friends had raised a substantial sum of money for him to live on, in fact only very limited funds were available to him. His friends had taken Constance for a fool but, as Oscar knew well, that was one thing Constance could never be accused of.

Writing to Robbie Ross, Oscar now reminded him of the letter in which he instructed Robbie not to go against Constance's wishes. It was, of course, far too late.

'You were very wrong not to do so,' he rebuked his friend.

> Again how silly the long serious letters advising me not to surrender my rights over my children . . . My rights! I had none. A claim that a formal appeal to the judge in Chambers can quash in ten minutes . . . How much better if you had done as I asked you, as at that time my wife was kind and ready to let me see my two children and be with them occasionally . . . My wife was very sweet to me, and now she, very naturally, goes right against me. Of her character also a wrong estimate was made. She warned me that if I let my friends bid against her she would proceed to a certain course, and she will do so.[21]

By May 1897, Hargrove had drawn up a deed of separation that saw the life assurance returned in full to Constance and offered Oscar an income of just £150 a year. Oscar attempted to push back on a clause that suggested this income was dependent on him not mixing with disreputable people. But even in this he failed, and finally he was required not only to accept humbly what was offered but also to sign a deed of separation 'of the most pitifully stringent kind and of the most humiliating conditions'.

On 19 May 1897, Oscar Wilde left prison. He was so furious with More Adey over the management of his affairs with Constance that he had attempted to prevent his friend meeting him and accompanying him from the gaol, as had been planned. This inclination on Oscar's part had perhaps been heightened by the fact that Constance, against all the odds, made an unexpected last-minute gesture of kindness. Made aware that talk about substantial funds raised for Oscar were in fact not going to be forthcoming, she herself made sure that his immediate expenses would be covered as he began his new life. Oscar revealed to his friend Reggie Turner that 'The person who has sent me money to pay for my food and expenses on going out is my dear sweet wife.'[22]

And so with his wife's money in his pockets Oscar left Reading gaol on 18 May and travelled by cab to Twyford station with two prison guards. He took the train to London, where he spent a final night in Pentonville prison. On the morning of 19 May, Oscar met More Adey and the Revd Stewart Headlam (who had stood him bail two years earlier) and took a cab to the latter's house. That afternoon he went to Newhaven with Adey and then took the night ferry to Dieppe.

By the time he arrived in France, Oscar had assumed his new identity. He was to be known as Sebastian Melmoth, a name inspired by the novel written by his forebear Charles Maturin, *Melmoth the Wanderer*. He wrote instantly to Constance. She received the letter four days later and told Otho it was 'full of penitence'. By return Constance sent Oscar photographs of Cyril and Vyvyan and a note suggesting that they should meet.

15

Life is a terrible thing

ON 22 JUNE 1897, Queen Victoria celebrated her diamond
jubilee. It was her sixtieth year on the throne, and both Oscar
and Constance – true Victorians in spite of everything else they were
– celebrated with her.

Oscar threw a party for the local children in the northern French
town of Berneval-sur-Mer, where he had been staying since his
arrival in France a month earlier. He put on a turquoise shirt for the
benefit of fifteen 'gamins', and from half-past four in the afternoon
until seven o'clock that evening he treated his young guests to
strawberries and cream, 'apricots, chocolates, cakes and sirop de
grenadine'. Oscar had commissioned a 'huge iced cake with Jubilé
de la Reine Victoria in pink sugar just rosetted with green, and a great
wreath of red roses round it all'.[1] All the children were given presents
from an assortment of accordions, trumpets and horns, and during the
party Oscar encouraged them to play the British national anthem.

Meanwhile, in Italy, Constance was back in Nervi, staying this
time at the Ranee's Villa Raffo. The day before the jubilee she had
written to Vyvyan. 'Why do you specially keep St Louis's day at your
school, and which St Louis is it?' Constance asked.

> Mind you answer this when you write next. I saw two processions on
> Corpus Christi day, one at 10 o'clock in the morning in Genoa,
> where I had gone to see the book that the Ranee is giving to our
> Queen. The other procession was here after vespers and we . . . threw
> flowers as the Host passed. I saw a beautiful service once on Corpus
> Christi day at the Oratory, the biggest of the many Catholic Churches
> in London where Cardinal Vaughan led the Te Deum that was sung

in all the catholic churches yesterday all through England in honour of the Queen's accession.[2]

'I hope you remember you are an English boy,' Constance continued, 'and are proud of your queen as you should be, for she is a good woman. It is 60 years since she came to the throne, and to-morrow is to take place the great procession through London, where every-one who can will see the Queen!! I have ordered a book of the procession to be sent to you.'

Since May 1896, when Constance had first visited Heidelberg with the boys, she had split her time between that city, Nervi, where she was close to the Ranee, and Otho's chalet in Bevaix. It was a pattern of life that she would repeat for the year ahead too.

After their first summer term at Neuenheim College, the boys had remained with Constance in the environs of Heidelberg for their summer holidays. They were staying in the Hotel Schloss, in the hills immediately above the city, so Constance felt she was at least saving the expense of travelling. The hotel was secluded, surrounded by woods and was accessed by a little funicular railway that ran from the main market-place in the city.

Constance and the boys settled in well. She became friendly with the proprietors, Herr and Frau Kohler. While Frau Kohler and Constance sewed together, the boys would talk stamps with Herr Kohler, who was fanatical about philately and would show Cyril and Vyvyan his extensive stamp collection, much to their delight.

With the commencement of the autumn term the boys returned to the college, and Constance headed back to Bevaix to stay with her brother. Remote from the busy social world she had once inhabited and all its fads and fashions, she nevertheless tried to keep up with some of the latest crazes. Many British newspapers were running graphology services, inviting their readers to submit examples of their handwriting for analysis. Constance duly sent off examples of her hand to both the *Evening News* and *Pearson's Weekly and Home Notes*.

'Calligro' from the former publication responded that the handwriting of a certain C. M. Holland 'denotes neatness order and persevering nature. You have a good temper and a well balanced mind – and affection is marked. You are not demonstrative nor do you wear your heart on your sleeve . . . You are easily led but cannot be driven.' Otho noted this summary of his sister was 'excellent, excepting that Constance was impatient and irritable from ill health and distress'.[3] However, he deemed the analysis that was sent from *Pearson's* perfect.

> You have an artistic appreciation of form and beauty and are a good deal influenced by outward appearances; your tastes are culti-vated and refined, you have some literary ability and a keen sense of humour and are an acute observer. Your moods are a little uncertain, one day you will be in high spirits, the next a prey to despondency. You are generous in some ways, affectionate, loyal and fairly unselfish.

Although Cyril was settled and fitting in well to the rough and tumble of school life, Constance was receiving troubling reports from Vyvyan, who remained unhappy at his new school. 'My darling Vyvyan,' she wrote to him from Bevaix, 'I enclose stamps for you from Otho . . . Are you learning to be less babyish? I do hope so Darling. You are quite old enough now, & of course what you really will have most difficulty in learning is consideration for other people's feelings & that you are not the centre of everything!'[4]

Despite her and the school's best efforts, by Christmas Constance realized that Vyvyan would have to be removed from Neuenheim College. In December she travelled back to Heidelberg and collected him, and together they spent a few days in Verona together as plans were made to put him into a Jesuit college in Monaco at the begin-ning of the new year.

Constance had been given the address of the college in Monaco by her old family friend Mrs Cochrane. Constance had decided to try and hire a villa near Nervi, and make the Italian Riviera her home in the mid-term at least. Mrs Cochrane had recognized that a school in Monte Carlo, close by, would be very practical.

Despite their greatly reduced means, the legacy of their formerly privileged life still brought the Holland family some adventures. Princess Alice of Monaco was both a close friend of the Ranee and had been on very good terms with Oscar. Although she and Constance were not acquainted, once she heard from the Ranee that Oscar's son was at school in her principality, she made a point of meeting him. Vyvyan was accordingly presented at the grand Grimaldi Palace.

'I was so glad to hear all about your visit to the Princess,' Constance wrote to Vyvyan at the end of February. 'Did she speak English or French to you? And was she kind & did you like her? I have never seen her & only know about her by name.'[5] Constance was finally growing to appreciate her younger son. He was more similar to her than perhaps she had imagined. He was proving something of a linguist, like his mother, writing to her in Italian from the moment he was installed in Monaco. He was also developing a profound interest in religion and a strong appetite for Catholicism, which pleased her enormously. Her letters to him reveal a lively dialogue between them that ranged across religion, stamp collecting and world politics.

'Aunt Mary and Lizzie go tomorrow,' Constance wrote to Vyvyan from the hotel in Nervi, where in the first few months of 1897 she was once again staying. Her aunt and cousin had been to Japan, where cousin Lilias now lived with her new husband, who was in the diplomatic service there.

> It has been very nice having them here as otherwise it is very lonely. I am afraid there is no news to tell you as nothing ever happens here but we are wildly interested about affairs in Crete & would like to see the island taken away from the Turks who are horrid and given to the Greeks who are splendid . . . I like your little pictures so much that you send me & they go into my Bible.[6]

As Constance's hunt for an appropriate villa near Nervi continued, she moved from the Hotel Nervi to become a guest in the Ranee's own Villa Raffo, which must have been a relief for Constance, who was now continuously worried about money.

'The kind Ranee is having me with her now & of course I like being here very much,' she wrote to Vyvyan.

> I am going to try and get something near here to live in & have a resting place not a hotel. If the Villa Bigatli where Mr Hardcastle was last year is big enough & is to be had I shall get that as there seems nothing unfurnished to be had which of course I should prefer. I think I shall stay at Nervi till the Ranee goes next month & then go to Otho for a month. We shall probably spend the holidays somewhere in Switzerland but I have not made up my mind where.[7]

At the Villa Raffo, Constance took more Kodaks.

> I photograph a great deal now & have learned to develop & to print. The Ranee takes beautiful photos now, and she has taken charming things of me! I can only take things out of doors in the sun but she takes beautiful heads 'a pose' in Harry's room . . . We have very little sun here lately & I don't get out much, but then I should not get out much if it were sunny as I cannot walk properly.[8]

It was no longer just Constance's legs that were failing her. Her handwriting from this period reveals the difficulty she was now having in holding a pen properly. Her once even, easily legible hand, was becoming spidery and disjointed and looked more like something written by an eighty-year-old than that of someone in their late thirties. Constance discovered a typewriter at the Villa Raffo and found that easier than using a pen.

On his release from gaol Oscar had written to Constance inviting her and the boys to Dieppe to see him. In fact the pair were corresponding regularly. But Constance, who in the past had crossed continents to see her husband in prison, now delayed. She had conceded that she and Oscar would meet, but when and whether with the boys was something she could not immediately commit to. The massive deterioration in her mobility once again may well have contributed to her reluctance to rush and meet Oscar. The fact that the boys were mid-term in their boarding-school may have been another practical consideration for her. But this was no time for practicalities. It was time for a grand gesture. That Constance failed to grasp this proved a fatal mistake.

'It is a terrible punishment,' Oscar wrote to Robbie Ross, describing his wife's reticence, 'and oh! how I deserve it. But it makes me feel disgraced and evil and I don't want to feel that.'[9] However evil and disgraced he felt, a part of Oscar still wanted to impress the woman he had so let down. On leaving gaol he had almost immediately written an article on the treatment of children in prison. It was published at the end of May in *The Chronicle,* and straight away Oscar asked for a copy to be sent to Constance.

But although Oscar wanted to impress his wife, he was also in desperate need of love and craved respect once more after the humiliation of prison life. While he now waited to see Constance, there were others who were bombarding him daily with letters – none more so than Bosie Douglas. Very quickly Oscar developed the impression that Constance no longer cared properly for him, whereas the love of others continued to burn brightly.

Quite quickly Oscar also refined those views about homosexuality he had expressed in prison. Homosexuality itself was not a disease; it was materialism and over-indulgence that had been his sin, he now stated. This he explained in July in a letter to his old friend Carlos Blacker, a man once so close to Oscar that the latter had dedicated *The Happy Prince* to him: 'I was living a life unworthy of an artist, and though I do not hold with the British view of morals that sets Messalina above Sporus, I see that materialism in life coarsens the soul, and that the hunger of the body and the appetites of the flesh desecrate always, and often destroy.'[10]

It was Constance who had provided Blacker with Oscar's address. Blacker was also living in exile, in Freiburg in Germany. He and his wife, Carrie, had been on the Continent ever since the Duke of Newcastle accused him of cheating at cards, an accusation that in the nineteenth century clearly warranted flight. In June, Blacker had written to Constance asking for Oscar's address in Berneval, which she readily provided, urging him to write.

Blacker, like so many others, now began to involve himself in

Constance's and Oscar's affairs. After spending July in Bevaix with Otho, Constance met the boys in August, once their school terms had ended, and took them for a holiday in the Black Forest. 'It is exquisitely lovely with wonderful air,' she told Otho. 'Here we are high above everything . . . this is the highest parish in Germany, 3750 feet high, so you see you are not so much higher after all.'[11] She then joined the Blackers in Freiburg for the best part of September.

Photographs Constance took on her little Kodak of this holiday still survive. Blacker and his wife sit on a swing amid their and Constance's children. They stand on a dusty road, turn and smile to the camera. Everyone is relaxed and natural. It seemed a particularly happy time, with reports of Cyril riding a new bicycle that one of Constance's Napier cousins had sent from England. It was too small, and Blacker became entrusted with organizing a replacement.

Although Constance's correspondence with Oscar during this period no longer exists, it is clear that Oscar continued to press his desperate wish to see his sons during their school holidays. Blacker, however, now adopting some form of diplomatic role on behalf of the couple, suggested that, rather than Constance travelling to Dieppe with the boys to see Oscar, he should come and join them all once Constance was settled into her new villa. Constance was excited by this prospect. After all, she had finally secured the Villa Elvira, at Bogliasco, just outside Nervi. Their meeting there could be private, without the prying eyes of a hotel. It seemed like a perfect plan.

Sitting on a site that overlooked the sea, with a large terrace that hung over a steep cliff falling into the Mediterranean, the Villa Elvira was ideal for Constance. It had the cool marble floor and high ceilings one would expect of the region, and four bedrooms, one of which was used by the servants. It had a large hall, which Constance used as a dining room, and a small drawing room. And with this villa Constance was determined to rebuild a new kind of life.

'I have 2 servants, a delightful cook to whom I pay 45 fs a month and a maid who gets 35 fs out of me & does everything for me personally,' Constance boasted contentedly.[12] Her great friend the Ranee was close by, and what was more, to her joy, Otho and Mary were proposing to move to the region from Switzerland to be nearer to her.

Constance arrived back in Nervi after holidaying with the Blackers at the end of September and moved into the Villa Elvira within days. She seems to have been lulled into a false sense of security regarding Oscar over the summer months, and remained quite sure that plans for Oscar to meet her at the villa were indeed confirmed, even though she had not had a letter from Oscar, as she had anticipated.

'Not a sign of Oscar or a word from him,' she wrote quite happily to Blacker, 'but I have an idea that he will turn up some day without writing. Thank you immensely – both of you – for all your kindness to me and to the boys while I was at Freiburg.'[13]

Having not yet had time to purchase new linen for her home, she hired linen from the local hotel in readiness for Oscar's arrival and even decided that there would be no pretence over Oscar's identity. She had written to Oscar and asked him to confirm when he would be arriving. In the same missive she pointed out that, when he visited her, he was to come as her husband. 'The people who live here know my brother and know that I have no other,' she explained to Blacker. 'Besides, I hate telling lies more than this terrible thing called life makes necessary.'[14]

But the day after she wrote so joyfully to Blacker, everything went wrong. On 26 September 1897, Constance received her long-awaited letter from Oscar. She was shattered to read that he had decided to delay his visit to her by a month, until late October. This was odd, given Oscar's desire to see the boys. They would be back at their schools in late October. But more worrying to Constance was the postmark on the letter. As the horror dawned on her, she immediately wrote to Blacker with her concerns: 'I have this morning received a letter from Naples saying that my letter has been forwarded from Paris . . . Question: has he seen the dreadful person at Capri? No-one goes to Naples at this time of year, so I see no other reason for his going, and I am unhappy . . . Write to me and tell me what to do.'[15]

In fact, Constance did not wait for Blacker's advice. Another letter sent in a different post but on the same day reveals the fury that began to take hold of her. She didn't need telling what the postmark meant. All those instincts that she had had about Bosie before and which she had suppressed she now understood immediately, and this time she recognized them for what they were. Oscar had gone to stay with Bosie in Naples. In doing so, he had chosen Bosie, not only over her but also over her sons, despite his protestations of his ardent desire to see them. The nightmare had returned. It all felt horribly familiar. This time she was having none of it. She wrote to Oscar and demanded to know whether he was with Bosie again. Her furious letter contained many harsh words. She accused Oscar of not caring for his children.

To Constance's horror, but presumably not to her surprise, within days Blacker was able to confirm that Oscar was with Bosie once more, sharing a villa in Naples. Oscar was 'as weak as water', Constance, observed.[16] She was revolted by him.

Oscar replied to Constance's letter. Although the letter itself no longer exists, one gets a sense of it from one he wrote to Robbie Ross, who had also already berated Oscar for going back to Bosie. Now in this letter the damaging influence of Bosie is evident. The humility and charm that Oscar displayed in Berneval had deserted him. In its place were bile and arrogance, mixed, no doubt, with a degree of pain that his wife failed to show him the level of adoration and urgency that Lord Alfred Douglas readily displayed.

'I am awaiting a thunderbolt from my wife's solicitor,' Oscar told Robbie.

> She wrote me a terrible letter, but a foolish one, saying 'I forbid you' to do so and so: 'I will not allow you' etc: and 'I require a distinct promise that you will not' etc. How can she really imagine that she can influence or control my life? She might as well just try to influence and control my art. I could not live such an absurd life

– it makes one laugh. So I suppose she will now try to deprive me of my wretched £3 a week. Women are so petty, and Constance has no imagination. Perhaps for revenge she will have another trial: then she certainly may claim to have for the first time in her life influenced me. I wish to goodness she would leave me alone. I don't meddle with her life. I accept the separation from the children: I acquiesce. Why does she want to go on bothering me, and trying to ruin me?[17]

Constance reacted as one might expect. 'Had I received this letter a year ago . . . I should have minded, but now I look upon it as the letter of a madman who has not even enough imagination to see how trifles affect children, of unselfishness enough to care for the welfare of his wife,' she wrote to Blacker. 'It rouses all my bitterest feelings, and I am stubbornly bitter when my feelings are roused. I think the letter had better remain unanswered and each of us make our own lives independently. I have latterly (God forgive me) an absolute repulsion to him.'[18]

The thunderbolt that Oscar expected did indeed come. Under the terms of their separation, if Oscar kept notorious company he could expect his annual income from Constance to be stopped. This was duly done. 'I am being freed from the necessity of paying the allowance so now anything I give is a free gift which is much more satisfactory,' she conceded to Otho.[19]

Constance spent the winter months in the Villa Elvira concentrating on what was positive in her life. She tried to put Oscar out of her mind. She made cushions for the villa and had its ugly red walls painted yellow. Photographs she took of the rooms there reveal her mantelpiece full of remembrances of an earlier life. There is the photograph of her and Cyril, another of Watts's portrait of Lady Mount-Temple. Her skills as a photographer improved greatly, but she did not allow herself to be content with one hobby alone, and so also set about learning macramé. Impressed by the typewriter she had sampled at the Villa Raffo, Constance bought one for herself. From October 1897 onwards her correspondence is practically all typewritten.

Even though she could no longer venture out, Constance received visitors. The Ranee was, of course, a regular guest. Other visitors included the American socialite Princess Salm (widow of the Prussian Prince Felix Salm-Salm) and none other than Oscar's distant relative Father Maturin, who had now very controversially converted to Catholicism.

As Christmas approached, Constance prepared to spend the festive season. She received some gifts from London, including books from Arthur Humphreys. If she and Humphreys had ever had a future together, Oscar's disgrace and her subsequent flight had made a relationship that was already clandestine impossible to pursue. Humphreys, however, was meticulous in sending both Constance and the boys all the books they wanted, and his letters to her remained deeply affectionate. In the one he wrote to her that Christmas, Constance was overcome by this continuing affection. His words, 'I confess made me ashamed', she admitted. 'However it is much better to be thought too well of; then one has an ideal to live up to!'[20]

In addition to Arthur Humphreys' gifts, Constance also had a photograph of a kitten from Lady Mount-Temple, and a photograph of a painting by Arnold Böcklin from the Blackers. Cyril arrived from Germany on 22 December, although Vyvyan stayed at his school.

In January, Constance bought a silver photograph frame that would serve as a late Christmas present to her from Vyvyan. In February she visited him in Monaco, staying in the Hotel Bristol. Finally she saw Vyvyan as a success story. He was 'very happy, as clever as he can be, very sure of himself as always, and mad about stamps', she reported back to Otho. 'He is also mad about coins,' she added.[21]

In this quiet life Oscar remained a spectre who haunted Constance. Her feelings towards him shifted between affection and pain. In January she heard from Adrian Hope that Oscar and Bosie had separated. 'But I have not the ghost of an idea where he is and I can't imagine how he is living,' she told Otho.[22] Then in February 1898, three months after their terrible letters to one another,

Constance saw a copy of the *Ballad of Reading Gaol*, which Oscar had just had published. This extraordinary poem, the tale of a murderer who has committed a *crime passionnel* and subsequently walked to the gallows, reduced her to tears.

Constance could no longer bear not knowing what had become of her former husband. She had been told that Oscar was in Paris and urged Carlos Blacker find out more. 'He has, as you know, behaved exceedingly badly both to myself and my children,' she explained,

> and all possibility of our living together has come to an end, but I am interested in him, as is my way with anyone that I have once known. Have you seen his new poem, and would you like a copy, as if so I will send you one? His publisher lately sent me a copy which I conclude came from him. Can you find this out for me and if you do see him tell him that I think the Ballad exquisite, and I hope that the great success it has had in London at all events will urge him on to write more.[23]

Constance's best intentions, however, caused more trouble for her. The man she had once loved so dearly no longer existed. Instead, a husk of the great man responded to her inquiries with demands, as she revealed to Blacker:

> The result of your writing to O is that he has written to me more or less demanding money as of right. Fortunately for him hearing that he was in great straits, I had yesterday or rather the day before sent him £40 through Robbie Ross. He says that I owe him £78 and hopes I will send it. I know that he is in great poverty, but I don't care to be written to as though it were my fault. He says that he loved too much and that that is better than hate! This is true abstractedly, but his was an unnatural love, a madness that I think is worse than hate. I have no hatred for him, but I confess that I am afraid of him.[24]

In March, Blacker visited Oscar in Paris and found a sad and devastated figure. Two of the last letters between Blacker and Constance reveal the pathetic level to which Oscar's relations with his wife were finally reduced.

14 Villa Elvira
18.3.98

Dear Mr Blacker

. . . your account of Oscar is a very sad one. Still I am glad he is in Paris, for I know that he does require intellectual stimulus always. He would have been bored to death with family life, though he does not seem at present to realize this.[25] What could either the children or I have given him? Vyvyan, though clever, is a baby, and Cyril, thank heaven, goes in as at his age he should, for sports . . . Have you see Arthur Symons' review of the *Ballad* in the last *Saturday Review*? I think it I excellent and the best that has appeared and I would like to know what you think of it when you have seen it. Also I would be most grateful to you if you would send me the *Mercure de France* when it appears as I don't know how to get hold of it. Also I wonder if you could get hold of for me a copy of the French translation of *Dorian Gray*? I had one, but lent it, and like most things one lends, one rarely sees them again![26]

15 Villa Elvira
20.3.98

Dear Mr Blacker

I did send £40 to Mr Ross but he would not . . . send more than £10 at a time to him. I enclose your letters that I have had from Robbie which at any rate are truthful which I know that Oscar is not. The actual sum that I owe him, if you call it owing, is at the rate of £12.10 a month £62.10 and not £80. This is counting from the month of November when I stopped giving him his allowance to the end of this present month. I have said that I would give him £10 a month so at the most I owe him little more than £20! By his own account to me he received £30 from Smithers and he seems to have had money since. Also he has had £10 of mine which he more than ignores in his letter to you, for he says that he has had nothing from me. Oscar is so pathetic and such a born actor, and I am hardened when I am away from him. No words will describe my horror of that BEAST for I will call him nothing else AD. Fancy Robbie receiving abusive letters from him and you know perfectly well that they are sent with Oscar's knowledge and consent. I do not wish him dead, but considering how he used to go on about Willie's extravagance and about his cruelty in forcing his mother to give him money, I think he might leave his wife and children alone. I beg that you will not let him know that you have seen these letters, only I wish you to realise that he knew perfectly well that he was forfeiting his income, small as it was, in going back to Lord A, and that it was absurd of him to say now that I acted without his knowledge. He owes I am certain more than £60 in Paris, and if I pay money now he will think that he can write to me at any time for more. I have absolutely no one to fall back upon, and will not get into debt for anyone. The boys' expenses will go on increasing until they are grown up and settled, and I <u>will</u> educate them and give them what they reasonably require. As Oscar will not bargain or be anything but exceedingly extravagant why should I do with my own money what is utterly foreign to my nature . . . But Oscar has no pride. When he had this disastrous law-suit he borrowed £50 from me, £50 from my cousin and £100 from my aunt. The £50 I repaid my cousin, the £100 never has been and I suppose never will be repaid. I was left penniless and borrowed £150 from Burne-Jones, and have never borrowed a penny since. I still owe money in London which I am trying to pay, but all these things are nothing to Oscar as long as someone supports him! . . . You will say in the face of this why did I ask you to go and see him in Paris? Well, I thought you would have nothing to do with his money affairs, and I strongly advise you to leave them alone . . . I was silly enough to think that you would merely give him the intellectual stimulus he needed. I don't know what name he is living under in Paris. Is it his own or the name he took when he left England? If he was fixed anywhere, I could make an arrangement to pay 10 francs a day for his board to the hotel, not to him for I know that he would never pay it. In the winter I paid at the hotel here 9 francs a day. Of course the good hotels are about 18 francs but I knew I could not afford that and did not go to them. He ought to go to a 'pension' and live a great deal cheaper than this, for you see it only leaves him around 12 francs a month.[27]

These letters, a sad mix of love, pride, infuriation and practical housekeeping, are the tragic remnants of a relationship. For all this, they remain extraordinary in the residual love and concern that even now they display.

Quite why Constance continued to show pride in her husband's work, in spite of his condemnation of her, and quite why she continued to provide for him are difficult questions. Before the terrible events that led to Constance's exile, she had written a very revelatory letter to Lady Mount-Temple that perhaps offers some explanation. Back in September 1893 Constance had urged Georgina not to 'trouble about me. I cannot say my <u>small</u> troubles, but in a way one's life troubles are easier to take up and bear than the small ones which are so trying. My motto for many years has been "Qui patitur vincit" – He conquers who endures – and so I will endure and fight my battle and try to take up my cross.'[28]

'Qui Patitur Vincit' had, of course, been Constance's name of choice as a member of the Golden Dawn, and it remained her motto subsequently. Oscar constantly wrote in his fairy tales poignant stories of sacrifice. In 'The Happy Prince' he told the story of the bird which gives its heart to the statue of the Prince and, having carried out the Prince's wishes for the love of him, dies at his feet. In 'The Nightingale and the Rose', Oscar imagined a nightingale that bleeds to death to give a young lover a red rose for his sweetheart, and whose sacrifice to love goes unnoticed.

If he had had the appropriate perspective, sitting in his cafés in Paris in 1898, Oscar might had recognized that the themes he chose in those fairy tales were those by which Constance lived her life. That Oscar, so wrapped up in the consequences of his allowing his own life to become a work of fiction, could not see that his wife had become a poem to love and constancy, is perhaps the real tragedy at the heart of this story.

In April 1898, Georgina Mount-Temple wrote to Constance. It was, after all, Easter time, a time that in the past they had always spent together. But some days later, to her surprise, her letter was returned in another. She must have sensed instantly why. The black border around the writing paper instantly warned of the tragedy that would be recounted within its pages. It was a letter from Otho. Constance, who had turned forty that January, was dead.

Unbeknown to her friends and family, Constance had returned to

Signor Bossi's clinic in early April to have another operation. Before she booked herself in, she wrote to Vyvyan. 'Try not to be hard on your father,' she wrote. 'Remember that he is your father and he loves you. All his troubles arose from the hatred of a son for his father, and whatever he has done he has suffered bitterly for.'[29]

Then on Saturday 2 April she underwent another operation. Details are murky. Anecdotally the operation was on her spine, relieving pressure on nerves there that was causing her creeping paralysis. However, Otho had referred to his sister's tumours, and the fact that Bossi was a gynaecologist suggests perhaps that the growths were uterine. Constance had gone into the clinic with her Italian maid, Maria Segre. On her arrival, and with writing now so painful for her, Constance dictated a post card in Italian to Maria for Otho, informing him of her whereabouts. He received it on Tuesday 5 April. But to his horror, the very next day he received a telegram with a far more urgent message: 'I want to see you at once. I am very ill. Will pay journey & hotel.'[30]

In the final hours of her life Constance had summoned both her brother and the Ranee, but neither got to her bedside in time. Otho made his way from Switzerland in a day, arriving on Thursday the 7th at seven in the evening. He 'was told at the door quite cheerfully by a young sister of mercy that she was dead. I have never had such a shock.'[31] After the operation, the creeping paralysis she was suffering, rather than being redressed, accelerated. Constance's heart just stopped.[32]

'It has all been so dreadful,' Otho informed Lady Mount-Temple,

for there seems to be no doubt that Constance was never warned of the danger she ran; she told almost no one that she was going, not one of her family knew it, and to the two friends in Nervi to whom she either wrote or named it she spoke of it as a mere nothing which would soon be over. I will not say what I think of the doctors who were responsible – the head one as soon as he was telephoned to that she was dead went right away from Genoa: his assistant read me from a telegram that he was in Savona, and said he wd be absent for three or four days: last night the British consul's clerk was informed that he is in Spain and will not be back till Friday next. Needless to say I wait here until I have seen him. Of the friends around her not one was allowed to realize her danger; the Ranee only divined it the evening before, and the one person who was beside her when she died – of those who knew her I mean, was her devoted Italian maid, Maria Segre. Everyone who knew her is indignant with the doctors.

'You knew Constance thoroughly,' Otho continued,

and you know how good she has always been to me; and when there are only two, just brother and sister, part of oneself is dead when she dies. And Constance to whom I always gave many years of life over mine, and whom so many loved and esteemed & would have done anything in the world to help. But of all of them you were spiritually the nearest and I dread to think of the shock I am causing to your heart.[33]

Constance was buried at four o'clock on the afternoon of 9 April in the Protestant section of Genoa's Campo Santo cemetery, which lies outside the city, in the foothills of the surrounding mountains. Otho, who had to make arrangements hurriedly, chose a plain cross inlaid with ivy leaves. Her association with the once famous Oscar Wilde was not alluded to. Rather, it was noted simply that she was 'Constance Mary, daughter of Horace Lloyd QC'.

The boys did not attend their mother's funeral. The news of her demise was broken to them by their respective schools. Their lives were now frozen in limbo while their guardian, Adrian Hope, thought about what would be best for their futures.

One month later Otho wrote a second letter to Babbacombe Cliff. Its contents were much to be expected. He brought Georgina up to date with news of the boys and provided a sense of the other letters he had received in memoriam of his sister. In the very final paragraph, before signing off, he noted almost casually that he had come across a friend of Oscar Wilde's who had told him that Oscar 'had not given a hang for the death of his wife'.[34]

Otho had developed a profound dislike for Oscar for his treatment of his sister. This is why he perhaps chose to convey this about Oscar to Constance's great friend rather than the response Oscar himself had sent him on hearing the news: 'Am overwhelmed with grief. It is the most terrible tragedy.'[35]

The version of Oscar that Otho chose to share with Georgina is closest to that which history has adopted more generally with regard to Oscar's relationship with his wife. This version is, of course, incomplete. Oscar also wrote to Carlos Blacker after Constance's death and said, 'I don't know what to do. If we had only met once, and kissed each other.'[36] In this ambiguous sentence lies a far more appropriate sentiment from a man who some say should have never married.

By 7 April the press, once so infatuated with Constance, had got the story of her death. The brevity of the announcements of her death reflects the general distaste with which the whole Oscar business was still handled. 'A Torquay telegram states Mrs Oscar Wilde died on Thursday week on the Riviera under distressing circumstances,' *Reynolds's* newspaper announced.[37] *Lloyd's Weekly Newspaper* had little more to add other than the context that 'After recent events she retired with her two sons to the Continent.'[38]

Constance's circle of close friends and family were devastated by her death – none more so than the Napiers. The Hopes had the dreadful duty of breaking the news to them. 'We received the telegram on Friday and went to the Napiers that afternoon,' Laura Hope related. 'They had heard nothing whatsoever and had no idea Constance was ill – beyond the usual poor health she had had of late years, & were terribly shocked. Her last letters had been brighter – & full of a visit she hoped to have paid the Napiers in London shortly.'[39]

On 12 April, Constance's friends John and Jane Simon invited some of her London friends to their home in Kensington Square to remember her. Most of them felt that such a sorry end could have been avoided. Jane Simon insisted that Constance had been advised time and again in England that surgery was not appropriate for her condition. And Aunt Mary Napier had 'been most urgent in advising her to avoid operations'.[40]

But Constance had wanted to be able to enjoy life with her sons.

She had made a brave and bold decision that she thought would benefit Cyril and Vyvyan. Such bravery was characteristic of her. Her relatives noted, however, that it was typical of a woman who would 'go her own way, as is the case of the marriage which wrecked the happiness of her life'. In this regard the consensus among Constance's friends and family was that her death, despite her relative youth, was for the best. Many, like the Simons, felt that 'death for her must have been the solution of almost intolerable misery'. At the end they 'all felt that she was safe. Safe from him – safe from herself.'[41]

A few years later one writer who had known Oscar and Constance rewrote the outcome of their story, offering a version of their tragedy that was more palatable to a judgemental society than the actual events. It was less that Constance had been saved by death than that Oscar should have saved her and the boys by killing himself. In her novel *The Rose of Life*, Mary Braddon's character Daniel Lester fraudulently embezzles from a friend. When his friend discovers his crime and threatens to reveal it, Lester faces prison and ruin. He considers flight but in the end chooses suicide, although the latter course is so carefully executed that the coroner returns a verdict of natural death. In this manner Lester is redeemed, for his actions have been taken for the sake of his wife. She has been spared the shame and ignominy that his incarceration would have visited on her.

Bosie Douglas also offered an assessment of the Wildes' tragic story, although he was as harsh in his judgement of Constance as most others were in theirs of Oscar. 'As to his wife,' Bosie said, 'he married her for love and if she had treated him properly and stuck to him after he had been in prison, as a really good wife would have done, he would have gone on loving her to the end of his life . . . Obviously she suffered a great deal and deserves every sympathy, but she fell woefully short of the height to which she might have risen.'[42]

These judgements passed upon Oscar and Constance by their society were brutal. For their children, however, death offered little comfort. Otho told Lady Mount-Temple: 'Cyril has deeply felt the loss of his mother, I think there is no doubt of that, though boy like he was at a loss for words to express himself, and I believe her memory will for a very long time have a hold on his mind, and perhaps for ever. At first he hardly realized very likely what it meant for him that his mother was gone, and he must have had many a pang as it slowly came home to him that he could not look forward any more to seeing her again.'[43] Writing years after her passing, Vyvyan recalled: 'My grief for my mother was very genuine and deep. I worshipped her, and all the weight of the world seemed to descend upon me after her death.'

Under the terms of Constance's will Oscar was restored his income of £150 a year. It was a provision that was in the end barely used, since he himself died within two years of his wife. On 25 February 1899, just months before his own demise, Oscar visited Constance's grave.

'It was very tragic seeing her name carved on a tomb – her surname, my name not mentioned of course – just Constance Mary, daughter of Horace Lloyd QC,' Oscar wrote to Robbie Ross. 'I brought some flowers. I was deeply affected – with a sense also of the uselessness of all regrets. Nothing could have been otherwise and life is a terrible thing.'[44]

Epilogue

Afte separating from Bosie in Naples, Oscar based himself in Paris, where his life was coloured by meagre means and perpetual debt, although he continued to be supported by a small circle of devoted friends and well-wishers. He established himself first in rooms in the Hôtel de Nice in the rue des Beaux-Arts, and later in the Hôtel d'Alsace. Throughout he complained constantly of being penniless and unable to meet his bills. In addition, his health was poor, and the punishment for his crimes seemed unending. Even in Paris, Oscar suffered the humiliation of seeing former friends and colleagues shun him in public.

When not in Paris, much as his wife and children had done Oscar moved through Europe's fashionable resorts, taking people up on their offers of hospitality wherever possible. In the autumn of 1898 he travelled to the south of France at the recommendation of his friend Frank Harris, and then in the spring of 1899 he stayed in Switzerland with another well-wisher, Harold Mellor. It was *en route* to Mellor's that Oscar took a detour to Genoa, where he spent three days with a young Italian actor he met there, call Didaco. The primary purpose of his visit to the city, however, was to pay a visit to Constance's grave.

By May 1899, Oscar had tired of Switzerland and was in rooms above a restaurant in Santa Margherita, an Italian resort close to Nervi, where his wife and family had spent so much time in the previous years. Here he became bored and drank, and in the end Robbie Ross, perhaps the most devoted of all his friends, dashed out to return him to the French capital.

Throughout the course of 1898 and 1899 Oscar worked slowly on a number of literary projects. *The Importance of Being Earnest* and *An Ideal Husband* were both published during this time, and Oscar also entered an agreement with Frank Harris to collaborate on a play, *Mr and Mrs Daventry*, which eventually went into production at London's Royalty Theatre in November 1900.

But in the first year of the new century Oscar's health went into rapid decline. Early in the year he complained persistently of food poisoning and blood poisoning, and although he rallied sufficiently to visit Italy with Harold Mellor in the spring, during which time he took a trip to Rome and received a blessing from the Pope, on his return to Paris he was once more terribly unwell.

Although Oscar continued to see Bosie from time to time, the latter had made a return to London society – a privilege that would never again be extended to Oscar himself. Back home in England, Bosie may well have noted the sale of a group of artworks at Messrs Foster of Pall Mall. On 1 August 1900 eleven pictures came under the hammer, raising just over £60. These were Constance's pictures, being sold on behalf of her estate by Mr Hargrove. Three etchings of Venice by Whistler, which in early descriptions of Tite Street hung in the drawing room there, must have been removed by Constance from her former home before the bailiffs moved in. Each one sold spoke of a period in Constance's life. Hanging in the Villa Elvira, they must have served as a reminder of her past and the friends she continued to hold dear. In addition to Whistler's Venetian scenes there was an etching of a geisha by Mortimer Menpes, a portrait of Sarasate by Whistler, two pencil drawings by Edward Burne-Jones, a proof engraving and a photogravure by Watts (one, if not both, almost certainly of his portrait of Georgina Mount-Temple) and a photograph of Tennyson and his friends, by Henry Herschel Hay Cameron.

While these sad relics of a lost life went under the hammer in London, in Paris Oscar was spending more and more time confined to his small room in the Hôtel d'Alsace. He was having great trouble with his ear, almost certainly as the result of a fall he had had in prison that had done permanent damage to it. By October the ear was terribly painful, and in the end Oscar agreed to have an operation on it, which was undertaken in his hotel room. Robbie Ross and Reginald Turner cared for him during this period. But despite their best efforts, within three weeks Oscar had developed a post-operative abscess in the ear and meningitis had set in. Although Robbie left Oscar's bedside on 12 November to visit his mother in the south of France, he returned at the end of the month, alerted by Reggie to the fact that Oscar's condition had become terminal. On 29 November 1900 Robbie fetched a Catholic priest, and Oscar was taken into that faith. The very next day he died. Bosie, summoned by Robbie, failed to reach Oscar's bedside in time. He did, however, take the place of chief mourner at the funeral, although it was Robbie Ross who was holding Oscar's hand as he passed away. Oscar was buried in the cemetery in Bagneux in a temporary concession. In 1909 his remains were removed to a permanent resting place in the Père Lachaise cemetery in Paris.

Oscar never got to see his sons after Constance's death. The Lloyd and Napier family closed ranks around the boys. Although they had so often been separated by their parents, and had little in common in terms of interest and temperament, Cyril and Vyvyan found themselves united by the tragedy of their circumstances and specifically by Constance's premature demise. From that moment on, according to Vyvyan, they 'walked along shoulder to shoulder'. After their school terms finished in the summer of 1898, they returned home to England and were brought up by Aunt Mary Napier and her daughter Lizzie. Although Adrian Hope was their appointed guardian, he adopted this role with a degree of distance.

Vyvyan, whose fascination with Catholicism continued, was sent to Stonyhurst College. Despite Constance's positive letter from the Admiralty in 1895, Cyril was denied a place in the navy and was instead sent to Radley College with a view to going into the army.

Having endured the death of their mother, the boys suffered a second trauma when news of Oscar's death broke. The Napiers had done their best to make his sons forget Oscar. Vyvyan claimed he had been told his father was already dead, and so when the school rector delivered the news that in fact he was newly deceased, Vyvyan was utterly perplexed. Cyril, on the other hand, read about Oscar's death in the newspaper. On hearing that Robbie Ross had sent flowers on the boys' behalf to the funeral, Cyril sent a letter of thanks in which he noted the deep pain that Oscar had inflicted on his family, for which Cyril hoped his father was truly penitent.

Oscar's story informed Cyril's life. Determined to win back some respectability, he cast himself as a masculine hero keen to win sports trophies for his school. After Radley he went to the Royal Military Academy at Woolwich, and then into the army, initially serving in India. There is some suggestion by his brother that he worked as a spy in the years leading up to the First World War. Cyril's German was perfect, a fact not lost on the authorities. In 1914 Cyril's regiment arrived in France. On 9 May 1915 he was shot dead by a German sniper during the Neuve-Chapelle offensive, just before the battle of Festubert.

Vyvyan also served in the army in the First World War. As with his brother, the legacy of his years in exile had at least provided him with an unusual facility for languages. He served first as a second lieutenant in the Interpreters' Corps and later in the Royal Field Artillery. He was awarded an OBE thereafter. Before the war he studied law at Cambridge University, but he went on to become a translator and author.

When Adrian Hope succumbed to an early death in 1904, the main barrier to Oscar's friends reacquainting themselves with his sons was lifted. Robbie Ross made a point of befriending the boys, and Vyvyan attended Oscar's reburial in 1909. Despite becoming friendly with Robbie Ross and many others from Oscar's circle, and despite writing about being the son of Oscar Wilde, Vyvyan Holland never changed his name back to that of his Irish forebears. He had experimented with using the name Wilde just once, for about a month before the First World War when on a trip to Venice, and was so bothered by Italian reporters that he decided to never repeat the exercise. He died in 1967 aged eighty, leaving a son, Merlin, who has become an acknowledged Wilde scholar.

Willie Wilde pre-deceased his brother, dying in March 1899 from an alcohol-related illness. Lily Wilde, his second wife and widow, subsequently married the journalist and translator Alexander de Teixeira de Mattos. Her and Willie's daughter, Dorothy, grew up to be a well-known socialite. She drove an ambulance in the First World War. Like her father, she had a susceptibility to alcohol, and died young in 1941.

Lady Mount-Temple survived Constance and died in 1901. Her daughter Juliet Deschamps, who had initially been so damning of Oscar when he was gaoled, wrote to Oscar in warm terms in October 1898 to inform him of the death of her husband, Eugène. Oscar had seen Eugène during his exile. In her letter Juliet restated how much she had valued Constance's friendship. She also went on to speculate that, now united with Constance in the afterlife, her husband might have brought her 'tidings of you whom she so dearly loved and for whose good she prayed and suffered'.[1]

Bosie's father, the Marquess of Queensberry, died in January 1900, at which point Bosie inherited a significant sum. After his return to London society in 1898 he married the heiress Olive Custance in March 1902, and they had a son, Raymond. In 1911 he converted to Catholicism. Bosie continued to get embroiled in libel cases, losing a case he himself brought against Arthur Ransome in 1913, and finding himself sued successfully for libel by Winston Churchill in 1923. This last led to a six-month gaol sentence.

Robbie Ross became Oscar's literary executor and worked tirelessly to acquire the copyright to his work. Within a few years of Oscar's demise he had paid his debts and returned his estate to credit. Adrian Hope had deemed that Oscar's sons should not benefit from his literary estate, but after Hope's death Robbie was able to restore any financial benefit from his work to Cyril and Vyvyan. In 1905 Ross published an abridged version of Oscar's long confessional letter to Bosie, *De Profundis*. It ran to five editions in the first year of publication. In the same year Richard Strauss produced an operatic version of *Salome* in Dresden. Subsequently Robbie oversaw the publication of Oscar's collected works in 1908. In 1909 George

Alexander revived *The Importance of Being Earnest* at the St James's to great success, and nine years later, when he died, the copyright of both this play and *Lady Windermere's Fan* was restored to Vyvyan in Alexander's will.

In 1900 Ross, along with More Adey, joined the management of the Carfax Gallery, which had been founded by Arthur Clifton. Living together for fifteen years, they both continued to move in circles of artists and poets for whom homosexuality was a predominant theme.

Relations between Bosie and Robbie Ross deteriorated dramatically during this time as the former went on to embrace a more conventional lifestyle and in doing so turned against his former homosexual friends. Bosie attempted to have Robbie arrested for indecency, and in 1914 the latter was forced to sue Bosie for criminally libelling him as a practising homosexual.

After Bosie, Ross fell foul of the right-wing, homophobic MP Noel Pemberton Billing, who believed that Robbie's circle were at the heart of national treachery. Billing published an article in which he suggested that an actress, Maud Allen, then appearing in a private production of *Salome* organized by Ross, was a lesbian associate of conspirators. When Allen sued Billing for libel over the allegations, Bosie actually testified in Billing's favour.

The pressures that Bosie and Billing between them brought down on Ross proved too great, and he died unexpectedly in 1918, aged just forty-nine. In 1950, on the fiftieth anniversary of Wilde's death, Ross's ashes were added to Wilde's tomb. More Adey outlived his lover by a great many years, and died in a mental institution in 1942.

Otho Lloyd Holland survived More Adey by a year. He eventually returned from exile and spent his dotage living in Bournemouth. He published a number of translations of Greek texts, including the *Olynthiacs* and *Philippics* of Demosthenes in 1901 and Sophocles' *Antigone* in 1931. He had three children with his second wife, Mary. Horace, a brother to Eugene and Hester, was born after Constance died. Of his two sons from his first marriage, to Nellie, Fabian Lloyd went on to become a well-known avant-garde artist who went under the name of Arthur Cravan. A darling of the Dada and Surrealist group of artists, he wrote a controversial article in 1913 claiming that Oscar Wilde was still alive and had visited him. Cravan finally disappeared in mysterious circumstances in 1918, when, having set out on a sailing trip from Mexico to Argentina, his boat never arrived and it was presumed he had drowned at sea.

Among Otho's papers left to his family was a newspaper cutting regarding Signor Bossi, the surgeon whom Otho blamed for his sister's death. Under the headline 'Woman's Surgeon Shot, A Consulting Room Mystery', the *Daily Mail* reported on 3 February 1919 that the Genoese gynaecologist had been found shot dead: 'He was seated at his desk in his professional rooms with his pen still grasped in his hand.' The *Mail* added that also in the room 'were the body of an unknown man, who had been shot dead, and a woman lay mortally wounded'.

Otho's descendants continued to take an interest in the story of their forebear, and in 1963 they added the words 'Wife of Oscar Wilde' to Constance's grave in Genoa.

Notes

Introduction

1. Merlin Holland and Rupert Hart-Davis, *The Complete Letters of Oscar Wilde* (Fourth Estate, London, 2000), p. 633. This note is undated, and it remains conjecture that it was written on 28 February, although the schedule of events as presented in this chapter suggest that it was.
2. *The Illustrated London News* (12 Jan 1895).
3. *The Ladies' Treasury* (1 Feb 1895).
4. Constance to Lady Mount-Temple, undated. University of Southampton, Broadlands Archive (BR) 57/14/6.
5. *The Lady's Pictorial* (12 Jan 1895).
6. Marie-Jacqueline Lancaster (ed.), *Letters of Engagement 1884–1888: The Love Letters of Adrian Hope and Laura Troubridge* (Tite Street Press, London, 2000), p. 103.
7. Constance to Lady Mount-Temple, 5 Jan 1895. BR 57/22/8.
8. *The Young Woman*, to which Constance contributed in 1895, had been carrying a regular column called 'An Ideal Husband' since October 1894 which aired these views. Authors of the column included Lady Jeune and John Strange Winter, both friends of the Wildes.
9. *The Illustrated London News* (23 Feb 1895).
10. 'I want him to go off to stay at Tangier with Walter Harris as soon as possible. He has not been well for such a long time.' Constance to Lady Mount-Temple, 4 Dec 1894. BR 57/22/3.
11. Constance to Robert Ross, 28 Jan 1895. Library of William Andrews Clark Jr at the University of California in Los Angeles (Clark Library).
12. In a letter to Lady Mount-Temple on New Year's Eve Constance notes that the doctor was due on that day to give her 'some electricity'. BR 57/22/7.

13. Letter to Otho Lloyd Holland, 22 Jan 1895. MSS collection of Merlin Holland.

14. *The Complete Works of Oscar Wilde* (Collins, London, 2003), p. 534.

Chapter 1: The sins of the parents

1. This is how Captain John was described in Dublin's *Freeman's Journal and Daily Commercial Advertiser* on the announcement of Ada's second marriage, in 1878.

2. Otho explains the family lineage and how Horace and Ada were related in a note to A. Symons, 22 May 1937: 'John Lloyd . . . married "Molly" a sister of Holland Watson, a JP for the counties of Lancashire and Cheshire . . . John Lloyd's son John Horatio married his first cousin Caroline 7th daughter of the above Holland Watson; and their son Horace, Constance's and my father, also took to wife a cousin, his second cousin by the same Watson branch, Adelaide Barbara Atkinson of Dublin; her paternal grandmother *née* Judith Watson was one of Holland Watson's many sisters. Holland Watson's and their mother had been a Miss Judith Holland, a descendant of the well known "Lancashire Hollands".' Clark Library.

3. Ibid.

4. Otho made these comments scribbled in the back pages of his personal copy of Leonard Cresswell Ingleby's *Oscar Wilde* (T. Werner Laurie, London, 1907). MSS collection of John Holland.

5. Notes in the MSS collection of John Holland.

6. Constance to Otho, 14 Jan 1882. MSS collection of Merlin Holland.

7. Constance to Otho at Oriel College, 31 Oct 1878. MSS collection of Merlin Holland.

8. Otho to A. J. Symons Clark, 22 May 1937. Clark Library.

9. Patrick Byrne, *The Wildes of Merrion Square: The Family of Oscar Wilde* (Staples Press, London, 1953), p. 91.

10. Ibid., p. 111.

11. Notebook of Otho. MSS collection of John Holland.

12. Notes from Otho in his copy of Ingleby's *Oscar Wilde*. MSS collection of John Holland.

13. Constance to Otho, 25 July 1878. MSS collection of Merlin Holland.

14. Notes from Otho, undated. MSS collection of John Holland.
15. Otho to A. J. Symons, 22 May 1937. Clark Library.
16. Constance to Otho, 3 Sept 1878. MSS collection of Merlin Holland.
17. Undated letter from Constance to Otho, marked private. MSS collection of Merlin Holland.
18. Otho lists these friends in his notebook. MSS collection of John Holland.
19. Rossetti painted Mrs Morris wearing such a peacock-blue dress with puffed sleeves.
20. Undated letter from Constance to Otho. The reference to her mother's marriage, however, indicates it was written in the autumn of 1878.
21. Ibid.
22. Constance to Otho, 21 Sept 1878. MSS collection of Merlin Holland.
23. Ibid.
24. Constance to Otho, 31 Oct 1878. MSS collection of Merlin Holland.
25. Constance to Otho, 21 Sept 1878. MSS collection of Merlin Holland.
26. Constance to Otho, 3 Sept 1878. MSS collection of Merlin Holland.

Chapter 2: Terriby bad taste

1. C. R. Elrington (ed.), *Paddington, Bayswater*, vol. 9 of *A History of the County of Middlesex*, Victoria History of the Counties of Britain (Oxford University Press, Oxford, 1989), pp. 204–12.
2. Merlin Holland, *The Complete Works of Oscar Wilde* (Collins, London, 2003) p. 18.
3. Constance to Otho, 10 June 1881. MSS collection of Merlin Holland.
4. Constance to Otho, 18 Nov 1881. MSS collection of Merlin Holland.
5. Sir William Abdy had lent Belt the not insignificant sum of £2,000. When he failed to repay his debt, Belt presented Abdy with an investment opportunity. The sculptor had made the acquaintance of a Mrs Morphy, who Belt claimed had been part of a sultan's harem. The sultan had given his mistress wonderful diamonds, which she now needed to sell to support herself. Belt brokered the sale of these precious jewels to Sir William, who promptly sued Belt when he discovered that they were nothing more than cheap stones he had sourced from a pawnbroker. In Oscar's *An Ideal Husband* the blackmailing Mrs

Cheverley is undone when it is discovered that a diamond brooch she has was in fact stolen by her in her youth. This crime is leveraged against her, and she is forced to yield the letter with which she is blackmailing Lord Chiltern.

6. Notebook of Otho. MSS collection of John Holland.
7. Constance to Otho, 3 Sept 1878. MSS collection of Merlin Holland.
8. Otho's notes in the back of Ingleby's *Oscar Wilde*. MSS collection of John Holland.
9. Constance's signature, along with that of John Horatio, Aunt Emily and Otho, is still visible in the Royal Oak's guest book.
10. Constance to Otho, 9 Sept 1879. MSS collection of Merlin Holland.
11. *The Shield* cites one such meeting occurring in February 1883, at which Mary Fedden was one of the speakers.
12. Otho's notebook. MSS collection of John Holland.
13. Constance to Otho, undated (probably 1879). MSS collection of Merlin Holland.
14. Charlotte Gere with Lesley Hoskins, *The House Beautiful: Oscar Wilde and the Aesthetic Interior* (Lund Humphries in association with the Geffrye Museum, London, 2000), p. 14.
15. Lillie Langtry, *The Days I Knew* (Hutchinson, London, 1925), p. 60.
16. As noted in *The Illustrated London News* (November 1878).
17. Hope-Nicholson (ed.), *Life amongst The Troubridges: Journals of a Young Victorian, by Laura Troubridge, 1873–1884* (Tite Street Press, London, 1999), p. 151.
18. Langtry, *The Days I Knew*, p. 87.
19. Constance to Otho, 1 Aug 1880. MSS collection of Merlin Holland.
20. Constance to Otho, undated (1880). MSS collection of Merlin Holland.
21. Constance to Otho, 7 June 1881. MSS collection of Merlin Holland.
22. A Mrs Arbuthnot appears in Wilde's play *A Woman of No Importance*. Many of his characters' names are based on those of real acquaintances or places that he found amusing or just convenient to use.
23. Constance to Otho, 10 June 1881. MSS collection of Merlin Holland.
24. Otho to A. J. Symons, 22 May 1937. Clark Library.
25. Constance to Otho, 10 June 1881. MSS collection of Merlin Holland.
26. Constance to Otho, 7 June 1881. MSS collection of Merlin Holland.
27. Constance to Otho, undated. MSS collection of Merlin Holland.
28. *The Era* (7 May 1881).

29. Constance to Otho, June 1881. MSS collection of Merlin Holland.
30. *Complete Letters*, p. 110.
31. Constance to Otho, undated. MSS collection of Merlin Holland.
32. Constance to Otho, 10 June 1881. MSS collection of Merlin Holland.
33. Constance to Otho, 10 June 1881. MSS collection of Merlin Holland.
34. Ibid.

Chapter 3: The sunflower and the lily

1. Constance to Otho, 27 Nov 1881. MSS collection of Merlin Holland.
2. *Freeman's Journal and Daily Commercial Advertiser* (17 July 1882).
3. 'Constance used to keep all her letters from Oscar in a little blue leather case': Anne Clark Amor, *Mrs Oscar Wilde: A Woman of Some Importance* (Sidgwick & Jackson, London, 1983). Amor claims the box was stolen from Tite Street when the contents of the house were auctioned in 1895. Although Constance's brother preserved a fair amount of her correspondence, this box and its contents seem to have been lost. It may alternatively have been destroyed at the time of the scandal or by the family after Constance's death.
4. *The Saturday Review* (23 July 1881).
5. Oscar to Violet Hunt, 22 July 1881. *Complete Letters*, p. 114.
6. Neil McKenna, *The Secret Life of Oscar Wilde* (Arrow Books, London, 2004), p. 26.
7. Constance to Otho, 18 Nov 1881. MSS collection of Merlin Holland.
8. Constance to Otho, 27 Nov 1881. MSS collection of Merlin Holland.
9. Constance to Otho, 10 Jan 1882. MSS collection of Merlin Holland.
10. Constance to Otho, 10 June 1881. MSS collection of Merlin Holland.
11. Constance to Otho, 29 March 1882. MSS collection of Merlin Holland.
12. Gere with Hoskins, *The House Beautiful*, p. 86.
13. Constance to Otho, 31 March 1883. MSS collection of Merlin Holland.
14. Constance to Otho, 28 April 1883. MSS collection of Merlin Holland.
15. 'Work for All', *The Girls Own Paper* (22 Dec 1883).
16. Constance to Otho, 18 Aug 1882. MSS collection of Merlin Holland.
17. Constance to Otho, 20 Aug 1882. MSS collection of Merlin Holland.
18. Ibid.
19. Constance to Otho, 22 Aug 1882. MSS collection of Merlin Holland.

20. Constance to Otho, 23 Aug 1882. MSS collection of Merlin Holland.

21. Constance to Otho, 27 March 1883. MSS collection of Merlin Holland.

22. Constance to Otho, 4 Sept 1880. MSS collection of Merlin Holland.

23. BL Eccles 81690.

24. Ibid.

25. Ibid.

26. Clark Library.

27. BL Eccles 81690.

28. Clark Library.

29. Oscar to Robert Sherard, May 1883. Merlin Holland and Rupert Hart-Davis (eds), *The Complete Letters of Oscar Wilde* (Fourth Estate, London, 2000), p. 211.

30. Oscar wrote to Steele Mackaye in May asking for a loan of £200 to be honoured as he found himself once again with 'a great many expenses'. *Complete Letters*, p. 209.

31. BL Eccles 81731.

32. Constance to Otho, undated. MSS collection of Merlin Holland.

33. Ibid.

34. Joy Melville, *Mother of Oscar: The Life of Jane Francesca Wilde* (John Murray, London, 1994), p. 179.

35. Constance to Otho, written from Norfolk House, Folkestone, 28 Sept 1883.

36. BL Eccles 81690.

37. Constance to Otho, 23 and 24 Nov 1883. MSS collection of Merlin Holland.

38. Constance to Otho, 26 Nov 1883. MSS collection of Merlin Holland.

Chapter 4: 'Bunthorne is to get his bride'

1. Constance to Otho, 26 Nov 1883. MSS collection of Merlin Holland.

2. Maria Luisa Borras, the biographer of Otho's son Fabian Lloyd, claims that, while in Lausanne, Nellie looked after two little girls of the neighbouring Hutchinson family. She was of an obscure background, and so they lent her their name so that she would be sufficiently respectable to marry Otho. She thus became known as Clara St-Clair Hutchinson.

Maria Luisa Borras, *Arthur Cravan: une stratégie du scandale* (Editions Jean-Michel Place, Paris, 1996), p. 19.

3. Constance to Otho, 26 Nov 1883. MSS collection of Merlin Holland.

4. Constance to Oscar, addressed from 1 Ely Place and dated Thursday 8.30 p.m. (therefore Thursday 27 Nov 1883). BL Eccles MS 81690.

5. Constance to Otho, 27 Nov 1883. MSS collection of Merlin Holland.

6. Ada Swinburne-King to Lady Wilde, 30 Nov 1883. Clark Library.

7. Clark Library.

8. 'I know nothing about Oscar's means whatsoever but as I shall not be able to marry while poor Grandpa is alive, I shall have enough for us both to start on.' Constance to Otho, 28 Nov 1883. MSS collection of Merlin Holland.

9. Clearly John Horatio had increased his initial allowance of £150 per annum bestowed on Constance in 1878.

10. BL Eccles 81690.

11. *Complete Letters*, p. 224.

12. BL Eccles 81690.

13. Ibid.

14. Ibid.

15. Clark Library.

16. Ibid.

17. BL Eccles 81690.

18. Langtry, *The Days I Knew*, p. 94.

19. Basil Cochrane's grandfather was Lieutenant-Colonel Edward FitzGerald, and it is tempting to speculate that the mysterious Mr Fitzgerald with his military background who was Oscar's rival for Constance's affections may well have been a cousin of the Cochranes.

20. BL Eccles 81690.

21. Ibid.

22. Ibid.

23. 'Feminine Fashions and Fancies', *The Newcastle Courant* (28 March 1884).

24. Anna Kingsford to Speranza, 11 March 1884. BL Eccles 81731.

25. Under the influence of their highly artistic household, the Nettleships' daughter Ida would in due course go to art school and ultimately marry the painter Augustus John.

Chapter 5: Violets in the refrigerator

1. *New York Times* (8 June 1884).
2. Ada Leverson, *Letters to the Sphinx from Oscar Wilde: With Reminiscences of the Author* (Duckworth, London, 1930), p. 44.
3. Constance to Otho, 3 June 1884. MSS collection of Merlin Holland.
4. Ibid.
5. Louise Jopling, *Twenty Years of My Life: 1867 to 1887* (John Lane, London, 1925).
6. Marie-Jaqueline Lancaster (ed.), *Letters of Engagement: The Love Letters of Adrian Hope and Laura Troubridge* (Tite Street Press, London, 2001), p. 115.
7. In a letter to Lady Mount-Temple, Constance signed herself 'Constanza Cantankeray' adding, 'Oscar thinks that a very wicked name for me and he laughed immensely over it!' 17 Feb 1894, BR 57/19/3.
8. *The Lady's Pictorial*, quoted in 'The Household (A Column for the Ladies)', *The Derby Mercury* (3 Sept 1884).
9. A friend of Whistler's called Miss Reubell.
10. Constance to Otho, 3 June 1884. MSS collection of Merlin Holland.
11. *The Ladies Journal* [Toronto] (1 Oct 1884).
12. 'Society Gossip', *Hampshire Telegraph and Sussex Chronicle* (2 May 1885).
13. A shade of green identified with the grey-green leaves of the plant of the same name.
14. 'Society Gossip', *Hampshire Telegraph and Sussex Chronicle* (2 May 1885).
15. 'The Private View at the Grosvenor', *Daily News* (3 May 1886).
16. The use of beetle wings in embroidery was a consequence of Empire. Beetle-wing cases were collected in Burma and sold through Calcutta. In the hands of Mrs Nettleship beetle-wing embroidery reached new levels of creativity and exoticism. In 1888 she went on to make a beetle-wing-embroidered gown for Ellen Terry's Lady Macbeth. A creation that at once suggested soft chain-mail armour and the scales of a serpent, the beetle wings gave the impression of a shimmering sheath enveloping the actress.
17. *Hearth and Home* (15 Jan 1887).
18. Anna, Comtesse de Brémont, *Oscar Wilde and His Mother* (Everett & Co., London, 1911), p. 91.
19. 'Our Ladies' Column', *Preston Guardian* (9 May 1885).

20. Michael Field (Katherine Bradley and Edith Cooper), *Works and Days: From the Journal of Michael Field* (John Murray, London, 1933), p. 70.
21. Hope-Nicholson (ed.), *Life amongst the Troubridges*, p. 169.
22. Ibid., p. 38.
23. Ibid., p. 236.
24. *Ladies' Pictorial* (8 January 1887).
25. 'Our Ladies' Column', *The Preston Guardian* (9 May 1885).
26. Brémont, *Oscar Wilde and His Mother*, p. 68.
27. Constance to Otho, 10 Jan 1882. MSS collection of Merlin Holland.
28. Our Ladies' Column', *Bristol Mercury and Daily Post* (7 March 1885).
29. 'Dear Mr Godwin, Oscar asked me to let you know that Mr Sharp has only gone today to the "Healtheries" to get the Japanese things.' BL Eccles 81691. Correspondence between Constance and Godwin relating to the renovation of 16 and 14 Tite Street, 10 Nov 1884.
30. So Constance would have a further £6,000 invested from the estate, in addition to the £5,500 that John Horatio had already invested for her before his death.
31. Mary Braddon, *The Rose of Life* (Hutchinson, London, 1905), p. 107.
32. Oscar to Constance, 16 Dec 1884. *Complete Letters*, p. 241.
33. BL Eccles 81700.
34. BL Eccles 81732.
35. Constance to Otho, 6 May 1885. MSS collection of Merlin Holland.
36. Ibid.

Chapter 6: Ardour and indifference

1. *The Owl* (22 October 1885).
2. *Complete Letters*, p. 261.
3. Ibid.
4. Ibid., p. 258.
5. Ibid., p. 262.
6. V. Holland, *Time Remembered after Père Lachaise* (Gollancz, London, 1966), p. 129.
7. Marie-Jaqueline Lancaster (ed.), *Letters of Engagement* (Tite Street Press, London, 2001), p. 134.
8. *Complete Letters*, p. 264.

9. Constance to Otho, 25 June 1884. MS collection of Merlin Holland.

10. *The Illustrated London News* (4 June 1881).

11. Constance to Otho, 6 May 1885. The letter in the *Pall Mall Gazette* is signed simply 'CW'.

12. Henry Currie Marillier (1865–1951) was a Bluecoat boy attending Christ's Hospital school and had lodged in the same building in Salisbury Street as Oscar when Wilde was there in 1880 and 1881. At this time Marillier ran errands for Oscar and brought him his coffee.

13. Hengler's was subsequently converted into what is today the London Palladium.

14. *The Era* (22 May 1886).

15. Frank Harris, *Oscar Wilde* (Constable, London, 1938), p. 338.

16. Constance is inconsistent in her spelling of her son's name, but in the majority of instances she spells it 'Vivian'. However, after her death Vyvyan Holland, as he became, adopted the spelling that I have therefore used for the sake of consistency in this book.

17. Vyvyan Holland, *Son of Oscar Wilde* (Rupert Hart-Davis, London, 1954), p. 35.

18. Leverson, *Letters to the Sphinx*, p. 44.

19. Constance to Lady Mount-Temple, 8 Dec 1892. BR 57/18/2.

20. Douglas Ainslie went on to become a poet.

21. Constance to Otho, 15 Jan 1885. MSS collection of Merlin Holland.

22. *Complete Letters*, p. 267.

23. Ibid., p. 272.

24. Ibid., p. 282.

25. McKenna, *Secret Life of Oscar Wilde*, p. 111.

26. BL Eccles 81731.

27. Mrs Claude Beddington, *All That I Have Met* (Cassell & Co., London, 1929), p. 41.

28. There is a family anecdote handed down on Otho's side of the family that Mary Winter got her surname after having been found as a baby deserted in a handbag in deep midwinter – though this author has not sought to substantiate this story. It is amusing to think that Oscar may have adapted this story for *The Importance of Being Earnest,* where Jack Worthing also says he was discovered in a handbag as a baby.

29. Constance to Otho at Riposte Cottage, Lausanne, 26 July 1887. MSS collection of Merlin Holland.

30. Constance to Otho at Hotel Matanhoff, Interlaken, 27 Aug 1887. MSS collection of Merlin Holland.
31. Richard Ellman, *Oscar Wilde* (Alfred A. Knopf, New York, 1988), p. 275.
32. The file relating to Oscar's bankruptcy reveals Oscar borrowed £500 from Otho, secured against a life policy. PRO B9 429.
33. Constance to Otho, 26 July 1887. MSS collection of Merlin Holland.
34. *Complete Letters*, p. 297.

Chapter 7: A literary couple

1. *Funny Folks* (14 April 1888).
2. Vyvyan Holland, *Son of Oscar Wilde*, p. 50.
3. BL Eccles 81755.
4. Ibid.
5. Anna, Comtesse de Brémont, *Oscar Wilde and His Mother* (Everett & Co., London, 1911), pp. 87–8.
6. *Complete Letters*, p. 301. Later on Constance changed her 'at homes' to Wednesdays.
7. BL Eccles 81755.
8. Weldon became known for successfully suing her husband. They separated, and he attempted to have her committed to a lunatic asylum in order to avoid having to support her financially. She successfully fought her way out of the situation in the courts.
9. The *Preston Guardian* (December 1885) notes that Henriette Corkran was painting Constance's portrait in pastels. This picture is now lost.
10. *Lloyd's Weekly Newspaper* (27 Nov 1887).
11. Alice Corkran (ed.), *The Bairn's Annual 1887/88* (Leadenhall Press, London, 1887), pp. 65–74.
12. Constance to Otho, 9 Nov 1887. MSS collection of Merlin Holland.
13. J. H. Badley, the headmaster of Bedales, recalls being among the group of Cambridge students to whom Oscar told the story, while Mrs Claude Beddington passes on Harry Marillier's recollections in her memoir *All That I Have Met*, p. 35.
14. Beddington, *All That I Have Met*, p. 39.

15. 'I am trying to read a Dutch review of *Salome* for Oscar. It seems to have been translated into Dutch without his leave, & I hope to get hold of a copy. *Lady Windermere's Fan* was translated into Dutch and *The Happy Prince* with a beautiful view of Nelson's Column supposed to represent the statue of the Prince. So you see, the Dutch like Oscar & probably recognised that his name is most likely corrupted from Van der Welde. But it is a horrid language & I don't get on with my translation of the review.' Constance to Lady Mount-Temple, 16 Nov 1893. BR 57/47/14.
16. Intriguingly, the bound volume was put together by the 11th Marquess of Queensberry, the grandson of John Sholto Douglas and Bosie Douglas's nephew.
17. Oscar to George Kersley. *Complete Letters*, p. 352.
18. *Complete Letters*, p. 478.
19. Merlin Holland, *A Portrait of Oscar Wilde* (privately printed, Genoa, 2008), Chapter 4.
20. 'Jottings on Dress, Fashion, Music, Drama, Literature, Fashionable Doings & c.', *Weekly Irish Times* (2 Feb 1889).
21. F. E. Weatherly, M. A. Hoyer, Mrs Glasgow, Mrs Molesworth, Emily Bennett, Frances Compton and others, *Cosy Corner Stories* (Ernest Nister, London, 1895).
22. *Complete Letters*, p. 317.
23. *The Woman's World,* issue 1 (Nov 1887), p. 7. BL Eccles 418.
24. The other article Constance wrote was on the history of the muff.
25. *Rational Dress Society Gazette*, 1 (April 1888).
26. Ibid., p. 6.
27. *Rational Dress Society Gazette* (April 1889), p. 6.
28. Ibid.

Chapter 8: 'Not to kiss females'

1. Constance to Otho, March 1888. MSS collection of Merlin Holland.
2. Ibid.
3. 'Baby's birthday was last Thursday and though he is small I think he is quite strong now. He is frightfully spoilt and very self willed and does not say one mortal word, still grows a greater darling every day,

but baby is his father's pet.' Constance to Otho, 9 Nov 1887. MSS collection of Merlin Holland.

4. Vyvyan Holland, *Son of Oscar Wilde*, p. 53.

5. Constance to Lady Mount-Temple, 13 Nov 1891. BR 57/12/12.

6. There is evidence in Constance's letters to Otho that the Lloyds had hoped that he would go into the law and then Parliament. However, after the break-up of his first marriage and his elopement it seems that Otho attempted to live off the income left him by his grandfather, using it to make a series of speculative investments. He pursued his interest in Classics, meanwhile, and in the twentieth century published a number of translations.

7. Gladstone signed Constance's autograph book on Easter eve in 1888.

8. *Pall Mall Gazette* (17 April 1888).

9. On a trip to Florence in 1893 Constance related: 'I went to Dante's house again and into the little chapel where he married Gemma Donata. Poor wife, I pity her! Then lunch with Miss Cunninghame Graham and out to a lovely villa belonging to Mr Spenser Stanhope and to the Bello Sguardo to see Florence by the sunset-glow – such an exquisite picture.' Constance to Lady Mount-Temple, 11 Feb 1893. BR 57/46/15.

10. *Pall Mall Gazette* (17 April 1888).

11. *Northern Echo* (24 May 1889).

12. *Pall Mall Gazette* (24 May 1889).

13. *Birmingham Daily Post* (14 June 1889).

14. Bertha Vyver, *Memoirs of Marie Corelli* (Alston Rivers, London, 1930).

15. Sarasate signed Constance's autograph book in 1889, and Corelli the following year.

16. Corelli notes the shared popularity of Sarasate in her memoirs. In addition, in a letter to Lady Mount-Temple's daughter Juliet, Constance notes: 'I went to Marie Corelli's and talked to Sarasate, rather an ordeal.' Constance to Juliet Latour Temple, 19 June 1889. BR 57/11/1.

17. Marie Corelli, *The Silver Domino, or Side Whispers, Social and Literary* (Lamley & Co., London, 1892), p. 166.

18. Two women with whom Constance was acquainted, Annie Besant and Elizabeth Garrett Anderson, had taken up this opportunity.

19. *The Standard* (18 Dec 1888).

20. Constance to Mrs Stopes, undated. BL Add. MS 58454, Stopes Papers.

21. BL Add. MS 58454.
22. Constance to Otho, March 1888. MSS collection of Merlin Holland.
23. *Complete Letters*, p. 365.
24. Oscar mentions his wife's ill health has taken her to Brighton. In a letter to Mrs Stopes on 13 March 1889 Constance revealed that 'Mrs Charles Hancock is giving a drawing room meeting . . . I don't expect to be at it unless I am better.' BL Add. 58454.
25. Constance to Juliet Latour Temple, 19 June 1889. BR 57/11/1.
26. Ibid.
27. Ibid.
28. *Complete Letters*, p. 411.
29. Cyril inherited this tendency to over-reaction from Oscar, who was also known to be very sensitive and prone to tears. Lillie Langtry witnessed this deep sensitivity in Oscar: 'After a frank remark I made on one occasion, I happened to go to the theatre, and, as I sat in my box, I noticed a commotion in the stalls – it was Oscar who, having perceived me suddenly, was being led away in tears.' Langtry, *The Days I Knew,* pp. 82–3.
30. Constance to Emily Thursfield, 1 Sept 1889. Clark Library.
31. Ibid.
32. Constance to Lady Mount-Temple, 27 Nov 1890. BR 57/11/3. Russell Gurney, an eminent judge and Tory politician, and his wife, Emelia, were part of Lady Mount-Temple's set.
33. Constance lectured at the Somerville on 6 Nov 1888, on the topic: 'Clothed in our right minds'. *Women's Penny Paper*, 17 Nov 1888.
34. *Man About Town* notes her involvement in its issue of 15 Nov 1890.
35. *Belfast Newsletter* (16 Aug 1892). The writer also notes that the pioneer ladies were wearing a big smile at the prospect of a Gladstone government.
36. Israel Zangwill, *The Old Maids' Club* (Tait & Co., New York, 1892).

Chapter 9: Qui patitur vincit

1. *Belfast Newsletter* (1 Nov 1888).
2. *The York Herald* (21 Dec 1888).

3. Anna Kingsford to Speranza, 11 March 1884. BL Eccles 81731.

4. Anna Kingsford to Constance, 20 July 1884. Clark Library.

5. Molloy himself would become a member of the Golden Dawn, but not until 1893.

6. George Bernard Shaw, *The Diaries 1885–1897*, vols 1 and 2, ed. Stanley Weintraub (Pennsylvania State University Press, Philadelphia, 1986), p. 303.

7. This description based on A. E. Waites's memoir in the *Occult Review* (April 1919).

8. Ellic Howe (ed.), *The Alchemist of the Golden Dawn: The Letters of the Revd W. A. Ayton to F. L. Gardner and Others, 1886–1905* (Aquarian Press, Wellingborough, 1985).

9. R. A. Gilbert, *The Golden Dawn Companion* (Aquarian Press, Wellingborough, 1986), pp. 43–4.

10. Ibid., p. 31.

11. Brémont, *Oscar Wilde and His Mother*, p. 13.

12. Ibid.

13. W. B. Yeats, *Autobiographies: Reveries over Childhood and Youth and the Trembling of the Veil* (Macmillan & Co., London, 1926), pp. 230–31.

14. In 1893 Constance was in Italy and wrote to Myers: 'I am enjoying so thoroughly my first visit to Italy and just before your letter came I had been gazing at the Raphael fresco in the Vatican, of St Peter being led out of prison by the angel. Do you remember the photograph of it at Babbacombe, and how you said it was an allegory to us of the delivery of the soul from the bondage of materialism?' BL Eccles 8173. Constance's letters to Lady Mount-Temple indicate that she took her friends Sir Hugh and Lady Low to meet Myers at the Psychical Research Society.

15. Constance to Lady Mount-Temple, St Andrew's Day 1892. BR 57/17/6.

16. Yeats, *Autobiographies*, p. 135.

17. Constance to Juliet Deschamps, 8 June 1890. BR 57/11/12.

18. *The Sun* (17 Nov 1889).

19. *Complete Letters*, p. 426.

20. McKenna, *Secret Life of Oscar Wilde*, p. 123.

21. Amor, *Mrs Oscar Wilde*, p. 96.

22. Constance to Lady Mount-Temple, 23 Jan 1891. BR/45/2.

Chapter 10: My own darling mother

1. Richard Le Gallienne, *The Romantic '90s* (Putnam & Co., London, 1951), p. 103.
2. 'I had a delightful dinner with the Lows last evening and our conversation was chiefly on spiritual matters . . . they . . . (have) a great belief in spirituality as a Dynamite Force in the world. I think her enlightenment came through Professor Drummond as did mine too.' Constance to Lady Mount-Temple, 5 March 1891. BR 57/45/6.
3. Constance to Emily Thursfield, 2 Sept 1889. Clark Library.
4. Georgina's own diary indicates meetings with Oscar on at least two occasions during the course of the year – one imagines when she called on Constance at home.
5. Mr and Mrs Bowles, noted as talking at these Sunday lectures, were an apparently popular duo who also turned up in November 1889 talking to the Women's Liberal Association on 'The Difficulties of the Peace Question', according to the *Women's Penny Paper* (23 Nov 1889). This seems to indicate an interactivity and overlap between the political and religious groups to which Constance belonged.
6. Constance to Lady Mount-Temple, 26 Dec 1890. BR 57/11/4.
7. Constance to Lady Mount-Temple, 27 Dec 1890. BR 57/11/6.
8. Le Gallienne, *Romantic '90s*, p. 165.
9. Constance to Lady Mount-Temple, 2 Nov 1891. BR 57/12/4.
10. 'I see a great deal now of Paradise Walk but I feel hopeless to do anything there. Still you begged me once to work there and they all come to me now to help them, so at any rate your part of the wish is fulfilled.' Constance to Lady Mount-Temple, 23 Oct 1892. BR 57/48/13.
11. Constance to Lady Mount-Temple, 23 Jan 1891. BR 57/45/3.
12. *Aberdeen Weekly Journal* (16 July 1890).
13. Clark Library.
14. Noted in Georgina's diary, June 1890.
15. Constance to Lady Mount-Temple, 6 Feb 1891. BR 57/45/4.
16. Constance to Lady Mount-Temple, undated. BR 57/11/19.
17. 'I do not attempt any explanation, that on each occasion the ancestral silver from my father's side of the family was left untouched.' V. Holland, *Son of Oscar Wilde*, p. 42.
18. Clark Library.

19. BR 57/12/14.
20. Constance to Lady Mount-Temple, 15 Oct 1891. BR 57/13/12.
21. Constance to Lady Mount-Temple, 9 Oct 1891. BR 57/13/6.
22. Constance to Lady Mount-Temple, 21 Oct 1891. BR 57/13/14.
23. Lord Alfred Douglas, *Autobiography* (Secker, London, 1929), p. 59.
24. Constance to Lady Mount-Temple, 22 Oct 1891. BR 57/13/15.
25. Constance to Lady Mount-Temple, 26 Oct 1891. BR 57/12/1.
26. Some days were, by Constance's own admission, 'begun in deep depression'. Constance to Lady Mount-Temple, 12 Nov 1891. BR 57/12/10. Speranza's letters to Oscar at this time also relate that, despite her busy life, Constance felt lonely. In an account of a visit from Constance that November, her mother-in-law noted, 'She is so nice to me always. I am very fond of her. Do come home. She is very lonely, and mourns for you.' Clark Library.
27. Constance to Lady Mount-Temple, 28 Oct 1891. BR 57/12/2.
28. Constance to Lady Mount-Temple, 2 Nov 1891. BR 57/12/4.
29. Constance to Lady Mount-Temple, 15 Nov 1891. BR 57/12/13. The play was *Salome*.
30. Oscar was so evidently tempted by Rome as a young man that his half-brother Henry Wilson made it a specification in his will that Oscar would only qualify for a small legacy he had left him on the basis that he was still an Anglican.
31. Constance to Lady Mount-Temple, 12 Nov 1891. BR 57/12/10.
32. Constance to Lady Mount-Temple, 20 Nov 1891. BR 57/12/16.
33. Constance to Lady Mount-Temple, 27 Nov 1891. BR 57/14/4.
34. Constance to Lady Mount-Temple, 23 Nov 1891. BR 57/14/1.
35. Undated letter from Oscar to Lady Mount-Temple. Private collection.
36. 'While in London one hides everything, in Paris one reveals everything . . . the lowest dive interests me as much as the most elegant café.' McKenna, *Secret Life of Oscar Wilde*, p. 223.
37. Constance to Otho, 22 July 1892. MSS collection of Merlin Holland.
38. Constance to Lady Mount-Temple, undated. BR 57/15/16.
39. Constance to Lady Mount-Temple, 23 Aug 1892. BR 57/15/18.
40. Constance to Lady Mount-Temple, undated. BR 57/16/5. The line is in fact from Andrew Marvell's 'The Garden'. Either Oscar misattributed the line, or Constance misremembered what Oscar said.

41. Constance to Lady Mount-Temple, 1 Sept 1892. BR 57/16/6.
42. Constance to Oscar, 3 Sept 1892. Clark Library.

Chapter 11: A dark bitter forest

1. Constance to Lady Mount-Temple, undated. BR 57/14/93.
2. Constance to Lady Mount-Temple, 10 Aug 1883. BR 57/49/11.
3. Constance to Lady Mount-Temple, undated. BR 57/50/5.
4. Constance to Lady Mount-Temple, undated. BR 57/14/93.
5. Constance to Lady Mount-Temple, undated. BR 57/50/02.
6. Constance to Otho, 26 Oct 1892. MSS collection of Merlin Holland.
7. Constance to Lady Mount-Temple, 16 Aug 1892. BR 57/15/11.
8. Constance to Lady Mount-Temple, 17 Nov 1892. BR 57/17/10.
9. Constance to Lady Mount-Temple, 4 Dec 1892. BR 57/46/7.
10. Constance to Lady Mount-Temple, 12 Dec 1892. 57/18/6.
11. Ibid.
12. Constance to Lady Mount-Temple, 16 Dec 1892. BR 57/46/8.
13. Constance to Lady Mount-Temple, 21 Nov 1892. BR 57/17/12.
14. Constance to Lady Mount-Temple, 2 Feb 1893. BR 57/46/10.
15. Constance to Lady Mount-Temple, from via Michele, Florence, 4 Feb 1893. BR 57/46/11.
16. Constance to Lady Mount-Temple, 4 Feb 1893. BR 57/46/11.
17. Constance to Lady Mount-Temple, 11 Feb 1893. BR 57/46/15.
18. *Complete Letters*, p. 547.
19. *Complete Letters*, p. 556.
20. Constance to Lady Mount-Temple, 19 Feb 1893. BR 57/49/2.
21. *Complete Letters*, p. 691.
22. Ibid.
23. 'Saint C' was the pet name for John Ruskin used by Lady Mount-Temple and others of his close friends. In his book on Florence, Ruskin wrote: 'rise with the sun, and go to Santa Croce, with a good opera-glass in your pocket, with which you shall for once, at any rate, see an "opus" . . . Walk straight to the chapel on the right of the choir ("K" in your Murray's guide). When you first get into it, you will see nothing but a modern window of glaring glass, with a red hot cardinal in one pane – which piece of modern manufacture takes away at least

seven-eighths of the light (little enough before) by which you might have seen what is worth sight. Wait patiently till you get used to the gloom. Then guarding your eyes from the accursed modern window as best you may, take your opera glass and look to the right, at the uppermost of the two figures beside it. It is St Louis, under campanile architecture, painted by – Giotto . . . or the last Florentine painter who wanted a job – over Giotto?' John Ruskin, *Mornings in Florence* (George Allen, London, 1875), p. 3.

24. Constance to Lady Mount-Temple, 9 March 1893. BR 57/49/6.
25. *Freeman's Journal and Daily Commercial Advertiser* (20 April 1893).
26. Constance to Lady Mount-Temple, 9 Sept 1893. BR 57/50/7.
27. Constance to Lady Mount-Temple, 21 Aug 1893. BR 57/49/17.
28. *Complete Letters*, p. 693.
29. Constance to Lady Mount-Temple, undated. BR 57/50/02.
30. Constance to Lady Mount-Temple, 13 Sept 1893. BR 57/50/8.
31. Lord Alfred Douglas, *Oscar Wilde: A Summing Up* (Icon Books, London, 1962), p. 98.
32. Constance to Lady Mount-Temple, undated. BR 57/50/02.
33. E. Nister, *A Dandy Chair* (London, *c.* 1892)
34. Constance to Lady Mount-Temple, 30 Sept 1893. BR 57/50/11.
35. Constance to Lady Mount-Temple, 9 Oct 1893. BR 57/48/1.
36. Constance to Lady Mount-Temple, 10 Oct 1893. BR 57/48/2.
37. Constance to Lady Mount-Temple, 12 Oct 1893. BR 57/48/4.
38. *Complete Letters*, p. 693.
39. Constance to Lady Mount-Temple, 18 Oct 1983. BR 57/48/9.
40. Constance to Lady Mount-Temple, 18 Oct 1893. BR 57/48/9.
41. Constance to Lady Mount-Temple, 19 Oct 1893. BR 57/48/10.

Chapter 12: Modern-day Martha

1. *Complete Letters*, p. 693.
2. Lord Cromer was Agent and Consul-General in Egypt at this time.
3. *Complete Letters*, p. 575.
4. Constance to Lady Mount-Temple, 30 Oct 1893. BR 57/47/2.
5. Constance to Lady Mount-Temple, All Souls' Day 1893. BR 57/47/3.
6. Constance to Lady Mount-Temple, 10 Nov 1893. BR 57/47/11.

7. Constance to Lady Mount-Temple, 17 Nov 1893. BR 57/47/15.

8. Constance to Lady Mount-Temple, 22 Oct 1893. BR 57/48/12.

9. Constance to Lady Mount-Temple, 17 Nov 1893. BR 57/47/15.

10. Constance to Lady Mount-Temple, 29 Nov 1893. BR 57/47/17.

11. *Complete Letters*, p. 695.

12. Constance to Lady Mount-Temple, undated BR 57/19/10.

13. Constance to Lady Mount-Temple, undated BR 57/19/11.

14. Constance to Lady Mount-Temple, 11 March 1894. BR 57/20/2.

15. *New York Times* (10 Dec 1893).

16. Constance to Lady Mount-Temple, 10 Oct 1893? BR 57/17/3.

17. This scene was recounted in court by Wilde. McKenna, *Secret Life of Oscar Wilde*, p. 385.

18. Constance to Otho, 8 June 1892. MSS collection of Merlin Holland.

19. Constance to Arthur Humphreys, 1 June 1894. BL Eccles 81732.

20. Constance to Arthur Humphreys, 11 August 1894. BL Eccles 81732.

21. This sum is revealed in Constance's letter to her brother Otho dated 31 August 1894. MSS collection of Merlin Holland.

22. Henry Scott Holland, *A Lent in London: A Course of Sermons on Social Subjects Organized by the London Branch of the Christian Social Union and Preached during Lent 1895* (Longman, London, 1895).

23. Constance to Lady Mount-Temple, 11 Aug 1894. BR 57/20/11.

24. *Complete Letters*, p. 599.

25. Ibid., p. 623.

26. Oscar to Bosie, August 1894. *Complete Letters*, p. 598.

27. Constance to Lady Mount-Temple, 25 Aug 1894. BR 57/20/14.

28. Constance to Otho, 31 Aug 1894. MSS collection of Merlin Holland.

29. Ellmann, *Oscar Wilde,* p. 421.

30. Oscar to Bosie, 8 Sept 1894. *Complete Letters*, p. 607.

31. Constance to Otho, 31 Aug 1894. MSS collection of Merlin Holland.

32. Scribbled in the back pages of Otho's copy of Leonard Ingleby's *Oscar Wilde*. MSS collection of John Holland.

33. Constance to Arthur Humphreys, 22 Oct 1894. Clark Library.

34. Constance to Lady Mount-Temple, 10 Nov 1894. BR 57/21/16.

35. 'Your letter puzzles me very much, but I *have* finally come to the conclusion that your suggestion is for the best and that I will come to you later on after the boys go back to school.' Constance to Lady Mount-Temple, 8 Dec 1894. BR 57/22/4.

36. Constance to Lady Mount-Temple, 8 Dec 1894. BR 57/22/4.

37. The Clark Library holds a response to one such greeting from Florence Stoker, *née* Balcombe.

38. Vyvyan Holland, *Son of Oscar Wilde*, p. 55.

39. Constance to Lady Mount-Temple, 31 Dec 1894. BR 57/22/7.

40. BL Eccles 81727.

41. *Complete Letters*, p. 634.

42. Both Willie and Speranza also felt that Oscar should face the courts rather than flee, as a matter of honour.

43. Constance to Robbie Ross, 12 March 1895. Clark Library.

44. In letters between Jane Simon and Lady Mount-Temple after Constance's death, Laura recounted that Aunt Napier had strongly advised against surgery, as had Constance's doctors. BR 57/23/4.

45. This anecdote was copied by Otho from an unknown source. MSS collection of John Holland.

46. *Pall Mall Gazette* (28 March 1895).

47. Frank Harris, *Oscar Wilde* (Constable & Co., London, 1938), p. 138.

48. BL Eccles 81732.

49. Douglas, *Oscar Wilde: A Summing Up*, p. 97.

Chapter 13: The strife of tongues

1. *Complete Letters*, p. 637.

2. H. Montgomery Hyde, *Oscar Wilde: The Aftermath* (Methuen, London, 1963), p. 227.

3. Ellen Terry to Constance, 'Thursday', undated. MSS collection of John Holland.

4. MSS collection of John Holland.

5. Ibid.

6. Ibid.

7. Autograph letter to Juliet Latour Temple, undated. BR 54/13.

8. Susie to Constance, dated 7 April 1895. MSS collection of John Holland.

9. Vyvyan Holland, *Son of Oscar Wilde*, p. 61.

10. MSS collection of John Holland.

11. Vyvyan Holland, *Son of Oscar Wilde*, p. 61.

12. Philip Burne-Jones to Constance, 11 April 1895. MSS collection of John Holland.
13. Ibid.
14. Ibid.
15. Constance to Mrs Robinson, 19 April 1895. BL Eccles 8173.
16. Mrs Robinson to Constance, undated MSS collection of John Holland.
17. Speranza to Constance. MSS Collection of John Holland.
18. Vyvyan Holland, *Son of Oscar Wilde*, p. 62.
19. A subsequent letter from Arthur Clifton contained a cheque for £9 2s 9d, 'for the last two weeks hotel bills ending the 4th July', and another cheque for '£6 payable to Mme Schuwer'. These, it seems, were the expenses incurred by the boys and their French governess, now being met by the generosity of friends. Clifton went on to say that 'about £63 or £64 has been spent of the money raised for the children. £25 went in travelling and two months salary at the outset and since the boys started I have written cheques for £39.' Arthur Clifton to Constance, 14 July 1895. MSS collection John Holland.
20. Ada Leverson, *Letters to the Sphinx*, p. 41.
21. Bosie to Oscar, 15 May 1895. Clark Library.
22. Hyde, *Oscar Wilde: A Biography*, p. 293.
23. Georgiana Burne-Jones to Constance, 31 May 1895. MSS collection of John Holland.
24. Constance to Lady Mount-Temple, 10 June 1895. BR 57/22/10.
25. Bosie's elder brother Lord Drumlaurig, who died in a suspicious hunting accident, was rumoured to have had an affair with Rosebery. Some have speculated that while Rosebery's name was kept out of the Wilde trial, the prime minister continued to show particular interest in the case.
26. Arthur Clifton to Constance, 14 July 1895. MSS collection of John Holland.
27. Constance to Emily Thursfield, 25 June 1895. Clark Library.
28. MSS collection of John Holland.
29. Ibid.
30. Constance to Mary Holland, 15 Sept 1895. MSS collection of John Holland.
31. R. H. Sherard, *The Real Oscar Wilde* (Werner Laurie, London, 1917), p. 173.

350

32. Constance to Emily Thursfield, 12 Oct 1895. Clark Library.
33. Constance to Lady Mount-Temple, 18 Oct 1895. BR 57/22/12.
34. Juliet Deschamps to Constance, undated. MSS collection of John Holland.
35. Charles Brooke was the second white Rajah, inheriting the title from his uncle, who was made Rajah, or King, of Sarawak by the Sultan of Brunei in 1841.
36. Margaret Brooke, Ranee of Sarawak, *Good Morning & Good Night* (Constable, London, 1934), p. 258.
37. Constance to Lady Mount-Temple, 5 Dec 1895. BR 57/22/14.
38. Ibid.

Chapter 14: Madame Holland

1. Constance to Otho, 6 Jan 1896. MSS collection of Merlin Holland.
2. Constance to Lady Mount-Temple, 29 Dec 1895. BR 57/22/16.
3. Constance to Lady Mount-Temple, 11 Jan 1896. BR 57/22/17.
4. Undated letter. Clark Library.
5. Constance to Otho, 21 Feb 1896. MSS collection of Merlin Holland.
6. *Complete Letters*, p. 766.
7. *Complete Letters*, p. 652.
8. Constance to Otho, 31 March 1896. MSS collection of Merlin Holland.
9. Ibid.
10. *Complete Letters*, p. 654.
11. Constance to Lady Mount-Temple, 1 April 1886. BR 57/22/21.
12. When Constance refers to 'Hejlsberg College' in her letters, it is in fact clear that she is referring to the English Neuenheim College, since she notes that one of the staff attended Clifton College in Bristol, as Otho had done.
13. Constance to Otho, 19 July 1896. MSS collection of Merlin Holland.
14. Constance to Robbie Ross, 21 June 1896. Clark Library.
15. Adela Schuster to More Adey, 23 June 1896. Clark Library.
16. In a letter to Otho dated 17 Jan 1898 (MSS collection of Merlin Holland) Constance wrote: 'I am glad that Cyril goes away tomorrow as I am afraid that if he stayed here he might be got hold of. Apparently the Ranee had a letter sent her from Posilippo asking if I lived here or

something and she wrote a formal answer saying that I did not. She did not tell me till long afterwards and I have never seen the letter and don't know who sent it.'

17. Clark Library.
18. Clark Library.
19. Oscar to the Home Secretary, 2 July 1896. *Complete Letters*, p. 656.
20. *Complete Letters*, p. 675
21. *Complete Letters*, p. 784.
22. *Complete Letters*, p. 829.

Chapter 15: Life is a terrible thing

1. *Complete Letters*, p. 906.
2. Constance to Vyvyan, 21 June 1897. BL Eccles 81727.
3. Notes made in Otho's notebook. MSS collection of John Holland.
4. Constance to Vyvyan, 27 Sept 1896. BL Eccles 81727.
5. Constance to Vyvyan, 23 Feb 1897. BL Eccles 81727.
6. Ibid.
7. Constance to Vyvyan, undated. BL Eccles 81727.
8. Constance to Vyvyan, 27 May 1897. BL Eccles 81727.
9. *Complete Letters*, p. 865
10. *Complete Letters*, p. 912.
11. Constance to Otho, 5 Aug 1897. MSS collection of Merlin Holland.
12. Constance to Otho, 7 Oct 1897. MSS collection of Merlin Holland.
13. Constance to Blacker, 25 Sept 1897. BL Eccles 81727.
14. Constance to Blacker, 26 Sept 1897. BL Eccles 81727.
15. Ibid.
16. Constance to Blacker, 30 Sept 1897. BL Eccles 81728.
17. *Complete Letters*, p. 954.
18. Constance to Blacker, 1 Oct 1897. BL Eccles 81727.
19. Constance to Otho, 17 Jan 1898. MSS collection of Merlin Holland.
20. Constance to Arthur Humphreys, 24 Oct 1897. Clark Library.
21. Constance to Otho, 19 Feb 1898. MSS collection of Merlin Holland.
22. Constance to Otho, 17 Jan 1898. MSS collection of Merlin Holland.
23. Constance to Blacker, 4 Feb 1898. BL Eccles 81727.
24. Constance to Blacker, 10 March 1898. BL Eccles 81727.

25. Ironically, unbeknown to Constance, Oscar had already written *De Profundis*, a confessional letter to Bosie in which he admitted he had grown bored with married life.
26. Constance to Blacker, 18 March 1898. BL Eccles 81727.
27. BL Eccles 81728. Leonard Smithers was a publisher and bookseller who published Oscar's work, including *The Ballad of Reading Gaol*.
28. Constance to Lady Mount-Temple, 27 Sept 1893. BR 57/50/9.
29. Vyvyan Wilde, *Son of Oscar Wilde*, p. 130.
30. Otho quoting Constance's telegram in his letter to Lady Mount-Temple, 9 April 1898. BR 57/23/1.
31. Otho to Lady Mount-Temple, 9 April 1898. BR 57/23/1.
32. This account from Laura Hope to Lady Mount-Temple, based on Otho's explanation to her.
33. Otho to Lady Mount-Temple, 9 April 1898. BR 57/23/1.
34. Otho to Lady Mount-Temple, 29 May 1898. BR 57/23/6.
35. *Complete Letters*, p. 1055
36. *Complete Letters*, p. 1055
37. *Reynolds's Newspaper* (17 April 1898).
38. *Lloyd's Weekly Newspaper* (17 April 1898).
39. Laura Hope to Juliet Deschamps, 14 April 1898. BR 57/23/5.
40. Jane Simon to Lady Mount-Temple, 16 April 1898. BR 57/23/4.
41. Jane Simon to Lady Mount-Temple, 13 April 1898. BR 57/23/3.
42. Douglas, *Oscar Wilde: A Summing Up*, p. 99.
43. Otho to Lady Mount-Temple, 29 May 1898. BR 57/23/3.
44. Oscar to Robbie Ross, *c.* 1 March 1899. *Complete Letters*, p. 1128.

Epilogue

1. Juliet Deschamps to Oscar, 10 October 1898. Clark Library.

Select Bibliography

Manuscript Collections

The largest collection of Constance's autograph letters is of those between her and Lady Mount-Temple, held as part of the Broadlands Archive in the University of Southampton. Over a hundred letters from Constance to her brother Otho are in the private collection of Merlin Holland. The Library of William Andrews Clark Jr at the University of California in Los Angeles has some letters from Constance, while the British Library, as part of its Eccles collection, holds a significant number, not least those between Constance and the Blackers and from Constance to Vyvyan, all written during her period in exile on the Continent. The Morgan Library and Museum holds the MS of 'The Selfish Giant', written by Constance. Important original correspondence relating to Constance's flight from England and her time in exile is held in the private collection of John Holland.

Published Sources

Amor, Anne Clark, *Mrs Oscar Wilde: A Woman of Some Importance* (Sidgwick & Jackson, London, 1983)

Beddington, Mrs Claude, *All That I Have Met* (Cassell & Co., London, 1929)

Bentley, Joyce, *The Importance of Being Constance* (Robert Hale, London, 1983)

Borras, Maria Luisa, *Arthur Cravan: une stratégie du scandale* (Editions Jean-Michel Place, Paris, 1996)

Braddon, Mary, *The Rose of Life* (Hutchinson, London, 1905)

Brémont, Anna, Comtesse de, *Oscar Wilde and His Mother* (Everett & Co., London, 1911)

Byrne, Patrick, *The Wildes of Merrion Square* (Staples Press, London, 1953)

Cherry, Deborah, *Beyond the Frame: Feminism and Visual Culture, Britain, 1850–1900* (Routledge, London, 2000)

Corkran, Henriette, *Celebrities and I* (Hutchinson, London, 1902)

Douglas, Lord Alfred, *Oscar Wilde and Myself* (John Long, London 1914)

——, *Autobiography* (Secker, London, 1929)

——, *Without Apology* (Martin Secker, London, 1938)

——, *Oscar Wilde: A Summing Up* (Icon Books, London, 1962)

Ellmann, Richard, *Oscar Wilde* (Alfred A. Knopf, New York, 1988)

Field, Michael [Katherine Bradley and Edith Cooper], *Works and Days: From the Journal of Michael Field* (John Murray, London, 1933)

Fryer, Jonathan, *Robbie Ross: Oscar Wilde's Devoted Friend* (Carroll & Graf, New York, 2000)

Gere, Charlotte, with Lesley Hoskins, *The House Beautiful: Oscar Wilde and the Aesthetic Interior* (Lund Humphries in association with the Geffrye Museum, London, 2000)

Gide, André, *Oscar Wilde: in memoriam (souvenirs)* (Mercure de France, Paris, 1925)

Gilbert, R. A., *The Golden Dawn Companion* (Aquarian Press, Wellingborough, 1986)

Gregory, James, 'And May I Say Nothing', *The Oscholars*, vol. III, no. 12, issue 31; www.oscholars.com

Harris, Frank, *Oscar Wilde* (Constable & Co., London, 1938)

Holland, Merlin, *The Wilde Album* (Fourth Estate, London, 1997)

——, *Irish Peacock and Scarlet Marquess: The Real Trial of Oscar Wilde* (Fourth Estate, London, 2003)

——, and Rupert Hart-Davis (eds), *The Complete Letters of Oscar Wilde* (Fourth Estate, London, 2000)

——, *The Complete Works of Oscar Wilde* (Collins, London, 2003)

Holland, Vyvyan, *Son of Oscar Wilde* (Rupert Hart-Davis, London, 1954)

——, *Time Remembered after Père LaChaise* (Gollancz, London, 1966)

Hope-Nicholson Jacqueline (ed.), *Life amongst the Troubridges: Journals of a Young Victorian, by Laura Troubridge, 1873–1884* (Tite Street Press, London, 1999)

Howe, Ellic, *The Magicians of the Golden Dawn: A Documentary History of a Magical Order 1887–1923* (Routledge & Kegan Paul, London, 1972)

Hyde, H. Montgomery, *The Trials of Oscar Wilde* (Hodge, Edinburgh, 1948)

——, *Oscar Wilde: The Aftermath* (Methuen, London, 1963)

——, *Oscar Wilde: A Biography* (Eyre Methuen, London, 1976)

Ingleby, Leonard Cresswell, *Oscar Wilde* (T. Werner Laurie, London, 1907)

Jopling, Louise, *Twenty Years of My Life, 1867 to 1887* (John Lane, London, 1925)

Kingston, Angela, *Oscar Wilde as a Character in Victorian Fiction* (Palgrave Macmillan, Basingstoke, 2007)

Lancaster, Marie-Jaqueline (ed.), *Letters of Engagement: The Love Letters of Adrian Hope and Laura Troubridge* (Tite Street Press, London, 2000)

Langtry, Lillie, *The Days I Knew* (Hutchinson, London, 1925)

Le Gallienne, Richard, *The Romantic '90s* (Putnam & Co., London, 1951)

Leverson, Ada, *Letters to the Sphinx from Oscar Wilde: With Reminiscences of the Author* (Duckworth, London, 1930)

Lowndes, Marie Belloc, *Diaries and Letters, 1911–1947* (Chatto & Windus, London, 1971)

McKenna, Neil, *The Secret Life of Oscar Wilde* (Arrow Books, London, 2004)

Melville, Joy, *Mother of Oscar: The Life of Jane Francesca Wilde* (John Murray, London, 1994)

Newnham-Davis, Lieut.-Col., *Dinners and Diners* (Grant Richards, London, 1899)

Newton, Stella Mary, *Health, Art & Reason: Dress Reformers of the 19th Century* (John Murray, London, 1974)

Owen, Alex, *The Place of Enchantment: British Occultism and the Culture of the Modern* (Chicago University Press, Chicago, 2004)

Page, Norman, *An Oscar Wilde Chronology* (Macmillan, London, 1991)

Pearson, Hesketh, *The Life of Oscar Wilde* (Methuen, London, 1946)

Queensberry, Marquess of, *Oscar Wilde and the Black Douglas* (Hutchinson & Co., London, 1949)

Raffalovich, André, *L'Affaire Oscar Wilde* (A. Stork, Lyon, 1895)

——, *Uranisme et unisexualité* (Lyon, 1896)

Robb, Graham, *Strangers: Homosexual Love in the Nineteenth Century* (Picador, London, 2003)

Ruskin, John, *Mornings in Florence* (George Allen, London, 1875)

Schroeder, Horst, *Additions and Corrections to Richard Ellman's 'Oscar Wilde'* (privately printed, Braunschweig, 2002)

Shaw, George Bernard, *The Diaries, 1885–1897,* vols 1 and 2, ed. Stanley Weintraub (Pennsylvania State University Press, Philadelphia, 1986)

Sherard, Robert Harborough, *The Life of Oscar Wilde* (Werner Laurie, London, 1906)

Terry, Ellen, *Memoirs* (Gollancz, London, 1933)

Tollemache, Baron, *Some Reminiscences of the Early Life of Georgina, Lady Mount Temple, by Her Surviving Brother* (Helmingham, 1890)

Tweedie, Mrs Alec, *Hyde Park: Its History and Romance* (Eveleigh Nash, London, 1908)

Vyver, Bertha, *Memoirs of Maria Corelli* (Alston Rivers, London, 1930)

Wilde, Constance, *The Bairn's Annual* (Leadenhall Press, London, 1887)

——, *There Was Once: Grandma's Stories* (Ernest Nister, London, 1888)

——, *A Long Time Ago* (Ernest Nister, London, 1892)

——, *A Dandy Chair* (Ernest Nister, London, 1893)

——, *Cosy Corner* (Ernest Nister, London, 1895)

——, *Favourite Nursery Stories* (Ernest Nister, London, n. d.)

Wilde, Oscar, *The Complete Works* (HarperCollins, London, 2003)

Yeats, W. B., *Autobiographies: Reveries over Childhood and Youth and the Trembling of the Veil* (Macmillan & Co., London, 1926)

Illustration Acknowledgements

The William Andrews Clark Memorial Library, University of California, Los Angeles: 6 below/*Judy, or the London Serio-Comic Journal* December, 1886; 7 above left (Acc:BX-2N.2.16b); 12 above left/*Great Expectations!* cartoon by Phil May, 1895; 12 below/*New York Standard* 1895; 14 above (Acc:BX-3N.11).

Getty Images: 6 above; 7 below.

John Holland Collection: 2 above left and above right; 11 above right.

Merlin Holland Picture Archive: 1; 2 below left and below right; 3; 4 above left and above right; 5 below; 7 above right; 8; 9; 10; 11 above left; 13; 14 below left and below right; 15 above left and below; 16.

TopFoto: 4 below/Roger-Viollet; 5 above; 11 below/The Granger Collection; 12 above right; 15 above right.

Index